Lecture Notes in Artificial Intelligence 541

Subseries of Lecture Notes in Computer Science
Edited by J. Siekmann

Lecture Notes in Computer Science

Edited by G. Goos and J. Hartmanis

Lecture Notes in Artificial Intelligence 541

Subseries of Lecture Notes in Computer Science
Edited by J. Siekmann

Lecture Notes in Computer Science
Edited by G. Goos and J. Hartmanis

P. Barahona   L. Moniz Pereira   A. Porto (Eds.)

EPIA 91

5th Portuguese Conference on Artificial Intelligence
Albufeira, Portugal, October 1-3, 1991
Proceedings

Springer-Verlag

Berlin Heidelberg New York
London Paris Tokyo
Hong Kong Barcelona
Budapest

Series Editor

Jörg Siekmann
Institut für Informatik, Universität Kaiserslautern
Postfach 3049, W-6750 Kaiserslautern, FRG

Volume Editors

Pedro Barahona
Luís Moniz Pereira
António Porto
Departamento de Informática, Universidade Nova de Lisboa
2825 Monte da Caparica, Portugal

CR Subject Classification (1991): I.2.3-4, I.2.6, I.2.8

ISBN 3-540-54535-2 Springer-Verlag Berlin Heidelberg New York
ISBN 0-387-54535-2 Springer-Verlag New York Berlin Heidelberg

© Springer-Verlag Berlin Heidelberg 1991
Printed in Germany

Typesetting: Camera ready by author
Printing and binding: Druckhaus Beltz, Hemsbach/Bergstr.
2145/3140-543210 - Printed on acid-free paper

Preface

The Portuguese Association for Artificial Intelligence (Associação Portuguesa Para a Inteligência Artificial-APPIA) has been organizing Portuguese Conferences on Artificial Intelligence, now held every second year, since 1985.

The present Fifth Conference on Artificial Intelligence, like the previous one, was aimed at an international audience and at a high standard regarding accepted communications.

The international status of the Conference can be assessed from the fact that 62 contributions from 13 countries were received (26 contributions from Portugal). All of them were reviewed by at least three researchers of the appropriate scientific areas, and the reviews closely scrutinized by the Program Committee. To guarantee a high scientific standard, the Program Committee decided to accept only those papers significantly better than merely acceptable, and in fact most of them were judged definitely acceptable. As a result, only 20 papers were accepted and included in these proceedings.

We would like to thank all the people who made important contributions to the technical quality of this Conference, namely the Program Committee members and the referees, listed elsewhere in these proceedings.

We also thank our invited speakers Hassan Aït-Kaci, Robin Cooper, Mark Drummond, Catherine Lassez Vladimir Lipschitz, and Werner Schimanovich for their presentations, which significantly increased the interest and quality of the Conference.

Finally, we would like to thank the institutions who have contributed (financially or otherwise) to the organization of this Conference, namely Fundação Calouste Gulbenkian, Instituto Nacional de Investigação Científica, Junta Nacional de Investigação Científica e Tecnológica, Fundação Luso-Americana para o Desenvolvimento, Banco Espírito Santo e Comercial de Lisboa, Caixa Geral de Depósitos, Companhia Portuguesa Radio Marconi, Alcatel Portugal, IBM Portuguesa, Centro de Inteligência Artificial do UNINOVA, and Departamento de Informática da Universidade Nova de Lisboa.

Lisbon, July 1991

Luís Moniz Pereira
António Porto
Pedro Barahona

Conference Chair

Pedro Barahona

Program Chair

Luís Moniz Pereira
António Porto

Program Committee

Pedro Barahona	Universidade Nova de Lisboa
Pavel Brazdil	Universidade do Porto
Helder Coelho	Universidade Técnica de Lisboa
Gabriel Pereira Lopes	Universidade Nova de Lisboa
João Pavão Martins	Universidade Técnica de Lisboa
Fernando Pereira	ATT Bell Laboratories, New Jersey
Luís Moniz Pereira	Universidade Nova de Lisboa
António Porto	Universidade Nova de Lisboa

Referees

J. Alegria	J. J. Alferes	P. Barahona
A. Borges de Almeida	I. Braha	P. Brazdil
R. Camacho	L. Camarinha de Matos	J. Camões Silva
A. Cardoso	J. Cohen	H. Coelho
R. Cooper	E. Costa	J. Cunha
L. Damas	J. Duarte do Amaral	J. Esgalhado Valença
J. Falcão e Cunha	M. Filgueiras	G. Gaspar
M. Gomes	P. Guedes de Oliveira	T. Hichey
J. Hirschberg	J. M. Jacquet	D. Johnson
J. P. Leal	J. Legatheaux Martins	M. Mamede
A. Matos	M. Matos	F. Menezes
L. Moniz Pereira	L. Monteiro	E. Morgado
J. Nunes Aparício	A. Odlyzko	E. Oliveira
J. N. Oliveira	J. Pavão Martins	F. Pereira
G. Pereira Lopes	I. Pimenta Rodrigues	A. Pinho
A. Porto	M. Próspero dos Santos	C. Queiroz
C. Ramos	R. Ribeiro	A. Sernadas
C. Sernadas	L. Torgo	A. Traça de Almeida

Table of Contents

Temporal Reasoning

Planning

Diagnosis and Repair

Learning

Solving Linear Constraints on Finite Domains Through Parsing[*]

Miguel Filgueiras, Ana Paula Tomás

Centro de Informática, Universidade do Porto
R. do Campo Alegre 823, 4100 Porto, Portugal
email: mig@ncc.up.pt, apt@ncc.up.pt

Abstract

In this paper we present results from ongoing research which allows the use of parsing methods to solve a particular kind of constraints, namely linear constraints on finite domains. Solving this kind of constraints is equivalent to solving systems of linear Diophantine equations on a finite subset of the naturals. We associate, to such a system, a definite-clause grammar that can be used to enumerate its solutions, and define a class of grammars, the *connected grammars*, for which the set of successful derivations covers the set of non-negative solutions of the associated system. This definition is based on a study of cycles in context-free grammars using compiler construction concepts and techniques.

1 Introduction

The emergence of Constraint Logic Programming languages, namely Prolog III [Colmerauer 1987] and CHIP [Dincbas *et al.* 1988], [van Hentenryck 1989], and the definition of the CLP-scheme [Jaffar *et al.* 1986], [Jaffar and Lassez 1987], increased and renewed the importance of the study of methods for handling constraints and, in particular, methods for solving constraints [Cohen 1990].

---

[*]The research described in this paper was partially supported by Instituto Nacional de Investigação Científica.

In this paper we present results from ongoing research which allow the use of parsing methods to solve a particular kind of constraints, namely linear constraints on finite domains[1]. Solving this kind of constraints is equivalent to solving systems of linear Diophantine equations on a finite subset of the naturals. It is easily seen that such a system may be always transformed into an equivalent one with positive coefficients by an appropriate use of the bounds for the unknowns. We show that there is a natural correspondence between a system and a definite-clause grammar (DCG) [Pereira and Warren 1980], what enables us to trivially map the problem of solving linear constraints on finite domains into a parsing problem, and to try to use efficient parsing algorithms to solve the first one. How interesting this may turn out in practice depends on the results of a comparison with other methods. The soundness requirement that the set of successful grammar derivations covers the solution set of the system is proved for the class of *connected grammars*, a sub-class of context-free grammars introduced below. The results presented can be easily extended to a subset of the DCGs.

The next section gives a formal presentation of how successful derivations in a grammar can be related with a system of non-negative linear Diophantine (NNLD, for short) equations. In Section 3 notions concerning cycles in grammars are introduced that allow the definition, in Section 4 of the class of connected grammars. In order to prove (Section 6) that for this class the set of successful derivations covers the set of solutions of the associated system of equations, some other notions and results concerning subtrees and multisets of subtrees (*forests*) are described in Section 5. Finally, and before the Conclusions, an overview of how parsing can be used to solve linear constraints on finite domains is given.

2   Derivations and Systems of Equations

To every context-free grammar G it is possible to associate a system of linear equations on non-negative integers in which each variable stands for the number of applications of each production rule of G in a successful derivation. Let $G = (V_t, V_n, P, S)$ and for every $r_i \in P$, $1 \le i \le p$ let n_i be the number of times r_i is applied during a derivation of a string in $L(G)$, the language generated by G. Let

- $ip(A)$ denote the set of indices i of the rules r_i whose left-hand side is A[2],

---

[1]See also [Filgueiras 1990], [Filgueiras and Tomás 1990].

[2]Without loss of generality it will be assumed that for every non-terminal $A \in V_n$, $ip(A) \ne \emptyset$.

- $rhs(r)$ be the right-hand side of rule r,

- $occ(X, \alpha)$ be the number of occurrences of symbol X in the string α, and

- $n(x)$ be the number of occurrences of the terminal x in the string to be parsed.

In a successful derivation of a string $w \in L(G)$, the number of times a non-terminal symbol is expanded must be equal to the number of times it is produced (the start symbol obviously has one more occurrence). Similarly, the number of times a terminal symbol occurs in w must be equal to the number of times it is produced. As a consequence of these facts given a string $w \in L(G)$ the following equations must hold:

- non-terminal equations:
  for S, the start symbol of G

$$\sum_{i \in ip(S)} n_i - \sum_{k=1}^{p} occ(S, rhs(r_k)) * n_k = 1$$

  for every non-terminal $A(\neq S) \in V_n$

$$\sum_{i \in ip(A)} n_i - \sum_{k=1}^{p} occ(A, rhs(r_k)) * n_k = 0$$

- terminal equations:
  for every terminal $a \in V_t$

$$\sum_{k=1}^{p} occ(a, rhs(r_k)) * n_k = occ(a, w)$$

A particular string determines a set of solutions to the system. However, a solution in this set may either correspond to a successful derivation of a different string or to no derivation at all. The first situation arises because in the system there is no information about the order of symbols. The second one originates from the existence of cycles in the grammar: a solution may correspond to a sucessful derivation plus a certain number of cycles.

When our goal is to solve a system of NNLD equations by parsing, the first case is not really problematic because we can fix the order and the string to be parsed. In contrast, the second means that the set of solutions is not covered by the set of derivations, what makes the approach unfeasible. We now give some concepts that are needed to define a subclass of context-free grammars for which the second situation cannot occur.

3 Cycles in Grammars

Cycles appear in grammars as a consequence of recursive productions. Some concepts and results of the analysis of flow graphs usually applied in compiler construction, namely in code optimization techniques (see [Aho et al. 1986]), are useful in studying those cycles.

Let $G = (V_n, V_t, P, S)$ be a context-free grammar as above and let $V = V_t \cup V_n$. The derivation relation, its closure and positive closure will be denoted by $\Rightarrow$, $\Rightarrow^*$ and $\Rightarrow^+$. The conventions of [Hopcroft and Ullman 1969] concerning the denotation of grammar symbols and strings will be employed, namely, that Latin capital letters stand for non-terminals, Latin lower case at the beginning of the alphabet for terminals and at the end of the alphabet for strings of terminals, Greek lower case letters for strings of non-terminals and terminals.

3.1 Some Interesting Relations Between Non-terminals

We start by defining some relations between non-terminals that will enable us to characterize in a formal way the notion of cycle in a grammar.

Definition 1 (i-gives relation) *For any* $A, B \in V_n$, *A* **i-gives** *B (read as A immediately gives B) iff there exists a rule* $A \to \alpha_1 B \alpha_2$.

Definition 2 (gives relation) *The* **gives** *relation is the transitive closure of the i-gives relation. Alternatively, for any* $A, B \in V_n$, *A* **gives** *B iff* $A \Rightarrow^+ \alpha_1 B \alpha_2$.

Definition 3 (controls relation) *For any* $A, B \in V_n$, *A* **controls** *B iff either A is the same as B, or A gives B and every derivation* $S \Rightarrow^* \gamma_1 B \gamma_2$ *has the form* $S \Rightarrow^* \beta_1 A \beta_2 \Rightarrow^+ \beta_1 \delta_1 B \delta_2 \beta_2$.

The equivalent of this last relation in the analysis of flow graphs is named *dominates* and is denoted by dom — a different name is used here to avoid the confusion with notions found in grammatical and linguistic formalisms. X **controls** Y means that every path from the start symbol S to Y in the graph for the

i-gives relation contains the node X. An obvious conclusion is that the start symbol **controls** every non-terminal.

Figure 1 shows the graph of the **i-gives** relation for the following grammar

Grammar G_1

$$S \;\rightarrow\; aAb$$

$$A \;\rightarrow\; BC$$
$$A \;\rightarrow\; c$$

$$B \;\rightarrow\; dD$$
$$B \;\rightarrow\; aF$$

$$C \;\rightarrow\; aAaF$$

$$D \;\rightarrow\; aEb$$
$$D \;\rightarrow\; cAd$$

$$E \;\rightarrow\; dDe$$

$$F \;\rightarrow\; a$$

Note that although A controls F, neither B **controls** F, nor C **controls** F, because in the graph of Figure 1 F is reachable from S through either B or C, but in any case necessarily through A.

The graph in Figure 1 is a *reducible graph*[3] because it is possible to make a partition of its edges into two disjoint sets, the set of *forward edges* and the set of *back edges*, so that the two following properties hold:

- the set of nodes and the set of forward edges form an acyclic graph with a node from which all the others can be reached[4]

- every back edge reaches a node that **controls** the edge starting node[5].

---

[3]There are several different equivalent definitions for this notion, of which two will be used here. For more details the reader is, once more, kindly referred to [Aho et al. 1986].

[4]In graphs for grammars such a node corresponds to the start symbol, and therefore every non-terminal can be derived from the start symbol.

[5]In other words ([Aho et al. 1986]): the edge's head **controls** its tail.

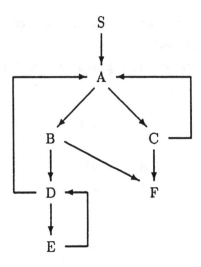

Figure 1: The graph for the **i-gives** relation.

In the present graph, the edges $C \mapsto A$, $D \mapsto A$ and $E \mapsto D$ are back edges, all the others being forward edges.

It may happen that the **i-gives**-graph for a grammar is not reducible, in which case it is always possible to transform the grammar into another one generating the same language and having a reducible graph. Such transformation is known as *node splitting*. To check whether a given graph is reducible the easiest method is by using what is called $T_1 - T_2$ analysis, which corresponds to another definition of reducible graphs: a graph is reducible if and only if the result[6] of successively applying, in any order, the transformations T_1 and T_2 until they cannot be applied, is a graph with a single node. The transformations T_1 and T_2 are

- T_1: delete an edge $X \mapsto X$.

- T_2: if Y has a unique predecessor X, X *consumes* Y by deleting Y and transforming every edge $Y \mapsto Z$ into $X \mapsto Z$.

When the result of the $T_1 - T_2$ analysis is not a single node, then a node splitting must be made[7]. After a finite number of node splitting operations a reducible graph is obtained.

---

[6]Which is a unique graph.

[7]Note that a node in the resulting graph corresponds to a sub-graph of the initial graph.

For reducible graphs an efficient algorithm exists to compute the **controls** relation (see Algorithm 10.16 of [Aho et al. 1986]).

3.2 Cycles

We assume for a given context-free grammar G, that its **i-gives**-graph is reducible and that its **controls** relation has been computed.

The following definitions are adopted from the corresponding ones in the analysis of loops in reducible flow graphs:

Definition 4 (Back production rule) *A production rule $A \rightarrow \alpha_1 B \alpha_2$ is called a* back production rule *from A to B if B* controls *A.*

Definition 5 (Cycle of back production rule) *The* cycle *of a back production rule r from A to B is the set of derivations $B \Rightarrow^* \alpha_1 A \alpha_2 \Rightarrow \beta_1 B \beta_2$ in which the last derivation step is the application of r, and no other application of a back production rule to B exists.*

Definition 6 (Header of cycle) *The* header *of a cycle of a back production rule from A to B, is the non-terminal B.*

Note that nothing prevents a certain non-terminal to be the header of several different cycles.

4 Connected Grammars

Let G be a context-free grammar as before, and, for any $A \in V_n$, let $G' = G \ominus A$ be the grammar obtained from G by deleting all the rules in which A occurs (on the left-hand, or the right-hand side). More formally, $G' = (V'_n, V_t, P', S)$ where $V'_n = V_n - \{A\}$, $P' = P - \{X \rightarrow \alpha \in P \mid (A = X) \vee (\alpha = \beta_1 A \beta_2)\}$.

Definition 7 (Connected grammar) *A* connected grammar *is any context-free grammar G whose **i-gives**-graph is reducible, and that fulfils one of the following conditions:*

- *the **i-gives**-graph of G does not contain back edges*
- *for any $A \in V_n$ such that A is the header of a cycle, the grammar $G \ominus A$ has no successful derivations.*

This definition implies that the grammar G_1 is not a connected one. In fact, its cycles have A and D as headers, and, although, on the one hand, it is obvious that $G_1 \ominus A$ has no derivations at all because it has no rules for the start symbol, on the other hand, there are successful derivations for the grammar $G_1 \ominus D$. One of them obtains from applying $S \rightarrow aAb$ and $A \rightarrow c$.

The class of languages generated by connected grammars is strictly contained in the class of context-free languages and is not comparable with the class of regular languages. This follows from the fact that the definition of connected grammars is a restriction of the definition of context-free grammars not preventing self-embedding, and from the case of the regular language denoted by the regular expression $(a \mid b^*)$ for which no connected grammar exists.

Before proving that any solution to the system of NNLD equations associated with a connected grammar corresponds to a successful derivation in the grammar, we need to establish a few facts concerning derivations.

5   Systems of Equations, Cycles and Forests

The following notions and results will be given in terms of context-free grammars. The notation conventions of the previous sections will be kept.

We will need the usual definitions of *derivation tree*, *subtree*, and *frontier* (also named *yield* or *result*) of a tree — see, for instance, [Hopcroft and Ullman 1969]. Note that the empty string (ε) may be the label of a leaf.

Definition 8 (Cyclic subtree) *A cyclic subtree for a grammar G is a subtree for G whose root is A and whose frontier has the form $w_1 A w_2$, with $w_1, w_2 \in V_t^*$.*

Definition 9 (Forest and forest border) *A forest for a grammar G is a (finite) multiset of subtrees for G, and the forest border of a given forest is the multiset sum[8] of the frontiers of its subtrees.*

Definition 10 (Even forest) *An even forest for a grammar G is a forest F for G such that every $A \in V_n$ has the same number of occurrences both in the multiset formed by the roots of the subtrees of F, and in the border of F.*

---

[8]The multiset sum takes two or more multisets as operands and yields the multiset in which the number of occurrences of each element is the sum of the number of its occurrences in each of the operands.

5.1 Cycles and Forests

Definition 11 (Composition of subtrees) *Given two subtrees T_1, T_2 for a grammar G, such that the root A of T_2 is an element of the frontier of T_1, a composition of T_1 and T_2, denoted by $T_1 \odot T_2$, is any subtree obtained from T_1 replacing one of the leaves of T_1 labelled A by the entire tree T_2.*

A subtree resulting from composing a subtree with another one having ε as its frontier, may, in most cases, be simplified by deleting leaves labelled ε and the edges leading to them.

We now prove the following theorem:

Theorem 1 (Cycles in even forests) *Every even forest for a grammar G either is, or may be reduced (through composition of its subtrees) to a multiset of cyclic subtrees for G.*

    Proof: Let F_0 be the an even forest for G. Apply the following transformation to F_0 until it cannot be applied:

- given an even forest F_k such that $T_2 \in F_k$ has frontier in V_t^*, choose arbitrarily a $T_1 \in F_k$ in whose frontier the root of T_2 occurs, and obtain the even forest $F_{k+1} = (F_k - \{T_1, T_2\}) \cup \{T_1 \odot T_2\}$.

Note that if there is a T_2 as described, there must also be a T_1 in the required conditions, because F_k is an *even* forest. The resulting forest must be even, because if the root of T_2 is A there will be in F_{k+1} one less occurrence of A both as a root and in its border. As forests are finite multisets, there is an even forest F_i, with $i \geq 0$ to which the transformation above cannot be applied because there are no more subtrees with a frontier in V_t^* — note that the number of applications of the transformation is, in general, greater than the number of such subtrees in F_0, because other ones can be arrived at through composition. The even forest F_i has, say, n elements each of which is a subtree whose frontier has exactly one non-terminal and 0 or more terminals. This is implied by the fact that in F_i there are n roots (one for each subtree), there must be n non-terminals in its border (because F_i is even), and each of these non-terminals must belong to the frontier of a different subtree (otherwise there would be at least one subtree with a frontier in V_t^*). As a consequence we can number from 1 to n each root in F_i and number (also from 1 to n) the non-terminals in the border of F_i in such a way that to each root labelled L there is a node labelled L in the border with the same number. The forest F_i can be seen now as a permutation of the integers 1 to n. As every permutation of a finite set may be decomposed in cycles, F_i can be partitioned into a set of even forests each of which results in a cyclic subtree by composing its elements in the order dictated by the permutation cycle. •

5.2 Systems of Equations and Forests

Let S be the system of NNLD equations associated with a context-free grammar G as described in Section 2. We recall that a solution to S gives for each production rule the number of times it must be applied in a successful derivation. It is clear that to each production rule there is a corresponding subtree. The following definition and theorem will be useful in the next section.

Definition 12 (Solving forest) *The* solving forest *associated to a solution $\vec{s}$ of the system of equations for a grammar G is the forest containing a number of occurrences of the subtree for each production rule of G that is equal to the number of times the rule should be applied as dictated by $\vec{s}$.*

Any solving forest F is "almost" an even forest: it would be one except for the start symbol occurring as the root of a subtree once more than the required number. Also, the frontier of F must contain all the symbols in the string to be derived.

Theorem 2 (Derivation tree from solving forest) *If F is a solving forest for a grammar G, it is always possible to build a derivation tree in G by composition of subtrees in F.*

> **Proof:** There are two possible cases:
>
> - if there is a subtree in F whose root is the start symbol S and whose frontier is in V_t^*, the thesis is trivially true.
> - otherwise, let T_1 be a subtree with root S and with a non-terminal A in its frontier. Then, by composing T_1 with a subtree T_2 with root A (which must exist in F as F is a solving forest) we obtain another solving forest F'. Taking now F', applying

the same procedure to $T_1 \odot T_2$, if it does not fall in the first case above, and iterating the procedure a derivation tree[9] must be reached as the number of elements in the successive forests is decreasing.

●

Note that what remains of a solving forest after building a derivation tree must be either the empty set, or an even forest.

5.3 Cyclic Subtrees and Headers

When dealing with a grammar G whose i-gives-graph is reducible, we may be interested in transforming a cyclic subtree T whose root is not the header of a cycle into another cyclic subtree T' whose root is a header, with T and T' corresponding to exactly the same derivation steps, although applied in different orders. This transformation, illustrated in Figure 2, is always possible as stated in the next theorem (see [Filgueiras and Tomás 1990] for a proof).

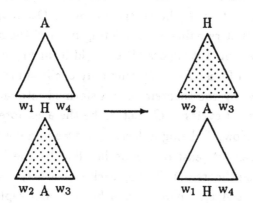

Figure 2: Transformation of a cyclic subtree.

Theorem 3 (Header as a root of cyclic subtree) *Every cyclic subtree T for a context-free grammar G whose i-gives-graph is reducible, may be transformed into another cyclic subtree T' for G, corresponding to exactly the same derivation*

---

[9]Which is a subtree with root S and frontier in V_t^*.

steps (even if applied in a different order) and such that the root of T' is the header of a cycle in G.

6 Connected Grammars and Systems of Equations

In this section we will consider a connected grammar G and the system S of NNLD equations associated to it in the way described in Section 2. Before presenting and proving our main result, we give an intermediate theorem that is trivially implied by the definition of connected grammar.

Theorem 4 (Headers in sucessful derivations) *Every successful derivation in a connected grammar G must use at least one production for each non-terminal which is the header of a cycle in G.*

Theorem 5 *To each solution of the system S of NNLD equations associated with a connected grammar G there corresponds a successful derivation in G.*

> **Proof:** Let F be the solving forest for a solution of S. By the theorem 2 it is possible to build a derivation tree T from F. If T contains all the elements of F the thesis is proved. Otherwise, let F_1 be the even forest that remains after deleting from F the subtrees used in T. By the theorem 1 it is possible to build from F_1, by tree composition, a new even forest F_2 containing only cyclic subtrees. All these subtrees may be, by the theorem 3, transformed into subtrees whose roots are headers of cycles in G. Let F_3 be the even forest formed by these subtrees. Now, T, being a derivation tree in a connected grammar, must contain at least one node labelled by the header of any cycle in G, by the theorem 4. Taking each element T_i of F_3, with root A_i and frontier $w_i A_i x_i$, where A_i is a header, and replacing a node labelled A_i in T by T_i, a new derivation tree is obtained containing all the subtrees in F, as we wanted. •

7 Solving Linear Constraints on Finite Domains

As we pointed out in the Introduction linear constraints on finite domains may be mapped into systems of NNLD equations with non-negative coefficients. Such systems have a finite number of solutions which can be enumerated by using a

DCG. The enumeration process will be complete if the DCG has a context-free backbone which is connected.

In fact, the final result of the previous section can be easily extended to a subset of the DCGs — taken here as a grammar formalism not to be confused with their usual Prolog implementation. The subset we are interested in corresponds to a use of DCG rule arguments that only restricts the language generated by the grammar by imposing bounds on the number of applications of each rule.

Because of space limits we just present an example of a DCG that can be used to enumerate the solutions of the following system:

$$\begin{cases} 4 * x \; + \; 3 * y \; + \quad\;\; z \;=\quad 9 \\ 3 * x \; + \; 4 * y \; + \; 2 * z \;=\quad 8 \\ 5 * x \quad\qquad\qquad + \quad\;\; z \;=\; 11 \end{cases}$$

$$
\begin{aligned}
s(X, Y, Z) \quad &\longrightarrow\quad xstar(a, 0, X), ystar(a, 0, Y), zstar(a, 0, Z), \\
&\qquad\qquad xstar(b, 0, X), ystar(b, 0, Y), zstar(b, 0, Z), \\
&\qquad\qquad xstar(c, 0, X), zstar(c, 0, Z).
\end{aligned}
$$

$$
\begin{aligned}
xstar(T, N, M) \quad &\longrightarrow\quad x(T), xstar(T, succ(N), M). \\
xstar(\_, N, N) \quad &\longrightarrow\quad [\,].
\end{aligned}
$$

$$
\begin{aligned}
x(a) \quad &\longrightarrow\quad [a, a, a, a]. \\
x(b) \quad &\longrightarrow\quad [b, b, b]. \\
x(c) \quad &\longrightarrow\quad [c, c, c, c, c].
\end{aligned}
$$

$$
\begin{aligned}
ystar(T, N, M) \quad &\longrightarrow\quad y(T), ystar(T, succ(N), M). \\
ystar(\_, N, N) \quad &\longrightarrow\quad [\,].
\end{aligned}
$$

$$
\begin{aligned}
y(a) \quad &\longrightarrow\quad [a, a, a]. \\
y(b) \quad &\longrightarrow\quad [b, b, b, b].
\end{aligned}
$$

$$
\begin{aligned}
zstar(T, N, M) \quad &\longrightarrow\quad z(T), zstar(T, succ(N), M). \\
zstar(\_, N, N) \quad &\longrightarrow\quad [\,].
\end{aligned}
$$

$$
\begin{aligned}
z(a) \quad &\longrightarrow\quad [a]. \\
z(b) \quad &\longrightarrow\quad [b, b]. \\
z(c) \quad &\longrightarrow\quad [c].
\end{aligned}
$$

Note that the arguments in the rule for s force $xstar$ to be applied an equal number of times for each of a, b, and c, and similarly for $ystar$ and $zstar$. Therefore, the associated system must include equations stating these facts. Successful parses of a string of 9 as, followed by 8 bs, followed by 11 cs, with this DCG yield the solutions for the system above (as the interested reader may easily verify). Of course, other DCGs do exist that would serve the same purpose.

The DCGs used in this way are *depth-bounded*[10] [Haas 1989]. Each solution corresponds to a different parse of an appropriate string. If the system has m equations this string is in the language denoted by the regular expression $c_1^* \ldots c_m^*$ and the number of occurrences of the terminal c_i equals the right-hand side of the i-th equation. The time to get a parse of the string with the algorithm (based on Earley's) of [Haas 1989] is bounded by the cube of the length of the string.

Instead of the Haas algorithm the direct Prolog implementation of DCGs may be used. This implementation corresponds, in the case of a single equation, to the "Positive Diophantine" algorithm in [Mitra et al. 1970]. Both can be seen as generate and test methods.

8 Conclusions

We presented a method and its theoretical justification for solving linear constraints on finite domains through parsing with DCGs. The question whether or not this method is of practical significance remains open and will be settled by a thorough comparison with more standard algorithms for linear Diophantine equations, such as those in [Chou and Collins 1982], [Bradley 1970], [Greenberg 1971], [Huet 1978], [Guckenbiehl and Herold 1985], [Boudet et al. 1990], [Pottier 1990], as well as for constraints on finite domains, like those in [Dincbas *et al.* 1988], [van Hentenryck 1989]. Our study of the former is under way and has already led us to the formulation of a new algorithm for solving NNLD equations (for a description, see [Tomás and Filgueiras 1991a], [Tomás and Filgueiras 1991b]).

References

[Aho et al. 1986] Alfred V. Aho, R. Sethi and J. D. Ullman, *Compilers — Principles, Techniques and Tools*. Addison-Wesley, 1986.

---

[10]A depth-bounded grammar is a unification grammar such that every parse tree for any string of a given length has a depth which is bounded.

[Boudet et al. 1990] Alexandre Boudet, E. Contejean and H. Devie, A new *AC* Unification algorithm with an algorithm for solving systems of Diophantine equations. In Proceedings of the 5th Conference on Logic and Computer Science, IEEE, 1990.

[Bradley 1970] Gordon Bradley, Algorithm and Bound for the Greatest Common Divisor of n Integers, *Comm. ACM*, 13(7), 1970.

[Chou and Collins 1982] Tsu-Wu J. Chou and G. E. Collins, Algorithms for the solution of systems of linear Diophantine equations. *SIAM J. Comput.*, 11(4), 687-708, 1982.

[Cohen 1990] Jacques Cohen, Constraint Logic Programming Languages. *Comm. ACM*, 33(7), 1990.

[Colmerauer 1987] Alain Colmerauer, Opening the Prolog III Universe. *Byte*, 12(9), 1987.

[Dincbas *et al.* 1988] M. Dincbas, P. van Hentenryck, H. Simonis, A. Aggoun, T. Graf, F. Berthier, The constraint Logic Programming language CHIP. In *Proceedings of the International Conference on Fifth Generation Computer Systems*, ICOT, 1988.

[Filgueiras 1990] Miguel Filgueiras, Systems of Linear Diophantine Equations and Logic Grammars, Centro de Informática da Universidade do Porto, 1990.

[Filgueiras and Tomás 1990] Miguel Filgueiras, Ana Paula Tomás, Relating Grammar Derivations and Systems of Linear Diophantine Equations. Centro de Informática da Universidade do Porto, 1990.

[Greenberg 1971] H. Greenberg, *Integer Programming*, Academic Press, 1971.

[Guckenbiehl and Herold 1985] Thomas Guckenbiehl and A. Herold, Solving Linear Diophantine Equations. Memo SEKI-85-IV-KL, Universität Kaiserslautern, 1985.

[Haas 1989] Andrew Haas, A parsing algorithm for Unification Grammar. *Computational Linguistics*, 15(4), 1989.

[Hopcroft and Ullman 1969] John E. Hopcroft and J. D. Ullman, *Formal Languages and Their Relation to Automata*. Addison-Wesley, 1969.

[Huet 1978] Gérard Huet, An algorithm to generate the basis of solutions to homogeneous linear Diophantine equations. *Information Processing Letters*, 7(3), 1978.

[Jaffar *et al.* 1986] Joxan Jaffar, J.-L. Lassez and M. Maher, Logic Programming language scheme. In D. DeGroot and G. Lindstrom (eds.), *Logic Programming: Functions, Relations, and Equations*, Prentice-Hall, 1986.

[Jaffar and Lassez 1987] Joxan Jaffar and J.-L. Lassez, Constraint Logic Programming. In *Proceedings of the 14th POPL Conference*, 1987.

[Mitra et al. 1970] G. Mitra, D. B. C. Richards and K. Wolfenden, An improved algorithm for the solution of integer programs by the solution of associated Diophantine equations. *R.I.R.O.*, 1970.

[Pereira and Warren 1980] F. Pereira and D. H. D. Warren, Definite Clause Grammars for language analysis — a survey of the formalism and a comparison with Augmented Transition Networks. *Artificial Intelligence*, 13, 1980.

[Pottier 1990] Loïc Pottier, Solutions Minimales des Systèmes Diophantiens Linéaires: Bornes et Algorithmes. Rapport de Recherche no. 1292, I.N.R.I.A., 1990.

[Tomás and Filgueiras 1991a] A. P. Tomás and M. Filgueiras, A New Method for Solving Linear Constraints on the Natural Numbers. This volume.

[Tomás and Filgueiras 1991b] A. P. Tomás and M. Filgueiras, A Congruence-based Method for Finding the Basis of Solutions to Linear Diophantine Equations. Centro de Informática da Universidade do Porto, 1991.

[van Hentenryck 1989] P. van Hentenryck, *Constraint Satisfaction in Logic Programming*, MIT Press, 1989.

Constraint Solving in Finite Domains under User Control

Francisco Menezes   Pedro Barahona
(fm@fct.unl.pt)   (pb@fct.unl.pt)

Departamento de Informática
Universidade Nova de Lisboa
2825 Monte da Caparica
Portugal

Abstract

Constraint logic programming languages extend logic programming by providing constraint solving capabilities on particular domains, which are more powerful than normal unification. However, these capabilities are usually general-purpose and embedded in the language. In this paper we make a case for extending the user interaction with the constraint solver, namely to achieve better performances. More specifically we present for finite domains, an inference rule (SLAIR) which subsumes previously defined ones and improves their interactivity. Additionally, experimental results show that this rule leads to significant speedup in execution time.

1 Introduction

The efficiency of logic programming can be greatly improved, if general unification is replaced by constraint solving in some adequate domains. This has motivated the specification of several constraint logic programming languages, namely CLP [JaLa87] (for the domain of real numbers), Prolog-III [Colm90] (for the domains of rational numbers, boolean terms and trees) and CHIP [DVHS88] (for finite domains, rational numbers and boolean terms).

In all these languages, a form of test and generate paradigm is supported, in that constraints on variables of the appropriate domains may be stated completely before the generation of values, and are used actively by a constraint solver to reduce the search space *a priori*.

For some languages, only general purpose methods are used by constraint solvers for the intended domains. For example both CLP(R) and Prolog-III use the constraint satisfaction phase of the simplex algorithm to efficiently handle linear constraints on rational numbers [JaMi87]. The decision on which methods to include in the constraint solver usually takes into account the trade-off between the generality and completeness of the method and the efficiency of its implementation.

Furthermore, the constraint solver is embedded in the language, and is made invisible to the user. Hence, he/she has no possibility of specifying better constraint solving methods, which could be quite useful to solve particular problems, but are not general enough to have been included in the language implementation. In such cases, constraints are delayed until enough information is available. For example a non-linear constraint such as $X^2 \leq 36$ is typically delayed until X becomes ground, even if it can be applied much earlier to impose that $X \geq -6$ and $X \leq 6$.

This is thus a potential source of inefficiency and has led us to investigate ways of allowing the user to interact with the constraint solver, in some appropriate manner. In particular, our research has been focussed on constraint solving problems, where variables range over finite domains.

CHIP is of course a language that supports constraint solving on these domains. Moreover, the user has some possibilities of defining special purpose constraints and deciding when such constraints are to be activated, by means of forward and lookahead *meta-level* declarations.

[Hent89] defines two inference rules, the LAIR (Looking-Ahead Inference Rule) and the FCIR (Forward Checking Inference Rule) which provide the formal support for user defined constraints over finite domains in looking-ahead and forward-checking modes, respectively. The application of a constraint is delayed until its signature fulfills certain prerequisites (the applicability condition). LAIR delays a constraint until each of its arguments is either ground or a domain variable. FCIR has a stronger prerequisite, allowing at most one domain variable.

For example, a forward constraint such as $X + Y \neq 5$ is delayed until the value V of one of the variables is known, in which case the value $5 - V$ is removed from the domain of the other variable. Furthermore, when a constraint reduces the domain of a variable to a single element, that variable becomes ground (i.e. it is assigned this element), which in turn may cause the activation of other (delayed) constraints. Due to this delay mechanism, all constraints may be stated completely before the generation process, making programming style much more declarative since one need not worry with control aspects such as when each constraint should be applied.

With the use of special meta-level declarations, CHIP enables the programmer to decide which inference rule a constraint should be handled with. The choice is however limited to FCIR and LAIR. In our view, this limitation should be removed, and more flexibility should be given to allow the specification of particular activation strategies for user defined constraints, in order to take advantage of specific knowledge on the constraints in hand (but without jeopardizing the declarative nature of logic programming).

To this purpose we have implemented a prototype where the activation strategy (and thus the control of execution of a program) may be meta-programmed by the user. In this paper, we will therefore describe the main features of our prototype and provide some examples of results achieved with its use.

The structure of the paper is the following. In the next section, we will further comment on the limitations of the FCIR and LAIR rules mentioned above and justify the need for allowing the user to specify more flexible strategies for constraint handling. In section 3, after presenting some definitions and constructs of our system, we define its operational semantics. In section 4, we discuss ways of introducing user defined constraint solving methods in our system, which are however not implemented. In section 5, we present and discuss some experimental results obtained with our system. Finally, we present the main conclusions and summarize directions in which we intend to proceed in our future work.

2 Flexible constraint handling over finite domains

As mentioned above, CHIP enables the programmer to decide which inference rule a constraint should be handled with, the choice being limited to FCIR and LAIR. Since they are general inference rules, they are not adequate to handle efficiently all situations.

For example, a particular constraint may be activated too early if it is declared as lookahead. In such case, in most of its activations the amount of pruning achieved on the variables domains does not pay off the time spent to achieve such pruning (in the worst case, no pruning at all is achieved, and thus all time spent is purely wasted).

On the other hand, if the constraint is declared as forward it might be activated too late, i.e. not all the times where pruning could occur, forcing the program to consider a much larger search space than it probably should.

To overcome the limitations of these two rules, in the prototype that we have implemented, the activation strategy (and thus the control of execution of a program) may be specified by the user. Furthermore, this specification does not jeopardize the declarative nature of logic programming, in that it is made through meta-programming declarations using *guards* (loosely borrowed from committed-choice parallel logic programming languages [Shap89]).

Of course, an adequate activation strategy depends highly on the constraint solver used, which often results from the above mentioned trade-off between efficiency and generality. Although built-in methods are used to optimize certain constraints, such as equality (=) of linear terms, other constraints could be more efficiently solved by specific methods. For example a constraint such as $A = 3 * (B - C)$, could be handled very efficiently by removing all values from the domain of A which are not multiples of 3. This removal is very efficient, although it would not be complete, in the sense that, depending on the domains of B and C, other values could possibly be remove from A's domain (to allow this type of incomplete constraint solving methods, CHIP has a special inference rule - the PLAIR- that we also use in our prototype). Nevertheless, this situation is not sufficiently general, and so, this handling would therefore be typically left for the user.

Although we intend to address this issue in the near future, our prototype does not allow yet the user-defined constraint solving methods. For the time being, the user may only choose between alternative built-in methods of constraint solving, and thus tune constraint activation accordingly.

To some extent, our work is thus an extension to CHIP's constraint handling over finite domains. We intend to overcome CHIP restriction of only solving user defined constraints by general methods supplied by the language. The way we propose to achieve this goal is by taking LAIR as the most general inference rule and to identify where and how it can be refined by the user to create a more adequate inference rule for particular constraints (notice that FCIR itself fits in this approach since it behaves just like LAIR if the applicability condition of a constraint is restricted to when at most one domain variable remains not ground). This is described in more detail in the next section.

3 Operational semantics

In this section we present the operational semantics of extensions to LAIR that we have made. We begin by presenting the LAIR itself, trying to highlight the parts that can be specialized. Some of the following definitions where adapted from [Hent89].

Definition 1 (Domain variable) A domain variable is a variable V ranging over a finite domain. The attribution of a domain to a variable is accomplished using the :: operator as in $V :: Domain$, where $Domain$ is either a list of constants or an integer range specification of the form $M..N$, being M and N integer expressions and $M < N$.

Lookahead checking is the only general method available in our prototype to handle constraints. Consequently, there is a single type of constraint declaration.

Definition 2 (Constraint declaration) A n-ary predicate p is a *constraint* if submitted to a unique declaration of the following form:
:- constraint $p(a_1, \ldots, a_n)$.
each a_i is either a 'g', a 'd' or a 'h'.

Definition 3 (Checkable constraint) A constraint $p(t_1, \ldots, t_n)$ is *checkable* if all its arguments specified as 'g' in the constraint declaration are ground and all arguments specified as 'd' are either ground or domain variables. 'h' arguments may be anything.

Definition 4 (Lookahead variables) In a checkable constraint, uninstantiated variables corresponding to a 'd' in the constraint declaration, are called *lookahead variables*.

Two versions of the LAIR, the *exhaustive* LAIR and the *partial* LAIR, are presented in definition 5, which differ on steps 2 and 4, below. The latter is used in the definition of some built-in constraints where specific methods are used which, for efficiency reasons, are not complete (not all inconsistent values from the domains of some variables are removed).

Definition 5 (LAIR) Let P be a program, $G_i =\leftarrow A_1, \ldots, A_m, \ldots, A_k$ a resolvent, and A_m the atom selected by some selection rule. The LAIR will derive G_{i+1} from G_i and P using the substitution θ_{i+1} if:

1. *Activation test*
   A_m is a checkable constraint and $x_1, \ldots, x_n$ are the lookahead variables of A_m, which range respectively over $d_1, \ldots, d_n$.
2. *Constraint checking*
   2.a) *Exhaustive LAIR*
   $$(\forall x_j), e_j = \{v_j \in d_j \mid (\exists v_1 \in d_1, \ldots, v_{j-1} \in d_{j-1}, v_{j+1} \in d_{j+1}, \ldots, v_n \in d_n),$$
   $$P \vdash A\theta \text{ with } \theta = \{x_1/v_1, \ldots, x_n/v_n\}\} \neq \emptyset.$$
   2.b) *Partial LAIR*
   $$(\forall x_j), e_j \supseteq \{v_j \in d_j \mid (\exists v_1 \in d_1, \ldots, v_{j-1} \in dj - 1, v_{j+1} \in d_{j+1}, \ldots, v_n \in d_n),$$
   $$P \vdash A\theta \text{ with } \theta = \{x_1/v_1, \ldots, x_n/v_n\}\} \neq \emptyset.$$
3. *New substitution*
   $\theta_{i+1} = \{x_1/z_1, \ldots, x_n/z_n\}$ where each z_j is the constant c if $e_j = \{c\}$, otherwise a new variable ranging over e_j.

4. *Reintroduction (of the constraint) test*
>   4.a) *Exhaustive LAIR*
>
>   if at most one z_i is a domain variable
>
> $\quad$ then $\;\; G_{i+1} =\leftarrow (A_1,\ldots,A_{m-1},A_{m+1},\ldots,A_k)\theta_{i+1}$ $\qquad$ (discard)
>
> $\quad$ else $\;\; G_{i+1} =\leftarrow (A_1,\ldots,A_k)\theta_{i+1}$ $\qquad\qquad\qquad\qquad$ (reintroduce)
>
>   4.b) *Partial LAIR*
>
>   if no z_i remains a domain variable (i.e. they are all ground)
>
> $\quad$ then $\;\; G_{i+1} =\leftarrow (A_1,\ldots,A_{m-1},A_{m+1},\ldots,A_k)\theta_{i+1}$ $\qquad$ (discard)
>
> $\quad$ else $\;\; G_{i+1} =\leftarrow (A_1,\ldots,A_k)\theta_{i+1}$ $\qquad\qquad\qquad\qquad$ (reintroduce)

When a constraint is reintroduced in the new resolvent, its immediate activation would not produce any new information. Therefore, although being checkable, the constraint is not selected again until at least one of its argument is subjected to further changes.

3.1 The SLAIR

By looking to the LAIR definition, one can detect three potential sources of inefficiency: the activation test, the constraint checking process and the reintroduction test. In this section the definition of SLAIR (Specialized Locking-Ahead Inference Rule) is given. It specializes the LAIR by refining each of those three components.

The activation test is our main concern in this paper and is discussed in the next subsection. The constraint checking process and the reintroduction test are discussed less thoroughly in section 4 since although we already provide ways to improve constraint checking, further work must be done.

3.1.1 The activation test

The fact that a constraint is checkable does not mean that its activation will produce any significant pruning, at least to compensate the overhead of the constraint checker. In the worst case it will waste time to achieve no pruning at all.

Take for example a checkable constraint like $X < Y$, and let max_x, max_y, min_x, min_y denote the maximum and minimum values of their domains. If $min_x < min_y$ and $max_x < max_y$ then the activation of the constraint will have no consequence. If later alterations, caused by other constraints, restrict the domains of X or Y, but leaving min_x and max_y unchanged, the reactivation of $X < Y$ will still be useless.

A more suitable activation test should thus be used for certain constraints to avoid this inefficiency. The specification of an *activation guard* in the constraint declaration is the way in which our prototype allows the programmer to use his/her knowledge to refine the activation test. Let us now reformulate definitions 2 and 3 to include these features.

Definition 6 (Constraint declaration) A n-ary predicate p is a *constraint* if submitted to a unique declaration of the following form:
$\quad$:- constraint $p(a_1,\ldots,an) <-$ *Activation Guard.*

The activation guard is optional and is just like a normal rule body. Each a_i is either a 'g' , a 'd' or a 'h' or may take the form $g(Arg)$, or $d(Arg)$, or $Arg :: Dom$, or $h(Arg)$, where Arg and Dom are variables. The first format corresponds to a 'g' , the second and the third to a '*d*' and the last to a '*h*'. These specifications allow the binding between constraint arguments and the variables in the activation guard.

Definition 7 (Checkable constraint) A constraint $p(t_1, \ldots, t_n)$ is checkable if a) all its arguments specified as '*g*' or a $g(Var)$ in the constraint declaration are ground and all arguments specified as '*d*', $d(Var)$ or $Var :: Dom$ are either ground or domain variables, and b) the activation guard succeeds. '*h*' or $h(Arg)$ arguments may be anything.

In this context, SLAIR is the inference rule resulting from a specialization of LAIR with this new definition of *checkable constraint*.

With the specialization of the activation test one can easily define FCIR (the forward checking inference rule) from SLAIR, by stating an activation guard that only succeeds when at most a domain variable is still not ground. Program 1 shows a general method to implement FCIR in our prototype, for an arbitrary n-ary constraint *c*.

```
:- constraint c(d(A1), ..., d(An)) <- atmost([A1, ..., An], 1).

% definition of c/n
c(A1, ... ,An) :- ...
  ...
```

Program 1: definition of a forward constraint

The predicate $atmost(List, N)$ is a built-in predicate, which only succeeds if *List* does not contain more than N variables. Using this predicate in an activation guard one can control the maximum number of allowed lookahead variables before a constraint is activated. This will allow the specification of intermediate constraint activation regimes, between lookahead checking (which delays activation the least) and forward checking (which delays it the most).

Although other activation guards can be considered, in the examples of section 5 we will only use activation guards of this type which are quite useful and illustrates adequately our proposal.

4 Constraint checking and reactivation

4.1 The constraint checker

The constraint checker processes the second step of the LAIR, which is the most complex process of the constraint solver. In order to detect which values may remain and which should be discarded from each domain of the lookahead variables this step may, in the worst case, be implemented as a generation and test of several variable tuples.

This implementation exhibits an exponential time complexity, and is the main cause of LAIR inefficiency. On the other hand, when a constraint is handled in forward checking mode, and since only one domain is involved, the constraint checking process is proportional to this domain size.

As such, forward checking is usually preferable since it presents a more efficient behavior of the constraint handler. However, in a test and generate paradigm, the delay of constraint satisfaction just readdresses the combinatorial problem to the generation process. Failure detection is postponed and the generation process may have to perform too many backtracks.

The inefficient behavior of the constraint checker is of course due to its general scope. When dealing with a specific constraint there may be several properties that can be explored to make constraint checking efficient. Built-in constraints that languages usually provide are handled with specific methods.

For instance, the satisfaction of $X < Y$ just takes two linear steps. Given d_x, d_y, respectively the domains of X and Y, min_x, the least value of d_x , and max_y , the greatest value of d_y then the new domains to be computed are respectively $e_x = \{v \in d_x \mid v < max_y\}$ and $e_y = \{v \in d_y \mid v > min_x\}$.

We have not yet defined a general and declarative way of defining user constraint checkers. Since there are several built-in constraints that are handled with specific methods, our prototype allows a special specification, with the operator :=, of a constraint defined as a single built-in constraint call. With this specification, the constraint is handled by the built-in constraint checker instead of the general one. This enables the programmer to combine the use of guards with the efficient handling of built-in constraints. Program 2 shows a case of such specification, taken from an example of the next section (cf. program 5). We shall call such constraint as a *guarded built-in constraint*.

```
:- constraint add_digits(d(A), d(B), d(C), d(D), d(E))
        <- atmost([A,B,C,D,E], 3).

add_digits(Dig1, Dig2, CarryIn, Result, CarryOut) :=
        Dig1+Dig2+CarryIn = Result+10*CarryOut.
```

Program 2: example of a guarded-built-in constraint

4.2 The reintroduction test

After being checked, step 4 of the LAIR states that a constraint should be reintroduced in the resolvent if more then one lookahead variable remains non ground and discarded otherwise. Although this procedure is sound in the sense that only useless constraints (i.e. those satisfied by all tuples of the variables' domains) are discarded, it is not complete since it does not ensure that all useless constraints will be discarded.

For example, let X and Y be two domain variables and max_x and min_y denote respectively the maximum value of X's domain and the minimum value of Y's domain. If a constraint $X < Y$ is activated when $max_x < min_y$ (due to the action of other constraints), then $X < Y$ will trivially succeed removing no values from the variables' domains and will be reintroduced in the resolvent since more than one lookahead variable remains uninstantiated. Whenever the domain of X or Y is changed, this constraint is reactivated again, although being completely useless.

To avoid this inefficiency, the reintroduction of such a constraint should only be made if $max_x \geq min_y$. At present, the specification of flexible reintroduction tests is not possible in our prototype, but this is a topic we intend to carry out in future research.

5 Experimental results

The following examples where executed in our prototype, implemented with Quintus Prolog (and running on a 3 Mips, VAXSation 3540). It should not be regarded as a particularly efficient prototype, but rather as an experimental tool to compare algorithms and different approaches to solve constraints over finite domains.

1st problem

The first problem consists of finding four different integers, (between 1 and 56), for which the multiplication of any two of them is divisible by the addition of the other two. Constraint c/4 defined in program 3 specifies this property.

It is a normal user-defined constraint, so it is handled by the general constraint checker. The program has been executed under several activation regimes, which differed on the maximum number of lookahead variables allowed (by the *atmost/2* predicate).

Table I shows the results obtained on these executions, where N indicates the number of lookahead variables, *Time* the execution time (in seconds), *Backtracking* the number of backtracks made on the value generator (predicate *indomain/1*), *Activations* the number of activations of constraint c/4 and *Tests* the number of constraint tests made with c/4 (i.e. calls to c with all parameters ground).

```
:- constraint c(d(A), d(B), d(C), d(D)) <- atmost([A,B,C,D],2).

c(A,B,C,D) :- (A*B) mod (C+D) = 0, (A*C) mod (B+D) = 0,
              (A*D) mod (B+C) = 0, (B*C) mod (A+D) = 0,
              (B*D) mod (A+C) = 0, (C*D) mod (A+B) = 0.

solve([A,B,C,D]::1..56) :- A<B, B<C, C<D, c(A,B,C,D),
                           labeling([A,B,C,D]).

labeling([]).
labeling([H|T]) :- indomain(H), labeling(T).
```

Program 3: 1st problem

As expected, lookahead checking ($N=4$) with the general constraint checker, does not pay off. Although the search space is pruned so successfully that the generation process becomes almost deterministic, this pruning is achieved by means of an excessive number of constraint tests.

As explained before, although a constraint logic program replaces the generate and test paradigm by a test and generate, the general constraint checker (which performs the tests)

N	Time	Backtracking	Activations	Tests
4	7 837.30	3	19	21 913 017
3	433.57	7	17	1 193 592
2	382.53	372	367	913 138
1	464.58	9904	9 540	325 823

Table 1: statistics

is itself implemented as a generate and test procedure. In fact the results obtained with
$N=4$ are worse than with a standard backtracking program (where predicates indomain
are called before the less than ($<$) comparisons and constraint $c/4$), which took only 1600s
to execute. An early activation of a constraint (when it has too many domain variables)
is therefore too costly, given the high number of constraint tests performed.

Forward checking ($N=1$) is generally more compensatory, and this is indeed the case
for this program. Much more activations of the constraint are made, because the constraints are activated too late, i.e. when the bad choices for the variables were already
made, and thus a significant amount of backtracking occurs in the generation phase.
However, each activation only performs an average of 34 constraint tests (the maximum
domain size of a variable is 56), against an average of 1 153 317 constraint tests for each
activation in lookahead checking.

In general the number of constraint tests grows very rapidly with the number of allowed
lookahead variables, when the general constraint checker is used. Nevertheless, the results
obtained with forward checking may be bettered.

For example, with $N=3$ an effective pruning is also achieved, in fact almost as good as
with lookahead checking, with much less work of the constraint checker. Although more
constraint tests were made than for $N=1$, the pruning achieved is sufficient to cause a
speedup of 1.07 in the overall execution time. The best result is however achieved with
$N=2$ (a 1.21 speedup), which is the best trade-off between the amount of backtracks and
the constraint testing.

Of course, the improvements on forward checking are not very impressive given the
inefficiency of the constraint checker. The early pruning thus achieved does not pay off
very significantly. The next examples use a specific and more efficient constraint checker,
in which case the anticipation of constraint activation is much more worthwhile.

2nd problem

The second problem is the classic crypto-arithmetic problem of assigning different decimal
digits to the letters $G, E, R, A, L, D, O, N, B$ and T in order to satisfy the equation:

$$
\begin{array}{ccccccc}
 & G & E & R & A & L & D \\
+ & D & O & N & A & L & D \\
\hline
 & R & O & B & E & R & T \\
\end{array}
$$

Program 4 depicts the specification of this problem. The *crypto*/10 predicate is
a guarded-built-in constraint allowing several activation regimes, where the maximum
number of lookahead variables allowed is controled with the *atmost*/2 predicate. The

```
:- constraint crypto(d(G), d(E), d(R), d(A), d(L),
                     d(D), d(O), d(N), d(B), D(T))
        <- atmost([G,E,R,A,L,D,O,N,B,T], 7).

crypto(G,E,R,A,L,D,O,N,B,T) :=
            100000*G + 10000*E + 1000*R + 100*A + 10*L + D +
            100000*D + 10000*O + 1000*N + 100*A + 10*L + D =
            100000*R + 10000*O + 1000*B + 100*E + 10*R + T.

solve(L) :- L = [G,E,R,A,L,D,O,N,B,T]::0..9,
            alldifferent(L), G\=0, D\=0, R\=0,
            crypto(G,E,R,A,L,D,O,N,B,T),
            labeling(L).
```

Program 4: 2nd problem

N	Time	Backtracking	Activations
10	3.73	16	121
9	3.73	16	121
8	3.42	16	114
7	2.67	17	90
6	3.05	49	89
5	10.95	313	354
4	50.40	1 931	1 819
3	234.60	10 089	8 281
2	2 491.88	139 534	97 135
1	5 123.57	333 801	194 268

Table 2: statistics

alldifferent/1 predicate, guarantees that no two elements of a list are equal, by means of constraint \=.

Table II reports the behavior of finding the first solution under the influence of each activation guard, where N, *Time* and *Backtracking* are as before, and *Activations* is the number of activations of constraint *crypto*/10.

Notice that this time the column with the number of constraint tests was not included, since *crypto*/10 is a guarded-built-in constraint, which is handled by specific methods, that exploit some properties of linear equations. In particular, for each activation the time it takes for the constraint to be checked is proportional to the number of domain variables involved, since only the maximum and minimum values are considered (i.e. it is a case of Partial SLAIR).

Lookahead checking presents now a better behavior than forward checking, given the efficiency of the constraint solver. Notice, however, that better results may still be achieved with activation strategies that lie somewhere between these two extremes. In this case, $N=7$ is the best result obtained, with a 1.4 speedup over lookahead checking ($N=10$).

Furthermore, notice that, given the above mentioned efficiency of the constraint solver, the execution time of this problem is now, by and large, closely related to the number of activations of the constraint crypto (and not the number of tests performed by the constraint solver). In fact, the number of backtracks (and activations of constraint \=, not shown in the table), explains the fact that this problem executes faster with $N=7$ than with $N=6$.

3rd problem

The last problem is again a crypto-arithmetic puzzle, taken from [Hent89], of the following form:

```
  B A I J J A J I I A H F C F E B B J E A
+ D H F G A B C D I D B I F F A G F E J E
  ─────────────────────────────────────
  G J E G A C D D H F A F J B F I H E E F
```

Since this puzzle represents a 20 decimal digits addition, it would overflow if a single constraint as the previous one were used. Therefore, the solution adopted, is the perhaps more "natural" one of taking the addition of each pair of digits separately, using 19 extra variables to propagate the carry values, as shown in program 5.

```
:- constraint add_digits(d(A), d(B), d(C), d(D), d(E))
            <- atmost([A,B,C,D,E], 3).

add_digits(Dig1,Dig2,CarryIn,Result,CarryOut) :=
            Dig1+Dig2+CarryIn = Result+10*CarryOut.

solve(L) :- L = [A,B,C,D,E,F,G,H,I,J] :: 0..9,
            Carries = [C1,C2,C3,C4,C5,C6,C7,C8,C9,C10,C11,
                       C12,C13,C14,C15,C16,C17,C18,C19] :: 0..1,
            alldifferent(L), B\=0, D\=0, G\=0,
            add_digits(A, E,   0, F,   C1),
            add_digits(E, J,  C1, E,   C2),
                        ...
            add_digits(A, H, C18, J, C19),
            add_digits(B, D, C19, G,   0),
            labeling(Carries), labeling(L).
```

Program 5: 3rd problem

The statistics gathered with this problem with different activation guards is presented in Table III, where N, *Time*, *Backtracking* and *Activations* are as before. Notice that, instead of a single constraint on many variables, this problem uses now several constraints on much less variables, i.e. it requires 20 calls to *add_digits*/5 guarded built-in constraint.

Nevertheless, the results obtained show that, again, a number of lookahead variables which lies somewhere between pure lookahead checking ($N=5$) and forward checking

N	Time	Backtracking	Activations
5	3.42	1	174
4	2.33	1	121
3	1.75	1	91
2	3.43	54	173
1	3.10	91	117

Table 3: statistics

(N=1), is likely to get better execution times than these extreme strategies. In particular, with N=3 a speedup of 1.77 and 1.95 is achieved, when compared with forward and lookahead checking, respectively.

6   Conclusions and further work

In this paper we have discussed ways of extending the user interaction with the constraint solver, in order to achieve better performances on constraint logic programs, on finite domains. Our starting point, was the Look Ahead Inference Rule (LAIR) used in CHIP, the first constraint logic programming language defined over finite domains.

We have shown that this rule is very general, and by allowing the user to (meta-) programming it, better results could be achieved. With this purpose, a Specialized Look Ahead Inference Rule (SLAIR) is proposed, which will eventually allow the user to control a) the activation of constraints, b) the solving methods used on them and c) the need for their reactivation.

So far only the first of these capabilities is fully formalized (and implemented). The use of different constraint solvers has also been implemented, but their programming is not allowed (i.e. they must be built-in). Nevertheless, the experimental results already obtained with various activation strategies, partially reported in the paper, show that it pays off to tune the control of activation of the program constraints. In particular, we have shown that significant speedups are achieved with our system using activation regimes which allow a variable number of lookahead variables. The results show that these number should be closer, but different, to all (used by CHIP's lookahead checking) if an efficient constraint solver is used and closer to one (used by CHIP's forward checking) otherwise.

These encouraging results are a good motivation to proceed our work further in two other issues, namely allowing the user to meta-program both the constraint solving methods and reactivation of constraints.

Acknowledgements

This work was developed at the AI Centre of UNINOVA and funded by INIC. Francisco Menezes owns a scholarship from JNICT. We would like to thank these institutions for their support. We also like to thank our colleagues both at the Department of Computer Science and at UNINOVA, for all fruitful discussions and advice.

References

[Colm90]   A. Colmerauer, *Prolog III Universe*, Communications of the ACM, Vol.33, Number 6, June 1990.

[DVHS88]   M. Dincbas, P. Van Hentenryck, H. Simonis, A. Aggoun, T. Graf and F. Berthier, *The Constraint Logic Programming Language CHIP*, Proceedings of the International Conference on Fifth Generation Computer Systems (FGCS'88), Tokyo, December 1988.

[Hent89]   P. van Hentenryck, *Constraint Satisfaction in Logic Programming*, The MIT Press, Cambridge, MA (1989).

[JaLa87]   J. Jaffar and J.-L. Lassez, *Constraint Logic Programing*, Proceedings of the 14th ACM POPL Symposium , Munich, January 1987.

[JaMi87]   J. Jaffar and S. Michaylov, *Methodology and Implementation of a CLP System*, Proceedings of the 4th ICLP , Melbourne, May 1987.

[Shap89]   Ehud Shapiro, *The Family of Concurrent Logic Programming Languages*, ACM Computing Surveys, Vol.21, Number 3, September 1989.

A New Method for Solving Linear Constraints on the Natural Numbers*

Ana Paula Tomás, Miguel Filgueiras

Centro de Informática, Universidade do Porto
R. do Campo Alegre 823, 4100 Porto, Portugal
email: apt@ncc.up.pt, mig@ncc.up.pt

Abstract

In the recent past much attention has been given to the handling of constraints. The focus of this paper is solving linear constraints on the natural numbers, a problem that is also of great importance in AC-unification. We describe a new algorithm that is faster than the methods we compared it with, and that may well contradict the view that this kind of algorithms is too expensive to be of practical use, for instance in the implementation of Constraint Logic Programming languages.

1 Introduction

In the recent past much attention has been given to the handling of constraints in relation with the design of new programming language formalisms, such as CLP [Jaffar et al. 1986], [Jaffar and Lassez 1987], new programming languages, like CONSTRAINTS [Steele and Sussman 1982], Prolog III [Colmerauer 1987], or CHIP [van Hentenryck 1989]. Solving constraint satisfaction problems is also the traditional subject of several subfields of both Artificial Intelligence and Operations Research.

Dealing with constraints has several aspects, as, for instance, obtaining canonical forms, making simplifications and eliminating redundancies, testing the consistency, or solvability, of a set of constraints, adding or removing constraints from a set, and finding the solutions.

---

*The research described in this paper was partially supported by Instituto Nacional de Investigação Científica.

The latter aspect is the focus of this paper for a particular kind of constraints: linear equations over natural numbers, also known as non-negative linear Diophantine (NNLD) equations. Developing better methods for treating particular problems is important in the implementation of CLP languages, because the usual implementation strategy relies on specific methods for specific problems, rather than on general, but less efficient, methods (see, for instance, [Cohen 1990], [van Hentenryck 1989]). Methods for solving NNLD equations are also important for tackling constraints on finite domains, like those introduced in CHIP.

In the context of Operations Research, and more recently of CLP, linear arithmetic constraints are of special interest because their treatment leads, in most situations, to algorithms that are efficient. In this respect it is worth mentioning the linear programming problem, for which some years ago a polynomial algorithm has been found (see, for instance, [Tarjan 1980], and the references in [Lassez and McAloon 1989]).

Nevertheless, this is not the case when solving linear equations on the natural numbers, a problem which is known to be NP-complete. Efficient algorithms do exist when the domain is the integers (see, for instance, [Chou and Collins 1982]). Restricting the domain to the naturals makes these algorithms unsuitable, unless they are used as a basis for generate-and-test methods.

Apart from studies in Integer Programming, most of the effort we are aware of on finding methods for solving NNLD equations is related to the so-called *AC-unification*, which means unification of terms having associative-commutative function symbols. In the seventies Stickel proposed an algorithm which reduces the problem of AC-unification to that of solving a NNLD equation [Stickel 1981]. Since then several algorithms for the latter problem have been developed.

In this paper we present a new algorithm for solving NNLD equations, called CBA (for *congruence-based algorithm*), which is faster than the other algorithms we have compared it with. Its development was initially motivated by our study of the relationship between parsing and constraints on finite domains [Filgueiras 1990], [Filgueiras and Tomás 1990], [Filgueiras and Tomás 1991].

The following sections describe CBA in its basic form, how this basic form may be improved, and some implementation details. Before the conclusions, a comparison with other methods is given.

2 The basic version of CBA

A homogeneous NNLD equation has either only one solution (the null solution) or an infinity of them. The set of solutions can be generated by a (unique) finite basis such that any solution is a (unique) non-negative linear combination of the elements of the basis[1]. The basis is the set of all (non-null) *minimal solutions*, minimal in a component-wise ordering. The algorithms for solving this kind of equation usually just compute the basis.

When the equation is not homogeneous, the same algorithms may still be of use (see, for instance, [Guckenbiehl and Herold 1985] for a detailed treatment of this case).

Most of the algorithms we know of generate either candidate solutions which are then tested for minimality, or just tuples that are tested, first for being solutions and then for being minimal ones. The generation process consists in increasing the components of previous candidates by a certain order. Some bounds for the components have been established (see, for instance, [Pottier 1990]).

In contrast, in CBA we use some simple facts about congruences to efficiently solve NNLD equations in three unknowns. For the general case, this is combined with an enumeration process for the other unknowns. In this way, CBA generates a relatively small number of candidate solutions, which must be tested for minimality only when more than three unknowns are non-zero.

2.1 Equations in Three Unknowns

Any minimal solution (x_0, y_0, z_0) of Diophantine equation (1)

$$(1) \qquad a.x = b.y + c.z \quad a, b, c > 0$$

corresponds biunivocally to a minimal solution (y_0, z_0) of congruence (2)[2]:

$$(2) \qquad b.y + c.z \equiv 0 \pmod{a}$$

Taking $y_{max} = a/\gcd(a, b)$ and $z_{max} = a/\gcd(a, c)$ ($\gcd(x, y)$ stands for the greatest common divisor of x and y), we note that the residues of $b.y + c.z$ are cyclic with periods y_{max} in y and z_{max} in z. The search for the minimal solutions is therefore restricted to a rectangle of dimensions $y_{max} \times z_{max}$. Solutions with

---

[1] For the details, see, for instance, [Guckenbiehl and Herold 1985].

[2] By solution of a congruence we intend the actual values that satisfy it, not the residue class they are in.

exactly n non-zero components will be called *order n* solutions. The minimal order 2 solutions are $(b/\gcd(a,b), y_{max}, 0)$ and $(c/\gcd(a,c), 0, z_{max})$ and can be computed directly. The following facts[3] allow us to find a minimal solution of order 3 to (1).

Proposition 1 *Congruence (3)*

(3)
$$b.y \equiv c.z \pmod{a}$$

has a solution for some y iff $z = t.\gcd(a,b)/\gcd(a,b,c)$ for any integer t.

Proposition 2 *The solutions to congruence (3) with positive y and z are given by*

$$(t.m_b . \frac{c}{\gcd(a,b,c)} \bmod y_{max}, t. \frac{\gcd(a,b)}{\gcd(a,b,c)})$$

where m_b satisfies $b.m_b + a.m_a = \gcd(a,b)$ for some integer m_a, t ranges over the positive integers, and $n \bmod m$ denotes the remainder of n/m.

The algorithm of Figure 1, founded on the above results, computes the set S of minimal solutions of the equation $a.x = b.y + c.z$, given a, b and c positive. Apart from a function for evaluating the gcd of two integers, it uses a function *multiplier(n,m)* that computes a multiplier m_1 such that $\gcd(n,m) = m_1.n + m_2.m$, for some m_2. The **mod** operator is taken to always yield a non-negative value.

2.2 Equations with a Single Negative Coefficient

We now analyse an equation of the form (4):

(4)
$$a.x = \sum_{j}^{M} b_j . y_j \quad a, b_j > 0 \ M > 2$$

Any minimal solution of order $k+1$ with $k > 2$ has k non-zero unknowns in the equation right-hand side. Taking two of them as being the distinguished unknowns y and z, we enumerate the possible values for the others, and we get the equation (5).

(5)
$$a.x = b.y + c.z + \sum_{j'} b_{j'} . y_{j'}$$

---

[3]For the proofs please refer to [Tomás and Filgueiras 1991].

Input: *The positive coefficients a, b and c.*
Output: *The set S of minimal solutions.*

```
gb := gcd(a,b);   gc := gcd(a,c);   G := gcd(gb,c);
ymax := p := a/gb;   zmax := a/gc;
S := {(b/gb, ymax, 0), (c/gc, 0, zmax)};
dz := gb/G;   dy := (c*multiplier(b,a)/G) mod ymax;
y := z := 0;
while z+dz < zmax and p > 1 do begin
    z := z+dz;   y := (y+dy) mod ymax;
    if ymax-y < p then begin
        p := ymax-y;
        S := S ∪ {((b*p+c*z)/a, p, z)};
    end
end
```

Figure 1: Finding the minimal solutions of $a.x = b.y + c.z$.

Note that, for any j', $1 \le y_{j'} < a/\gcd(a, b_{j'})$, because the solution with $x = b_{j'}/\gcd(a, b_{j'})$, $y_{j'} = a/\gcd(a, b_{j'})$, and all the other components zero, is always minimal.

For each tuple in this enumeration, let $v = \sum_{j'} b_{j'}.y_{j'}$. Each minimal solution of (5) is now a minimal solution to (6).

(6) $$b.y + c.z \equiv -v \pmod{a}$$

The converse is not always true, as candidate solutions having different values for the y_j's may be comparable.

The following proposition justifies the algorithm of Figure 2 which computes the set S of minimal solutions of order 3 of the equation $a.x = b.y + c.z + v$, given a, b, c and v, positive.

Proposition 3 *Suppose $\gcd(a, b, c)$ divides v. Then, the least non-negative integer z_0 that solves the congruence (6) is the remainder from the division of $-v.M_c/\gcd(a, b, c)$ by $\gcd(a, b)/\gcd(a, b, c)$, where M_c is any integer satisfying $b.M_b + c.M_c + a.M_a = \gcd(a, b, c)$, for some integers M_a, and M_b. The value y_0*

for that solution is the remainder from the division of $(-v - z_0.c).m_b/\gcd(a, b, c)$
by $y_{max} = a/\gcd(a, b)$, *with* m_b *defined as in Proposition 2.*

Input: *The positive values* a, b, c *and* v.
Output: *The set* S *of minimal solutions of order 3.*

```
gb := gcd(a,b); gc := gcd(a,c);  G := gcd(gb,c);
S := {};
if v mod G = 0 then begin
    ymax := p := a/gb;  zmax := a/gc;
    dz := gb/G;  dy :=(c*multiplier(b,a)/G) mod ymax;
    z := (-v*multiplier(c,gb)/G) mod dz;
    y := ((-v-z*c)*multiplier(b,a)/gb) mod ymax;
    while z < zmax and p > 1 do begin
        if y < p and z > 0 and y > 0 then begin
            s := ((b*y+c*z)/a, y, z);  p := y;
            if for all s' in S, s' is not less than s then
                S := S ∪ {s};
        end;
        z := z+dz;  y := (y-dy) mod ymax;
    end
end
```

Figure 2: Finding the minimal solutions of order 3 of $a.x = b.y + c.z + v$, $v > 0$.

As stated above, not all the minimal solutions of $a.x = b.y + c.z + v$ correspond to minimal solutions of (5). As a consequence, we have to compare the solutions obtained by the last algorithm. For efficiency, we produce the solutions to (5) of order $n+1$ only after those of order n and ensure, by adopting an appropriate way of enumerating the y_j's, that no solution is less than a solution produced before. This implies that the set of minimal solutions to (5) is computed incrementally.

2.3 The General Case

The previous algorithms are used in CBA to compute the minimal solutions of an equation under the general form (7):

$$\sum_i^N a_i.x_i = \sum_j^M b_j.y_j \qquad (7)$$

For each i, CBA first solves $a_i.x_i = \sum_j^M b_j.y_j$, and for each j it finds the minimal solutions of order $n > 2$ to $b_j.y_j = \sum_i^N a_i.x_i$. It then solves subproblems in which at least two x_is, and two y_js are positive. They are given a form similar to that of (5) by assigning positive values to all but three components. There remains a problem $a.x = b.y + c.z + v$, but now v may be any integer. Clearly, if v is zero, no solution to this particular subproblem is a minimal solution to the initial one. When v is positive the problem reduces to the one described in the last subsection.

When v is negative we no longer have the guarantee that all the interesting solutions for (y, z) satisfy $1 \leq y < y_{max} = a/\gcd(a, b)$ and $1 \leq z < z_{max} = a/\gcd(a, c)$, respectively. CBA uses a combination of the last algorithm with a test for $x > 0$. When a solution with a negative value for x is found, CBA adds the minimum multiple of y_{max} to y that makes $x > 0$. Also, whenever a positive solution is found, CBA checks whether it is possible to subtract a multiple of y_{max} from y without making $x < 0$. Solutions with $x = 0$ are only used to find bounds to y.

3 Enumeration Bounds and Enhancements

Huet ([Huet 1978a]) and Lambert (as described in [Pottier 1990]) give bounds to the values of enumerated components. Two of them, by Huet and Lambert respectively, are (in the notation we have been using):

$$\forall_i x_i \leq max_j(b_j) \qquad \forall_j y_j \leq max_i(a_i)$$

$$\sum_i x_i \leq max_j(b_j) \qquad \sum_j y_j \leq max_i(a_i)$$

We have used the former in all our implementations of CBA, and the latter in two of them, which proved to be faster in problems with a great number of solutions (cf. next section).

Some enhancements may be introduced by considering bounds derived from minimal solutions obtained in previous steps of the algorithm. When there is a minimal solution whose non-zero components take the value 1, except one, say $y_r' = h$, we call such a solution *quasi-Boolean*. It is obvious that in any other minimal solution having at least the same non-zero components the value of y'_r must be less than h.

When all non-zero components take the value 1 we say we have a *Boolean solution*. It precludes the existence of any minimal solution having at least the same non-zero components, and can, therefore, be used to filter out some configurations of non-zero components.

4 Implementation

We have implemented CBA in C on a Sun 3/60 workstation. At present we have several versions. All of them make use of filtering by Boolean solutions, and Huet's bounds referred to above. For a fast access to the information concerning Boolean solutions and for speeding up the comparison between minimal solutions and candidates, we attach to each configuration of non-zero components a bit mask. In contrast with the implementation of [Huet 1978b], which uses recursion, our enumeration method is iterative.

The results presented below were obtained with versions $V0$, which is the basic one, and $V3$, which uses the bounds computed from quasi-Boolean solutions and incorporates Lambert's bounds described in the previous section.

Execution times of these versions are given in Figure 3. They are CPU-times obtained by making calls to the appropriate Unix system routines. For small problems, those taking less than 1/100 minute, we have used variants of the programs that repeat 100 times the computation of the solutions and give the average CPU-time spent. The values shown are the lowest CPU-times obtained in 3 consecutive runs of the programs[4] for each problem, with only one user active[5].

Figure 4 gives the numbers of candidate solutions rejected by these CBA versions. These numbers, which we think are quite informative, were obtained by slightly modified programs that count the numbers of generated candidates[6] that are liminarly rejected (by a simple test, like divisibility) and of those that are filtered after being compared to the minimal solutions already found.

From an analysis of these values together with experiments with the other versions we may conclude that:

---

[4]Compiled using the Unix standard *cc* command, with optimization (flag $-O$).

[5]What did not prevent some fluctuations from occurring, as there were other machines in the same local area network.

[6]Tuples with less components than the number of coefficients were not considered.

Problem	V0	V3
(2 1)(1 1 1 2 2 3)	5.7	6.0
(2 1)(1 1 1 2 2 10)	5.5	6.0
(9 5 2)(3 7 8)	30.3	17.3
(9 5 2)(1 2 3 7 8)	66.7	43.7
(3 3 3 2 2 2)(2 2 2 3 3 3)	133.3	133.3
(10 8 7 3)(9 5 2 10)	350.0	83.3
(8 7 3 2 1)(1 2 2 5 9)	466.7	233.3
(10 2 1)(1 1 1 2 2)	416.7	233.3
(653)(235 784 212)	416.7	100.0
(29 13 8)(42 15 22)	450.0	66.7
(29 13 8)(44 14 23)	1816.7	733.3
(11 11 12 13 14)(11 12 13 14 15)	11983.0	2966.7
(21 21 22 23)(21 23 24 25)	39683.0	26683.0

Figure 3: Execution times (ms) of CBA versions.

- using information from quasi-Boolean solutions reduces the number of candidates and increases the speed of the algorithms. In small problems the time spent in bookkeeping this information clearly outweighs the gain in speed.

- using Lambert's bounds may significantly increase the speed. Again, in small problems there is little or no advantage in this.

Some other tests shown that, in general, our CBA implementations have better performances when, for a given equation, the coefficients are in decreasing order in the left-hand side and in increasing order in the right-hand side.

5 Comparison with Other Methods

As we noted in the Introduction, most of the algorithms for solving NNLD equations originated from research on AC-unification methods. Abdulrab and Pécuchet describe the use of two Integer Programming algorithms in that context [Abdulrab and Pécuchet 1989]. Unfortunately they do not make a comparison with other, more specific, methods such as those by Huet [Huet 1978a] and

Problem	Min. Sols.	V0	V3
(2 1)(1 1 1 2 2 3)	19	0	0
(2 1)(1 1 1 2 2 10)	19	0	0
(9 5 2)(3 7 8)	65	1 192	41
(9 5 2)(1 2 3 7 8)	119	1169	84
(3 3 3 2 2 2)(2 2 2 3 3 3)	138	90	69
(10 8 7 3)(9 5 2 10)	152	14543	323
(8 7 3 2 1)(1 2 2 5 9)	345	5598	424
(10 2 1)(1 1 1 2 2)	349	4007	14
(653)(235 784 212)	37	111680	29996
(29 13 8)(42 15 22)	133	44081	2194
(29 13 8)(44 14 23)	216	133619	27890
(23 21 15)(19 17 12 11)	303	62184	12734
(11 11 12 13 14)(11 12 13 14 15)	1093	206818	31516
(21 21 22 23)(21 23 24 25)	3167	371875	107853

Figure 4: Number of rejected candidates in CBA versions.

Fortenbacher (described in [Guckenbiehl and Herold 1985]). Boudet, Contejean and Devie [Boudet et al. 1990] give a new method for solving systems of NNLD equations, based on Fortenbacher's, and although they state that their method is more efficient than previous ones, they do not provide data supporting their claim. More recently, Pottier, in [Pottier 1990], proposes a modification to this algorithm along with a novel one using concepts related with Gröbner bases, and for which an implementation is still under way [Pottier, *personal communication*, 1991].

At the moment we can compare the efficiency of CBA with Huet's and Fortenbacher's algorithms. For Huet's, we translated the Pascal implementation given in [Huet 1978b] to C, making minor adjustments so as to have a fair comparison. This allowed us to make CPU-time measurements which can be directly compared to those of CBA — see Figure 5. Notice that when running Huet's algorithm, we adopted the order of the coefficients that better suits it [Huet 1978a].

Problem	Huet's	CBA-V3
(2 1)(1 1 1 2 2 3)	3.3	6.0
(2 1)(1 1 1 2 2 10)	8.7	6.0
(9 5 2)(3 7 8)	189.8	17.3
(9 5 2)(1 2 3 7 8)	1536.0	43.7
(3 3 3 2 2 2)(2 2 2 3 3 3)	116.8	133.3
(10 8 7 3)(9 5 2 10)	6200.0	83.3
(8 7 3 2 1)(1 2 2 5 9)	11900.0	233.3
(10 2 1)(1 1 1 2 2)	1100.0	233.3
(653)(235 784 212)	2.00e6	100.0
(29 13 8)(42 15 22)	0.14e6	66.7
(29 13 8)(44 14 23)	0.10e6	733.3
(23 21 15)(19 17 12 11)	0.29e6	533.3

Figure 5: Execution times (ms) of Huet's algorithm and of CBA-V1.

Figure 6 shows a comparison of the numbers of rejected candidates. Instead of the total number of rejected candidates we present the numbers of those liminarly rejected and of those filtered by comparison with other solutions.

These results show that CBA generates much less candidates and, although it takes more time to generate a candidate, it is much faster in problems with coefficients that are not too small.

Problem	Sols.	Huet's		CBA-V3	
		L. rej.	Filt.	L. rej.	Filt.
(2 1)(1 1 1 2 23)	19	19	2	0	0
(2 1)(1 1 1 2 2 10)	19	69	0	0	0
(9 5 2)(3 7 8)	65	6008	637	35	6
(9 5 2)(1 2 3 7 8)	119	45911	6159	78	6
(3 3 3 2 2 2)(2 2 2 3 3 3)	138	546	24	69	0
(10 8 7 3)(9 5 2 10)	152	247927	4733	281	42
(8 7 3 2 1)(1 2 2 5 9)	345	214684	21094	396	28
(10 2 1)(1 1 1 2 2)	349	1914	1476	14	0
(653)(235 784 212)	37	121941872	305608	29793	203
(29 13 8)(42 15 22)	133	7265514	171871	1839	355
(29 13 8)(44 14 23)	216	4628052	11395	24119	3771
(23 21 15)(19 17 12 11)	303	13792434	614194	10976	1758

Figure 6: Number of rejected candidates in Huet's algorithm and CBA-V1.

Lisp implementations of Huet's and Fortenbacher's algorithms are compared in [Guckenbiehl and Herold 1985], which presents time measurements for several equations. However, the values given are averages of real time measurements, instead of CPU times. This fact is at the origin of some discrepancies with our data for Huet's algorithm. Also, the equations that were used have, in general, very small coefficients, which distorts the results of a direct comparison. Even so, and in the absence of more concrete data, we tried to compare Fortenbacher's algorithm and ours by comparing their speeds with those of Huet's as given by [Guckenbiehl and Herold 1985] and by test runs of the implementation we have — the first 8 problems of Figure 5 were taken from that paper. This led to the following values: the average speed-up when comparing Fortenbacher's and Huet's algorithms is 1.9, while when comparing Huet's to CBA-V0 and to CBA-V3 we get 4.1 and 7.7, respectively. The ranges for these speed-ups are: 0.5 to 10.5 in the former case, and in the other two, 0.2 to 25.5 and 0.2 to 74.4. CBA-V3 behaves badly when the coefficients are below 3 or 4, which happens in 11 of the 28 problems treated. All in all, our algorithm is faster than Fortenbacher's, at least when the coefficients are not too small.

6 Conclusions

We presented a new algorithm for finding the basis of minimal solutions of NNLD equations. It has the advantage of combining an enumeration process for some of the components with an efficient method for solving equations in 3 unknowns. Our algorithm proved to be faster than the methods we compared it with. In particular, the difference in speed is enormous for problems with large coefficients.

Although a more detailed study remains to be done, this algorithm may well contradict the view (put forth, for instance, in [Dincbas *et al.* 1988]) that this kind of mathematical tools is too expensive computationally and not adapted to solve real world problems. Also, for the case of finite domains our method will of course gain from the existence of bounds to the unknowns. This means that it appears to be possible its use in, for instance, the implementation of Constraint Logic Programming languages.

References

[Abdulrab and Pécuchet 1989] Habib Abdulrab and J.-P. Pécuchet, Solving systems of linear Diophantine equations and word equations. In N. Dershowitz (ed.) *Proceedings of the 3rd International Conference on Rewriting Techniques and Applications*, Lecture Notes in Computer Science, 355, Springer-Verlag, 530-532, 1986.

[Boudet et al. 1990] Alexandre Boudet, E. Contejean and H. Devie, A new *AC* Unification algorithm with an algorithm for solving systems of Diophantine equations. In Proceedings of the 5th Conference on Logic and Computer Science, IEEE, 1990.

[Chou and Collins 1982] Tsu-Wu J. Chou and G. E. Collins, Algorithms for the solution of systems of linear Diophantine equations. *SIAM J. Comput.*, 11(4), 687-708, 1982.

[Cohen 1990] Jacques Cohen, Constraint Logic Programming Languages. *Comm. ACM*, 33(7), 1990.

[Colmerauer 1987] Alain Colmerauer, Opening the Prolog III Universe. *Byte*, 12(9), 1987.

[Dincbas *et al.* 1988] M. Dincbas, P. van Hentenryck, H. Simonis, A. Aggoun, T. Graf, F. Berthier, The constraint Logic Programming language CHIP. In

Proceedings of the International Conference on Fifth Generation Computer Systems, ICOT, 1988.

[Filgueiras 1990] Miguel Filgueiras, Systems of Linear Diophantine Equations and Logic Grammars. Centro de Informática da Universidade do Porto, 1990.

[Filgueiras and Tomás 1990] Miguel Filgueiras and A. P. Tomás, Relating Grammar Derivations and Systems of Linear Diophantine Equations. Centro de Informática da Universidade do Porto, 1990.

[Filgueiras and Tomás 1991] Miguel Filgueiras and A. P. Tomás, Solving Linear Constraints on Finite Domains through Parsing. This volume.

[Guckenbiehl and Herold 1985] Thomas Guckenbiehl and A. Herold, Solving Linear Diophantine Equations. Memo SEKI-85-IV-KL, Universität Kaiserslautern, 1985.

[Huet 1978a] Gérard Huet, An algorithm to generate the basis of solutions to homogeneous linear Diophantine equations. *Information Processing Letters*, 7(3), 1978.

[Huet 1978b] Gérard Huet, An Algorithm to Generate The Basis of Solutions to Homogeneous Linear Diophantine Equations. Rapport de Recherche no. 274, I.R.I.A., 1978.

[Jaffar *et al.* 1986] Joxan Jaffar, J.-L. Lassez and M. Maher, Logic Programming language scheme. In D. DeGroot and G. Lindstrom (eds.), *Logic Programming: Functions, Relations, and Equations*, Prentice-Hall, 1986.

[Jaffar and Lassez 1987] Joxan Jaffar and J.-L. Lassez, Constraint Logic Programming. In *Proceedings of the 14th POPL Conference*, 1987.

[Lassez and McAloon 1989] Jean-Louis Lassez and K. McAloon, A Canonical Form for Generalized Linear Constraints. IBM Research Report, Yorktown Heights, 1989.

[Pottier 1990] Loïc Pottier, Solutions Minimales des Systèmes Diophantiens Linéaires: Bornes et Algorithmes. Rapport de Recherche no. 1292, I.N.R.I.A., 1990.

[Steele and Sussman 1982] G. Steele and G. Sussman, CONSTRAINTS - A constraint based programming language. *Artificial Intelligence*, 1982.

[Stickel 1981] M. E. Stickel, A unification algorithm for associative-commutative functions. *JACM*, 28(3), 1981.

[Tarjan 1980] Robert E. Tarjan, Recent Developments in The Complexity of Combinatorial Algorithms. Report No. STAN-CS-80-794, Stanford University, 1980.

[Tomás and Filgueiras 1991] A. P. Tomás and M. Filgueiras, A Congruence-based Method for Finding the Basis of Solutions to Linear Diophantine Equations. Centro de Informática da Universidade do Porto, 1991.

[van Hentenryck 1989] P. van Hentenryck, *Constraint Satisfaction in Logic Programming*, MIT Press, 1989.

A Constraint-Based Fuzzy Inference System

Kevin Lano *

Abstract

This paper describes an inference system for uncertain predicates, providing an alternative to the maximal entropy method used by Paris and Vencovska in [7], and of acceptable efficiency in practical examples. Implementation results and relationships to other systems are also described.

In the Appendix we give an example of the application of the process, and a formal definition of the logics that underlie the system.

Key words   Fuzzy logic, Inexact reasoning.

1   Introduction

It has been recognised that standard expert systems, designed around classical logic and relational languages, are inadequate in many cases for reasoning about uncertain or indeterminate predicates. Such systems use probabilistic language and degrees of certainty in presenting their results, but the methods for combining these values suffer from being ad hoc or unsystematic. Various solutions have been suggested, including the necessity of unsound reasoning systems, and the use of contradictions [16]. A preferable alternative is to work with sound inferences within a logic that accommodates the possibility of partial and ambiguous truth. These logics are generally known as *Fuzzy* logics, and have undergone rigorous development and application since the initial papers of Zadeh [17] and Goguen [15]. This is the basis of the FRIL system of Baldwin [1, 2]. A more general approach, but based on probability theory is that of Paris and Vencovska [7], whose *maximal entropy process* applies to determine the 'fairest' value of a given formula, under given constraints. We combine the approaches of the FRIL system and the Paris-Vencovska system to obtain a general fuzzy logic based inference system, described in section 3.

2   Existing Systems

The system FRIL [2, 3] developed by Baldwin, uses a series of rules to determine the range of possible values that a formula can have as a consequence of a database of *support*

---

*Oxford University Programming Research Group, 11 Keble Rd., Oxford, UK *logic* clauses, generalising PROLOG. Although such support logic programs are considerably more expressive than the classical horn clauses of PROLOG, and possess a more authentically logical negation, as opposed to 'negation by failure', nevertheless the system is restricted in expressiveness in that constraints on general logical formulae cannot be stated, for instance that predicates A, B have $w(A \wedge B) \leq \frac{1}{3}$, where $w(\theta)$ denotes the *value* of formula θ (under a certain database or theory). In addition the operations of conjunction and negation used in FRIL are not taken from the same logic; the *residuated* algebra [14] with conjunction interpreted by multiplication has a *strict* negation operation: $\neg\, a$ has value 0 unless $a = 0$, when $\neg\, a = 1$. The conjunction corresponding to the more natural implication

$$a \Rightarrow b = min(1,\ (1 - a + b))$$

is

$$a \cdot b = max(0,\ a + b - 1)$$

These are the *Lukasiewicz* operations [5], they have the fundamental property of *adjointness*:

$$a \cdot b \leq c \ \equiv\ a \leq (b \Rightarrow c)$$

Definitions
Let *Alph* denote a set of propositional variables, usually this set will be taken to be finite, and L_{Alph} the corresponding propositional language, written as $SL(A_1, \ldots, A_n)$ if $Alph = \{A_1, \ldots, A_n\}$.

A *constraint* is an equality or inequality of the form

$$\alpha_1 w(\theta_1) + \ldots + \alpha_n w(\theta_n) \ \Phi\ \beta$$

Where $\Phi \in \{=, \leq, \geq\}$, β is real, the α_i are rational, and the θ_i are formulae of the language L_{Alph}. Let CL denote the class of finite sets of constraints (from the given language).

In the papers of Paris and Vencovska [7, 8] a generalisation of rules based classical expert systems is developed, to solve the problem:

(V):

> Given sentences $\theta_1, \ldots, \theta_n$ of the propositional calculus, and linear constraints on their values (degree of truth or belief), what value should be given to the degree of truth of a sentence θ from the same language.

The natural properties that an inference system for solving these constraints should possess are defined; the consequences of these principles being that there is only one (apparently infeasible) method of arriving at a solution that satisfies these properties, namely the method of maximum entropy.

3 An Extended System

The inference system described here deals with an extension of problem (V), and adopts the FRIL concept that a range of values is the natural result of fuzzy constraints. It uses a genuine fuzzy logic valuation in place of the statistical basis of both FRIL and the Paris-Vencovska system. Using fuzzy logic instead of Bayesian probabilities or the Dempster-Shaffer method is defended as reasonable in the system Z-II [5]. "Human beings reason with inexact predicates as if computing ... according to the rules of fuzzy logic, a number of studies bear this out" (Zadeh). Paris and Vencovska themselves question whether the elaborate statistical reasoning of the maximal entropy method bears any relation to the expert reasoning of humans. Although the system loses certain information contained in the input constraints, its output ranges serve to guide the user as to the plausible values of the variables of the situation.

The value space [0,1], the real interval, with the Lukasiewicz operations, is commonly used in fuzzy mathematics, see [12, 6, 10] for a comparison with other operators. Generalising these logics we obtain *residuated logics* [13], of residuated algebras [14].

The problem considered here is a modification of (V):

(V'):

Given a set of constraints:

$$\{\alpha_{i,1} w(\theta_1) + \ldots + \alpha_{i,n} w(\theta_n) \; \Phi_i \; \beta_i : 1 \le i \le m\}$$

in the values of the sentences $\theta_1, \ldots, \theta_n$, where the $\alpha_{i,j}$ are rational, the β_j are real, and Φ_i is an operator $\le$, $\ge$ or $=$, what is the set of possible values for $w(\theta)$, for a formula θ in the same language.

In place of the conditions (*) of w as a probability measure assumed in [8]:

$w(\theta) = 1 \wedge w(\neg\,\theta) = 0$ each classical theorem θ
$w(\theta) = w(\phi)$ if θ, ϕ are classically equivalent
$w(\theta \vee \phi) = w(\theta) + w(\phi)$ if $\theta \wedge \phi$ is false

here w is explicitly given as the Lukasiewicz valuation on [0,1]:

(i) :
$$\begin{aligned}
w(\theta \wedge \phi) &= max(0, w(\theta) + w(\phi) - 1) \\
w(\theta \Rightarrow \phi) &= min(1, 1 - w(\theta) + w(\phi)) \\
w(\theta \vee \phi) &= max(w(\theta), w(\phi)) \\
w(\neg\,\theta) &= 1 - w(\theta)
\end{aligned}$$

All that are left undetermined are the values assigned to the atomic formulae. The conditions (i) yield the properties:

(i') :
If sentences ϕ, θ are logically equivalent in residuated logic, then $w(\phi) = w(\theta)$.

All residuated logic theorems are theorems of classical logic (Boolean algebras being particular cases of Heyting algebras, which are particular cases of residuated algebras), but the converse is not true; for instance the formula $A \Rightarrow (A \wedge A)$ is not valid in the Lukasiewicz semantics.

(ii') :

$0 \leq w(\phi) \leq 1$ for any formula ϕ, and if θ is a theorem of residuated logic then $w(\theta) = 1$ and $w(\neg \theta) = 0$. Additional properties such as $w(\theta) = w(\neg \neg \theta)$ are also valid in [0,1].

The problem (V') then becomes essentially a linear programming problem; to maximise and then minimise the value $w(\theta)$ as a function of the $w(X)$ for the propositional variables X of θ, under the given constraints. The Lukasiewicz operations, apart from yielding more natural and continuous negation/implication operators, also make the problem linear; as opposed to the *multiplicative* residuated calculus:

$$
\begin{aligned}
w(A \wedge B) &= w(A) * w(B) \\
w(A \Rightarrow B) &= \begin{array}{ll} 1 & \text{if} \quad w(A) \leq w(B) \\ w(B)/w(A) & \text{otherwise} \end{array} \\
w(\neg B) &= \begin{array}{ll} 1 & \text{if} \quad w(A) = 0 \\ 0 & \text{otherwise} \end{array}
\end{aligned}
$$

With disjunction interpreted by maximum again. That ranges of values should be the result of fuzzy constraints is clear; there will inevitably be imprecision in the supplied inequations, representing inputs to an expert system for example, so that precise values of the output predicate will not actually exist.

4   Implementation

The inference system for solving constraints of type (V') has been implemented in Prolog, using the Sup-Inf algorithm for Presburger formulae described in [11]. A new variable ν is created to represent the objective function $w(\theta)$, and the formula $w(\theta) = \nu$ is conjoined to the constraints. The combined constraints are converted into disjunctive normal form $D_1 \vee ... \vee D_n$ with each D_i a conjunction of inequalities $L_{i,k} \leq U_{i,k}$ in variables $a_1, ..., a_m$ representing the values of propositional variables $A_1, ..., A_m$. As is proved in [11], the value of $Sup(C, v)$ for a variable v and clause C of this type, is the greatest real value that v can take in C, and $Inf(C, v)$ is the least real value. Therefore $l_i = Inf(D_i, \nu)$, $u_i = Sup(D_i, \nu)$ are the lower and upper bounds for the value of $w(\theta)$ under the clause D_i. The answer is returned as a sequence of clauses and corresponding ranges: $(D_1, [l_1, u_1]), ..., (D_n, [l_n, u_n])$ where $Inf(D_i, \nu) = l_i$, $sup(D_i, \nu) = u_i$ and so forth, the final simplified solution is the union of these ranges.

The Sup-Inf algorithm is of complexity 2^N in the length of the formula, but it is of practical efficiency for small instances, and has been used in commercial program verification tools.

5 The Natural Principles of an Inference Process

There are seven principles that a legitimate inference process for solving problem (V) is supposed to obey: in the formulation of [8] an inference process is a mapping N that takes sets of constraints S into a weight assigning function w on formulae. Here instead N is a mapping that takes generalised constraints into a mapping $N(S) = w$ that assigns values (as ranges) in $[0,1]$ to formulae:

$$N : CL \to (SL \to \mathbf{P}[0,1])$$

If S is inconsistent, $N(S)(X) = \emptyset$ for any X, otherwise, if a propositional variable X does not occur in S, $N(S)(X) = [0,1]$ is assumed.

The inference process described above does satisfy principles 1,2,3,5 and 7 of [8], under suitable rephrasing; and 6 is only invalid because of the particular operations chosen (it would be valid in the case that the multiplicative algebra operations for $\wedge$ and $\Rightarrow$ were adopted). Proofs of these principles follow, the notation of [8] will be used.

PROPOSITION 1
The inference process based on the Sup-Inf method satisfies the principles 1,2,3,5 and 7 of [8], and principle 6 in a modified form. We define these properties below:

Principle 1
If CL denotes the set of all possible finite sets of constraints, and $S1, S2 \in CL$ are equivalent on the basis of properties (i) of w, then $N(S1) = N(S2)$.
Proof
Equivalence under (i) means that the two sets of constraints, when fully expanded out as conditions purely of the $w(A_i)$ for propositional variables $A_1, \ldots, A_n$ are (classically) logically equivalent; they are quasi-linear inequations (involving max, min, multiplication by constants, addition, subtraction). Thus the same bounds will be returned for any formula under $N(S1)$ and $N(S2)$.

Principle 2
The equivalence classes of the formulae of $SL(A_{i1}, \ldots, A_{in})$ with respect to logical equivalence under residuated logic form residuated algebras $R(A_{i1}, \ldots, A_{in})$. If g is an isomorphism between two such classes $R1, R2$ say, then g is in particular a bijection between the classes of atoms of $R1, R2$, the classes $\{[A_{it}] : 1 \le t \le m\}$ of propositional variables, and (since $[0,1]$ with the Lukasiewicz operations validates residuated logic), if formulae ϕ, ψ are equivalent under residuated logic, then $w(\phi) = w(\psi)$ for any valuation on $[0,1]$. We require that $N(S1)(\theta) = N(S2)(\Gamma)$ whenever $g([\theta]) = [\Gamma]$, and $S1$ denotes the constraints

$$\{\sum_{i=1}^{m} \alpha_{i,j} w(\theta_i) \ \Phi_j \ \beta_j : 1 \le j \le k\},$$

and $S2$ the constraints of identical form but with formulae Γ_j in place of θ_j for each j, where $g([\theta_j]) = [\Gamma_j]$. This holds since g is determined by its action on atoms, so the expansion of the constraints $S1$, $S2$ into inequations in the values of the respective atomic propositions have identical forms (g commutes with the operations of conjunction, disjunction and implication). Thus the values $N(S1)(\theta)$ and $N(S2)(\Gamma)$ are the same whenever $g([\theta]) = [\Gamma]$.

Principle 3

If $S1$, $S2$ are consistent sets of constraints with no common propositional variables, then the inequations of $S2$ cannot affect the values assigned to the variables of $S1$, so that $N(S1)(\theta) = N(S2 + S1)(\theta)$ for θ in the language of $S1$, as required.

Principle 4

If $S1$ and $S2$ below are consistent sets of constraints, then $N(S1)(\Omega \wedge \phi) = N(S2)(\Omega \wedge \phi)$, for any formula Ω.

$$S1 = \{\sum_j \alpha_{i,j} w(\theta_j \wedge \phi) \quad \mu_i \quad \beta_i : 1 \leq i \leq n\} \cup \{w(\phi) = \gamma\} \cup$$

$$\{\sum_j \delta_{k,j} w(\theta_j \wedge \neg \phi) \quad \pi_k \quad \tau_k : 1 \leq k \leq r\}$$

and

$$S2 = \{\sum_j \alpha_{i,j} w(\theta_j \wedge \phi) \quad \mu_i \quad \beta_i : 1 \leq i \leq n\} \cup \{w(\phi) = \gamma\} \cup$$

$$\{\sum_q \gamma_{s,q} w(\Gamma_q \wedge \neg \phi) \quad \pi'_s \quad \tau'_s : 1 \leq s \leq p\}$$

This principle is invalid, as can be seen from the example of

$$S1 = \{w(A \wedge \neg B) = \alpha, \quad w(B) = \gamma\},$$
$$S2 = \{w(A \wedge \neg B) = \beta, \quad w(B) = \gamma\}$$

These, if $\alpha, \beta > 0$ are assumed, lead to the equations

$$E1 = \{a = \alpha + \gamma, \; b = \gamma\},$$
$$E2 = \{a = \beta + \gamma, \; b = \gamma\}$$

where a denotes $w(A)$, b denotes $w(B)$. Then, under $S1$, $w(A \wedge B) = max(0, \alpha + 2\gamma - 1)$, and under $S2$, $w(A \wedge B) = max(0, \beta + 2\gamma - 1)$.

The reason is the close connection between the values of ϕ and $\neg \phi$; in the case that a strict negation operator was taken (ie $w(\neg \phi) \in \{0, 1\}$, and either $w(\phi) = 0$ or $w(\neg \phi) = 0$), then this principle will hold (using the same process of maximising and minimising possible values of formulae, but now with a different set of logical operations specified by (i)).

Principle 5

For $S1, S2$ in CL, if the valuation $N(S1)$ satisfies the constraints in $S2$, then each of the output clauses D linking the values of the $w(A_i)$ in the expansion of $S1$ also solves the constraints of $S2$, ie: D implies $S2$ classically, hence no extra restrictions will be placed on the ranges of the variables of $S1$ by $S2$ in $S1 + S2$.

Principle 6

In this case the solution of the constraints:

$$\{w(A_1 \wedge A_3) = \alpha,$$
$$w(A_2 \wedge A_3) = \beta,$$
$$w(A_3) = \gamma\}$$

is simply:

$$w(A_1 \wedge A_2 \wedge A_3) = max(0, \alpha + \beta - \gamma)$$

which is reasonable, although Paris and Vencovska require that

$$w(A_1 \wedge A_2 \wedge A_3) = (\alpha * \beta)/\gamma$$

Principle 7

If $S + \{w(\theta) > 0\}$ is consistent then $N(S)(\theta) > 0$.

This holds with $(\exists p > 0)(p \in N(S)(\theta))$ as the consequence, since the consistency implies that the possible range of values for $w(\theta)$ under the equations S contains a non-zero value. $\square$.

6 Applicability and Examples

As opposed to conventional rules-based systems, the process described above is suitable for deriving information from situations in which there are complex inter-relationships and feedback effects between the variables of the situation. Any propositional logical formula can be used in a constraint, so that the expressivity is close to natural language.

Conventional rule-based systems are subsumed by this process. In the appendix we give a large example of a rule-based system of constraints for deciding university faculties, taken from [18], and show how the above inference process can be applied to obtain realistic results.

7 Other Operations

Other operations for fuzzy logic and approximate reasoning have been discussed at length in the fuzzy sets literature, [10], [12], and it is generally accepted that no single logic or algebra is sufficient for all situations, instead for each situation a suitable fuzzy logic will be chosen; for instance the Łukasiewicz conjunction is appropriate when the values of both conjuncts must contribute to the value of the conjunction, as opposed to the minimum operator, which ignores the value of the more valid conjunct.

7.1 The Multiplicative Algebra

As indicated above, the alternative residuated calculus with implication and negation defined by:

$$w(a \Rightarrow b) \quad = \quad \begin{array}{ll} 1 & if \quad w(a) \leq w(b) \\ w(b)/w(a) & otherwise \end{array}$$

$$w(\neg a) \quad = \quad \begin{array}{ll} 1 & if \quad w(a) = 0 \\ 0 & otherwise \end{array}$$

and conjunction interpreted as multiplication, disjunction as maximum, could be taken, and would validate each of the principles above, including principle 4, and principle 6 in the form required:

$$w(A_1 \wedge A_2 \wedge A_3) \quad = \quad (\alpha * \beta)/\gamma$$

for $\gamma > 0$. However the constraints and objective function are now no longer linear, so that in practice the problem of determining maximum and minimum possible values for variables of the constraints would be more difficult (and the Sup-Inf algorithm is restricted to *Presburger* arithmetic, arithmetic without multiplication except by constants). In addition the strict negation is unnatural.

Under some further reasonable assumptions however, it can be shown that this is the unique valuation w that satisfies principles 1 to 7 and the properties (i'):

PROPOSITION 2 If w satisfies principle 6, and (i'), and ran $w = [0,1]$ then w is the multiplicative algebra valuation.
Proof
From these assumptions we can show that $w(\theta \Rightarrow \phi) = 1$ iff $w(\theta) \leq w(\phi)$. Using Principle 6 with $\gamma = 1$, $A_3 = true$, we obtain that multiplication interprets conjunction, and hence (from axioms (XIII) and (VI)), implication is interpreted by the above operation. From axioms (IX) and (VII) and (VIII) we obtain that disjunction is interpreted by max.   □.

7.2   Intuitionistic Logic

The linear order [0,1] forms a Heyting algebra with the operations interpreted by:

$$\begin{aligned}
w(A \wedge B) &= min(w(A), w(B)) \\
w(A \vee B) &= max(w(A), w(B)) \\
w(A \Rightarrow B) &= \begin{array}{ll} 1 & if \quad w(A) \leq w(B) \\ w(B) & otherwise \end{array} \\
w(\neg A) &= \begin{array}{ll} 1 & if \quad w(A) = 0 \\ 0 & otherwise \end{array}
\end{aligned}$$

Again the process can be adapted to these operations by redefining the properties (i) of w to be these; so that any Intuitionistically valid formula ϕ has $w(\phi) = 1$ for any w. Again constraints and objective functions are quasi-linear forms, and the principles above hold after reformulation; principle 4 holds since the negation is strict.

Principle 6 holds in the form:

$$\begin{aligned}
w(A_1 \wedge A_2 \wedge A_3) &= min(\alpha, \beta) \\
&= min(\alpha, min(\beta, \gamma))
\end{aligned}$$

8   Limitations

8.1   Computational Limitations

Returning to the first formulation of problem (V') above, certain fundamental bounds can be placed on the computational complexity of any solution to this problem, since it in particular yields a satisfiability and validity test for this particular (Lukasiewicz) semantics: If S, the set of constraints, is empty, then the range of possible values for a formula θ contains 1 if and only if θ is satisfiable in [0,1] under this semantics; it is [1,1] if and only if θ is valid under this semantics. This also yields a validity test for classical logic, since the restrictions of the Lukasiewicz operations to $\{0,1\}$ are the corresponding classical operations.

PROPOSITION 3 The problem (V') is of at least NP time complexity.

Proof Since any propositional formula θ containing variables $A_1, \ldots, A_n$ can be converted to a formula:

$$\Phi \triangleq \theta \wedge \Pi\{A_i \Rightarrow (A_i \wedge A_i) : 1 \leq i \leq n\}$$

of length polynomial in the length of θ, and such that θ is classically satisfiable if and only if Φ is satisfiable in $[0,1]$ under the Lukasiewicz semantics, which holds if and only if $1 \in N(\varnothing)(\Phi)$.

Since the satisfiability problem for classical propositional formulae is known to be NP complete (Cooks Theorem), this demonstrates that the problem (V') is NP hard. □.

Similar arguments show the same lower bound for the other two semantics discussed above. In this sense then there appears to be no real advantage in abandoning classical logic as the basis of inexact reasoning; however practical application of the method is still possible, and the logical theoretical basis of this system is closer to the intrinsic nature of uncertainty than statistical reasoning; precise weights are not assigned to formulae, and as in FRIL, if there is no information supplied in the constraints about a propositional variable X, then the range $[0,1]$, "completely uncertain" is returned as the answer for $w(X)$. In the Paris-Vencovska system, the value $\frac{1}{2}$ would be the result, which does not distinguish between *certain* knowledge that the value is $\frac{1}{2}$, and complete ignorance of the value.

Paris and Vencovska have since argued against the use of the above principles, on the basis that they lead to an apparently infeasible process of deduction [9]. However, efficient implementations of constraint-based logic-programming languages have now been developed [4], and we believe that the logical clarity and natural nature of the constraint representation is a sufficient advantage that it should be considered as a serious basis for reasoning, despite computational costs, which seem reasonable in many practical cases. The language used in the constraints can be extended to predicate calculus, since there are meaningful semantics for residuated predicate logics [13], however, the computational cost would be expected to rise as a result.

8.2 Limitations on Representation

There is an inherent limitation in using elements of a linear order to represent degrees of truth. If we are interested in predicates over a world X of individuals, the interpretation of these predicates is as subsets of X, and the 'degree of truth' of a predicate is some measure of the size of the interpretation of the predicate relative to the extent of X. The Lukasiewicz valuation arises naturally in this situation as the lower bound on the degree of truth of $A \wedge B$ and $A \vee B$ given the degree of truth of A and B: If we assume the following properties of the measure $v : \mathbf{P}(X) \rightarrow [0,1]$:

$$v(X) = 1$$
$$v(X \setminus A) = 1 - v(A)$$
$$v(X) \leq v(Y) \quad \text{if} \quad X \subseteq Y$$

and the interpretation $r : Fmla \to \mathbf{P}(X)$ of the logical connectives $\lor, \land, \neg$ is taken to be classical (this need not be the case, we could interpret the negation of a property as the interior $(X \setminus r(P))^\circ$ of the complement of the interpretation $r(P)$ of predicate P, under some suitable topology, in which case the law of excluded middle could fail). That is, we define:

$$r(\mathbf{true}) = X$$
$$r(A \land B) = r(A) \cap r(B)$$
$$r(A \lor B) = r(A) \cup r(B)$$
$$r(\neg A) = X \setminus r(A)$$

so that we obtain the following limitations on the combined map $w : Fmla \to [0, 1]$ defined as the composition $w = v \circ r$ of these valuations:

(iii) :

$$w(A) \lor w(B) \le w(A \lor B) \le (w(A) + w(B)) \land 1$$
$$w(\mathbf{true}) = 1 \qquad w(\neg A) = 1 - w(A)$$
$$(w(A) + w(B) - 1) \lor 0 \le w(A \land B) \le w(A) \land w(B)$$

Hence, for purely positive formulae at least, the Łukasiewicz valuation is the one that makes the minimal assumption about the truth of the formulae. In reasoning from knowledge

$$w(A \land B) = \alpha, \quad w(A) = \beta, \quad \alpha \le \beta$$

of $A \land B$ and A to knowledge of B, on the other hand, the valuation is the most 'optimistic':

$$\alpha \le w(B) \le (1 - \beta + \alpha) \land 1$$

since the upper bound here is attained if we assume that

$$\alpha = (w(B) + \beta - 1) \lor 0$$

Representing subsets by their sizes is an abstraction that discards information, so that no valuation can be perfect. The Paris-Vencovska system has the same limitation, however it uses the assumption that $w(\theta) = 1$ for any classical theorem θ, whereas we use less restrictive assumptions.

9 Context Dependent and Context-Independent Reasoning

There is considerable evidence that the context and subject-matter of an inference task affects critically the methods that humans use to solve this task [20]. Our inference process, in contrast, has a fixed evaluation of logical connectives and applies these regardless of other information. A more liberal approach would be to assume only the basic value limitations discussed in section 8.2 above, and to evaluate formulae under these assumptions.

The ranges of formulae returned would be less tightly constrained in general, however basic logical facts such as

$$w(A \wedge \textbf{false}) = 0, \qquad w(A \vee \textbf{true}) = 1,$$
$$w(A \wedge \textbf{true}) = w(A), \qquad w(A \vee \textbf{false}) = w(A)$$

will still be valid.

Then we can show that principles 1, 3, 5, and 7 still hold under suitable reformulation:

PROPOSITION 4 The inference process that calculates possible ranges for the values of formulae, based only on the restrictions (iii) above, satisfies the properties 1, 3, 5, and 7 of an inference process.

10 Approximate Methods and Optimisations

We can apply Principle 3 in practice to reduce the work needed to derive values of formulae from rule bases expressed as sets of constraints. If the formula θ that is our objective contains propositional variables $A_1, \ldots, A_n$ then we need only examine the smallest subset S of a set R of constraints such that $R \setminus S$ contains none of $A_1, \ldots, A_n$, and has no variables in common with S.

It will often be the case that the rule base S is expressed as a set of positive implications:

$$a_{1,1} \Rightarrow s_1 \geq \alpha_{1,1}$$
$$\ldots$$
$$a_{1,n_1} \Rightarrow s_1 \geq \alpha_{1,n_1}$$
$$\ldots$$
$$a_{m,n_m} \Rightarrow s_m \geq \alpha_{m,n_m}$$

where the s_i are single variables, the antecedents contain no negations or implications, and none of the s_i occur in their own antecedents $a_{i,j}$. If in addition we define a relation $\ll$ as the transitive closure of $\prec$ defined by:

$$s_i \prec s_j \equiv s_i \text{ occurs in some } a_{j,k}$$

and $\ll$ is an ordering on the variables of the rule base, then we can reduce the calculation of lower and upper bounds for specific variables to:

$$w(S)(s_i) = [\bigvee \{ w(S)(a_{i,j})_l \cdot \alpha_{i,j} : 1 \leq j \leq n_i \}, 1]$$

where $w(S)(a_{i,j})_l$ is the lower bound on the value of the antecedent. The time complexity of the calculation of the lower bound of a variable s_i depends on the number of variables s_j with $s_j \ll s_i$, and on the complexity of the antecedents, but is linear in the size (number of symbols) of the given constraints. In addition no contradiction can be derived from these equations.

11 Conclusions

We have shown how a system that generalises classical propositional inference can be used as an inference engine for a fuzzy expert system, and that this system obeys most of the 'natural properties of an inference process' as specified in [8]. The practical limitations have been given, and alternative valuations investigated. A key advantage of the system is that rules and properties of a situation can be entered in a natural way as generalised logical statements. Thus maintenance of such a set of rules is made more efficient. In addition the logical basis of the system gives us a precise way of validating a set of rules against a model of a real world situation or of comparing two different rule bases of the same situation.

In philosophical terms it seems that actual reasoning in areas of uncertainty, even that carried out by experts, is to a large extent unconscious and does not involve explicit fixed rules, but is instead a network of intricate decision processes, capable of extension, learning and adaption. A balancing of alternatives and possible likelihoods occurs.

APPENDIX

1. Application to Classical Problems

The following is an example of an expert system rule base, taken from [18], illustrating how the system can be applied to yield realistic results in the case of a set of constraints that are purely rule-based. -> denotes implication, => 'greater than or equal to'. The rule base represents a set of rules for determining recommendations for faculties in which a student should study, based on his interest and abilities in various subjects, and the employment prospects in related occupations. For example, the variables recmed, epmed, ovintmed represent "degree to which the medicine faculty is recommended", "employment prospects in medicine", and "overall interest in medicine", respectively.

```
med_r1:
    (epmed = good) -> recmed => 0.9;
med_r2:
    (ovintmed = high) -> recmed => 0.6;
med_r3:
    (osuitmed = good) -> recmed => 0.4;
```

plus similar rules for science and art, and:

```
eng_r1:
    (epeng = good) -> receng => 0.9;
eng_r2:
    (ovinteng = high) -> receng => 0.6;
eng_r3:
    (osuiteng = good) -> receng => 0.4;
exam_r1:
    ((resphys = good) \/ (resbio = good)) &
    (resmath = fairtogood)    ->  (eppsc = good)  => 1.0;
exam_r2:
```

```
  ((resphys = fairtogood) & (resmath = good))
  -> (epeng = good) => 1.0;
exam_r3:
  ((resbio = verygood) & (resphys = good)
  & (resengl = fairtogood) ) -> epmed = good   => 1.0;
exam_r4:
  (resengl = good &  reshist = good) ->
  (epart = good) => 1.0;
exam_r5:
  (markengl <= (40,50)) ->
  (resengl = bad)              => 1.0;
exam_r6:
  ((50) < markengl < (70)) ->
  (resengl = fair)            => 1.0;
exam_r7:
  ((70) <= markengl < (90)) ->
  (resengl = good)            => 1.0;
exam_r8:
  ((90) <= markengl) ->
  (resengl = verygood)        => 1.0;
interest_r1:
  (interestredscibom = high) ->
  (ovintpsc = high)           => 1.0;
```

plus other rules for **interest** and **job suitability**.

We are using the rules that

```
(x = good) -> (x = fairtogood) = 1;
(x = fair) -> (x = fairtogood) => 0.9;
(x = fair) -> (x = good) => 0.8;
(x = fair) -> (x = verygood) => 0.4;
```

and similarly for the comparison of fuzzy numbers in the rules for the result of english. Given the sample information:

```
(resphys = verygood) =  1.0;
(resbio = fair)  =  1.0;
(resmath = fair)  =  1.0;
teachingdes =  0.9;
(curiouspersonality = true) =  0.8;
(interestredscibom = high)  = 1.0;
markengl = 75;
doctordes = 0.2;
(intanahumbody = high)  =  0.9;
(intrednovofic = high)  =  0.7;
(reshist = fair)  =  1.0;
engdes = 1.0;
(intcompdes = veryhigh)  =  1.0;
afraidblood = 0.0
```

we can simplify the rules and obtain the overall conclusions:

recmed = [0.5,1];   recpsc = [0.8,1];

recart = [0.7,1];   receng = [0.7,1];

which is similar to the conclusion arrived at by the Z-II system.

Indeed the result delivered by taking the multiplicative algebra operations is very close to this:

recmed = [0.54,1];   recpsc = [0.81, 1];

recart = [0.72, 1];   receng = [0.72, 1];

2. Formal Definition of Residuated Logic

We will only describe the propositional part of the logic here, a predicate calculus also exists. The language of residuated logic has the usual propositional connectives. Let *Fmla* denote the class of formulae of this language. The basic logical axioms are as given in [13]:

Propositional

(I) $\alpha \wedge \beta \Rightarrow \alpha$

(II) $\alpha \wedge \beta \Rightarrow \beta \wedge \alpha, \ (\alpha \wedge \beta) \wedge \gamma \Rightarrow \alpha \wedge (\beta \wedge \gamma)$

(III) $(\alpha \Rightarrow \beta) \Rightarrow ((\alpha \wedge \gamma) \Rightarrow (\beta \wedge \gamma))$

(IV) $((\alpha \Rightarrow \beta) \wedge (\beta \Rightarrow \gamma)) \Rightarrow (\alpha \Rightarrow \gamma)$

(V) $\beta \Rightarrow (\alpha \Rightarrow \beta)$

(VI) $\alpha \wedge (\alpha \Rightarrow \beta) \Rightarrow \beta$

(VII) $\alpha \Rightarrow (\alpha \vee \beta)$

(VIII) $\alpha \vee \beta \Rightarrow \beta \vee \alpha, \ (\alpha \vee \beta) \vee \gamma \Rightarrow \alpha \vee (\beta \vee \gamma)$

(IX) $((\alpha \Rightarrow \gamma) \wedge (\beta \Rightarrow \gamma)) \Rightarrow (\alpha \vee \beta \Rightarrow \gamma)$

(X) $\neg \alpha \Rightarrow (\alpha \Rightarrow \beta)$

(XI) $\alpha \Rightarrow (\beta \Rightarrow (\alpha \wedge \beta))$

(XII) $\alpha \wedge (\beta \vee \gamma) \Rightarrow (\alpha \wedge \beta \ \vee \ \alpha \wedge \gamma)$

(XIII) $(\alpha \wedge \beta \Rightarrow \gamma) \equiv (\alpha \Rightarrow (\beta \Rightarrow \gamma))$

(XIV) $(\alpha \Rightarrow \beta) \wedge (\gamma \Rightarrow \delta) \Rightarrow (\alpha \wedge \gamma \Rightarrow \beta \wedge \delta)$

(XV) $(\beta \Rightarrow (\beta \wedge \neg \beta)) \Rightarrow \neg \beta$

we use the inference rule Modes Ponens, and adjoining the axioms

$(IL):$ $\alpha \Rightarrow (\alpha \wedge \alpha)$ for any α

yields Intuitionistic propositional logic.

References

[1] J.F.Baldwin, B.Pilsworth, T.Martin - The FRIL manual, Equipu-Air Ltd, Bristol.

[2] J.F.Baldwin, B.Pilsworth - Evidential Support Logic Programming, Fuzzy Sets and Systems Vol 24, 1987, pp 1 - 26.

[3] J.F.Baldwin - A Fuzzy Relational Inference Language, Fuzzy Sets and Systems Vol 14, 1984, pp 155 - 174.

[4] A.Colmerauer - An Introduction to Prolog III, Proceedings of the ESPRIT 90 Symposium on Computational Logic, Brussels, DG XIII Commission of the European Communities.

[5] K.S.Leung, W.S.Felix Wong, W. Lam - Applications of a novel fuzzy expert system shell, Expert Systems Vol 6 No.1, Feb 89.

[6] V.Novak, W.Pedrycz - Fuzzy set and t-norms in the light of Fuzzy Logic, in Machine Learning and Uncertain Reasoning, B.Gains, J.Boose (Eds), Academic Press 1990.

[7] J.B.Paris, A.Vencovska - A Note on the Inevitability of Maximum Entropy, Mathematics Department, Manchester University 1988.

[8] J.B.Paris, A.Vencovska - On the Applicability of Maximum Entropy to Inexact Reasoning, International Journal of Approximate Reasoning Vol 3, No. 1.

[9] J.B.Paris, A.Vencovska - A Model of Belief, Manchester University, Department of Mathematics. (1990).

[10] R.R.Yeager - On a general class of fuzzy connectives, Fuzzy Sets and Systems Vol 4 (1980), 3, pp 235 - 242.

[11] R.Shostak - The Sup-Inf method for Proving Presburger Formulae, JACM Vol. 24, No. 4, October 1977, pp 529 - 543.

[12] S.Gottwald - Fuzzy Propositional Logics, Fuzzy Sets and Systems Vol 3. No. 2, pp 181 - 192.

[13] K.C.Lano - Mathematical Frameworks for Vagueness and Approximate Reasoning, PhD thesis, Bristol University, 1988. Summary in Fuzzy Sets and Systems, 35(2), 1990.

[14] A.Pultr - Fuzziness and Fuzzy Equality, Aspects Of Vagueness, Ed H.Skala, S.Termini, E.Trillas, (D.Reidel 1984) pp 119 - 135.

[15] J. Goguen - The Logic of Inexact Concepts, Synthese 19 (1969) pp 325 - 373.

[16] D. Long, R. Garigliano - A Formal Model through Homogeneity Theory of Adaptive Reasoning, PRG Technical Monograph 71, Oxford University Programming Research Group.

[17] L. Zadeh - Fuzzy Sets, Information and Control No. 8 (1965) pp 338 - 353.

[18] K.S.Leung, W. Lam - A Fuzzy Expert System Shell using both Exact and Inexact Reasoning, Journal of Automated Reasoning Vol 5, No. 2, June 1989.

[19] Z.Cao, Z.Handel - Applicability of Some Fuzzy Implication Operators, Fuzzy Sets and Systems Vol. 31 No. 2, June 1989, pp 151 - 186.

[20] H.Gardner - The Minds New Science, Basic Books, 1987.

A Constraint-Based Language for Querying
Taxonomic Systems

Margarida Mamede[†]   Luís Monteiro
Departamento de Informática
Universidade Nova de Lisboa
2825 Monte da Caparica, Portugal

Abstract

This paper presents a language for querying taxonomic systems
which is essentially a variant of first-order logic with terms denoting
types instead of individuals. A query expressed in the language is
either a declarative or an interrogative sentence. Declarative
sentences correspond to the usual first-order formulae and require a
"yes" or "no" answer. Interrogative sentences are basically declarative sentences with some variables stipulated as "query" variables,
for which the required answers are type assignments to the query
variables making the sentences true. From the semantic point of
view, queries will be interpreted as type constraints on the query
variables, and answers as constraints in a specified normal form
called "solved" form. To that effect, the paper proposes a general
scheme for constraint programming based on the notions of
constraint satisfaction and constraint reduction, and shows how the
query language can be viewed as an instance of the scheme. This
constraint system is the basis of a constraint logic programming
system dealing with type information as described by taxonomies.

1 Introduction

The usefulness in computer science of organizing information in a hierarchical
fashion can not be overemphasized. It has been amply demonstrated in connection
with the notions of subtyping and inheritance in both the programming [A-KN86,

---

† Owns a scholarship from Instituto Nacional de Investigação Científica.

Car88, MP90, Weg86] and the knowledge representation fields [Tou86]. This paper is a contribution to the subject from the point of view of querying a hierarchical type system, also called a taxonomic system, in a logic programming framework.

This work is, in part, a merge of two streams of ideas. On the one hand, it is concerned with the notion of a "useful" or "informative" answer to a query and with how to formalize this notion in logical terms. This problem has been investigated before by Porto, mainly in connection with the semantics of natural language systems [Por88, PF84], and our work builds on his ideas. On the other hand, to put the whole subject on a firm logical basis, we rely on the ideas of constraint logic programming [JL87], a field which has received lately a great deal of attention. In this view, queries and answers are both seen as constraints, the latter in some standard "solved" form agreed upon beforehand, which represents the required formalization of the notion of a useful answer. A previous version of this work is reported in [MM91].

The query language we use in this paper is based on the language described in [Por88] and is essentially a variant of first-order predicate logic. It contains no function symbols of arity greater than zero, and the constant symbols denote types. Derived types can be defined by comprehension (λ-abstraction applied to formulae), and by forming unions, intersections and products of other types. The formulae, called here declarative sentences, are defined in the usual way, except that there is a new kind of formula to express type containment. The language also comprises interrogative sentences, which are basically declarative sentences with some variables stipulated as "query" variables.

The semantics of the query language is described by viewing the language as a constraint system. To that effect, the paper proposes a novel scheme for constraint programming based on the notions of constraint satisfaction and constraint reduction, and shows how the query language can be viewed as an instance of the scheme. This constraint system is the basis of a constraint logic programming system dealing with type information as described by taxonomies. In this paper, however, we refrain from presenting the logic programming system and concentrate on the description of the constraint system only.

The rest of the paper is organized as follows. The next three sections present respectively the query language, the notion of taxonomy that will be used in the paper, and how relation symbols are interpreted in terms of taxonomies. The fifth section describes the general scheme for constraint logic programming, and the next three sections are devoted to showing how the query language can be viewed as an instance of the scheme. Section 6 characterizes the atomic constraints, and sections 7 and 8 present the satisfaction and the reduction systems, respectively. Section 9 presents two detailed examples illustrating the main points of the theory. Finally, section 10 indicates some directions of future work.

2 The Query Language

The query language we use in this paper is a 4-tuple L=<Type,Rel,Quant,Var> of pairwise disjoint sets of atomic types $N \in$ Type, relation names $r \in$ Rel, quantifiers $Q \in$ Quant (we only consider here the universal and the existential quantifiers), and variables $v \in$ Var. There are four kinds of language expressions: *declarative sentences* D, *multiple types* M, *singular types* S, and *interrogative sentences* I. The abstract syntax can be described as follows, where e is an atomic type or a variable:

$$D \rightarrow r(e_1,...,e_n)^1 \mid (e_1,...,e_n):M^1 \mid D_1 \wedge D_2 \mid D_1 \vee D_2 \mid \neg D \mid (Qv:S)D$$
$$M \rightarrow (S_1,...,S_n) \mid \lambda v_1,...,v_n.D \mid M_1 \& M_2 \mid M_1 + M_2$$
$$S \rightarrow N \mid \lambda v.D \mid S_1 \& S_2 \mid S_1 + S_2$$
$$I \rightarrow (?v:S)D \mid (?v:S)I$$

Occurrences of variables may be bound by a quantifier Q, by λ or by ?, otherwise they are free. In the expressions of the form $(e_1,...,e_n):M$ the variables occurring among $\{e_1,...,e_n\}$ may not be free variables of M, and in $(Qv:S)D$, $(?v:S)D$ and $(?v:S)I$, v may not occur free in S.

Except for type sentences, declarative sentences have the usual syntax. A type sentence states that a tuple of atomic types and variables belongs to a multiple type. A multiple type can be a tuple (a cartesian product) of singular types, an abstraction of a declarative sentence in some of its variables, an intersection or a union of two multiple types. A singular type is an atomic type, an abstraction of a declarative sentence in one of its variables, an intersection or a union of two singular types. An interrogative sentence is similar to a quantified declarative sentence, except that it specifically inquires about which elements of the singular types marked with ? satisfy the sentence.

Let us give the intuitive meaning of some sentences, assuming that bird and fish belong to Type, and eat and attack are relation names of arity two:

— All birds eat fish.   (all x:bird) (some y:fish) eat(x,y)
— What birds eat fish ?   (? x:bird) (some y:fish) eat(x,y)
— Which birds eat which fish ?   (? x:bird) (? y:fish) eat(x,y)
— All birds eat the fish they attack.   (all x:bird)(all y:fish&λb.attack(x,b)) eat(x,y)

The expected answers are: yes or no, for the first and last sentences; a set of atomic types, for the second; and a set of atomic type pairs, for the third.

---

[1] All the variables occurring among $e_1,...,e_n$ are distinct.

3 Taxonomies

A taxonomy is a partially ordered set $\langle T, \leq \rangle$ of types, with a greatest type T, that satisfies two additional properties. Further types can be defined by taking arbitrary subsets of T, interpreted as the union of its members. However, to give complete and concise answers to queries, we will restrict ourselves to those subsets of T that contain only the most generic types.

As an example, suppose $T=\{T,U,A,B,C,V\}$, with the $\leq$ relation presented in Figure 1. Everything is of type U or V, and U is the disjoint union of types A, B and C. In this context, the sets $\{U\}$, $\{U,A\}$ and $\{A,B,C\}$ contain the same "information", but we will only consider the first one since it is the most generic representation of that information.

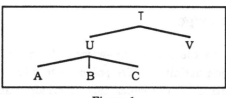

Figure 1

Definition (Ideal and Filter)

For every $X \subseteq T$, the ideal and the filter generated by X are, respectively, $\downarrow X = \{t \in T \mid (\exists x \in X)\, t \leq x\}$ and $\uparrow X = \{t \in T \mid (\exists x \in X)\, x \leq t\}$.

Intuitively, the closure of a set X, ΔX, is the biggest set with the same information as X. A type $t \in T$ doesn't add any information to X ($t \in \Delta X$) if every minimal subtype of t is also of type t', for some t' in X. This is formalized by the requirement that every minimal type of $\downarrow\{t\}$ is a minimal type of $\downarrow X$. For example, $\Delta\{A,B,C\}=\{A,B,C,U\}$. The minimal types of U are A, B and C, and all belong to $\downarrow\{A,B,C\}$. Note that $T \notin \Delta\{A,B,C\}$ because its minimal types are A, B, C and V, and $V \notin \downarrow\{A,B,C\}$. We conclude that T has some information not included in $\{A,B,C\}$, namely the type V.

Definition (Closure)

The closure of $X \subseteq T$ is $\Delta X = \{t \in T \mid$ minimal types of $\downarrow\{t\} \subseteq$ minimal types of $\downarrow X\}$.

Definition (Taxonomy)

A taxonomy is a triple $\langle T, \leq, T \rangle$ such that:
- $\langle T, \leq \rangle$ is a partially ordered set.
- T is the greatest element of T.
- Every chain has a least upper bound and a greatest lower bound.
- For every $X \subseteq T$, ΔX is closed for least upper bounds, i.e.,
$$\{a_1,a_2,...\} \subseteq \Delta X,\ a_1 \leq a_2 \leq ... \Rightarrow \vee\{a_1,a_2,...\} \in \Delta X.$$

It's easy to see that $X \equiv Y \Leftrightarrow \Delta X = \Delta Y$ is an equivalence relation. We will work on $\wp(T)/\equiv$, choosing the maximal elements of a closed set to represent each class. The maximal part of $X \subseteq T$ is $\Uparrow X = \{t \in X \mid (\forall x \in X) \; t \leq x \Rightarrow t = x\}$. The next result shows that our type system supports boolean reasoning.

Proposition 1

Let $<T, \leq, T>$ be a taxonomy. $M(T) = \{\Uparrow \Delta P \mid P \subseteq T\}$ is a Boolean algebra where, for every $X, Y \in M(T)$, $X \leq Y \Leftrightarrow (\forall x \in X)(\exists y \in Y) x \leq y$, $\bot = \varnothing$, $\top = \{T\}$, $X \vee Y = \Uparrow \Delta (X \cup Y)$, $X \wedge Y = \Uparrow (\downarrow X \cap \downarrow Y)$, $\neg X = \Uparrow (T - \Uparrow \downarrow X)$. ♦

Note that if $<T, \leq, T>$ is a taxonomy, T^k $(k > 0)$ is also a taxonomy whose greatest element is $(T,...,T)$ and $(a_1,...,a_k) \leq (b_1,...,b_k) \Leftrightarrow (\forall 1 \leq i \leq k) \; a_i \leq b_i$.

By convention $T^0 = \{T\}$ which is a taxonomy with the induced order relation.

4 The System Knowledge

In this paper, we assume the system answering the queries knows somehow the taxonomy and the relation definitions. We postpone to a later work the description of the language and data structures in which this knowledge can be expressed. For each $t \in$ Type there is a corresponding element in the taxonomy. And with every $r \in$ Rel, of arity k, is associated a finite set $R_r \in M(T^k)$ that defines it.

For simplicity, in the sequel we will not distinguish between T and Type, assuming that $<\text{Type}, \leq, T>$ is the taxonomy to be considered. Therefore, the definition of a relation is an element of $M(\text{Type}^k)$. Note that the constraint satisfaction and reduction systems presented below for the query language sentences take into account these given structures.

5 A Theory of Constraints

Our scheme for constraint programming is based on an abstract set of "atomic" constraints that is given from the outset. A constraint is defined as a finite set of atomic constraints. Two sets of notions, of a "model-theoretic" and of a "proof-theoretic" nature, are then introduced to study constraints. The model-theoretic notions are those present in the definition of a satisfaction system, whose main purpose is to characterize the set of "satisfiable" constraints. The proof-theoretic notions are embedded in the definition of a reduction system, which specifies the set of "solvable" constraints. The model- and proof-theoretic notions are related by the definitions of "soundness" and "completeness" of a reduction system with respect to a satisfaction system. The general idea is that soundness means that solvability implies satisfiability, and completeness that satisfiability implies solvability.

Definition (Constraint)

Let Atom be a set of *atomic constraints*. A constraint is a finite subset of Atom.

The intended meaning of a constraint is the conjunction of the atomic constraints comprising it. In particular, the empty constraint is interpreted as true, and {A} will be identified with $A \in$ Atom.

Constraint Satisfaction Systems

Definition (Constraint Satisfaction System)

A constraint satisfaction system over Atom is a pair $<\Sigma, Val>$, where Σ is a set of mappings $\sigma:Atom \rightarrow Atom$ called *substitutions*, and $Val \subseteq Atom$ is the set of *valid* atomic constraints. It is required that Val be stable under Σ, that is $\sigma(Val) \subseteq Val$ for every $\sigma \in \Sigma$.

Definition (Satisfiable Constraint)

A constraint C is satisfiable if there is $\sigma \in \Sigma$ such that $\sigma(C) \subseteq Val$; we then say that σ *satisfies* C. Let Sat be the set of all satisfiable constraints.

Proposition 2

Sat verifies the two following properties:
- $\emptyset \in$ Sat.
- If $C \in$ Sat and $C' \subseteq C$ then $C' \in$ Sat. ♦

Definition (Entailment)

If C and C' are satisfiable constraints, we write $C \models C'$, and say that C entails C', if every substitution satisfying C also satisfies C'.

Note that $C \models C'$ if and only if $C \models A$ for every $A \in C'$.

Proposition 3

We have the following obvious properties:
- If $C \models A$ then $C \cup \{A\} \in$ Sat.
- If $C \in$ Sat and $A \in C$ then $C \models A$.
- If $C \models C'$ and $C' \models A$ then $C \models A$. ♦

Propositions 2 and 3 together show that $<Atom, Sat, \models>$ constitutes an information system [Sco82].

Constraint Reduction Systems

Definition (Constraint Reduction System)

A constraint reduction system over Atom is a pair $<\rightarrow, Sol>$, where $\rightarrow$ is a *reduction* relation on constraints and Sol is a set of constraints in *solved form*, containing the empty constraint and closed at forming subsets (this means that $\varnothing \in$ Sol and that $C \subseteq C' \in$ Sol implies $C \in$ Sol).

Definition (Reduction)

If C and C' are constraints, we say C *reduces in one step* to C', and write $C \Rightarrow C'$, if there exist constraints B, B' and D such that $B \rightarrow B'$, $C = B \cup D$ and $C' = B' \cup D$. The reflexive and transitive closure of $\Rightarrow$ will be written as usual $\Rightarrow^*$, and if $C \Rightarrow^* C'$ we say C *reduces* to C'.

Definition (Soundness)

The reduction system $<\rightarrow,$ Sol$>$ is *sound* with respect to $<\Sigma,$ Val$>$ if it satisfies the two following properties:

- Every constraint in solved form is satisfiable, except possibly one whose intended meaning is false.
- If $C \Rightarrow^* C'$ and C' is satisfiable then $C' \models C$.

Intuitively, if we interpret a substitution satisfying C as a "solution" of the constraint C, then in a reduction $C \Rightarrow^* C'$, any solution of C' is also a solution of C. Conversely, completeness of the reduction system means that every solution of C is a solution of some such C' in solved form.

Definition (Completeness)

$<\rightarrow,$ Sol$>$ is *complete* with respect to $<\Sigma,$ Val$>$ if, for every constraint C and every $\sigma \in \Sigma$ satisfying C, there exists $C' \in$ Sol such that $C \Rightarrow^* C'$ and σ satisfies C'.

6 Atomic Constraints

The set of atomic constraints has all the declarative and interrogative sentences of the query language. We will see that the constraints of the form $(v_1,...,v_n):(N_{11},...,N_{1n})+...+(N_{k1},...,N_{kn})$, where the possible atomic types for the variables are explicitly stated, have a special role in the constraint reduction system. For example, since the declarative sentence $r(v_1,...,v_n)$ constrains the variables $v_1,...,v_n$, in the sense that this expression is true just in case $\{(v_1,...,v_n)\} \leq R_r$, if $R_r = \{(N_{11},...,N_{1n}),...,(N_{k1},...,N_{kn})\}$ the associated constraint in solved form will be $(v_1,...,v_n):(N_{11},...,N_{1n})+...+(N_{k1},...,N_{kn})$.

Now suppose $R_r = \varnothing$. To still represent the constraint in a similar way we will admit the empty sequence $M_1+...+M_k$ denoting it by the symbol ε. (Note that ε is the syntactical counterpart of $\bot$, the bottom of the lattice).

On the other hand, a closed declarative sentence does not restrict any variable; it is a proposition. In order to have a uniform way to represent any solved atomic constraint we will admit two new constraints, considered as declarative constraints, ():T and ():ε, whose intended meaning is true and false, respectively.

To summarize, the atomic constraints $A \in$ Atom are as follows ($n \geq 1$, $k \geq 0$):

$$A \rightarrow D \mid I$$
$$D \rightarrow r(e_1,...,e_n) \mid (e_1,...,e_k):M \mid D_1 \wedge D_2 \mid D_1 \vee D_2 \mid \neg D \mid (Qv:S)D$$
$$M \rightarrow (S_1,...,S_n) \mid \lambda v_1,...,v_n.D \mid M_1 \& M_2 \mid M_1 + M_2 \mid \epsilon$$
$$S \rightarrow N \mid \lambda v.D \mid S_1 \& S_2 \mid S_1 + S_2 \mid \epsilon$$
$$I \rightarrow (?v:S)D \mid (?v:S)I$$

In the sequel, the letters D, M, S and I will denote constraint language expressions instead of query language expressions. And to avoid some repetitions, T will stand for a singular or a multiple type.

7 Constraint Satisfaction System

Definition (Substitution)

A substitution $\sigma \in \Sigma$ is a function from $V \subseteq Var$ into Type and we write as usual $v\sigma$ instead of $\sigma(v)$. V will be called the *domain* of σ, denoted by Dom(σ).

- If σ is a substitution, $v \in$ Dom(σ) and $t \in$ Type, $\sigma[v/t] \in \Sigma$ is such that:

$$Dom(\sigma[v/t]) = Dom(\sigma), \qquad u(\sigma[v/t]) = \begin{cases} t \Leftarrow u = v \\ u\sigma \Leftarrow u \neq v \end{cases}$$

- If $\sigma \in \Sigma$, $\{v_1,...,v_n\} \subseteq Dom(\sigma)$, the substitution $\sigma[-v_1,...,v_n]$ is defined by:

$$Dom(\sigma[-v_1,...,v_n]) = Dom(\sigma) - \{v_1,...,v_n\}, \qquad u(\sigma[-v_1,...,v_n]) = u\sigma$$

Let Σ_V be the set of all substitutions with domain V. Note that $\sigma \leq \tau \Leftrightarrow (\forall v \in V) \ v\sigma \leq v\tau$ is a partial order on Σ_V, whose greatest element is the constant function equal to T, denoted by T_V.

To simplify the notation, we will apply a substitution σ to every variable and every atomic type e, assuming that $e\sigma = e$ when $e \notin$ Dom(σ).

When we apply a substitution to an atomic constraint A, we obtain an atomic constraint A'. Let us see first the declarative case. Except for quantified and abstracted variables that remain unchanged, A' is obtained as usual, replacing the variables that belong to the domain of the substitution by their corresponding atomic types.

Before addressing the interrogative case recall that we interpret a substitution as a possible solution of a constraint: σ is a solution of I when $\sigma(I) \in$ Val. As we will see later, only declarative constraints belong to the set of valid atomic constraints. Hence a substitution applied to an interrogative constraint will return a declarative constraint. Suppose I asks for those birds which are dangerous: $(?v:bird)dangerous(v)$. The substitution σ is a solution of I if σ is a solution of $v:bird \wedge dangerous(v)$, that is $v\sigma$ is a subtype of bird, for instance bird of prey, and dangerous(bird of prey) holds.

Definition (Substitution Mapping)

The application of the substitution σ to an atomic constraint is defined as follows:

Declarative Constraints

$$\sigma(r(e_1,...,e_n)) = r(e_1\sigma,...,e_n\sigma)$$

$$\sigma((e_1,...,e_k):M\,) = (e_1\sigma,...,e_k\sigma):\sigma(M)$$

$$\sigma(D_1 \wedge D_2) = \sigma(D_1)\wedge\sigma(D_2)$$

$$\sigma(D_1 \vee D_2) = \sigma(D_1)\vee\sigma(D_2)$$

$$\sigma(\neg D) = \neg\sigma(D)$$

$$\sigma((Qv:S)D) = (Qv:\sigma(S))\,\sigma[-v](D)$$

Types

$$\sigma((S_1,...,S_n)) = (\sigma(S_1),...,\sigma(S_n))$$

$$\sigma(\lambda v_1,...,v_n.D) = \lambda v_1,...,v_n.\sigma[-v_1,...,v_n](D)$$

$$\sigma(T_1 \& T_2) = \sigma(T_1)\&\sigma(T_2)$$

$$\sigma(T_1+T_2) = \sigma(T_1)+\sigma(T_2)$$

$$\sigma(\varepsilon) = \varepsilon$$

Interrogative Constraints

$$\sigma((?v:S)D) = \sigma(v:S)\wedge\sigma(D)$$

$$\sigma((?v:S)I) = \sigma(v:S)\wedge\sigma(I)$$

We will now define the denotation of a declarative or type expression E when the atomic types associated with its free variables are specified by the substitution σ, abbreviated to the *denotation of E under* σ and denoted by $[\![E]\!]\sigma$. We assume that all free variables of the expression are in the domain of the substitution.

The denotation domain of an expression depends on its kind. A declarative constraint is true or false. A type is associated with an element of $M(\text{Type}^k)$, with k=1 for singular types, sometimes identified with an element of $M(\text{Type})$. The denotation of E under σ is defined in Figure 2. As a matter of notation, we abbreviate $\Uparrow\!\Delta\{...\}$ to $\{...\}$.

Declarative Constraints

$$[\![r(e_1,...,e_n)]\!]\sigma=\{(e_1\sigma,...,e_n\sigma)\}\leq R_r$$

$$[\![(e_1,...,e_k):M]\!]\sigma=\{(e_1\sigma,...,e_k\sigma)\}\leq[\![M]\!]\sigma$$

$$[\![D_1 \wedge D_2]\!]\sigma=[\![D_1]\!]\sigma\wedge[\![D_2]\!]\sigma$$

$$[\![D_1 \vee D_2]\!]\sigma=[\![D_1]\!]\sigma\vee[\![D_2]\!]\sigma$$

$$[\![\neg D]\!]\sigma=(\forall\tau\leq\sigma)\,\neg[\![D]\!]\tau$$

$$[\![(\text{some } v:S)D]\!]\sigma=[\![S]\!]\sigma\wedge\{x\in \text{Type} \mid [\![D]\!]\sigma[v/x]\}\neq\perp$$

$$[\![(\text{all } v:S)D]\!]\sigma=[\![S]\!]\sigma\leq\{x\in \text{Type} \mid [\![D]\!]\sigma[v/x]\}$$

Types

$$[\![(S_1,...,S_n)]\!]\sigma=\Uparrow\!\Delta([\![S_1]\!]\sigma\times...\times[\![S_n]\!]\sigma)$$

$$[\![\lambda v_1,...,v_n.D]\!]\sigma=\{(x_1,...,x_n) \mid [\![D]\!]\sigma[v_1/x_1]...[v_n/x_n]\}$$

$$[\![T_1 \& T_2]\!]\sigma=[\![T_1]\!]\sigma\wedge[\![T_2]\!]\sigma$$

$$[\![T_1+T_2]\!]\sigma=[\![T_1]\!]\sigma\vee[\![T_2]\!]\sigma$$

$$[\![\varepsilon]\!]\sigma=\perp$$

$$[\![N]\!]\sigma=\{N\}$$

Figure 2

We can now identify the valid constraints. If D is a declarative constraint with free variables F⊆Var, we want D to belong to Val if $[\![D]\!]\sigma$ holds for every σ∈Σ such that F⊆Dom(σ), which means, intuitively, that D is true for all the possible values of its free variables. But this is equivalent to verify that $[\![D]\!]T_{Var}$ is true.

Definition (Valid Atomic Constraints)

The set of valid atomic constraints is Val=$\{D \mid [\![D]\!]T_{Var}\}$.

Proposition 4

$<\Sigma,\text{Val}>$ is a constraint satisfaction system over Atom. $((\forall\sigma\in\Sigma)\ \sigma(\text{Val})\subseteq\text{Val}.)$ ◆

8 Constraint Reduction System

Only declarative constraints of the form $(v_1,...,v_n):(N_{11},...,N_{1n})+...+(N_{k1},...,N_{kn})$ are allowed in the set Sol. All the other atomic constraints will be reduced to this form. For the answer to be concise, $P=\{(N_{11},...,N_{1n}),...,(N_{k1},...,N_{kn})\}$ should belong to M(Type^n). But we require $P\neq T$, which represents truth, and $P\neq\bot$, when n>0, because the contradiction is written in the simpler form ():ε. One last condition inhibits variables shared by atomic constraints. If v belongs to X:P and Y:Q, the possible types for v must satisfy both constraints, meaning that the final solution has not yet been found.

Definition (Constraints in Solved Form)

The set of constraints in solved form, Sol, has all the sets C of constraints of the form $(v_1,...,v_n):(N_{11},...,N_{1n})+...+(N_{k1},...,N_{kn})$ (n,k≥0) that verify the three following properties:

- $\{(N_{11},...,N_{1n}),...,(N_{k1},...,N_{kn})\}\in$ M(Type^n)$-\{T\}$.
- $(v_1,...,v_n):\varepsilon\in C \Rightarrow$ n=0, C=$\{():\varepsilon\}$.
- No variable occurs in more than one atomic constraint of C. If $(v_1,...,v_k):M_1$ and $(w_1,...,w_m):M_2$ are two distinct atomic constraints of C,
$$\{v_1,...,v_k\}\cap\{w_1,...,w_m\}=\varnothing.$$

In the sequel, a constraint $(v_1,...,v_n):(N_{11},...,N_{1n})+...+(N_{k1},...,N_{kn})$ (n,k≥0) such that $\{(N_{11},...,N_{1n}),...,(N_{k1},...,N_{kn})\}\in$ M(Type^n) will be called a *standard* constraint O. A tuple of distinct variables is a *reference*. To simplify the notation, we will deal with the sequence $(N_{11},...,N_{1n})+...+(N_{k1},...,N_{kn})$ as though it was the set $\{(N_{11},...,N_{1n}),...,(N_{k1},...,N_{kn})\}$ and ε the empty set.

Definition (Reference Change)

The reference change turns a standard constraint X:P, X=$(v_1,...,v_k)$, into a standard constraint Y:Q, Y=$(w_1,...,w_m)$, by changing the reference X into Y, Y:Q=(X:P)$_Y$. Note that if the variable w_i doesn't belong to X, the restriction introduced is $w_i\leq T$ (1≤i≤m).

m>0: $\quad Q=\{(q_1,...,q_m)\mid\exists(p_1,...,p_k)\in P, q_i=\begin{cases} p_j & \Leftarrow (\exists 1\leq j\leq k)\ w_i=v_j \\ T & \Leftarrow \text{otherwise}\end{cases}$ for 1≤i≤m\}

m=0: $\quad Q=\begin{cases}\varnothing & \Leftarrow P=\varnothing \\ \{T\} & \Leftarrow \text{otherwise}\end{cases}$

For example, $((A,B,C):(a_1,b_1,c_1)+(a_2,b_2,c_2))_{(D,C,A)} = (D,C,A):(T,c_1,a_1)+(T,c_2,a_2)$.

Definition (Variable Substitution)

The substitution of the variable v_i by w, in the standard constraint $(v_1,...,v_k):P$, is defined by $(X:P)[v_i \backslash w] = (v_1,...,v_{i-1},w,v_{i+1},...,v_k):P$, if $w \in Var-\{v_1,...,v_k\}$ $(1 \leq i \leq k)$.

Definition (Variable Discharge)

Let X:P be a standard constraint with $X=(v_1,...,v_k)$ and $1 \leq i \leq k$. $(X:P)-v_i=(X:P)_{(X-v_i)}$ where $X-v_i=(v_1,...,v_{i-1},v_{i+1},...,v_k)$.

Definition (Constraint Negation)

The negation of the standard constraint X:P is $\neg(X:P)=X:(\neg P)$.

Definition (Constraint Conjunction and Disjunction)

Let X:P and Y:Q be two standard constraints, and Z a reference with all the variables in X and Y. If $(X:P)_Z=Z:P'$ and $(Y:Q)_Z=Z:Q'$ then:

- $(X:P) \wedge (Y:Q)=Z:(P' \wedge Q')$.
- $(X:P) \vee (Y:Q)=Z:(P' \vee Q')$.

In the reduction process we assume that negation, conjunction and disjunction on standard constraints, and the closure $\{N\}$, with $N \in$ Type, are basic operations. A singular or multiple type will be reduced to an expression of the form $\lambda v_1,...,v_n.O$, an abstraction of a standard constraint in some variables.

Definition (Reduction Relation)

The reduction relation, $\rightarrow$, is defined by the following rules.

Constraints

(1) $\{r(e_1,...,e_n)\} \rightarrow \{(e_1,...,e_n):E_1+...+E_k\} \Leftarrow R_r=\{E_1,...,E_k\}$.

(2) $\{(e_1,...,e_i,...,e_n):M\} \rightarrow \{(all \; v:e_i)(e_1,...,v,...,e_n):M\} \Leftarrow e_i \in$ Type $(1 \leq i \leq n)$, v is a new variable.

(3) $\{(v_1,...,v_k):M\} \rightarrow \{(v_1,...,v_k):M'\} \Leftarrow M \notin M(Type^k)$, $\{M\} \rightarrow \{M'\}$.

(4) $\{(v_1,...,v_k):\lambda w_1,...,w_k.O\} \rightarrow \{O'\} \Leftarrow O'=O[w_1 \backslash v_1]...[w_k \backslash v_k]$.

(5) $\{D_1 \; op \; D_2\} \rightarrow \{D'_1 \; op \; D_2\} \Leftarrow op \in \{\wedge,\vee\}$, $\{D_1\} \rightarrow \{D'_1\}$.

(6) $\{O_1 \; op \; D_2\} \rightarrow \{O_1 \; op \; D'_2\} \Leftarrow op \in \{\wedge,\vee\}$, $\{D_2\} \rightarrow \{D'_2\}$.

(7) $\{O_1 \wedge O_2\} \rightarrow \{O_3\} \Leftarrow O_3=O_1 \wedge O_2$.

(8) $\{O_1 \vee O_2\} \rightarrow \{O_3\} \Leftarrow O_3=O_1 \vee O_2$.

(9) $\{\neg D\} \rightarrow \{\neg D'\} \Leftarrow \{D\} \rightarrow \{D'\}$.

(10) $\{\neg O\} \rightarrow \{O'\} \Leftarrow O'=\neg O$.

(11) $\{(op \; v:S)A\} \rightarrow \{(op \; v:S)A'\} \Leftarrow op \in \{all,some,?\}$, $\{A\} \rightarrow \{A'\}$.

(12) $\{(op \; v:S)O\} \rightarrow \{(op \; v:S')O\} \Leftarrow op \in \{all,some,?\}$, $\{S\} \rightarrow \{S'\}$.

(13) $\{(some \; v:\lambda v_1.O_1)O_2\} \rightarrow \{O_3\} \Leftarrow O_3=(O_1[v_1 \backslash v] \wedge O_2)-v$.

(14) $\{(all \; v:\lambda v_1.O_1)O_2\} \rightarrow \{O_3\} \Leftarrow O_3=\neg((O_1[v_1 \backslash v] \wedge \neg O_2)-v)$.

(15) $\{(? \; v:\lambda v_1.O_1)O_2\} \rightarrow \{O_3\} \Leftarrow O_3=O_1[v_1 \backslash v] \wedge O_2$.

Types

(t1) $\{(S_1,...,S_i,...,S_n)\} \rightarrow \{(S_1,...,S'_i,...,S_n)\} \Leftarrow \{S_i\} \rightarrow \{S'_i\}, 1 \le i \le n.$

(t2) $\{(\lambda v_1.O_1,...,\lambda v_i.O_i,...,\lambda v_n.O_n)\} \rightarrow \{\lambda v_1,...,v_n.O\} \Leftarrow O=O_1 \wedge ... \wedge O_i \wedge ... \wedge O_n.$

(t3) $\{\lambda v_1,...,v_n.D\} \rightarrow \{\lambda v_1,...,v_n.D'\} \Leftarrow \{D\} \rightarrow \{D'\}.$

(t4) $\{T_1 \text{ op } T_2\} \rightarrow \{T'_1 \text{ op } T_2\} \Leftarrow \text{op} \in \{\&,+\}, \{T_1\} \rightarrow \{T'_1\}.$

(t5) $\{\lambda v_1,...,v_n.O_1 \text{ op } T_2\} \rightarrow \{\lambda v_1,...,v_n.O_1 \text{ op } T'_2\} \Leftarrow \text{op} \in \{\&,+\}, \{T_2\} \rightarrow \{T'_2\}.$

(t6) $\{\lambda v_1,...,v_n.O_1 \& \lambda w_1,...,w_n.O_2\} \rightarrow \{\lambda v_1,...,v_n.O_3\} \Leftarrow O_3=O_1 \wedge O_2[w_1 \backslash v_1]...[w_n \backslash v_n].$

(t7) $\{\lambda v_1,...,v_n.O_1 + \lambda w_1,...,w_n.O_2\} \rightarrow \{\lambda v_1,...,v_n.O_3\} \Leftarrow O_3=O_1 \vee O_2[w_1 \backslash v_1]...[w_n \backslash v_n].$

(t8) $\{\varepsilon\} \rightarrow \{\lambda v.(v):\varepsilon\} \Leftarrow v$ a is a new variable.

(t9) $\{N\} \rightarrow \{\lambda v.(v):(N_1)+...+(N_n)\} \Leftarrow \{N\}=\{N_1,...,N_n\}, v$ is a new variable.

Special Cases

(s1) $\{(v_1,...,v_k):(T,...,T)\} \rightarrow \varnothing \Leftarrow k \ge 0.$

(s2) $\{(v_1,...,v_k):\varepsilon\} \rightarrow \{():\varepsilon\} \Leftarrow k \ge 1.$

(s3) $\{():\varepsilon\} \cup C \rightarrow \{():\varepsilon\} \Leftarrow C \ne \varnothing.$

(s4) $\{O_1,O_2\} \rightarrow \{O_3\} \Leftarrow O_1 \ne O_2, O_1$ and O_2 share a variable, $O_3=O_1 \wedge O_2.$

Proposition 5

$<\rightarrow,\text{Sol}>$ is a constraint reduction system over the set Atom. $(\varnothing \in \text{Sol}, C \subseteq C' \in \text{Sol} \Rightarrow C \in \text{Sol}.)$ ♦

Proposition 6

The reduction system $<\rightarrow,\text{Sol}>$ is sound with respect to $<\Sigma,\text{Val}>$. (Note that $\{():\varepsilon\}$ is the only constraint in solved form not satisfiable.) ♦

Proposition 7

The reduction system $<\rightarrow,\text{Sol}>$ is complete with respect to $<\Sigma,\text{Val}>$. ♦

9 Examples

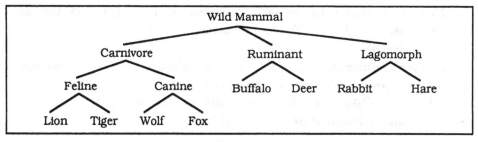

Figure 3

Let us see two examples, based on the taxonomy illustrated in Figure 3. For simplicity, we assume that the taxonomy is complete, in the sense that the classes associated with the represented types are the union of the classes of their subtypes. Consider two binary relations eat and attack, defined by:

- $R_{eat}=\{(\text{Carnivore},\text{Ruminant}),(\text{Canine},\text{Lagomorph})\};$

- R_{attack}={(Feline,Ruminant),(Wolf,Ruminant),(Fox,Lagomorph)}.

We will show how to solve the declarative sentence "all the wild mammals that are eaten are attacked by the eater", written as {(all y:λz.eat(x,z))attack(x,y)}. The corresponding constraint in solved form, in the free variable x, specifies the eaters for which the given sentence is true.

- {(all y: λz.eat(x,z)) attack(x,y)} $\rightarrow$

  By rule 11, first we reduce the inner declarative sentence, attack(x,y), whose reduction rule, 1, "substitutes" the relation name by the relation definition.

- {(all y: λz.eat(x,z))

  (x,y):(Feline,Ruminant)+(Wolf,Ruminant)+(Fox,Lagomorph)} $\rightarrow$

  Accordingly to rule 12, we should reduce the type, λz.eat(x,z). By t3, we need to solve the declarative expression, eat(x,z), that requires rule 1 again.

- {(all y: λz.(x,z):(Carnivore,Ruminant)+(Canine,Lagomorph))

  (x,y):(Feline,Ruminant)+(Wolf,Ruminant)+(Fox,Lagomorph)} $\rightarrow$

  Now, we must solve a universal quantification, using rule 14. As specified by the rule, solving a universal quantification consists first in determining the types for which the quantified sentence is false, second discharging the quantified variable, and finally finding the complementary constraint. Let O_1 be the constraint of the type and O_2 the constraint of the sentence. Note that the abstracted variable z and the variable of the quantification y should be unified. So, the restrictions to take into account are $O_1[z\backslash y]$ and O_2.

  $O_1[z\backslash y]$ (x,y): (Carnivore,Ruminant)+(Canine,Lagomorph)

  O_2 (x,y): (Feline,Ruminant)+(Wolf,Ruminant)+(Fox,Lagomorph)

  Next, we calculate the tuples of $O_1[z\backslash y]$ that don't belong to O_2.

  $\neg O_2$ (x,y): (Ruminant,Wild Mammal)+(Lagomorph,Wild Mammal)+
  (Wild Mammal,Carnivore)+
  (Feline,Lagomorph)+(Wolf,Lagomorph)+(Fox,Ruminant)

  $O_1[z\backslash y]\wedge\neg O_2$ (x,y): (Wolf,Lagomorph)+(Fox,Ruminant)

  Now we discharge the variable y. As we work always with the maximal elements, instead of (Wolf)+(Fox) we obtain (Canine).

  $(O_1[z\backslash y]\wedge\neg O_2)$-y (x): (Canine)

  So the quantified sentence is false for the canines and the restriction associated with x is given by the complementary constraint.

  $\neg((O_1[z\backslash y]\wedge\neg O_2)$-y) (x): (Feline)+(Ruminant)+(Lagomorph)

- {(x):(Feline)+(Ruminant)+(Lagomorph)}$\in$ Sol.

Now we will illustrate the reduction of {(op x:carnivore) (all y: λz.eat(x,z)) attack(x,y)}, for op$\in$ {all,some,?}.

- {(op x:Carnivore) (all y: λz.eat(x,z)) attack(x,y)} $\rightarrow^3$

  Note that by rule 11 the reduction of {(all y: λz.eat(x,z)) attack(x,y)} is required, whose result has been evaluated in three steps in the previous example.

- {(op x:Carnivore) (x):(Feline)+(Ruminant)+(Lagomorph)} $\rightarrow$

Next we reduce the type, Carnivore, and we obtain $\lambda v.(v):(\text{Carnivore})$, by t9.

- $\{(\text{op } x: \lambda v.(v):(\text{Carnivore})) \ (x):(\text{Feline})+(\text{Ruminant})+(\text{Lagomorph})\} \rightarrow$

  The following constraints are involved in the next operation, that depends on the value of op:

  $$O_1[v\backslash x] \qquad (x) : (\text{Carnivore})$$
  $$O_2 \qquad (x) : (\text{Feline})+(\text{Ruminant})+(\text{Lagomorph})$$

op=?   *What are the carnivores that attack all the wild mammals they eat ?*

    The tuples of the domain that verify the property are given by (rule 15):

$$O_1[v\backslash x]\wedge O_2 \qquad (x) : (\text{Feline})$$

- $\{(x):(\text{Feline})\}\in \text{Sol}.$

op=some   *Some carnivores attack all the wild mammals they eat .*

    An existential quantification (rule 13) is true for the tuples of the domain that verify the property: $O_1[v\backslash x]\wedge O_2$. But the variable of the quantification should also be discharged. In this case, since there are no more variables in the constraint, the result is $\top$ because the input type is not empty.

$$(O_1[v\backslash x]\wedge O_2)\text{-}x \qquad () : (\text{Wild Mammal})$$

- $\{():(\text{Wild Mammals})\}\rightarrow \varnothing$ (rule s1). This sentence is true.

op=all   *All carnivores attack all the wild mammals they eat .*

    We apply the same formula as before (rule 14):

$$\neg O_2 \qquad (x) : (\text{Canine})$$
$$O_1[v\backslash x]\wedge\neg O_2 \qquad (x) : (\text{Canine})$$
$$(O_1[v\backslash x]\wedge\neg O_2)\text{-}x \qquad () : (\text{Wild Mammal})$$
$$\neg((O_1[v\backslash x]\wedge\neg O_2)\text{-}x) \qquad () : \varepsilon$$

- $\{():\varepsilon\}\in \text{Sol}.$ The sentence is false.

10 Conclusions and Future Work

The main goal of this work was to provide a formalization of useful answer, when the system knowledge is structured in a hierarchical fashion. To this end we have introduced a query language and a definition of hierarchical type system, called taxonomy, which relates a set of names denoting atomic types. In order to formalize the sets of atomic types that are associated with useful and informative answers, we have defined a closure operation that measures the information contained in a set. Then, we have built a boolean algebra on the set of answers (any maximal part of a closed set).

On the other hand, since queries and answers can be both seen as constraints (the latter being solved) we have presented a general scheme for constraints systems and we have shown that the query language is an instance of the scheme. The answers obtained solving the constraints specified by the queries are "informative" because constraint satisfiability and solvability are defined in the boolean algebra.

Concerning the future work, we wish to extend the notion of taxonomy in order to cater for incomplete information: we would like to be able to specify whether an atomic type is, or is not, the union of its subtypes, which seems a desirable feature from the point of view of artificial intelligence since the information a reasoning system possesses about the world is seldom complete. We would also like to treat exceptions, and be able to give answers in negated form.

Also, lots of work must be done in the implementation of the system. The existing prototype, made by António Porto, implements a slightly different query language.

Acknowledgments

We thank António Porto for his pioneering work on useful answers for taxonomic systems, and his willingness to discuss with us every aspect of his ideas. This work was partially supported by Instituto Nacional de Investigação Científica and Junta Nacional de Investigação Científica e Tecnológica.

References

[A-KN86]
H. Aït-Kaci, R. Nasr. Login: A Logic Programming Language with Built-in Inheritance. *Journal of Logic Programming*, 3:185-215. 1986.

[Car88]
L. Cardelli. A Semantics of Multiple Inheritance. *Information and Control*, 76:138-164. 1988.

[JL87]
Joxan Jaffar, Jean-Louis Lassez. Constraint Logic Programming. In *Proc. 14th ACM POPL Conference*, Munich, 1987.

[MM91]
Margarida Mamede, Luís Monteiro. Answers as Type Constraints. Presented at the International Workshop on Non-standard Queries and Non-standard Answers, Toulouse, France. July 1-3, 1991.

[MP90]
Luís Monteiro, António Porto. A Transformational View of Inheritance in Logic Programming. In *Logic Programming: Proceedings of the Seventh International Conference*, D.H.D. Warren and P. Szeredi (eds.), MIT Press, Cambridge MA, 1990.

[Por88]

António Porto. A Framework for Deducing Useful Answers to Queries. In M. Tokoro (ed.), *Proc. IFIP WG 10.1 Workshop on Concepts and Characteristics of Knowledge-Based Systems*, North-Holland, 1988.

[PF84]

António Porto, Miguel Filgueiras. A Logic Programming Approach to Natural Language Semantics. In *Proc. International Symposium on Logic Programming*, IEEE Press, 1984.

[Tou86]

D.S. Touretzki. *The Mathematics of Inheritance Systems*. Pitman, London, 1986.

[Weg86]

P. Wegner. Classification in object-oriented systems. In *Proc. Object-Oriented Programming Workshop*, ACM Sigplan Notices 21 (10), 173-182. 1986.

[Sco82]

D. Scott. Domains for Denotational Semantics. In *Proc. ICALP 82*, Springer Verlag, New York, 1982.

HEURISTIC PARSING AND SEARCH SPACE PRUNING

José António Mendes †
Pedro Rangel Henriques
INESC-Braga, Universidade do Minho
Largo do Paço, 4719 Braga - Portugal

ABSTRACT

When parsing a Language the search space is traversed in a pre-defined way – top-down or bottom-up, depth-first or breath-first, typically. However, these might not be the ideal strategies: there are languages for which that process is very expensive or even, some valid sentences are not parsed straightly. Our aim is to describe an alternative method where the traversal may be heuristically defined during the process of parsing, depending only on the linguistic phenomena being analyzed. Such parser is data-driven by the string, and heuristically-driven by the annotated grammar rules. This makes it possible to mix top-down and bottom-up and also, to alternate parsing to the left or to the right of the symbol which causes the rule to be triggered. A bidirectional chart parsing was implemented in Prolog to express this idea. The results then obtained gave us some rules of thumb to get the best annotation of a grammar rule set and showed us the gain in time analysis by the spectacular pruning (65% in average for any phenomenon) of the search space.

1. INTRODUCTION

For a given grammar and for a given string, parsing is the process which verifies if the string belongs to the Language, which is generated by the grammar rule set and, if so, it assigns a structure to the string (accordingly to the hypotheses in the grammar). Parsing is, therefore, a search process to match an instance with a set of structural patterns.

The grammar rule set defines the search space. The search strategy defines the way that space is traversed. The search space path is defined by the rules which are verified until the structure of the string is found.

The depht-first strategy creates backtracking problems. By going back and attempt trough another path, it causes a duplication of effort since it tries to prove multiple instances of the same evidence. Another problem is that it may cause an infinite cycle when, depending on the variant of the method used, either left or right recursive rules are used.

In the breath-first strategy there is a duplication of efforts since multiple instances of alternative solutions, which belong to different paths, are found. This implies high cost of memory space since all alternative paths waiting to be analyzed are kept.

---

† Prof.Assistant in Esc. Superior de Tecnologia de Tomar doing a Ph.D. at the University of Minho

The top-down strategy is predictive and so it can parse rules which derive in the empty string. However it may formulate all hypotheses and traverse the whole search space, even when there is no need to try some hypotheses.

Bottom-up as a data-driven strategy constrains the search space, but it cannot straightly parse the null string since there is no lexical evidence[2]. Besides, the rules are always triggered by the first category on the right hand side (RHS) of the rule and, nothing tells us that such category is the best one to trigger the rule in any circumstances.

The method we will use to parse, in the context of ambiguous sentences, is Chart-Parsing, [Win83a] and [Tho85a]. By using charts the evidence are corroborated only once and then kept [Men90a]. So, the evidence may be shared by all hypotheses which need to be corroborated. Therefore, there is no duplication of efforts, there is a reduction of memory space and, very important, backtracking is avoided. The problems of top-down and bottom-up strategies are solved.

We will analyze a strategy based on the idea (coming from [SD87a]) of mixing standard search strategies, combining them not in a pre defined way but in a way that takes into account the string (phenomenon) being analyzed. This idea implies the concept of annotated context-free grammar, which means to annotate a rule by saying if it is to be triggered top-down or bottom-up (in the latter case, also saying which is the best evidence in the RHS to do that triggering), [Men91a].

If the rules are to be triggered by the best evidence (not necessarily the left-most category of the RHS) then the chart parser needs to be modified also to the left of the category that makes the triggering [DE86a], in order to corroborate hypotheses against such constituents[3]. This gives rise to the so called bidirectional chart parser [SD87a].

In the next section we present a brief review of search and strategies. In section 3 the concept of *annotation of a grammar rule set with heuristics* is discussed and some criteria to get the best annotation is presented [MD88a]. Then, in section 4 we talk about chart parsing discussing the modifications to get a bidirectional chart parser. The gain in efficiency due to an heuristic mixed strategy during parsing is analyzed in section 5 [4].

2. SEARCH AND STRATEGIES

Parsing the string *I saw a girl with a telescope* will produce a phrase structure tree (PST) as in Fig.1; another PST, in Fig.2, can be derived which show us ambiguity, i.e., there are two

---

2 *As the left-to-right bottom-up parser is the most used, from now on we will refer to standard bottom-up, or just bottom-up, assuming that it relies on the first symbol on the right hand side of the rule. Problems here presented as inherent to bottom-up strategy can be solved using well known techniques but, one would get a deterministic parser which is not our goal.*
3 *Some substructure which belongs to the string.*
4 *The examples presented follow the grammar defined on page 13*

possible structures assigned to that string. This means that at a certain step there are two possible rules which can be triggered successfully [5].

The PST's in Fig.1 and Fig.2 are the final result of traversing the search space but nothing is said about how that space was traversed [6] to achieve that result.

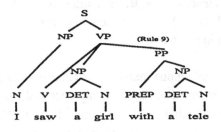

FIG.1 - A PHRASE STRUCTURE TREE (PST)

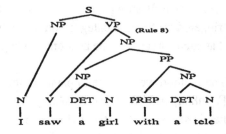

FIG.2 - ANOTHER PST SHOWING AMBIGUITY

Any traversal search path may be used to get those solutions: vertical, horizontal, from top to bottom or from bottom to top (Fig.3). Also, any combination of those can be thought, e.g. vertical from top to bottom. By analogy, in Fig.3 we may identify the well known depht-first and breath-first strategies from the graphs theory, and also identify the top-down and bottom-up strategies.

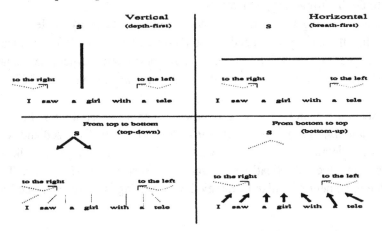

FIG.3 - STRATEGIES : PATHS THROUGH THE SEARCH SPACE

The parsing may start from left to the right or vice versa - the process evolution depends on the order that the rules are used. However this is not relevant, since the search space path is not altered [7] [AU72a].

---

5 *Suppose the existence of a grammar with the rules:* $VP \rightarrow V\,NP\,PP$ *and* $VP \rightarrow V\,NP$
6 *Which rules and in which order where used.*
7 *The search space is related to whether a rule is used or not.*

2.1 Depth-First

When parsing the example string *I saw a girl with a telescope*, the problems of backtracking and duplication of efforts inherent to the use of depth first strategy may be seen in Fig.4.

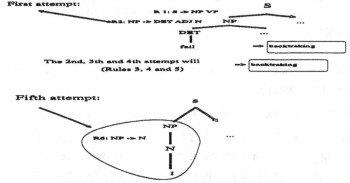

FIG.4 - PROBLEMS PARSING DEPTH-FIRST

2.2 Breath-First

In Fig.5 is showed the problem of finding multiple instances of the same evidence when parsing breath-first, which causes duplication of effort and high memory costs.

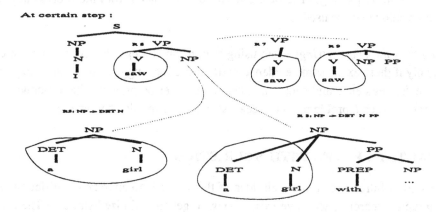

FIG.5 - PROBLEMS PARSING BREATH-FIRST

2.3 Top-Down and Bottom-Up Strategies Problems

Explosion of hypotheses: each non-terminal category, X, has usually its coordination $X \rightarrow X$ COORD X. Parsing top-down means that any time the analyzer looks for an X it should look for its coordination too. Parsing bottom-up means that anytime the evidence X is present, the analyzer should create the hypothesis of its coordination. Therefore one may say that the number of triggered rules is at least doubled. Both strategies present the same shortcoming: there is an explosion of hypotheses which become very expensive during the parsing process[8].

---

8 *Left-factoring the grammar rules is a thechnique which solves this problem. Again we would get a deterministic parser. Besides that is a trick which is far away from the natural form that a Linguist would represent the coordination phenomenon.*

Best evidence: grammar rules define a hierarchical structure of categories to be corroborated. Usually they are proved in a pre-defined sequential order which is the same as they appear in the string. Parsing bottom-up, in the sense we defined in introduction, means that the rules are triggered by the left-most category on the RHS of the rule. However, nothing ensures that such category is the best evidence as opposed to any other one on the same RHS.

Consider the rules (althoug the *coordination* bellow presented is quite odd we include it just to ilustrate our reasoning):

NP→ DET N   NP→ DET ADJ N   NP→ DET N RELCL   DET→ DET COORD DET

See that all rules start by DET on the RHS. If DET is corroborated bottom-up, all of the rules would be triggered and an attempt of their proof is made (because of the presence of a DET in the string). It should be possible to trigger the rules by other category than DET. The *best evidence* (above underlined) to trigger each rule seems to be:

NP→ <u>DET</u> N   NP→ DET <u>ADJ</u> N   NP→ DET <u>N</u> RELCL   DET→ DET <u>COORD</u> DET

With this choice, in presence of a DET in the string, only the first rule would be triggered (during bottom-up parsing). The others would be eliminated from the process at this step, and may would never be used.

Dealing with the empty string: when using bottom-up strategy the hypotheses are created if and only if there exists some evidence in the string that suggests it. As an *empty string* it has no lexical evidence and such *null string* may never be proved. The top-down strategy does not have such a problem, and it deals straightly with this phenomenon.

3. ANNOTATE RULES WITH HEURISTICS

As we said in Introduction, the main idea of this paper is to analyze the different ways of mixing typical search space traversals, in view to get an optimized strategy. The final goal is to prune the search space path. To do that we suggest an annotated grammar rule set. That is, a grammar which tells rule by rule, when each one should be triggered, i.e., considered as an hypothesis of belonging to the PST.

The alternative annotations are: top-down, corresponding to predictive situations (when one should create an hypothesis); and bottom-up, corresponding to inference acts (syntheses) coming from evidence which have just been corroborated.
A rule is annotated Top-Down Standard (TDS) when it proves useful to predictively define the path to prove some constituent : when the parser needs to prove the occurrence of X, and X is on the LHS of a rule annotated TDS then, that one is triggered.

On the other hand, a rule is annotated bottom-up when it is believed that the rule should be triggered once the constituent in which it is annotated, exists in the string (has just been found). In this general case we say that the rule is annotated on the best evidence (Best bottom-Up for Mixing-BUM). A particular case of this is the one annotated on the first category of the RHS which we call Bottom-Up Standard (BUS).

We shall represent TDS annotations with a down arrow on the right side of the category of the LHS of the rule. The annotations BUS and BUM are presented with an up arrow on the right side of the category (best evidence) of the RHS of the rule. For example,

$$\text{TDS: } X\downarrow \rightarrow X \text{ COORD } X;$$
$$\text{BUS: } X \rightarrow X\uparrow \text{ COORD } X;$$
$$\text{BUM: } X \rightarrow X \text{ COORD}\uparrow X$$

A grammar rule set may be annotated in order to get TDS (all rules annotated down on the LHS), BUS (all rules annotated down on the left-most category of the RHS), or Best Mixed Annotation - BMA (some rules TDS, others BUS and others BUM).

A problem involved in annotating rules is the possibility of getting an unsafe annotation which can cause the loss of solutions.
For example consider all rules where a PP is on the RHS (these rules are annotated BUM on PP):

$$\text{NP} \rightarrow \text{DET N PP}\uparrow$$
$$\text{VP} \rightarrow \text{V NP PP}\uparrow$$

Suppose that there is no grammar rules such that a PP produces a terminal symbol. Therefore, the above two rules can never be straightly triggered by evidence present in the string; they can only be triggered after being proved a PP. In order to prove PP, suppose that in our grammar the only rule defining that category is PP → PREP NP

Consider that rule annotated TDS, thus: PP↓ → PREP NP

This annotation means that the rule is triggered only when a PP is awaiting to be corroborated. However, since there is no other rules having a PP, that would never happen. With the annotation just described those three rules would never be triggered and so any string containing a PREP would never be parsed –it is an unsafe annotation since it will loose solutions.

The safety problem can be solved by bi-annotating the rules, i.e., annotate rules with both top-down and bottom-up triggers instead of annotate them with just one triger. This would require to change the algorithm of chart-parsing (described in section 4) to 'only propose when there is nothing to combine' in order to avoid duplications. An exhaustive analyses of this method has not yet been done.

3.1 Criteria to Annotate Rules

From a linguistic point of view some phenomena (e.g. the empty string) are better analyzed predictively (top-down) whilst others (e.g. coordination), are better analyzed from the evidence present in the string (bottom-up). Let us see how the annotation fits, phenomenon by phenomenon, these point of view.

Mendes [Men87a] defined a grammar to represent some English linguistic phenomena. Having chosen a set of strings representative of different phenomena he got some criteria to annotate the rules which we present below.

•annotate ↑ on the category less frequent in the grammar as a whole;

$$S \rightarrow NP\ VP\uparrow$$

• given a rule subset representing some phenomenon, annotate ↑ on the category which distinguishes one rule from another;

NP → DET↑	NP → DET ADJ↑ N
NP → DET N↑ R/N	NP → DET N PP↑

• Never annotate ↓ left or right recursive rules;

• In rules evolving pre-terminal categories, annotate ↑ those categories (the coordination is a particular case of this);

NP → N↑	NP → NP COORD↑ NP
VP → V↑	S → S COORD↑ S
VP → V↑ NP	VP → VP COORD↑ VP
VP → V↑ NP PP	N → N COORD↑ N
PP → PREP↑ NP	PP → PP COORD↑ PP

• annotate ↓ rules which evolve slashed categories[9] but the unreduced clause [SD87a];

S/N↓ → NP VP/N	S/N↓ → NP/N VP
VP/N↓ → V NP/N	
NP/N↓ → []	
R/N↓ → NP VP/N	

The *unreduced* clause has the presence of a relative pronoun and may have the *empty string* in both *subject* and *object* position.

The *reduced* clause has no lexical evidence and may have the *empty string* only in the *object* position. It makes sense to look for a reduced clause whenever there is a subject in the string.

---

9 *To represent rules which derive, directly or not, in the null string we shall use the so called slashed categories [Gaz85a]. Consider the rule S/N → NP/N VP. "S/N" denotes one slashed category meaning that there may be S missing N somewhere. The occurrence of a "NP/N" on the RHS means that the N which will be missing is evolved in the proof of an NP (see example strings 8,9 and 10 in section 5).*

Let us represent these clauses by the rules:

$$R/N \rightarrow RELPRO\uparrow\ S/N \qquad \text{'unreduced'}$$

$$N \rightarrow DET\ N\uparrow\ R/N \qquad \text{'reduced'}$$
$$R/N\downarrow \rightarrow NP\ VP/N$$

Note that the above annotation corresponds to the reasoning done to justify the existence of both clauses. The unreduced clause rule shall be chosen only when there is a RELPRO in the string; whenever there is an N the parser will try to prove the reduced clause rule (which will cause triger top-down the rule $R/N \rightarrow NP\ VP/N$).

• *The best annotation is the join of the best annotations for each phenomenon.*

4. CHART PARSER

A Chart is a data structure built up from edges (vertexes and links between them) - it is an oriented weighted graph. An edge has a start vertex and an end vertex and their link has a label - it defines a substring.

The labels, or weights, are used to keep information about the constituent that may derive in the associated substring: its found and the not-found substructures. The label has two distinctive parts: The GOAL constituent which one wants to prove (having the structure found so far) and, the NOT-FOUND part which represents the constituents needed to corroborate the goal.

An edge is called active if its not-found part is non-null. These edges are hypotheses predicting a constituent (the goal) which are awaiting to be corroborated.

In a so called complete edge the not-found part is empty. It represents constituents which are already corroborated (evidence) – they are well-formed substrings.

4.1 Combine and Propose

Consider i, j, k vertexes; X, Y, Z variables over categories and A, B, C, D variables over strings (may be null) of categories and words.

The operation COMBINE allows to corroborate an hypothesis, or part of it, and the operation PROPOSE allows to create hypotheses to be corroborated.

COMBINE concerns two edges, one complete and the other active. Its definition is as follows:

```
[i]  X(A)       | Y B      [j]
[j]  Y(D)       | []       [k]
[i]  X(A,Y(D))| B          [k]
```

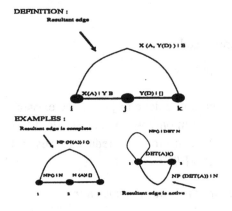

DEFINITION :

Resultant edge

EXAMPLES :

Resultant edge is complete

Resultant edge is active

FIG.6 - THE OPERATION COMBINE

If X is to be proved between i and j (substring A is already discovered and a YB is still needed to prove it) and there is the evidence Y between j and k (with structure D), then one may assume the corroboration of Y (previously missing in X) – X becomes corroborated between the vertexes i and k, with substructures A,Y(D) still having B to be proved (Fig.6).

The definition of PROPOSE depends on the strategy top-down or bottom-up. Propose creates new edges based on a known edge and on the grammar rule set. That known edge is complete when parsing bottom-up, and active when parsing top-down.

PROPOSE when parsing TOP-DOWN :

```
[i] X(A) | Y B    [j]
        Y  -> Z Q
[j] Y( ) | Z Q     [j]
```

When, between i and j, an Y is required in order to prove an X, all rules with an Y on the LHS must be searched and, for each one, an edge will be created on the vertex j with Y as the goal (the not-found part will be the RHS of the rule) (Fig.7). Note that the edge which causes the operation is an active one.

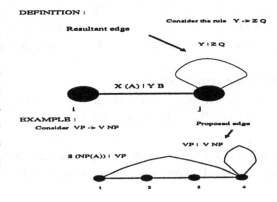

DEFINITION :

Consider the rule Y -> Z Q

Resultant edge

Y | Z Q

X (A) | Y B

EXAMPLE :
Consider VP -> V NP

Proposed edge

VP | V NP

S (NP(A)) | VP

FIG.7 - THE OPERATION PROPOSE TOP-DOWN

PROPOSE when parsing BOTTOM-UP :

```
[i]   X(A) |  []   [j]
       Y  ->   X Q
[i]Y( ) | X Q     [i]
```

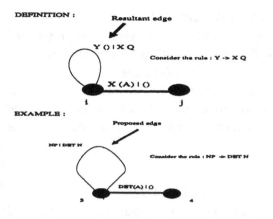

DEFINITION :

Resultant edge

Y O I X Q

Consider the rule : Y -> X Q

X (A) I O

i   j

EXAMPLE :

Proposed edge

NP I DET N

Consider the rule : NP -> DET N

DET(A) I O

3   4

FIG.8 - THE OPERATION PROPOSE BOTTOM-UP

The methodology of creating hypotheses is as follows: when, between i and j, there is an X already corroborated one has to search all rules where X is the first category on their RHS and for each rule, must create on the vertex i an edge whose Goal is the LHS and the Not-found part is the RHS (Fig.8). Note that the edge which causes the operation is a complete one.

4.2 The Process of Parsing

There are two data structures in which the chart parsing process is based : the Agenda which can be seen as a stack where next Goals are awaiting, and the Chart-Proper which can be seen as an oriented graph where it is kept information about the analysis being done.

The process of parsing starts with an initialization of the agenda which depends on the strategy.

If parsing top-down, the hypothesis of the start symbol of the grammar must also be added to the agenda ([1] ( ) | S [1]). Otherwise the agenda is only initialized with all the evidence present in the string – complete edges got from each word of the string.

All edges are kept temporarily in the Agenda. Then they are added one by one, to the chart-proper and at that time the operations Combine and Propose occur. The edges resulting from those operations are added to the agenda, and so on until the agenda becomes empty. After the initialization of the Agenda, the parsing algorithm can be synthesized as a cycle through the following steps:

• Add to the chart-proper the edge on the top of agenda;
• Combine the added edge with those on the chart-proper and keep the newly created ones on the agenda;
• Propose (according to the chosen method) based on the added edge and on the grammar rules, and keep the newly created edges on the agenda.

Note: From the newly created edges in Combine and Propose only those which do not exist (in the agenda or in the chart-proper) are kept in the Agenda – this avoids repetitions.

The parsing process ends when the agenda is empty. It succeeds if, at the end, there is a complete edge from the start vertex to the end vertex whose Goal is the start symbol of the grammar.

4.3 Modifying the Chart from Uni to Bidireccional

We have said that the capability of triggering rules bottom-up, by anyone category on the RHS of the rule, would require the modification of the Chart Parser algorithm just described in the previous section. We shall consider that in this section.

Apart from the Goal, the label of the edge must now have two Not-found parts: the left-not-found and the right-not-found one. Note that to represent the left-not-found we write the symbols to the left of the category which triggered the rule, in reverse order, e.g. if the rule

$$X \to A B C D E$$

is triggered by C then the new edge would be

$$B A \mid X (C) \mid D E$$

where B A is the left-not-found, X( ) is the goal with C as the structure already discovered (10) , and D E is the right-not-found.

The complete edges are those which their left-not-found and right-not-found are empty

The active edges may now be active-to-left, active-to-right or bi-active when active both left and right. In Fig.9 these types of active edges, resulting from different annotations of the same rule, are represented.

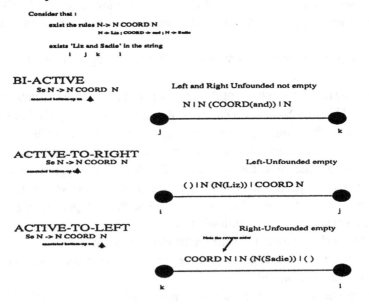

FIG.9 - ACTIVE EDGES

The Combine operation concerns a complete and an active edge. Therefore, it may happen as a result of adding from the agenda to the chart-proper, a complete or an active edge.

The combine operation resulting from adding to the chart-proper an active-to-right and an active-to-left edge, is represented in Figures 10 and 11.

---

10 *The evidence (complete edge) which makes the rule being triggered.*

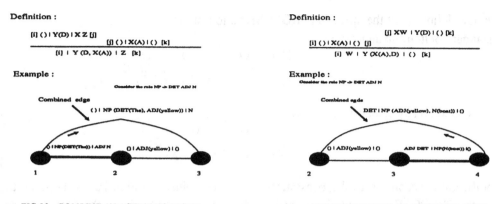

FIG.10 - COMBINE AN ACTIVE-TO-RIGHT

FIG.11 - COMBINE AN ACTIVE-TO-LEFT

If we add a bi-active edge from the agenda to the chart-proper (Fig.12) and if we combine it to both left and right, duplicated edges will occur in later steps. We have to restrict the direction of combining a bi-active edge, say only combine to the left. On the other hand, the combine operation resulting from adding a complete edge from the agenda to the chart-proper, has to be restricted, according to the previous constraint for bi-active edges, in order to avoid duplicated edges (see Fig.12).

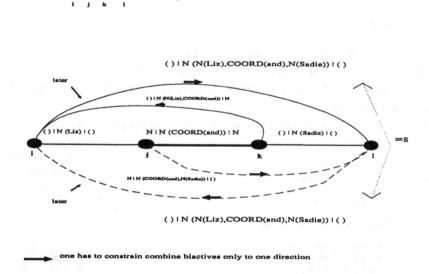

FIG.12 - COMBINE AND DUPLICATIONS

With the restriction of combining bi-actives only to the left and the restriction of not combining completes with bi-actives, one can see during the parsing process the bi-active edges behaving as 'islands of evidence', i.e. partial evidence awaiting to be corroborated first to the left and then (when they become active-to-right only) to the right.

The new definition of the operation PROPOSE bottom-up is:

a) standard bottom-up annotation

$$\frac{[i] \quad () \quad | \quad Z(A) \quad | \quad () \qquad [j]}{[i] \quad () \quad | \quad Y() \quad | \quad Z \; Q \quad [i]} \quad Y \; -> \; Z\uparrow \; O$$

b) annotated on any category

$$\frac{[i] \quad () \quad | \quad Z(A) \quad | \quad () \qquad [j]}{[i] \quad R \quad | \quad Y(Z(A)) \quad | \quad Q \quad [j]} \quad Y \; -> \; R \; Z\uparrow \; Q$$

Modifications according to the constraints for the combine operation has to be done to have the PROPOSE top-down, i.e. bi-active edges are proposed only on the first category of their left-not-found part, as illustrated bellow:

a) active-to-right edge (for active-to-left is similar)

$$\frac{[i] \quad () \quad | \quad X \quad | \quad Y \; W \; [j]}{[j] \quad () \quad | \quad Y \quad | \quad Z \; Q \; [j]} \quad Y\downarrow \; -> \; Z \; Q$$

b) bi-active edge

$$\frac{[i] \quad Y \; W \quad | \quad X \quad | \quad R \quad [j]}{[i] \quad Q \; Z \quad | \quad Y \quad | \quad () \quad [i]} \quad Y\downarrow \; -> \; Z \; Q$$

5. RESULTS

In [Men87a] Mendes describes a bidirectional chart parser implemented in PROLOG to compare different strategies. He defined a grammar, listed bellow, whose rules represent a considerable number of linguistic phenomena. He also defines a set of strings embedding the phenomena shown bellow.

Consider the following productions of an example Context Free Grammar:

	With the Best Mixed Annotation
a) to analyze the frequency of constituents	
R1: S -> NP VP	R1: S -> NP VP↑
b) to analyze the discriminate constituent	
R2: NP -> DET ADJ N	R2: NP -> DET ADJ↑ N
R3: NP -> DET N R/N	R3: NP -> DET N↑ R/N
R4: NP -> DET N PP	R4: NP -> DET N PP↑
R5: NP -> DET N	R5: NP -> DET↑ N
R6: NP -> N	R6: NP -> N↑
R7: VP -> V	R7: VP -> V↑
R8: VP -> V NP	R8: VP -> V↑ NP
R9: VP -> V NP PP	R9: VP -> V↑ NP PP
R10: PP -> PREP NP	R10: PP -> PREP↑ NP

c) to analyze the reduced and unreduced clauses (null string)

R11: R/N -> RELPRO S/N	R11: R/N -> RELPRO↑ S/N
R12: R/N -> NP VP/N	R12: R/N↓ -> NP VP/N
R13: S/N -> NP/N VP	R13: S/N↓ -> NP/N VP
R14: S/N -> NP VP/N	R14: S/N↓ -> NP VP/N
R15: VP/N -> V NP/N	R15: VP/N↓ -> V NP/N
R16: NP/N -> []	R16: NP/N↓ -> []

d) to analyze coordination

R17: S -> S COORD S	R17: S -> S COORD↑ S
R18: NP -> NP COORD NP	R18: NP -> NP COORD↑ NP
R19: VP -> VP COORD VP	R19: VP -> VP COORD↑ VP
R20: N -> N COORD N	R20: N -> N COORD↑ N
R21: PP -> PP COORD PP	R21: PP -> PP COORD↑ PP

and the rules belonging to the dictionary considered separately

```
N      -> girl,man,woman,Celia,Liz,Sadie,saw,boat,TV,I;
V      -> saw,walk,walks,walked,sank,died,met;
PREP -> with;  DET -> a,the;  ADJ -> yellow;  COORD -> and;  RELPRO -> that.
```

The strategies compared are TDS, BUS and BMA. The measure of comparison is the number of edges created during parsing. That is a feasible measure since from one strategy to another the only variable is the annotation, keeping constant the grammar, the string, and the rule interpreter.

LINGUISTIC PHENOMENON			STRINGS PARSED	TOTAL NUMBER OF EDGES			
				TDS	BUS	BMA	Gain (Average)
CONSTITUENT FREQUENCY		1	The man saw Celia with a TV	96	134	55	52%
DISCRIMINATE CONSTITUENT		2	The man walks	90	50	20	71%
		3	The man saw Celia	109	86	35	64%
		4	The man and the woman walk	154	111	43	68%
		5	The yellow boat sank	72	50	21	66%
		6	The man and the yellow boat sank	136	111	44	64%
	(TWO SOLUTIONS)	7	Celia saw the man with a TV	168	141	55	64%
NULL STRING	(NO SOLUTION BUS)*	8	The man that saw Celia died	186	0	54	71%
	(NO SOLUTION BUS)*	9	The man that Celia saw died	142	0	52	63%
	(NO SOLUTION BUS)*	10	The man Celia saw died	113	0	44	61%
	(NO SOLUTION)	11	The man saw Celia died	0	0	0	
COORDINATION	(TWO SOLUTIONS)	12	Celia and Sadie saw a girl	148	130	52	63%
		13	Celia and the man walk	123	78	35	65%
		14	Celia walks and the man died	161	83	42	66%
GLOBAL		15	Celia saw the man and saw the boat	262	215	92	61%
		16	Celia walks	59	27	13	70%
		17	The boat sank	90	50	20	71%
	(TWO SOLUTIONS)	18	The man saw the boat with a TV	204	173	67	64%
	(TWO SOLUTIONS)	19	I saw a girl with a TV	168	141	55	64%

Gain of the best mixed annotation strategy, 65% in average

TDS - Top Down Standard; BUS - Bottom Up Standard; BMA - Best Mixed Annotation

In Fig.13 a graphic shows the results of parsing the *example strings* applying TDS, BUS and BMA strategies. The gain in efficiency when parsing BMA for any phenomenon without loss of solutions is significant.

We confirm that, generally, the BUS strategy is more efficient than the TDS. Also, parsing BUS does not allow to deal straightly with the empty string (see strings 8 to 11 in Fig.13)

Parsing top-down, the number of complete edges is lesser than those produced in any other strategy which makes that one more efficient in this sense. This is because all the well-formed substrings are discovered when parsing BUS or BMA (where that number is equal).

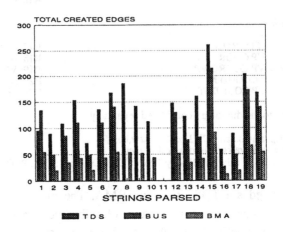

FIG.13 - COMPARISON OF TDS, BUS AND BMA

BMA strategy offers a significant gain in the number of active edges created. It creates hypotheses only when necessary. Another significant gain of the BMA strategy is on the number of repeated edges created - they are virtually eliminated for any phenomenon.

6. CONCLUSIONS

Parsing with Charts solves the depth-first and breath-first strategies problems. This is attained because duplicated edges are not kept, and because a well-formed substring is discovered only once. So a duplication of efforts is avoided, the need for memory space is reduced and the backtracking is eliminated.

Top-down and bottom-up strategies, being heuristically mixed, provide a search strategy through the optimum path designed during the parsing process. This solves the problem of the explosion of hypotheses (TDS) and the problem of not dealing straight with the empty string (BUS). Top-down is used to predict the null, otherwise bottom-up is used because it constrains the search space (data-driven).

Having rules annotated on the best evidence we get, not a pre-defined global strategy, but a locally mixed defined strategy (heuristically-driven). This will only depend on the string being parsed. It works as the directions depth-first and breath-first, and top-down and bottom-up get heuristically mixed in function of the string[Men90b]. This is an intelligent methodology of parsing: it creates only strictly necessary hypotheses without repetitions.

The path traversed through the search space to achieve the solution was reduced 65% in average for any phenomenon.

The Chart-Parser was modified from uni to bi-directional in order to fit different annotations of the grammar rule set: TDS, BUS, any Mixed Annotation and BMA. The benefits of using Charts and the generative power of the rules are still kept.

As one can define different grammar annotations the best is the one which minimize the search space without loss of solutions.

Some criteria to annotate a grammar rule set to obtain their corresponding best annotated set (BMA), were defined. We point out a level of independence over subsets of rules representing different phenomena. This makes it possible to reach the best annotation as the join of the best annotations on each phenomenon.

One may think that there might exist some grammar properties, identified globally and on each phenomenon subset rules, that allow us to automatically define its corresponding best annotated. Given a grammar, find its corresponding best annotated (uni or bi) and proving its completeness, is the research topic Mendes is developing. He is also studying Portuguese linguistic phenomena to analyze the applicability of heuristically parsing Portuguese Natural Language.

ACKNOWLEDGMENTS

We would like to thank the unknown referees for their valuable comments on this paper. And also our thanks to Leonor Barroca and Filomena Louro for proof-reading this text.

REFERENCES

[AU72a] Aho,A. and Ullman,J., "The Theory of Parsing, Translation, and Compiling", vol.1, Prentice-Hall, 1972

[DE86a] Du Boulay,B. and Elsom-Cook,M., "A Pascal program Checker", ECAI, 1986

[Gaz85a] Gazdar,G. and Kleine,E. and Pullum,G. and Sag,I., "Generalized phrase structure grammar", Blackwell, 1985

[Men90a] Mendes,J., "Reconhecimento com Charts", Department of Computer Science, University of Minho, 1990.

[Men90b] Mendes,J., "Reconhecimento:Pesquisa e Estratégias", Department of Computer Science, University of Minho, 1990.

[Men91a] Mendes,J., "Reconhecimento: estratégias heurísticas de pesquisa usando o chart bidireccional", Department of Computer Science, University of Minho, 1990.

[MD88a] Mendes,J., and DeRoeck,A., "Suport for Bidirectional Chart Parsing and Search Space Pruning", Department of Computer Science, University of Essex, 1988

[Men87a] Mendes,J., "Comparison of three parsing strategies", M.Sc. Dissertation, Department of Computer Science, University of Essex, 1987.

[SD87a] Steel,S. and DeRoeck,A., "Bidirectional Chart Parsing", Department of Computer Science, University of Essex, 1986; Proc. 1987 Conf.Soc.for Artificial Intelligence and Simulation of Behaviour; reprinted in Hallam and Mellish(eds): Advances in AI 1987, John Wiley, pags 223-235.

[TR84a] Thompson,H. and Ritchie,G. *Implementing Natural Language Parsers*, in O'Shea and Eisenstadt (eds), "Artificial Intelligence", Harper and Row, New York, 1984.

[Win83a] Winograd,T., "Language as a Cognitive Process", Vol. 1, Chapter 3, Addison Wesley, 1983.

Wave-shaping in Multiprocessor Bidirectional Heuristic State Space Search

Peter C. Nelson

Dept. of Electrical Engineering and Computer Science
University of Illinois
Chicago, Illinois 60680, USA
Phone: (312) 996-3259
Email: nelson1@uicbert.eecs.uic.edu

Anestis A. Toptsis

Dept. of Computer Science and Mathematics
York University, Atkinson College
Toronto, Ontario M3J 1P3, Canada
Phone: (416) 736-5232
Email: anestis@yetti.yorku.ca

ABSTRACT

Parallel bidirectional heuristic island search combines forward chaining, backward chaining, and parallelism to search a state space. The only algorithm in this category to date (PBA*) has been demonstrated to exhibit excellent performance in practice (superlinear speedup in all tested cases) [Nels90d]. This paper introduces the concept of wave-shaping for parallel bidirectional heuristic island search. The resulting algorithm improves the performance of PBA* by dynamically redirecting the local search processes that run concurrently on PBA*, toward quick path establishment. Experimental results on a uniprocessor, as well as a multiprocessor machine (Intel iPSC/2 hypercube) demonstrate the viability of the proposed method.

1. Introduction

Fast search techniques are crucial in almost all AI systems. AI search techniques can be categorized as *unidirectional* and *bidirectional*. Given an origination point S in the state space and a termination (goal) point G, the **unidirectional** algorithms perform a search from S to G. There is a plethora of unidirectional algorithms. Some notable examples are A* [Hart68], IDA* [Korf85], and island search algorithms I [Chak86], and I_n, I_{np} [Nels90b]. In bidirectional algorithms, there are two ongoing processes during the execution of the algorithm. One process - the *forward* process - performs the search from S to G, and the other process - the *reverse* process - performs the search from G to S. The idea is to have the two processes (forward and reverse) meet in the middle of the solution path, and thus reduce the number of nodes expanded exponentially. **Bidirectional** search has been introduced by Pohl [Pohl71]. In this method, the search builds two subgraphs, one originating from the source node (forward search) and the other from the goal node (reverse search). When expanding a node, the algorithm must decide whether to pick a node from the subgraph containing the source node, or from the subgraph containing the goal node. When the two subgraphs intersect with each other, then a solution has been found since the common node lies in the path from source to goal. A problem with Pohl's algorithm reported in [DeCh77,DeCh83,Pohl71,Poli84] is that the two opposing subgraphs may not intersect in the middle. This may occur, for example, when more than one path exists between source and goal, and the two searches follow different paths. This anomaly was remedied by DeChampeaux, and Politowski and Pohl [DeCh77,DeCh83,Poli84]. The proposed methods have the side effect of either increasing the execution time in favor of expanding fewer nodes [DeCh77,DeCh83], or increasing the number of nodes expanded [Poli84] in favor of reducing the execution time [Poli84]. Another variation of Pohl's algorithm [Pohl71] was given by [Kwa89] using pruning techniques to speed up the search. Kwa's algorithm concentrates on finding an optimal path rather than finding a(ny) path fast.

The availability and promising potentials of parallel computers made the development of parallel AI search algorithms a thriving area of research during the last decade. The two above mentioned categories (unidirectional, bidirectional) can be further divided to *uniprocessor* and *multiprocessor*, according to the number of processors that are used to perform the search. Thus, we have unidirectional uniprocessor, bidirectional uniprocessor, unidirectional multiprocessor, and bidirectional multiprocessor AI search algorithms. It is yet to be shown, but it is our belief that algorithms in the fourth category (bidirectional multiprocessor) constitute a promising approach in AI search. This belief is based on two facts.

(1) Bidirectionalism has the potential of reducing the number of nodes expanded by the unidirectional search algorithms exponentially [Pohl71].

(2) Parallel processing in AI search has been shown to deliver excellent performance which in *practical* cases is translated to superlinear speedup of the parallelized algorithm over its uniprocessor equivalent [Kuma88c,Rao87b,Rao87c,Topt91].

The existing **unidirectional multiprocessor** heuristic search techniques are parallelizations of the conventional A* algorithm and branch-and-bound techniques. Algorithms PA*$_1$ [Rao87d] and PIDA*[1] [Rao87a,Rao87d] are parallelizations of A* and IDA*, respectively. In these algorithms many processors assume the task of finding a path from source to goal. This is done by splitting the search space into subspaces (which, however, may be intersecting) and assigning one processor to progress the search in each subspace. By splitting the search space into subspaces, a processor might be assigned a subspace whose nodes are "far away" from the goal node, or a sparse subspace, i.e. one with a small number of nodes. As a result, this processor will perform wasted computation, or it will run out of work very soon. To remedy this, load balancing techniques were introduced [Kuma88c,Kuma89a] so that all processors have the same amount of work and also expand nodes of equivalent quality, i.e. of equal probability of finding a solution. Experimental results on a BBN parallel machine revealed many cases where superlinear speedup was achieved [Rao88a]. Another approach in parallelizing A* is by using a special data structure, a concurrent heap [Rao88b,Rao88c], in order to manipulate the globally shared OPEN list efficiently. The use of a concurrent heap proved beneficial, but also revealed certain bottlenecks due to congestion incurred near the root of the heap.

Bidirectional multiprocessor search algorithms intend to take advantage of both the bidirectionalism in the search, and the use of parallel processing in order to speed up the search. To the best of our knowledge, the only algorithm in this category to date is algorithm PBA* [Nels87,Nels88,Nels89b]. Our current research focuses on the study and further development of this algorithm.

Section 2 reviews algorithm PBA* and earlier experimental results of PBA* [Nels90d]. Section 3 presents an improvement on PBA* by introducing the concept of wave-shaping for parallel bidirectional island search. The method dynamically directs the local search processes that run concurrently in PBA*, toward quick path establishment. Section 4 presents some experimental results from the implementation of the new algorithm on an Intel iPSC/2 hypercube computer. Section 5 summarizes our findings and suggests further research directions.

2. Multiprocessor Bidirectional Heuristic Search

Bidirectional multiprocessor heuristic search has been introduced by [Nels87], first for 2 processors as a parallelization of Pohl's algorithm [Pohl71], and it was later generalized for N processors, N > 2 [Nels88,Nels89b]. The N-processor algorithm, PBA*, uses intermediate nodes of the search space, called *islands* or *X-nodes*[2] in order to divide the search space into smaller subspaces. In this section we review

---

[1]The names of the algorithms referenced in this category are set up by the authors of this paper for ease of reference.
[2]The terms *islands* and X-nodes are equivalent for the purposes of this paper. Historically, the term island nodes first appeared in [Chak86] to denote intermediate nodes in the search space, with the property that an optimal path passes through at least one of them. The term *X-nodes* was introduced in [Nels86] to denote intermediate nodes in the search space but not requiring that an optimal path passes through at least one of them. Also, since the algorithm described in [Nels88] requires two search processes (one forward and one reverse) to emanate from each node, the term *X-node* was coined as a reminder of the bidirectionalism in the search (see Figure 1). The main difference between the terms X-node and island node is that, while an island makes an excellent X-node, an X-node might not make a very good island. Throughout this paper, the terms *islands* and *X-nodes* are used interchangeably, and mean intermediate nodes of the search space, some of which may participate in a path (not necessarily optimal) connecting the source and goal nodes. Note, some of these intermediate notes may not participate in a solution. Actually this is especially true in [Chak86] where only one of the island nodes participates in the solution.

algorithm PBA* together with some of its properties, and also briefly discuss the potential speedup of this algorithm.

2.1. Algorithm PBA*

PBA* relies on[3] *(a)* bidirectionalism in the search, *(b)* use of many processors and "island" nodes which split the search space into smaller subspaces, *(c)* use of "reference" nodes for directing the partial searches toward fast convergence, and *(d)* use of special algorithms that reduce the amount of data communicated among the processors, and thus keep the communication cost at a reasonable level[4]. As illustrated in Figure 1, in addition to the parallel searches conducted from the source node S and the goal node G, two parallel searches are conducted from each X-node; a *forward* search towards the goal node G, and a *reverse* search towards the source node S.

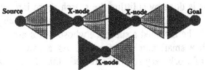

Figure 1: Parallel bidirectional search with islands

A solution is found as soon as a set of search spaces intersect in such a way that a path can be traced from S to G. The complexity of PBA* was analyzed in [Nels88,Nels89b]. In the case where the X-nodes are placed equidistantly on an optimal path from source to goal, the complexity of PBA* is

$$O(b^{\frac{n}{2(|X|+1)}}) \qquad (1)$$

where b is the branching factor of the problem, n is the length of an optimal path from source to goal, and $|X|$ is the number of X-nodes (or islands). This situation is illustrated in Figure 2 for $|X| = 2$.

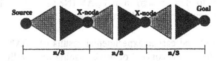

Figure 2: Algorithm PBA* in the best case

In the general case where X-nodes are not placed equidistantly on an optimal path from source to goal, the complexity of PBA* is

$$O(b^{\frac{\max\{\text{dist}(X_i, X_j), \text{dist}(X_i, E)\}}{2}}) \qquad (2)$$

where X_i and X_j range over all participating X-nodes, and E is either the source or the goal node. This situation is illustrated in Figure 3 for two X-nodes.

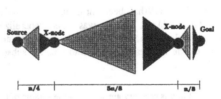

Figure 3: Algorithm PBA* in a general case

There are two main issues regarding the efficiency of PBA*. First is the search space management, that is, how to efficiently detect intersections among the many distributed search spaces. Second is the X-node generation, that is, how to find X-nodes that belong to a path from source to goal.

---

[3] A full description of the PBA* algorithm and its variations appears in [Nels88,Nels89a,Nels89b].
[4] Simulation results reported in [Nels88,Nels89a,Nels89b], show that these special algorithms incur only 1 % of the data traffic that it would have been caused if no algorithms were used.

In the first case (search space management), the difficulty arises from the fact that when N searches are concurrently in progress, it is very time consuming to have each process test if one of its generated nodes is identical to some node generated by any other process[5]. As shown in Figure 4, additional nodes, called *reference* nodes, are designated into the search space, in order to "guide" the search.

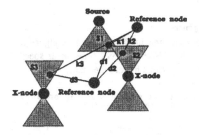

Figure 4: Reference nodes in PBA*

In Figure 4[6] $k_1 = k_2 < k_3$ and $d_1 = d_2 = d_3$. This leads to the prediction that the search spaces S_1 and S_2 are most likely to intersect, while search space S_3 does not. Given N reference nodes, each search space is represented by a N-dimensional polyhedron with 2^N corners. Each corner has coordinates

$$(R_{1i}, R_{2i}, ..., R_{Ni}),$$

where R_{ji}, is either the minimum or the maximum distance of the X-node corresponding to that search space, from the reference node R_j, j = 1, ..., N. Two search spaces S_a and S_b may contain a common node when there is an overlap of their corresponding polyhedra. A common node between two search spaces is not possible to exist, until such an overlap occurs [Nels88].

In the second case (X-node generation), the difficulty comes from the fact that poorly chosen X-nodes may not lie on an optimal (or near optimal) path from source to goal, and even worse they may not be equidistantly (or near equidistantly) placed on such a path. As implied by the complexity formula (2) and Figure 3 above, this will cause a bottleneck in PBA*'s performance. To date, the X-node generation problem has resisted any general solution and it is only addressed on a problem-by-problem basis. For some problems (such as the robot motion planning and the city travel), X-nodes can be naturally identified in the search space [Chak88,Nels88], whereas in other problems (such as the 15-puzzle), they cannot and random X-node generation may be forced [Nels88]. If an island set can be found for a particular problem, then the islands are a natural choice as origination points for these new search spaces. However, the criteria for selecting these nodes can be somewhat relaxed in a multiprocessor environment. Below, we summarize the advantages of parallel island search over sequential island search.

(1) In sequential island search, improperly selected islands may unnecessarily increase the running time since the cost of computing h_i is the *sum* of the times spent for computing h_i for each X-node. This is not true in the parallel island search since all processors compute h_i concurrently. In this case, the total time spent for the computation of h_i is the time spent by the *slowest*[7] processor (among all processors of the parallel machine) to compute the h_i for its associated X-node.

---

[5]In the 2-processor case, checking of common nodes is fairly inexpensive, since there are only two searches in progress.. As an attempt to ease this task, *multi-dimensional-heuristics* were introduced [Nels88,Nels89b].
[6]The distances k_1, k_2, k_3, d_1, d_2, and d_3 in Figure 4 are computed using some heuristic. Although it is not necessary, this heuristic can be the one used by the local A*-type searches.
[7]By *slowest processor* it is meant the processor that takes longer to perform the task under discussion. Note, this does not mean that this processor is less powerful than the other processors in a multiprocessor machine (in fact it is usually the case that all processors are of equal power in a parallel computer). It rather means that the *slowest* processor delays the

(2) In the sequential island search, improperly positioned islands may unnecessarily increase the running time since the time spent by the processor on doing search on behalf of a misplaced island, will procrastinate rather than help getting closer to the goal. This situation does not apply in the parallel method, for two reasons. First, a processor running on behalf of a misplaced island will stop as soon as a broadcast "solution found" is detected. Second, the wasted time of that processor is not counted *additively* but only in *parallel* in the total execution time.

2.2. Summary of Earlier Results

Earlier extensive experimentation with the implementation of algorithm PBA* on an Intel iPSC/2 hypercube [Nels90c,Nels90d], demonstrated that PBA* achieves superlinear speedup for *all* tested cases. Figure 5 is an example of the speedup achieved for various hypercube sizes.

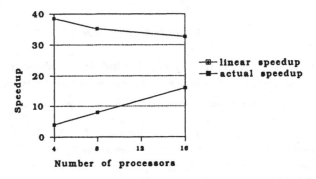

Figure 5: Speedup of PBA*

The *actual speedup* curve in this figure is the ratio

$$\frac{\text{time to execute uniprocesor version of PBA *}}{\text{time to execute PBA * on the iPSC / 2}}$$

The time for the uniprocessor version of PBA* is the time spent to execute PBA* on a Sun 3/160 using the iPSC/2 Simulator Version 3.0. Figure 5 shows that as the number of processes running per processor decreases, the speedup of PBA* also decreases[8]. However, we have also shown that this may be balanced by increasing the number of reference nodes, or by placing (if possible) the reference nodes on/near an optimal path connecting S and G. Other results from our experiments (not shown here) demonstrated that *(a)* as the number of X-nodes increases, the performance of PBA* improves; therefore, island search is a promising technique, *(b)* as the number of reference nodes increases, the speedup of PBA* over its sequential version also increases, *(c)* the positioning of reference nodes does not greatly affect PBA*'s performance although positioning a reference node on/close to an optimal path connecting S and G gives the best speedup, and *(d)* the positioning of X-nodes is best on an optimal path connecting nodes S and G. Random placement of X-nodes causes degration of PBA*'s performance, although superlinear speedup is still observable.

3. Wave-Shaping in Parallel Bidirectional Heuristic Search

As it stands, PBA* has the characteristic that any node expansion aims only to either the goal node (if the expanded node belongs to the search space of a forward search process), or the source node (if the expanded

---

computation of h_j since it performs other types of computation (e.g. expanding a node) before engaging in the computation of h_j.

[8]This observation is consistent to the analysis of the potential speedup of PBA*, appearing in [Nels90d].

node belongs to the search space of a reverse search process). This may cause the bidirectional search anomaly demonstrated in Figure 6.

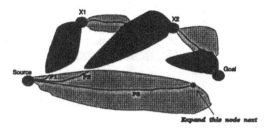

Figure 6: Bidirectional anomaly in PBA*

Although paths P1, P2, and P3 have been established and contain nodes very close to the search spaces of the X-nodes X1 and X2, a node far away from these search spaces is to be expanded next. If the algorithm had the ability to recognize that the end-node of path P1 instead of the end-node of path P3 should be expanded, then a path connecting S and G would have been established faster. The idea behind wave-shaping in parallel bidirectional island search is to try to form many partial paths connecting X-nodes (islands) in such a way that a path from source to goal is formed by joining the partial paths. Algorithm WS_PBA*, described next, performs this task.

3.1. Description of WS_PBA* (Wave-Shaping PBA*)

Algorithm WS_PBA* is an enhancement of algorithm PBA* described in [Nels88]. The enhancement aims at adding *wave-shaping* power to algorithm PBA*. The main difference between algorithms PBA* and WS_PBA* is that while in algorithm PBA* all local search processes *aim* to either the source or the goal nodes (depending on the direction of each search process), in algorithm WS_PBA* some processes change their targets *dynamically* and may *aim to X-nodes*. In algorithm WS_PBA*, a search process S_i (originating from X-node X_i) may aim toward X-node X_j (which roots search process S_j) if it is predicted that by doing so a path connecting the X-nodes X_i and X_j will be established quickly. The idea is to establish *partial* paths P_1, P_2, ... P_k, that will form a complete path connecting nodes S and G.

As in algorithm PBA*, in algorithm WS_PBA* a Central Control Process (CCP) coordinates the activity of the search processes running on the processors of a parallel machine. As soon as the CCP detects that the search spaces of two processes S_a and S_b of opposite direction (forward and reverse) are "close" to each other, it instructs S_a and S_b to *re-aim* toward the X-nodes rooting S_a and S_b respectively.

Two search spaces S_a and S_b start re-aiming activity as soon as they come close, up to a predetermined closeness value. The closeness of S_a and S_b is determined by the estimate of the distance of the two N-dimensional polyhedra corresponding to S_a and S_b. For example, assuming two reference nodes, let a_1, a_2, a_3, a_4 be the four corners of the rectangle corresponding to S_a, and let b_1, b_2, b_3, b_4 be the four corners of the rectangle corresponding to S_b. The closeness of S_a and S_b is $\min\{\text{dist}(a_i, b_j)\}$, i, j = 1, 2, 3, 4. [9]

---

[9]Note, this definition of closeness has the anomaly shown in Figure 7. The search spaces S_1 and S_2 are closer to each other than the search spaces S_1 and S_3. However, our closeness definition will instead dictate that S_1 and S_3 are closer to each other than any other pair (since $d_2 < d_1$).

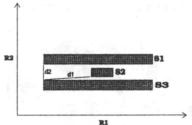

Figure 7: "Closeness" anomaly

Once two search spaces S_a and S_b are detected to be close to each other, the CCP instructs S_a and S_b to re-aim toward each other, and start expanding those nodes from their local search spaces that are closer to the opposing search space. The re-aiming is done as follows. Let dist(a_1, b_1) is the distance that determines that S_a and S_b are close (note, this distance is a heuristic estimate). Then, do:

(1) For all nodes n in S_a's local A*, re-evaluate the f-values. That is,
$$f_{new}(n) = g(n) + dist(n, X_b).$$
Do the same for all nodes in S_b's local A*, i.e.
$$f_{new}(n) = g(n) + dist(n, X_a).$$
The meaning of this re-evaluation of f-values is that process S_a re-aims to node X_b, and process S_b re-aims to node X_a.

(2) Until further notice, all node expansions from S_a and S_b are based on h-value dist(n, X_b), and dist(n, X_a), respectively, where n is a node to be expanded or inserted into the local OPEN list of S_a or S_b.

The above operations, namely estimation of closeness and re-aiming, incur an overhead for algorithm WS_PBA*, as discussed below.

Cost of operations in WS_PBA* which are in excess to regular PBA*.

(1) **Determining closeness of pairs S_a, S_b.** Let $|P|$ be the number of search spaces (number of processes in the algorithm), and $|Ref|$ be the number of reference nodes. Each search space polyhedron has $2|Ref|$ corners. Thus, to compute the distance between two search spaces, amounts to computing $(2|Ref|)^2$ distances (and choosing the minimum among them). Since there are $|P|$ search spaces, there are $1+2+ ... + |P|-1 = |P|(|P|-1)/2$ search space pairs (symmetric pairs of type (S_a, S_b), (S_b, S_a) are counted once). Therefore, the cost of computing the distances among all pairs of search spaces, is
$$\frac{|P| \cdot (|P|-1)}{2} \cdot (2^{|Ref|})^2 = O(|P|^2 \cdot 2^{|Ref|}).$$
Note, $|P| = 2(|X|+1)$, where $|X|$ is the number of X-nodes (two search processes per X-nodes, plus one from the source node, plus one from the goal node). Therefore, the above cost formula can be rewritten as $O(|X|^2 \, 2^{|Ref|})$. This cost is incurred at the CCP site.

(2) **Re-aiming search spaces.** Re-aiming amounts to re-evaluating the f-values of a local OPEN list. This incurs cost O($|OPEN|$), where $|OPEN|$ is the size of an (any) OPEN list of a search space. This cost is incurred at the local A* algorithms.

4. Performance Evaluation

4.1. Evaluation Methodology

We choose a simplified planar robot motion planning problem to test algorithm WS_PBA*[10]. In the robot motion planning problem there exists a plane broken up into a rectangular grid. On this grid there exist two designated points, S and G. S is the starting position of the robot, and G is the desired (or goal) position of the robot. The islands (X-nodes) are some points on the grid. The existence of X-nodes is a natural assumption, as there are usually obstacles on the grid and thus the X-nodes are assumed to be the endpoints of those obstacles. At any point on the grid, the robot can move north, south, east, or west, but not diagonally. Each move is assumed to be of *unit* cost. The Euclidean distance

$$d(P_1, P_2) = \sqrt{(x_1 - x_2)^2 + (y_1 - y_2)^2}$$

between two points $P_1 = (x_1, y_1)$ and $P_2 = (x_2, y_2)$ is used for the heuristic function. (Note, this is an underestimate of the actual distance and thus the admissibility of the individual A* searches is guaranteed.) The results presented in this section constitute a partial evaluation of the performance of algorithm WS_PBA*. As it has been demonstrated by earlier experiments [Nels90c,Nels90d], the performance of algorithm PBA* degrades when the X-nodes are not placed on an optimal path from S to G, which is a more realistic case. This is because partial paths are not formed for all consecutive X-nodes, and some local A* searches take longer until they encounter the first X-node in their search. One of the ideas behind WS_PBA* is to remedy this deficiency. Therefore, we compare the performance of WS_PBA* to PBA* when the X-nodes are positioned *randomly* on the grid.

As our analysis of the extra cost incurred due to wave-shaping in algorithm WS_PBA* showed in the previous section, increasing the number of reference nodes incurs overhead for WS_PBA*. On the other hand, by increasing the number of reference nodes, algorithm WS_PBA* gains a better "understanding" of the state space and thus it is expected to make more reliable estimates of the closeness of the evolving local search spaces. Therefore, we investigate the behavior of WS_PBA* (vs PBA*) when the number of reference nodes present on the grid increases.

The above tests compare WS_PBA* to PBA* when both algorithms are simulated on a uniprocessor machine. For the multiprocessor case, we present the achieved speedup of WS_PBA* over its uniprocessor version, and compare WS_PBA* to PBA* when both algorithms are executed on a multiprocessor machine.

4.2. Computing Environment

Two different machines, one uniprocessor and one multiprocessor, are used for the experiments. The *uniprocessor* machine is a workstation featuring a 33 MHz Intel 80386 processor with 4 MB of main memory. Its CPU/memory subsystem is rated at 7.12 MIPS. The operating system is the SCO XENIX 386 Release 2.3. Intel's iPSC/2 Simulator Version 3.0 is used to simulate the iPSC/2 on this machine. The *multiprocessor* machine is an Intel iPSC/2 hypercube. This consists of a *host* computer and 32 attached *nodes* connected in a hypercube topology. The host has a 16 MHz Intel 80386 processor, an Intel 80387 coprocessor, and 8 MB of main memory. Its operating system is AT&T UNIX System V/386, Release 3.2. Each node is based on the Intel 80386 processor, has a 80386 coprocessor, 4 MB of main memory, and runs the NX/2 operating system (Intel proprietary).

4.3. Experimental Results

The following parameters are used in the experiments:

|X| the number of X-nodes on the grid.
|Ref| the number of reference nodes on the grid.

---

[10]The reader should note that the purpose of this paper is to demonstrate that algorithm WS_PBA* is an efficient *general* purpose heuristic search algorithm, but not to claim that is the best algorithm for the robot motion planning problem. This problem was chosen as our testbed since it has naturally identifiable islands [Chak88].

In all tests, a 300 x 300 grid is used. The X-nodes and the reference nodes are positioned *randomly* on the grid. The timings that appear or implied in all figures consist of the sum

$$t_u + t_s,$$

where t_u is the time spent for actual computation, and t_s is the time spent on system calls on behalf of the user's process.

The results of the experiments are shown in Figures 8, 9, 10, and 11. Figures 8 and 9 present runs of WS_PBA* and PBA* both simulated[11] on the uniprocessor machine. Figures 10 and 11 show the performance of WS_PBA* on the iPSC/2. The speedup of WS_PBA* shown in Figure 10 is the ratio

$$\frac{\text{time to execute uniprocesor version of WS\_PBA*}}{\text{time to execute WS\_PBA* on the iPSC/2}}$$

Figure 8 compares WS_PBA* to PBA* when an increasing number of X-nodes are placed randomly on the grid.

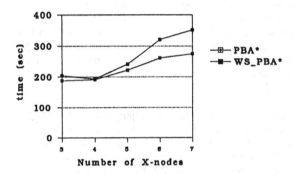

Figure 8: WS_PBA* vs PBA*. Randomly placed X-nodes

As we speculated in the *Evaluation Methodology* subsection of this section, figure 8 shows that algorithm WS_PBA* takes advantage of this situation over algorithm PBA*. The reason for this is that when the X-nodes are placed *randomly* in the search space, algorithm WS_PBA* manages to adjust the shapes of the individual search processes so that node expansions are aiming toward the closest X-node. On the other hand, this is not the case with algorithm PBA*, where all node expansions aim to either the source or the goal node. If all the X-nodes were placed on the straight line segment connecting the source with the goal node, algorithm PBA* would easily detect search space intersections, since it tends to establish a path aligned with the line defined by the X-nodes. However, when the X-nodes are placed randomly, the bidirectional search anomaly (described earlier in the paper) comes in effect, and algorithm PBA* finds it more difficult to detect search space intersections[12].

Figure 9 investigates the tradeoff "extra cost for |Ref| vs better wave-shaping ability". As it is shown in this figure, the extra cost incurred by increasing the number of reference nodes is overshadowed by the benefits incurred by a more reliable wave-shaping (in WS_PBA*) for up to a high number of reference nodes (50). Beyond that, the overhead in WS_PBA* is too high and algorithm PBA* exhibits better performance. However, we would like to point out that even in this case (|Ref| > 50) algorithm WS_PBA*) still maintains a reasonable performance (close to the one of PBA*) regardless of the exponential cost on |Ref|. This is due

---

[11]By *simulated* it is meant that a copy of the algorithm identical to the one running on the iPSC/2, is run under the Intel iPSC/2 Simulator Version 3.0 on the uniprocessor.

[12]Random distribution appeares to have made a poor placement of the X-nodes on the grid. This causes both algorithms to degrade. Nevertheless, we see that algorithm WS_PBA* is less affected by this situation.

to the increasing reliability in predicting the closeness of search space pairs.When a less expensive closeness estimation algorithm is devised, we expect that the performance of WS_PBA* to be significantly better than the one shown in Figure 9[13].

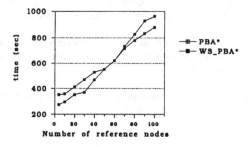

Figure 9: WS_PBA* vs PBA*. Effect of |Ref|.

Figures 10 and 11 show the performance of algorithm WS_PBA* on an iPSC/2 hypercube. As it is demonstrated by Figure 10, WS_PBA* achieves superlinear speedup over its uniprocessor version.

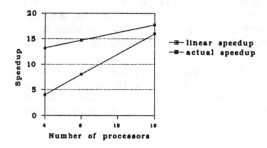

Figure 10: Speedup of WS_PBA*

Figure 11 compares WS_PBA* to PBA* when both algorithms execute on the Intel iPSC/2 hypercube. We see that WS_PBA* is about 20% faster than PBA*.

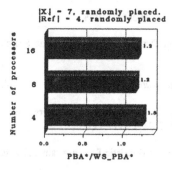

Figure 11: WS_PBA* vs PBA* on the iPSC/2

---

[13]This figure is almost implying that if |Ref| = 0, the algorithms achieve their best performance. We would like to caution the reader that this is not the case. Earlier experiments have demonstrated that when |Ref| = 0, parallel bidirectional search is up to 10 times worse than in the case when |Ref| is nonzero [Nels88], pp. 70-77.

In summary, the following conclusions are drawn from the above Figures.

(1) Random placement of X-nodes favors algorithm WS_PBA* over PBA* (algorithm PBA* is at its best when all X-nodes lie on an optimal path from source to goal). This is important, since placement of the X-nodes on an optimal path from S to G is problem dependent and impossible in most cases (e.g. 15-puzzle [Nels88]).

(2) WS_PBA* makes good use of a plethora of reference nodes *randomly* distributed in the search space. This is important since it is always possible to have as many reference nodes as desired, and random placement of reference nodes is problem independent.

(3) As Figure 11 demonstrates, given the wave-shaping power of WS_PBA*, the algorithm runs faster on a parallel machine than its predecessor, algorithm PBA*.

5.   Conclusion

We introduced algorithm WS_PBA* as an enhancement of algorithm PBA*, the only parallel bidirectional island search algorithm available to date. WS_PBA* provides wave-shaping power to PBA*, by redirecting the concurrent search processes toward fast convergence. Simulation of WS_PBA* on a uniprocessor machine, as well as its implementation   on an Intel iPSC/2 hypercube demonstrate that WS_PBA* performs well without requiring knowledge of the shape of the search space for the positioning of the X-nodes and the reference nodes. It also makes good use of the presence of large numbers of reference nodes, thus utilizing the multidimensional heuristic concept introduced in [Nels89a]. When WS_PBA* runs on a distributed memory multiprocessor (iPSC/2), it is about 20% faster than the earlier PBA* algorithm.

The performance evaluation presented here only intends to demonstrate the viability of the wave-shaping approach in parallel bidirectional island search. The algorithm is subject to more extensive and detailed benchmarking. Since wave-shaping is shown to be promising, further research aiming to the development of efficient search space re-aiming directives that can be incorporated into algorithm PBA* (and the current version of WS_PBA*) would be useful.

ACKNOWLEDGEMENTS
The iPSC/2 Simulator used for this research was provided by Intel Corporation. The Intel iPSC/2 computer time used for this research was provided by the Theory Center of Cornell University. We are especially thankful to both. Thanks also go to John Dillenburg for allowing us to use some of his programs for generating input data.

References

[Chak86] Chakrabarti, P.P., Ghose, S., and Desarkar, S.C., "Heuristic Search Through Islands", *Artificial Intelligence*, 29, (1986) : 339-348.

[Chak88] Chakrabarti, P.P., *Personal communication with Peter C. Nelson*, 1988.

[DeCh77] DeChampeaux, Dennis, and Sint, Lenie, "An Improved Bidirectional Heuristic Search Algorithm", *Journal of the ACM*, Vol. 24, No 2, (1977) : 177-191.

[DeCh83] DeChampeaux, Dennis, "Bidirectional Heuristic Search Again", *Journal of the ACM*, Vol. 30, No 1, (1983) : 22-32.

[Hart68] Hart, P., Duda, R., and Raphael, B., "A Formal Basis for the Heuristic Determination of Minimum Cost Paths", *IEEE Trans. on SSC*, vol. 4, (1968) : 100-107.

[Korf85] Korf, Richard E., "Depth-First Iterative-Deepening: An Optimal Admissible Tree Search", *Artificial Intelligence*, Vol. 27, (1985) : 97-109.

[Kuma88c] Kumar, Vipin, Ramesh, K., and Nageshwara, Rao V., "Parallel Best-First Search of State-Space Graphs: A Summary of Results", *AAAI 1988* : 122-127.

[Kuma89a] Kumar, Vipin, and Nageshwara, Rao V., "Load Balancing on the Hypercube Architecture", *Proc. 4th Conf. on Hypercubes, Concurrent Computers and Applications*, March 1989.

[Kwa89] Kwa, James B.H., "BS*: An Admissible Bidirectional Staged Heuristic Search Algorithm", *Artificial Intelligence* 38 (1989) : 95-109.

[Nels86] Nelson, Peter C., "A Parallel A* Algorithm", *MS Thesis*, Northwestern University, 1986.

[Nels87] Nelson, Peter C. and Henschen, Lawrence J. "Parallel Bidirectional Heuristic Searching", *Proc. Canadian Information Processing Society 5* (1987) : 117-124.

[Nels88] Nelson, Peter, "Parallel Bidirectional Search Using Multi-Dimensional Heuristics", *Ph.D. Dissertation*, Northwestern University, June 1988.

[Nels89a] Nelson, Peter, and Henschen, Lawrence, "Multi-Dimensional Heuristic Searching", *IJCAI '89 - International Joint Conf. on Artificial Intelligence*, August 1989, 316-321.

[Nels89b] Nelson, Peter, "Parallel Heuristic Search Using Islands", *Proc. 4th Conf. on Hypercubes, Concurrent Computers and Applications*, 1989.

[Nels90b] Nelson, Peter C., and Dillenburg, John F., "Multiple Level Island Search", *5th Rocky Mountain Conf. on Artificial Intelligence*, June 1990.

[Nels90c] Nelson, Peter C., and Toptsis, Anestis A., "Artificial Intelligence, Parallel Processing, and Bidirectional Heuristic Search", Submitted for publication.

[Nels90d] Nelson, Peter C., and Toptsis, Anestis A., "Superlinear Speedup in Multiprocessor Bidirectional Heuristic State-Space Search", Submitted for publication.

[Pohl71] Pohl, Ira, "Bi-Directional Search", *Machine Intelligence* 1971, 127-140.

[Poli84] Politowski, G. and Pohl, I. "D-Node Retargeting in Bidirectional Heuristic Search.", *Proc. AAAI 4* , (1984) : 274-277.

[Rao87a] Rao, Nageshwara, V., Kumar, Vipin, and Ramesh, K., "A Parallel Implementation of Iterative-Deepening-A*", *AAAI 1987*, 178-182.

[Rao87b] Rao, Nageshwara, and V., Kumar, Vipin, "Parallel Depth First Search. Part I. Implementation", *International Journal of Parallel Programming*, 16 (6) (1987) : 479-499.

[Rao87c] Rao, Nageshwara, and V., Kumar, Vipin, "Parallel Depth First Search. Part II. Analysis", *International Journal of Parallel Programming*, 16 (6) (1987) : 501-519.

[Rao87d] Rao, Nageshwara, V., Kumar, Vipin, and Ramesh, K., "Parallel Heuristic Search on a Shared Memory Multiprocessor", *Tech. Report. AI Lab, TR-87-45*, Univ. of Texas at Austin, January 1987.

[Rao88a] Rao, Nageshwara, V., and Kumar, Vipin, "Superlinear Speedup in State-Space Search", *Tech. Report. AI Lab, TR-88-80*, Univ. of Texas at Austin, June 1988.

[Rao88b] Rao, Nageshwara, V., and Kumar, Vipin, "Concurrent Insertions and Deletions in a Priority Queue", *1988 Inter. Conf. on Parallel Processing*, Vol. 3, (1988) : 207-210.

[Rao88c] Rao, Nageshwara, V., and Kumar, Vipin, "Concurrent access of priority queues", *IEEE Trans. on Computers* Vol. 37, (1988) : 1657-1665.

[Topt91] Toptsis, Anestis A., "Parallel Bidirectional Island Search in Distributed Memory Multiprocessors", *Ph.D. Dissertation*, Univ. of Illinois, Chicago, February 1991.

The Extended Stable Models of Contradiction Removal Semantics

Luís Moniz Pereira   José J. Alferes

Joaquim N. Aparício

AI Centre, Uninova and DCS, U. Nova de Lisboa

2825 Monte da Caparica

Portugal

Abstract

Our purpose is to define a semantics that extends Contradiction Removal Semantics just as Extended Stable Model Semantics extends Well Founded Semantics, thus providing the notion of Contradiction Free Extended Stable Models. Contradiction Removal Semantics extends Well Founded Semantics to deal with contradictions arising from the introduction of classical negation. Because the Extended Stable Models structure of a program is useful for expressing defaults and abduction, it is important to study in what way the structure of the Extended Stable Models is affected by Contradiction Removal Semantics when the Well Founded Model is contradictory. Given that the Contradiction Removal Semantics is useful for expressing belief revision and counterfactual reasoning, dealing with the structure of such models is expected to be useful for mixing together all four mentioned kinds of reasoning within a single common framework.

The Contradiction Free Extended Stable Semantics is an extension to the definition of Contradiction Removal Semantics, provided here in a form independent from the Well Founded Semantics, in terms of a fixpoint operator, instead of in terms of the Well Founded Semantics of transformed programs as before. This definition also clarifies how the semantics is useful for Belief Revision.

Nevertheless, we also define a single program transformation such that the Extended Stable Models of a transformed program correspond exactly to the Contradiction Free Extended Stable Models of the original one. By relying on the Well Founded Semantics of the transformed program no new model determining procedures are needed.

Introduction

Well Founded Semantics (WFS) (introduced in [VGRS90]) is a 3-valued semantics extending previous logic program semantics to the class of all normal programs. This semantics has been proven equivalent to a natural extension to 3 values of the 2-valued Stable Model

Semantics of [GL88], i.e. the 3-valued (or extended) Stable Model Semantics (XSMS) of [PP90, Prz90]. The WF Model (WFM) of a program P is the smallest XS Model of P. In [Prz90], an extension of WFS encompassing programs with classical negation is proposed, similar to the extension of [GL90] to deal with classical negation within Stable Model Semantics. This approach transforms a program with classical negation into another without it, by replacing every occurrence of each classically negated literal by a positive literal with a new predicate symbol. Afterwards the program models are obtained as usual. Finally, every contradictory model[1] is rejected. This seems quite reasonable for noncontradictory programs, i.e. those whose WFM is noncontradictory. But for contradictory ones it seems too strong to throw out all models. Consider for example the statements: *Birds, not known to be abnormal, fly. Tweety is a bird and does not fly. Socrates is a man.* which can be naturally represented by the program[2]:

$$fly(X) \; \leftarrow \; bird(X), \sim abnormal(X). \qquad bird(tweety)$$
$$\neg fly(tweety). \qquad\qquad\qquad man(socrates).$$

The [Prz90] WFS approach to classical negation provides no model for this program, which in our opinion is inadequate. We should at least be able to say that *Socrates* is a *man*. In our view, it is also reasonable to conclude that *tweety* is a *bird* and doesn't *fly*, because the rule stating it doesn't *fly*, being a fact, makes a stronger statement than the one concluding it *flies*, since the latter relies on the assumption of non-abnormality enforced by the Closed World Assumption (CWA) treatment of the negation as failure involving the abnormality predicate. In fact, whenever an assumption leads to a contradiction it seems logical to be able to take it back in order to remove the contradiction.

More recently, in [PAA91a], a semantics was defined that extends WFS to programs with classical negation, which avoids the absence of models caused by contradictions brought about by closed world assumptions – the Contradiction Removal Semantics (CRS). This extension relies on allowing to take back such contradiction originating CWA assumptions about literals, by making their truth value become undefined rather than false, and thus permiting noncontradictory models to appear. Such assumptions can be withdrawn in a minimal way, in all alternative ways of removing contradictions. Moreover, a single unique model that defines the semantics of a program is identified. This model is included in all the alternative contradiction removing ones. Since CRS extends WFS to deal with contradictions arising from the introduction of classical negation, and since the XSM structure of a program is useful for expressing defaults and abduction [PAA91f, PAA91e], it is important to study in what way the structure of the XSMs is affected by CRS when the WFM is contradictory and redefined by CRS as the CRWFM. Given that the CRS is useful for expressing belief revision and counterfactual reasoning [PAA91c], dealing with such models is expected to be useful for mixing together all these four kinds of reasoning within a single common framework.

The definition of these models is an extension to the definition of CRS, here provided in a form independent of the WFS, in terms of a fixpoint operator, instead of in terms of the WFS of transformed programs as before. This definition also clarifies how the semantics is useful for Belief Revision.

---

[1] By contradictory model we mean one that has some literal p and its classical corresponding negative literal $\neg p$ both true in it. A contradictory program is one having a contradictory WF Model.

[2] Here, and throughout the paper, $\sim$ stands for the negation as failure and $\neg$ for classical negation.

Nevertheless, we also define a single program transformation such that the XSMs of a transformed program correspond exactly to the Contradiction Free Extended Stable Models (CFXSMs) of the original one. By relying on the WFS of the transformed program no new model determining procedures are needed; they can be found in [Prz89, War89, PAA90, PAA91d].

The structure of this paper is as follows: in section 1 we define the language used and a program transformation similar to the ones in [GL90] and [Prz90] for dealing with classical negation, but also adumbrating integrity constraints. In section 2 we define some useful sets for establishing the causes of and the removal of contradictions within WFS. Afterwards we define Contradiction Free Extended Stable Models based on a fixpoint operator. In section 4 we formalize a notion of families of CRXSMs and examine some problems of ordering between models and families. Section 5 states some important links with the WFS. Finally, in section 6, we define the single program transformation refered above.

1 Language

In what follows a program is a set of rules of the form:

$$H \leftarrow B_1, \ldots, B_n, \sim C_1, \ldots, \sim C_m. \quad m \geq 0, n \geq 0.$$

The symbol $\sim$ stands for negation as failure, i.e. negation in the sense of WFS. $H, B_1, \ldots, B_n, C_1, \ldots, C_m$ are classical literals. A classical literal is either an atom A or its classical negation $\neg A$. A literal is a classical literal L or its negation as failure $\sim L$.

As in [GL90] and in [Prz90], we first transform such programs into ones obtained by replacing every occurrence of every classically negated literal, say $\neg l(X)$, by another with the same arguments and a new predicate name, say $'\neg l'(X)$. Then we introduce, for every atom $a(X)$ of the program, the integrity constraint $\perp \leftarrow a(X), '\neg a'(X)$, where $\perp$ stands for not true[3].

After the above transformation, contradiction removal is tantamount to preventing the appearance of literal $\perp$ in the WFM. This notion of contradiction can be extended to encompass the prevention of integrity constraint (IC) violation, if each IC is of the form $\leftarrow A_1, \ldots, A_n$ and transformed into the rule $\perp \leftarrow A_1, \ldots, A_n$.

Throughout the paper we consider partial (or 3-valued) interpretations. A partial interpretation [PP90] I of a language $\mathcal{L}$ is a pair $< T; F >$ where T and F are disjoint subsets of the Herbrand base $\mathcal{H}$ of $\mathcal{L}$. The set T contains all ground atoms true in I, the set F contains all ground atoms false in I and the truth value of the remaining atoms, those in $U = \mathcal{H} - (T \cup F)$, is undefined(or unknown).

We represent a partial interpretations $< T; F >$, equivalently, by a set of literals I such that:

- $A \in I$ iff $A \in T$

- $\sim A \in I$ iff $A \in F$

---

[3]Because, according to WFS, a literal can only be true if it has at least one rule defined for it, we need only add these $\perp$-rules for every pair of atoms $a(X)$ and $\neg a(X)$ that figure (both) as conclusions of rules in the program.

By contradictory interpretation we mean one that has $\perp$ true in it. A contradictory program is one having a contradictory WF Model.

2 Contradiction Support Sets and Contradiction Removal Sets

In this section we present the (assumptive) Contradiction Support Sets and (assumptive) Contradiction Removal Sets which were first defined in [PAA91a]. These sets are the main new constructs required by Contradiction Removal Semantics.

Informally, Contradiction Support Sets are sets of $\sim$negative literals present in the WF Model which are sufficient to lend support to $\perp$ in the WFM (and thus support a contradiction)[4], i.e. given their truth the truth of $\perp$ is inevitable. Contradiction Removal Sets are built from the Contradiction Support Sets. Intuitively, they are minimal sets of literals chosen from the Support Sets such that any support of $\perp$ registrers at least one literal in the set. Consequently, if all literals in some Contradiction Removal Set were to become undefined in value no support of $\perp$ would exist. We shall see how such literals can be made undefined, through revising a contradictory program by means of a transformation.

Example 1 Consider the program:

$$p \leftarrow \sim q. \qquad p \leftarrow \sim r. \qquad \neg p \leftarrow \sim t. \qquad a \leftarrow \sim b.$$

Its contradiction support sets are $\{\sim q, \sim t\}$ and $\{\sim r, \sim t\}$, and its contradiction removal sets are $\{\sim q, \sim r\}$ and $\{\sim t\}$.

Suppose we had q and r both undefined. In that case $\perp$ would also be undefined, the program becoming noncontradictory. The same would happen if t alone became undefined. No other set, not containing one of these two alternatives, has this property. $\square$

Definition 2.1 *Support Set[5]*
A Support Set of a literal L belonging to the WF Model M_P of a program P, represented as $SS_P(L)$, or $SS(L)$ for short, is obtained as follows:

- *If L is an atom:*

  - *Choose some rule of P for L where all the literals in its body belong to M_P. One $SS(L)$ is obtained by taking all those body literals plus the literals in some SS of each body literal.*

- *If $L = \sim A$:*

  - *If there are no rules defined for A in P then the only SS of L is $\{L\}$.*

---

[4]This notion can be seen as a special case of the notion of Suspect Sets, both of wrong and missing solutions, in declarative debugging [PC88, PCA90].

[5]An alternative definition of support sets [PAA90] relies on a notion of derivation for a literal in the WFS, and doesn't require the previous availability of the WF Model.

- *Otherwise, choose from each rule defined for A, a literal such that its complement[6] belongs to M_P. A $SS(L)$ has all those complement literals, and the literals of a SS of each of them.*

By considering all possible rules of P for a literal all its SSs are obtained.

This definition of Support Set in the WFM, can easily be extended to XSMs. For this we have only to consider the model M_P above as being some XSM. In this case, we dub the sets, *Extended Support Sets (XSS)*.

Example 2 Consider the program:

$$p \leftarrow \sim q, r. \qquad p \leftarrow \sim b. \qquad r \leftarrow a. \qquad b \leftarrow q, c. \qquad a.$$

whose WF Model is $M_P = \{p, r, a, \sim q, \sim b, \sim c\}$. Let's compute the SSs of p.

By the first rule for p, because $\sim q, r \in M_P$ they belong to a $SS(p)$. As there are no rules for q the only SS of $\sim q$ is $\{\sim q\}$. From the single rule for r we get that the single SS of r is $\{a\}$, since the only SS of a is $\{\}$. So one $SS(p) = \{\sim q, r, a\}$. With the second rule for p we get the only other $SS(p) = \{\sim b, \sim q, \sim c\}$. □

Proposition 2.1 *Existence of Support Sets*
Every literal L belonging to the WF Model of a program P has at least one support set $SS_P(L)$.

Proof: The proof follows from the definition of WFM as in [PP90], and is omitted for brevity. ◊

We have a special interest in those negative literals true by CWA, i.e. those for each there are no rules defined for their complement. With the purpose of identifying such literals we define the Assumption Support Set of a literal in the WF Model.

Definition 2.2 *Assumption Support Set*
An Assumption Support Set (ASS) of a literal L in the WFM is the (possibly empty) subset of some $SS_P(L)$, which contains exactly all its $\sim$negative elements having no rules for their complement. We represent an ASS of a literal L in a program P as $ASS_P(L)$, or $ASS(L)$ for short. For simplicity we represent these sets using the literal's complements (i.e. with atoms).

Example 3 The two $ASS(p)$ in example 2 are $\{q\}$ and $\{q, c\}$. □

Definition 2.3 $\perp$-*Assumption Support Set*
A $\perp$-Assumption Support Set ($\perp ASS$) is an $ASS(\perp)$.

These are sets of atoms false by CWA in the WF Model of the program, involved in supporting contradiction (i.e. $\perp$) in the program[7].

Having defined the sets of CWA literals that together support some literal, it is easy to produce sets of CWA literals such that, if all become undefined, the truth of that literal necessarily becomes ungrounded.

---

[6]The complement literal of an atom A is $\sim A$; that of a literal of the form $\sim A$ is A.
[7]Note that there is a close relationship between the SSs of $\perp$ and the sets of *NOGOODS* of Truth Maintenance Systems.

Definition 2.4 *Removal Sets*

A Removal Set (RS) of a literal L belonging to the WFM of a program P is a set of atoms formed by the union of some nonempty subset from each $ASS_P(L)$. If the empty set is an $ASS_P(L)$, then the only $RS(L)$ is the empty set. Note that a literal not belonging to the WFM of P has no RSs defined for it.

In view of considering minimal changes to the WF Model, we next define those RSs which are minimal in the sense that there is no other RS contained in them.

Definition 2.5 *Minimal RS*

A RS of a literal L, $RS_m(L)$, in a program P, is minimal iff there exists no $RS_i(L)$ in P such that $RS_m(L) \supset RS_i(L)$. We represent a minimal RS of L in P as $MRS_P(L)$.

Definition 2.6 *Contradiction Removal Sets*

A Contradiction Removal Set (CRS) of program P is a minimal Removal Set of the (special) literal $\perp$, i.e. a CRS of P is a $MRS_P(\perp)$.

3   Contradiction Free Extended Stable Models

Next we define Combined Removal Sets (CombRSs), based on the CRSs, to obtain the contradiction removal 3-valued stable models (CFXSMs). The CombRSs are the sets of literals which, if made undefined, generate the noncontradictory models of interest (i.e. the CFXSMs).

Definition 3.1 *Combined Removal Sets*

Let $Lits_{CRS}$ be the set of all atoms in some CRS of a program P, i.e. $Lits_{CRS} = \bigcup_i CRS_i$. A Combined Removal Set (CombRS) of P is a set of atoms formed from the union of a CRS with a subset of $Lits_{CRS}$. If there are no CRSs for P then, by definition, its only Combined Removal Set is the empty set.

This notion is an obvious extension to the notion of CRS. It gives all the ways of removing contradiction, considering the literals that contribute to it, i.e. those that contain some CRS. CRSs are minimal CombRSs.

CFXSMs will be defined in such a way that in each CFXSM the literals of some CombRS are all undefined. This ensures that the models are noncontradictory. For this purpose we define the program transformation:

Definition 3.2 *Given a program P and a set A of atoms from its alphabet, we define P_A, and call it P sub A, as the program obtained by:*

- *Removing from P all rules whose head is an element of A.*

- *Replacing every occurrence of each atom A in P by the special atom $\mathbf{u}$[8].*

---

[8]The meaning of this special atom, introduced in [PP90], is that $\mathbf{u}$ is undefined in every model of any program.

The alphabet of P_A, $\mathcal{LIT}(P_A)$, is by definition, $\mathcal{LIT}(P) - \mathcal{LIT}(A)$.

Note that no XSM of the transformed program contains any element in A (i.e. all are undefined). However, because of the second item above, all the consequences of forcing them undefined are nevertheless obtained.

We can now define Contradiction Free Extended Stable Models (CFXSMs). The idea is that the CFXSMs of each program P are the XSMs of a program P_R obtained by the above transformation on P with respect to each CombRS R. The desired result is that the set of CFXSMs of a program P is the set of all noncontradictory XSMs of each P_R, when every CombRS is considered. More formally:

Definition 3.3 *Modulo transformation [PP90]*

Let P be a logic program and let I be a 3-valued interpretation. By the extended GL-transformation of P modulo I we mean a new (non-negative) program P/I obtained from P by performing the following three operations:

- *Removing from P all rules which contain a negative premise $L = \sim A$ such that $A \in I$.*

- *Removing from all the remaining rules those negative $L = \sim A$ which satisfy $L \in I$.*

- *Replacing in all remaining rules the negative premises $L = \sim A$ by $\mathbf{u}$.*

$\Gamma^*(P, I)$, *a generalization of the Γ operator [GL88], is defined as the 3-valued least model of P/I.*

Definition 3.4 *Contradiction Free Extended Stable Models*

A noncontradictory partial interpretation I is a Contradiction Free Extended Stable Model of a program P iff there exists some CombRS R of P such that $I = \Gamma^*(P_R, I)$. If such is the case we call R the Source Removal Set of I.

The need to impose noncontradiction on the XSMs is that literals undefined in it, even if the WFM is noncontradictory, still may originate an XSM of some transformed program P_{RS} with some contradiction, when they become defined. This matter will be further examined later.

Example 4 Consider the (contradictory) program $P = \{p \leftarrow \sim q; \; \neg p \leftarrow \sim r; \; a \leftarrow \sim b; \; b \leftarrow \sim a\}$, whose (contradictory) WF Model is $\{p, \neg p, \sim q, \sim r\}$. Its CRSs are $\{q\}$ and $\{r\}$, and its CombRSs are its CRSs and $\{q, r\}$.

The corresponding transformed programs are:

$$P_{\{q\}} = \{p \leftarrow \mathbf{u}; \; \neg p \leftarrow \sim r; \; a \leftarrow \sim b; \; b \leftarrow \sim a\}$$
$$P_{\{r\}} = \{p \leftarrow \sim q; \; \neg p \leftarrow \mathbf{u}; \; a \leftarrow \sim b; \; b \leftarrow \sim a\}$$
$$P_{\{q,r\}} = \{p \leftarrow \mathbf{u}; \; \neg p \leftarrow \mathbf{u}; \; a \leftarrow \sim b; \; b \leftarrow \sim a\}$$

For the first program we have the CFXSMs: $\{\neg p, \sim r\}$, $\{\neg p, \sim r, a, \sim b\}$ and $\{\neg p, \sim r, b, \sim a\}$. For the second program we have the CFXSMs: $\{p, \sim q\}$, $\{p, \sim q, a, \sim b\}$ and $\{p, \sim q, b, \sim a\}$. Finally, for the last program we have the CFXSMs: $\{\}$, $\{a, \sim b\}$ and $\{b, \sim a\}$.

These are the only CFXSMs. The first group of three correspond to the XSMs of the program, after removing the contradiction via undefining q. The second group correspond to the XSMs of the program, after removing the contradiction via undefining r. As there is no compulsory preference about which literal to remove, q or r, we should also consider undefining them both. In this case the modified XSMs of the program are those in the third group. □

Lemma 3.1 *If the empty set is a CRS of a program P then P has no CFXSMs.*

Proof: If the empty set is a CRS of P then there exists an empty $\perp$-ASS, i.e. there exists one $SS(\perp)$ having no CWAs, and all CombRSs are $\{\}$. Since $P = P_{\{\}}$ has one $SS(\perp)$ having no CWAs then its WFM is contradictory. So all its XSM are contradictory, i.e. non of them is a CFXSM. ◇

Lemma 3.2 *If the empty set is not a CRS of a program P then there exists at least one CFXSM of P.*

Proof: By hypothesis, program P has no empty CRS. Two cases occur: if there are no CRSs the conclusion follows by theorem 5.1; otherwise there is at least one nonempty CRS, RS. By definition of Contradiction Removal Set, none of the previous $SS(\perp)$ exists in P_{RS}, because all atoms in RS are undefined in P_{RS}, and hence in all its XSMs[9]. Moreover as undefined literals cannot make any other literals true or false, no new $SS(\perp)$ are generated. ◇

With the two lemmas above, the next theorem, which expresses the completeness conditions for the semantics, follows easily.

Theorem 3.3 *A program P has at least one (noncontradictory) CFXSM iff the empty set is not a CRS of P.*

4 Ordering among CFXSMs

In this section we formalize the notion of family of CFXSMs and establish orderings among models and their families. In order to take advantage of previous results, we compare the orderings with the lattice of submodels of [PAA91a]. We also identify a single unique model that defines the semantics of a program. This model is proven equivalent to the one defined in [PAA91a].

Definition 4.1 *Two CFXSMs of a program P belong to the same family $[RS]$ if they have the same Source Removal Set RS.*

Intuitively, a family corresponds to the set of XSMs of the resulting program after one way of removing the contradiction.

Example 5 In example 4, each of the three groups of CFXSMs is one family. □

---

[9]One always exists, albeit the WFM of P_{RS}.

A set inclusion ordering among models of the same family can be defined: We say a model $M_1 \leq M_2$ iff $M_1 \subseteq M_2$. Given this ordering, we define the root model $root([RS])$ of a family $[RS]$ to be its least model, i.e. by the properties of XSM Semantics $root([RS])$ is the WFM of P_{RS}.

Theorem 4.1 *If a program P has at least one CFXSM then for every CombRS RS there exists a nonempty family* $[RS]$.

Proof: By theorem 3.3, this is the case when the empty set is not a CRS of P. In all (possible contradictory) XSMs of P_{RS} all atoms in RS are undefined. By definition of Contradiction Removal Set, in every $SS(\perp)$ of P, at least one element was removed (i.e. became undefined) in P_{RS}. So none of the $SS(\perp)$ remains in P_{RS}. As undefined literals cannot make any other literal true or false, no new $SS(\perp)$ are generated. Thus at least the WFM of P_{RS} is noncontradictory and so is a CFXSM with Source Removal Set RS. ◇

Definition 4.2 *We say* $[RS_1] \leq [RS_2]$ *iff* $root([RS_1]) \subseteq root([RS_2])$. *In order to ensure this set inclusion ordering is a lattice we include as top element the family comprised of the (contradictory) WFM of the original program.*

Example 6 The families of example 5 and their ordering is represented by the lattice below.

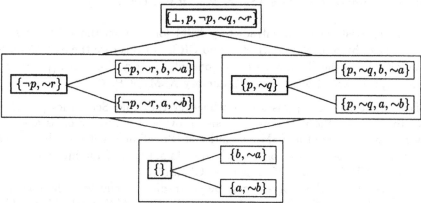

where families are $\leq$ from bottom to top, and models within a family are $\leq$ from left to right. □

A family reflects the XSMs structure of the original P after a specific contradiction removal. Its root model is its WFM. This suggests a close relation between root models and submodels (from [PAA91a]). In fact:

Proposition 4.1 *The root model of each family* $[RS]$ *of a program P is a submodel of P.*

Proof: $root([RS])$ is the WFM of P_{RS}, and P_{RS} is the program obtained from P after forcing literals in RS undefined. Because all atoms in RS are CWA literals, by definition root models are submodels. ◇

Proposition 4.2 *A root model of a maximal noncontradictory family (i.e. maximal family excluding the top element) is a maximal noncontradictory submodel, and vice-versa.*

Proof: The proof follows easily, given that the set of literals that became undefined are the same in both cases, i.e. the CRSs. ◇

Theorem 4.2 *Relation with Contradiction Removal Semantics*
   The Contradiction Removal Well Founded Model (as defined in [PAA91a]) is the root model, root([RS]), of the least family RS.

By establishing the connection with the definitions in [PAA91a], the notions of minimality of change defined there are inherited by the CFXSMs.

5   Relations with WFS

In this section will relate the CFXSMs with the (possibly contradictory) XSMs of any program[10]. In particular we prove that for noncontradictory programs they coincide.
   The next result expresses why the new semantics is an extension of XSM Semantics.

Theorem 5.1 *If there exists one noncontradictory XSM for a program P, then an interpretation I is a noncontradictory XSM of P iff it is a CFXSM of P.*

Proof: If there exists one noncontradictory XSM for P, then the WFM of P does not contain $\bot$. Then by proposition 2.1 P has no CRSs. In this case the only CombRS is $\{\}$. So by definition 3.4, the CFXSMs are the noncontradictory XSMs of $P_{\{\}}$ and as $P_{\{\}} = P$ by definition, they are also the noncontradictory XSMs of P. ◇

In fact this theorem expresses that whenever the XSM Semantics provides a noncontradictory model, the new semantics also provides the same models and vice-versa. Moreover, in cases where the XSM Semantics of [Prz90] does not provide any semantics, the new semantics does provide one, which consists not only of a unique noncontradictory model, the CRWFM, but also of some more CFXSMs.
   In the general case the program may be contradictory, and the relationship between the models of the XSM Semantics and those of the CFXSM Semantics is established via the families in the latter.
   A family can be viewed as the XSM structure pertaining to one way of removing contradiction. The relationship between CFXSMs in families and the (contradictory) XSMs of the original program, allows to establish results on the changes to the XSMs after contradiction removal. The CFXSMs can then be put to use for abductive, counterfactual, and default reasoning, as in [PAA91f, PAA91e, PAA91c].
   We next formalize the (partial) mapping from a given contradictory XSM CX of a program P, whose contradictory WFM is M_P, to a XSM FX of some family [RS].
   Let $Sup = CX - M_P$. If such a mapping exists the intended result is that FX results from $root([RS])$ in the same way as CX results from M_P (i.e. by defining the same set

---

[10]In what follows we consider that contradictory programs can have XSMs, not giving, for this purpose any special meaning to the atom $\bot$.

Sup of atoms[11]). In other words $CX - M_P = FX - root([RS])$, and so that CX maps into $FX = (CX - M_P) \cup root([RS])$.

Compared with CX, in FX (if it exists) there are some atoms that become undefined. The mapping is not defined if for some literal l in *Sup* all its Extended Support Sets $XSS(l)$ contain the complement of some atom in RS: in that case there could be no support for l in FX, and FX would not contain all of *Sup*.

Example 7 Consider the contradictory program $\{p \leftarrow \sim q; \quad \neg p; \quad b \leftarrow \sim a; \quad a \leftarrow \sim b; \sim q\}$. Its only CombRS is $\{q\}$. The XSM structure of the program and its only family $[\{q\}]$ are:

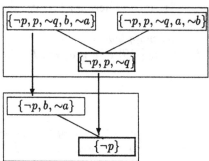

where the arrows express the desired partial mapping; note there is no mapping for the rightmost model because the only $XSS(a)^{12}$ in it contains $\sim q$, which becomes undefined in the family since $q \in RS$. □

The only case when a CX does not have a mapping is when it would map into a contradictory FX. This occurs only when there exists a $XSS(\perp)$ containing some element of *Sup* but not any complement literal of an atom in RS, i.e. such a contradiction is not removed by undefining the elements in RS (cf. formal definition below).

Example 8 Consider the contradictory program $\{p \leftarrow \sim q; \quad \neg p; \quad p \leftarrow \sim a; \quad a \leftarrow \sim b; \quad b \leftarrow \sim a\}$. Its only CombRS is $\{q\}$. The XSM structure of the program and the only family $[\{q\}]$ of the latter are:

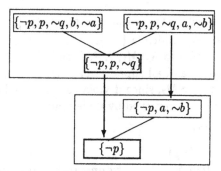

There is no mapping for the leftmost model because there is a $XSS(\perp) = \{\neg p, p, \sim a\}$ which persists even after making q undefined. □

---

[11]The literals in *Sup* are undefined in the WFM, thus not appearing in any SS and consequently in any CombRS.

[12]Note that in this case a is a member of *Sup*.

Definition 5.1 *Given a program P with WFM M_P and a family $[RS]$, we define the partial mapping $\xi : XSM \longrightarrow CFXSM$ such that $\xi(M_P, RS)(CX) = (CX - M_P) \cup root([RS])$ only if both two conditions below hold:*

- $\forall l \in Sup, \exists XSS(l) \mid \widehat{RS} \cap XSS(l) = \{\}$

- $\forall XSS(\bot), Sup \cap XSS(\bot) = \{\} \vee \widehat{RS} \cap XSS(\bot) \neq \{\}$

where $Sup = CX - M_P$ and $\widehat{RS}$ is the set of complement of the atoms in RS.

Proof of the theorem below is omitted here for brevity, but appears in [PAA91b].

Theorem 5.2 *Correctness of the mapping*
An element belongs to the family $[RS]$ of a program P with WFM M_P iff it belongs to the codomain of $\xi(M_P, RS)$.

Example 9 Consider the program:

$$\neg p. \qquad a \leftarrow \sim b, \sim q. \qquad c \leftarrow \sim d.$$
$$p \leftarrow b, c. \qquad b \leftarrow \sim a. \qquad d \leftarrow \sim c.$$
$$p \leftarrow \sim q.$$

whose only CRS is $\{q\}$. Its XSMs are:

$$
\begin{array}{ll}
\{\neg p, p, \sim q\} & WFM \\
\{\neg p, p, \sim q, a, \sim b\} & XSM_1 \\
\{\neg p, p, \sim q, b, \sim a\} & XSM_2 \\
\{\neg p, p, \sim q, c, \sim d\} & XSM_3 \\
\{\neg p, p, \sim q, d, \sim c\} & XSM_4 \\
\{\neg p, p, \sim q, a, \sim b, c, \sim d\} & XSM_5 \\
\{\neg p, p, \sim q, a, \sim b, d, \sim c\} & XSM_6 \\
\{\neg p, p, \sim q, b, \sim a, c, \sim d\} & XSM_7 \\
\{\neg p, p, \sim q, b, \sim a, d, \sim c\} & XSM_8 \\
\end{array}
$$

Let's construct now the CFXSMs of the only family $[\{q\}]$ of P.
Its root is the WFM of $P_{\{q\}}$ which is $\{\neg p\}$.
The mapping does not apply to XSM_1, XSM_5 and XSM_6, since they violate the first condition: all of them have a, and all supports of a fall when q becames undefined.
It also does not apply to XSM_7, since it violates the second condition: b and c in that model cause a contradiction not removed by undefining q.
Thus the CFXSMs of $[\{q\}]$ are:

$$
\begin{array}{ll}
\{\neg p\} & root([\{q\}]) \\
\{\neg p, b, \sim a\} & \text{by applying } \xi \text{ to } XSM_2 \\
\{\neg p, c, \sim d\} & \text{by applying } \xi \text{ to } XSM_3 \\
\{\neg p, d, \sim c\} & \text{by applying } \xi \text{ to } XSM_4 \\
\{\neg p, b, \sim a, d, \sim c\} & \text{by applying } \xi \text{ to } XSM_8 \\
\end{array}
$$

$\square$

6   A single transformation giving all CFXSMs

Now we present an equivalent alternative definition of CR Semantics, based on a single transformation of any program P, that not only gives us the CRWFM but also the several CFXSMs. The WF Model of the transformed program is the CRWF Model of the original one. The other noncontradictory XSMs of the transformed program are the CFXSMs.

As we've seen in section 3, each CFXSM coresponds to one possible way of removing contradiction, by undefining at least all the elements of some CRS and optionally, additional elements of other CRSs. In order to make available the option of undefining or not some CWA-false literal of P, we can add to P, for that CWA literal's atom A, the rules $A \leftarrow \sim A'$ and $A' \leftarrow \sim A$, where A' is a new atom with the arguments of A. These rules have the effect of making A (and A') undefined in the WF Model, and of allowing XSMs with A (and $\sim A'$) and others with $\sim A$ (and A'). To prevent A being true in any XSM, we prevent A' being false in any model by also adding the rule $A' \leftarrow \sim A'$.

Definition 6.1 *CWA choice rules*
The CWA choice rules for a classical literal A are $A \leftarrow \sim A'$, $A' \leftarrow \sim A$ and $A' \leftarrow \sim A'$, where A' is a new atom with the arguments of A.

Proposition 6.1 *Let P be a program without rules defined for atom A. The truth value of A in the WF Model of P augmented with the CWA choice rules for A is undefined. There exists at least one XSM of the augmented program such that $\sim A$ belongs to it. There is no such XSM of the augmented program such that A belongs to it.*

Definition 6.2 *CR Program Transformation*
The CR Transformed Program of a contradictory program $CRTP(P)$ with CRSs $C_1, \ldots, C_n$ is the program obtained by adding to P all CWA choice rules for each element of each C_i $(1 \le i \le n)$[13].

Example 10 The CRTP of the program of example 4 is:

$$
\begin{array}{lll}
p \leftarrow \sim q. & q \leftarrow \sim q' & r \leftarrow r' \\
\neg p \leftarrow \sim r. & q' \leftarrow \sim q & r' \leftarrow r \\
a \leftarrow \sim b. & q' \leftarrow \sim q' & r' \leftarrow r' \\
b \leftarrow \sim a.
\end{array}
$$

and its XSMs (modulo r' and q'), are shown in the next figure, where its contradictory models have been discarded:

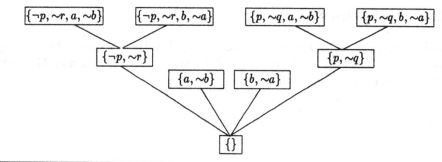

---

[13]Note that the union of all CRSs is equal to the union of all CombRSs.

Note that they correspond exactly to the CFXSMs found in example 4. □

To prove the correctness of this transformation, let's first state some lemmas.

Lemma 6.1 *There is a bijection between the noncontradictory XSM of $CRTP(P)$ (modulo new atoms introduced by CWA choice rules) and the CFXSMs of P.*

Proof: We prove this lemma by constructing for a given XSM of $CRTP(P)$ XM, a CombRS RS such that XM is also an XSM of P_{RS}, and thus a CFXSM.

By proposition 6.1, atoms in some subset S of $Lits_{CRS}$(c.f. definition 3.1) of P are false in XM, and atoms in $Lits_{CRS} - S$ are undefined in XM. Let $RS = Lits_{CRS} - S$. All XSMs of P_{RS} have, as noted before, all atoms in RS undefined and, as there are no rules for them, all atoms in S false. Thus, with respect to atoms of $Lits_{CRS}$, all XSMs of P_{RS} are equal to XM. The P sub RS transformation does not affect other literals, so if there is stability for them in XM, the same applies in one XSM of P_{RS}. ◇

Lemma 6.2 *If $[RS]$ is a family of a contradictory program P, then every model $M \in [RS]$ is a noncontradictory XSM of $CRTP(P)$ (modulo new atoms introduced by CWA choice rules).*

Proof: The proof of this lemma is similar to the one of lemma 6.1, but this time constructing the various XMs given RS. ◇

Theorem 6.3 *Correctness of the transformation*
   An interpretation I is a CFXSM of a program P iff I (modulo new atoms introduced by CWA choice rules) is a noncontradictory XSM of $CRTP(P)$.

Proof: When the CR Semantics coincides with the WFS, i.e. under the conditions of theorem 5.1, there are no CRSs, and so $CRTP(P) = P$. In this case the result follows easily. For a contradictory program the result follows directly from lemmas 6.1 and 6.2 above. ◇

Corollary 1 *If the WFM of $CRTP(P)$ is noncontradictory then it coincides with the CRWFM of P.*

Acknowledgements

We thank ESPRIT BRA COMPULOG (no. 3012), Instituto Nacional de Investigação Científica, Junta Nacional de Investigação Científica e Tecnológica and Gabinete de Filosofia do Conhecimento for their support.

References

[GL88] M. Gelfond and V. Lifschitz. The stable model semantics for logic programming. In R. A. Kowalski and K. A. Bowen, editors, *5th International Conference on Logic Programming*, pages 1070–1080. MIT Press, 1988.

[GL90] M. Gelfond and V. Lifschitz. Logic programs with classical negation. In *ICLP'90*, pages 579–597, 1990.

[PAA90] L. M. Pereira, J. N. Aparício, and J. J. Alferes. Top-Down procedures for well founded semantics. Technical report, AI Centre/Uninova, 1990.

[PAA91a] L. M. Pereira, J J. Alferes, and J. N. Aparício. Contradiction removal within Well Founded Semantics. In *LPNMR'91*. MIT Press, 1991.

[PAA91b] L. M. Pereira, J. J. Alferes, and J. N. Aparício. The extended stable models of contradiction removal semantics. Technical report, AI Centre/Uninova, 1991.

[PAA91c] L. M. Pereira, J N. Aparício, and J. J. Alferes. Counterfactual reasoning based on revising assumptions. Technical report, AI Centre/Uninova, 1991.

[PAA91d] L. M. Pereira, J. N. Aparício, and J. J. Alferes. A derivation procedure for extended stable models. In *IJCAI'91*. Morgan Kaufmann Publishers, 1991.

[PAA91e] L. M. Pereira, J. N. Aparício, and J. J. Alferes. Hypothetical reasoning with well founded semantics. In *SCAI'91*. IOS Press, 1991.

[PAA91f] L. M. Pereira, J. N. Aparício, and J. J. Alferes. Nonmonotonic reasoning with well founded semantics. In *ICLP'91*. MIT Press, 1991.

[PC88] L. M. Pereira and M. Calejo. A framework for Prolog debugging. In K. B. R. Kowalski, editor, *ICLP'88*. MIT Press, 1988.

[PCA90] L. M. Pereira, M. Calejo, and J. N. Aparício. Refining knowledge base updates. In *Simpósio Brasileiro de Inteligência Artificial*, 1990.

[PP90] H. Przymusinska and T. Przymusinski. *Semantic Issues in Deductive Databases and Logic Programs*. Formal Techniques in Artificial Intelligence. North Holland, 1990.

[Prz89] T. Przymusinski. Every logic program has a natural stratification and an iterated fixed point model. In *8th Symposium on Principles of Database Systems*. ACM SIGACT-SIGMOD, 1989.

[Prz90] T. Przymusinski. Extended stable semantics for normal and disjunctive programs. In *ICLP'90*, pages 459–477. MIT Press, 1990.

[VGRS90] A. Van Gelder, K. A. Ross, and J. S. Schlipf. The well-founded semantics for general logic programs. *Journal of ACM*, pages 221–230, 1990.

[War89] D.S. Warren. The XWAM: A machine that integrats prolog and deductive databases. Technical report, SUNY at Stony Brook, 1989.

Modeling a Rational Cognitive Agent in SNePS

Deepak Kumar and Stuart C. Shapiro
Department of Computer Science
226 Bell Hall
State University of New York at Buffalo
Buffalo, NY 14260
kumard, shapiro@cs.buffalo.edu

Abstract

Our goal is to model a rational cognitive agent whose behavior is driven by its beliefs, desires, and intentions. In this paper we present a model of a simplified cognitive agent and its implementation. We use intensional propositional representations of beliefs, plans, and acts. The representations are expressed using the SNePS semantic network formalism. After giving a declarative specification of our model, we describe an implementation, and examples of its use.

1   Introduction

This paper presents details of one of the CASSIE projects[15, 20]. Our goal is to model a rational cognitive agent whose behavior is driven by its beliefs, desires, and intentions. We want our agent to do natural language understanding, reason about beliefs, act rationally based on its beliefs, do plan recognition, and plan based text generation. Doing all these tasks in a single coherent framework poses several constraints. In this paper we present a model of a simplified rational cognitive agent and its implementation. The simplifications are due to several assumptions made about the behavior of the agent. At the end we will discuss how a more sophisticated model can be arrived at by lifting various assumptions.

2   The Language

We will use the language of predicate logic with a few extensions. Predicate symbols will be written italicized beginning with an uppercase letter followed by all lowercase letters (e.g. *Intend, Believe* etc), function symbols will be written in italicized capital letters (e.g. *FRONT, REMOVE* etc). In addition to functions and predicate symbols, we have action symbols and state terms. Action symbols denote actions and will be written just like function symbols. Functions are also actions, however, they are not part of the agent's conscious vocabulary (hence we will call them *meta-actions*). In the description of the model you will see function symbols being used as function as well as action terms. The meaning of these terms will be clear from context. Action terms take terms as arguments and denote specific acts (e.g. $PICKUP(o)$ denotes the act of picking up an object o). State terms are described below.

2.1 Actions and predicates

To formally specify the architecture and the behavior of the agent we will use some actions and predicates. The actions referred to are those that the agent is capable of performing. The set of actions an agent is capable of performing will be denoted by $\mathcal{A}$. Predicates enable us to say things about the agent's states. Let $\mathcal{P}$ denote the set of predicates used in the specification of the agent. The predicates and actions comprising $\mathcal{P}$, and $\mathcal{A}$ will be described in the following sections.

A note about representations of actions and predicates: We will be using the SNePS semantic network processing system [13, 19, 17] to represent/model the actions and predicates described. SNePS networks represent entities (individuals, propositions, acts, and rules) using nodes. One characteristic feature of SNePS representations is that all nodes are terms of SWM, the formal logic underlying SNePS [11, 16]. Nodes are typed by the kind of entity they represent. In the description of predicates and actions below, you will notice that both actions, as well as predicates can take other actions and predicates as arguments. This enables the agent to talk about its actions and beliefs. However, as mentioned earlier, the modeled agent will not be able to represent all of the actions described below. To enable an implementation of an agent, some of the actions will be modeled at a meta-level (i.e. as functions). This will become clear later when we describe an implementation of the system.

2.2 States

We define three types of states—*mental states, intentions,* and *external world;* that will help us in specifying the beliefs, intentions, and behavior of the agent.

2.2.1 Beliefs

A mental state (or a *belief space*) represents the agent's beliefs about entities (individuals, propositions, acts, and rules). Let Δ denote the set of mental states of the agent at various instants of time. Let $\delta(i)$ denote the belief space of the agent at instant i. Beliefs are stored as *supported wffs (swffs)* in the syntax of the SWM logic [11]. We will use the following variables, and predicates to talk about the agent's beliefs about various entities:

e, p, p_i are universally quantified variables denoting proposition nodes.

a, a_1, a_2 are universally quantified variables denoting act nodes.

Believe$(p, \delta(i))$ means that p follows from $\delta(i)$ (i.e. $\delta(i) \vdash p$).

Precondition$(p, a, \delta(i))$ means the agent believes that swff p is the precondition of act a in belief-space $\delta(i)$.

Effect$(p, a, \delta(i))$ means the agent believes that swff p is the effect of act a in belief-space $\delta(i)$.

Plan$(a_1, a_2, \delta(i))$ means the agent believes that act a_1 is a plan for complex act a_2 in belief-space $\delta(i)$.

Primitive(a) means the agent believes that act a is primitive.

2.2.2 Intentions

The agent's intentions at any instant are represented by a set of acts the agent intends to perform. Let $\tau(i)$ represent the set of intentions of the agent at any instant i, and $\mathcal{T}$ denote the set of all sets of intentions. We will model $\tau(i)$ as a first-in-first-out queue, and define the following predicates and actions on it (As above, variable a ranges over acts, and $\mathcal{A}$ is the set of actions the agent can perform):

Empty$(\tau(i))$ means that in state i the agent has no intentions.

$FRONT : \mathcal{T} \to \mathcal{A}$ is a function (meta-action) that returns the next act to be performed.

$REMOVE : \mathcal{T} \to \mathcal{T}$ is a function (meta-action) that removes the next act from the agent's intentions.

$SCHEDULE : \mathcal{A} \times \mathcal{T} \to \mathcal{T}$ is a function (meta-action) that schedules an act on the agent's intentions.

Intend$(a, \delta(i))$ means that in the belief-space $\delta(i)$ the agent forms the intention of performing act a.

The functions are defined by the following axioms:

$$FRONT(\tau(i)) = \begin{cases} error & \text{if } Empty(\tau(i)) \\ a & \text{if } SCHEDULE(a, \tau(i-1)) \end{cases}$$

$$REMOVE(\tau(i)) = \begin{cases} error & \text{if } Empty(\tau(i)) \\ \tau(i+1) & \text{where } \tau(i+1) = \tau(i-1), \\ & \text{if } SCHEDULE(a, \tau(i-1)) \end{cases}$$

$$SCHEDULE(a, \tau(i)) = \tau(i+1), \text{such that } FRONT(\tau(i+1)) = a.$$

2.2.3 External world

At any given time the agent is situated in a state in the external environment. The agent is capable of bringing about changes in its environment. No one else can affect any changes in this environment. The agent cannot perceive its environment. There is another passive agent, U (for user) that is present. U can inform the agent about the environment. U can ask the agent to perform some actions. Let $\sigma(i)$ designate the state of the external world at instant i, and Σ be the set of all external states. To describe the agent's behavior in the external world, we will use a meta-action $EXECUTE$:

$$EXECUTE : \mathcal{A} \times \Sigma \to \Sigma$$

$EXECUTE$ denotes the *effectory function* on the external world. We will use the predicate *Done* to indicate that an act was performed in a given state. Thus,

$Done(a, \delta(i))$ means that the act a is performed while the agent believes exactly the swffs contained in the belief-space $\delta(i)$. i.e.
$$Done(a, \delta(i)) \equiv Done(EXECUTE(a, \sigma(i)), \delta(i))$$

All members of the sets Δ, Σ and $\mathcal{T}$ are terms of the language.

2.3 State transitions

At any given instant of time i the complete state of the world is specified by the triple $\langle \sigma(i), \delta(i), \tau(i) \rangle$ where $\sigma(i)$ designates the state of the external world at instant i, $\delta(i)$ designates the set of beliefs of the agent at instant i, and $\tau(i)$ is the agent's current set of intentions.

State transitions occur when actions (or meta-actions) are performed. We identify three types of actions—*external, mental,* and *control*; depending on the states they change (i.e. external world, mental states, and intentions, respectively). Only one of the states is allowed to change at any given time. This is stated in the following assumption:

The State Persistence Assumption: At any given time exactly one state is allowed to change. Thus, for any mental action a

if	$Done(a, \delta(i))$ results in		$\delta(i+1)$
then	$\sigma(i+1)$	will be the same as	$\sigma(i)$
and	$\tau(i+1)$	will be the same as	$\tau(i)$

and similarly for any external and control action.

3 The SNePS agent

A SNePS agent in an environment can now be defined as a 6-tuple

$$\langle \Sigma, \Delta, \mathcal{T}, \mathcal{A}, \mathcal{P}, Init \rangle$$

where

Σ is a set of states of the external world,

Δ is a set of belief spaces of the agent,

$\mathcal{T}$ is the set of intentional states,

$\mathcal{A}$ is a set of actions,

$\mathcal{P}$ is a set of predicates,

Init is an initial state designated by $\langle \sigma(0), \delta(0), \tau(0) \rangle$

Using the above definitions we can now specify the following axioms that govern the agent's behavior:

Axiom 1: An act is scheduled to be performed if and only if it is intended.

$$Done(SCHEDULE(a, \tau(i)), \delta(i)) \Leftrightarrow Intend(a, \delta(i))$$

This axiom models the concept of the agent forming an intention. From the definition of $SCHEDULE$ it follows that the act always gets scheduled on the front of the queue i.e.

$$Intend(a, \delta(i)) \Rightarrow FRONT(\tau(i+1)) = a$$

Notice the use of $SCHEDULE$ as an action term and $FRONT$ as a function term.

Axiom 2: A primitive act is removed from the agent's intentions if and only if it is performed.

$$Done(a, \delta(i)) \wedge Primitive(a) \Leftrightarrow Done(REMOVE(\tau(i)), \delta(i))$$

This axiom states that the agent remains committed to an intention to perform an act until it is performed. The only way to drop a commitment to an intented act is to perform it. Axiom 7 below states what it means to remove a non-primitive act from the agent's intentions.

Axiom 3: An act is performed in the current belief-space if and only if it was intended in an earlier belief-space, it is the next act to be performed, and its preconditions are satisfied in the current belief-space.

$$Done(a, \delta(i)) \Leftrightarrow \begin{aligned} &Intend(a, \delta(j)) \wedge (j < i) \\ &\wedge FRONT(\tau(i)) = a \\ &\wedge \forall p[Precondition(p, a, \delta(i)) \Rightarrow Believe(p, \delta(i))] \end{aligned}$$

This axiom guarantees that if an agent performed an act in a state, all the act's preconditions were believed to be true. The following axiom specifies what happens if some preconditions are not believed to be true.

Axiom 4: If an earlier intented act is about to be done and its preconditions are not satisfied in the current belief space, intend to do the act of achieving the preconditions.

$$Intend(a, \delta(j))$$
$$\wedge FRONT(\tau(i)) = a \wedge (j < i)$$
$$\wedge \exists p[Precondition(p, a, \delta(i)) \wedge \neg Believe(p, \delta(i))$$
$$\Rightarrow \forall p_i[Precondition(p_i, a, \delta(i)) \Rightarrow Intend(ACHIEVE(p_i), \delta(i))]]$$

where $ACHIEVE$ is a primitive action defined later. Note that the agent performs the intention of $ACHIEVE$-ing *all* the preconditions of the act even though some of them may be already believed to be true. This is because it is possible that some of the act's preconditions may be undone in the process of achieving some other ones. Note that the act is not performed, and since intentions are treated on a first-in-first-out basis, the agent will try to achieve all the preconditions of the act before attempting to do it again. Axiom 3 guarantees that unless all preconditions are true the act will not be performed. Thus, we are modeling a skeptical agent.

Axiom 5: When an act is performed all its effects are intended to be believed.

$$Done(a, \delta(i)) \Rightarrow \forall e[Effect(e, a, \delta(i)) \Rightarrow Intend(BELIEVE(e), \delta(i))]$$

where $BELIEVE : P \rightarrow \Delta$ is an action that adds the proposition e to the current belief space (i.e. $Done(BELIEVE(p), \delta(i)) \Rightarrow Believe(p, \delta(i+1)))$. Note that the effects intended to be believed are derived in the current belief space.

Theorem: All effects of an act are believed in a belief-space resulting after an act is performed in the current belief-space.

$$\forall e[Effect(e, a, \delta(i)) \wedge Done(a, \delta(i)) \Rightarrow Believe(e, \delta(i+k)) \wedge (k > 0)]$$

Proof: follows from above.

Axiom 6: The effectory component of an act is executed if and only if the act is performed and it is primitive.

$$Done(EXECUTE(a, \sigma(i)), \delta(i)) \Leftrightarrow Done(a, \delta(i)) \wedge Primitive(a)$$

Axiom 7: A non-primitive act is removed from the agent's intentions by intending to carry out a plan that decomposes that act.

$$FRONT(\tau(i)) = a_2 \wedge \neg Primitive(a_2) \wedge Done(REMOVE(\tau(i)), \delta(i))$$
$$\wedge \exists a_1[Plan(a_1, a_2, \delta(i)) \Rightarrow Intend(a_1, \delta(i+1))]$$

This axiom does not specify what happens when a plan does not exist for a complex act. In a situation where more than one plan may exist for a complex act the agent non-deterministically chooses one act.

4 The SNePS acting system

Using the above specification, we have implemented a model of an agent in SNePS (See [20, 7, 8] for more details). The architecture of the SNePS acting system is shown in Figure 1. As specified, the SNePS actor operates in a single-agent world

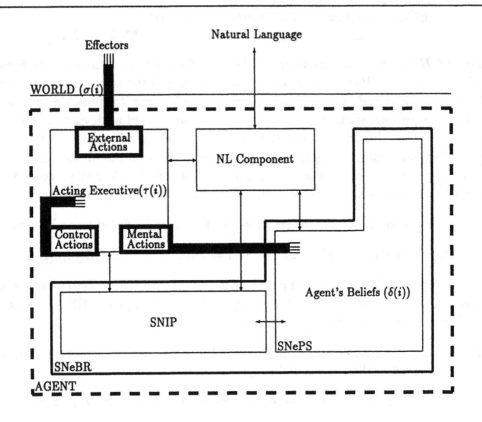

Figure 1: Architecture of The SNePS acting system

(it being the only agent). Beliefs of the agent are stored as SNePS propositions in the agent's belief space. The belief space is a SNeBR context (see [11]). SNeBR—the SNePS system for Belief Revision, an assumption-based truth maintenance system [10, 9, 11], ensures that the agent's belief space is always consistent. All interaction with the agent is done using the natural language component. Sentences are parsed by an ATN grammar and translated into SNePSUL(—the SNePS User Language) commands forming beliefs in the agent's belief space. World model rules for reasoning in the agent's belief space are also translated and represented as agent's beliefs.

4.1 Representations of plans, acts, and beliefs

We treat acts/plans as mental objects [18, 6]. This enables the agent to discuss, formulate, use, recognize, and reason about acts/plans. This is a significant advance over operator-based descriptions of plans. Operator-based formulations of actions tend to alienate the discussion of operators themselves since operators are usually specified in a different language from that used for representing beliefs about states. Moreover, plans (or procedural networks) constructed from these operators can only be accessed by specialized programs (critics, executors) and, like operators, are represented in still another formalism. Our representations for acts, goals, and plans build upon and add to the intensional propositional representations of SNePS. This framework enables us to tackle various tasks mentioned above in a uniform and coherent fashion. We now present SNePS representations for predicates and actions discussed earlier.

As mentioned above, a belief space ($\delta(i)$) in SNePS is a SNeBR context. In our current implementation we do not maintain the complete set Σ. At any time, only one belief space is available—the current one. When a mental act is performed, the current belief space is updated (using mental actions which are implemented as SNeBR operations to ensure consistency) appropriately.

Beliefs held by the agent are represented as SNePS propositions in the current belief space. The truth value of $Believe(p, \delta(i))$ is determined by performing a SNePS operation *deduce* which is an invocation of backward chaining using the SNePS inference engine (SNIP). The following describes the syntax of SNePS representations of other predicates defined in section 2 (Entities enclosed in {} are nodes. Entities in () are arcs emanating from the enclosing node and specify arc labels (written in teletype) and nodes at the end of the arcs [16]):

An act is represented as a molecular node[16] of the form

$$\{\langle \texttt{action}, \{action\}\rangle, \langle \texttt{object}, \{object\}\rangle\}$$

For actions having more than one object, we use the arc labels `object1`, `object2`, etc.

Precondition$(p, a, \delta(i))$ is represented as a molecular precondition-proposition node

$$\{\langle \texttt{precondition}, \{p\}\rangle, \langle \texttt{act}, \{a\}\rangle\}$$

Effect$(p, a, \delta(i))$ is represented as a molecular effect-proposition node

$$\{\langle \texttt{effect}, \{p\}\rangle, \langle \texttt{act}, \{a\}\rangle\}$$

$Plan(a_1, a_2, \delta(i))$ is represented as a molecular plan-act-proposition node

$$\{\langle \text{plan}, \{a_1\}\rangle, \langle \text{act}, \{a_2\}\rangle\}$$

$Primitive(a)$ is represented as a molecular proposition node

$$\{\langle \text{member}, \{a\}\rangle, \langle \text{class}, \{\text{primitive}\}\rangle\}$$

4.2 Intentions

Intentions are modeled using a module called the acting executive (see Figure 1). The acting executive maintains a queue $(\tau(i))$, and like Σ only the agent's current intentions are represented. The predicates $Empty(\tau(i))$ and the actions $FRONT$, $REMOVE$, and $SCHEDULE$ are procedurally modeled by the acting executive. Thus, like $EXECUTE$ (which is also modeled by the executive), these are also meta-actions. The acting executive is the following loop:

1. while act-queue is not empty do
2.   if   the first-act on the act-queue has preconditions
3.   and they are not currently satisfied
4.   then insert the achieving of them on the front of the act-queue
5.   else remove the first-act from the act-queue;
6.   deduce effects of first-act,
7.   and insert the believing of them on the front
8.   of the act-queue;
9.   if   first-act is primitive
10.   then perform it
11.   else deduce plans for carrying out first-act
12.   (using SNIP and available rules),
13.   choose one of them,
14.   and insert it on the front of the act-queue
15.   end if
16.   end if
17. end while

Referring back to the axioms in Section 3, the only place an act is performed by the executive is on line 10 which is in the else clause of the outer if (lines 5–16). This is where Axiom 2 is implemented. Axiom 3 is encoded in the same segment of the executive. Axiom 4 is implemented in lines 2–4; lines 6–8 implement Axiom 5; Axiom 6 is coded in lines 9–10; and lines 11–14 implement Axiom 7. Notice that the effects of the act about to be performed are retrieved and scheduled to be believed before the act is actually performed. This guarantees that proper effects of the act are retrieved depending on the context that exists at that time. This flexibility in dynamically determining the effects of acts is what enables us to avoid having multiple operators for the same action.

When preconditions for an act exist and some of them are found not to be true, we schedule the achieving of all of them on the queue. The intention to perform the act is now pushed behind the intention to achieve these preconditions. Once all the preconditions are achieved, and we are ready to perform the act, they are checked again (just in case achieving some precondition renders another one false). Later on, we intend to incorporate critics, that will enable detecting of such conflicts and more sophisticated reasoning about plans.

From the above loop, it can be seen that at this stage of our work, we are assuming that a plan will be found for every complex act, and that every act will be successful. These assumptions will be removed as we proceed. SNACTor can also be made to do classical planning in case it is not able to find a plan to achieve a goal. This is done in the spirit of STRIPS[4] by reasoning about effects of actions.

4.3   Control actions

We are now ready to examine the syntax and semantics of our current set of control actions. Recall that control actions, when performed, cause changes in the agent's intentional states.

Sequencing is represented using the structured act node

$$\{\langle \text{action}, \{SNSEQUENCE\}\rangle, \langle \text{object1}, \{a_1\}\rangle, \langle \text{object2}, \{a_2\}\rangle\}$$

(or $SNSEQUENCE(a_1, a_2)$) and is defined as

$$Done(SNSEQUENCE(a_1, a_2), \delta(i))$$
$$\Rightarrow FRONT(\tau(i+1)) = a_1 \wedge FRONT(REMOVE(\tau(i+1))) = a_2$$

i.e. a_2 is inserted on the front of the act queue, and then a_1 is inserted in front of it. Since both a_1 and a_2 can themselves be sequencing acts, we have a general structure for plans of sequential actions.

Choosing one act among a set of possible acts (as in the case where several plans are candidates for accomplishing a complex act) is called a *DoONE* represented as

$$\{\langle \text{action}, \{DoONE\}\rangle, \langle \text{object1}, \{(a_1, ..., a_n)\}\rangle\}$$

(or $DoONE(a_1, ..., a_n)$) and is defined as

$$Done(DoONE(a_1, ..., a_n), \delta(i)) \Rightarrow \exists k[(1 \le k \le N) \wedge Intend(a_k, \delta(i))]$$

i.e. it chooses one act and puts it on the front of the act queue. As currently implemented, the choice is arbitrary. However, we intend to implement a *DoONE* that will reason about the acts and pick the "best" one.

DoALL is similarly an act that makes the agent form the intention of doing all of its object acts in some unspecified order. It is represented as

$$\{\langle \texttt{action}, \{DoALL\}\rangle, \langle \texttt{object1}, \{(a_1, ..., a_n)\}\rangle\}$$

(or $DoALL(a_1, ..., a_n)$) and defined as

$$Done(DoALL(a_1, ..., a_n), \delta(i)) \Rightarrow \forall k[(1 \leq k \leq N) \wedge Intend(a_k, \delta(i))]$$

Conditional acts are represented using $SNIF((p_1, a_1), .., (p_n, a_n))$ i.e.

$$\begin{aligned}
&\{\langle \texttt{action}, \{SNIF\}\rangle, \langle \texttt{object1}, \\
&\{\langle \texttt{condition}, \{p_1\}\rangle, \langle \texttt{then}, \{a_1\}\rangle\}, ..., \\
&\{\langle \texttt{condition}, \{p_n\}\rangle, \langle \texttt{then}, \{a_n\}\rangle\}\rangle\}
\end{aligned}$$

defined as

$$\begin{aligned}
&Done(SNIF((p_1, a_1), ..., (p_n, a_n)), \delta(i)) \\
&\Rightarrow \forall k[Believe(p_k, \delta(i)) \Rightarrow Intend(a_k, \delta(i))]
\end{aligned}$$

Actually, a $DoALL$ of all the acts whose conditions are true is scheduled. This is based on Dijkstra's guarded-if [1].

Iteration, denoted as $SNITERATE((p1, a1), ..., (pN, aN))$ represented as

$$\begin{aligned}
&\{\langle \texttt{action}, \{SNITERATE\}\rangle, \langle \texttt{object1}, \\
&\{\langle \texttt{condition}, \{p_1\}\rangle, \langle \texttt{then}, \{a_1\}\rangle\}, ... \\
&\{\langle \texttt{condition}, \{p_n\}\rangle, \langle \texttt{then}, \{a_n\}\rangle\}\rangle\}
\end{aligned}$$

is defined, like Dijkstra's guarded-loops [1], as

$$\begin{aligned}
&Done(SNITERATE((p_1, a_1), ..., (p_n, a_n)), \delta(i)) \\
&\Rightarrow \exists k[(1 \leq k \leq n) \wedge Believe(p_k, \delta(i)) \wedge Intend(a_k, \delta(i))] \\
&\vee \forall k[(1 \leq k \leq n) \wedge \neg Believe(p_k, \delta(i))]
\end{aligned}$$

Actually, a $DoONE$ of all the acts whose p_i's are true is scheduled. Other control acts may be defined in the future, in particular a parameterized act that uses a sensory act to identify some object, and then performs some action on the identified object.

5 An example

A natural language understanding component has been implemented using a Generalized ATN grammar [14] and is used for analyzing sentences and for generating English responses. The agent begins with an empty knowledge-base. In the role of an informant, we interact with the agent using English sentences about the domain, instructing it about the various actions that it can do, and how to solve problems in that domain. A natural language generation grammar takes the new beliefs and expresses them back in English to show the agent's understanding to the informant. Requests to do some action are sent to an acting executive that may then generate and execute a plan to fulfill the request. The informant may also ask questions about plans and the way the system would solve various problems. The agent is capable of discussing its beliefs. For example, consider the queries

Is A on B?
```
Yes, A is on B.
```

Is A on C?
```
I really don't know if A is on C.
```

The answer to the second query above is inconclusive because there is no way for the agent to confirm or deny the queried fact. To be able to do so, we can instruct it about domain-specific rules in English. For example, to answer the above query conclusively it needs the following rule:

If a block is on a support then the block is not on another support.
```
I understand that if a block is on a support
then the block is not on another support.
```

Is A on C?
```
No, A is not on C.
```

Similarly, we can ask the agent to answer questions involving plans. SNIP, the inference procedure, is used to derive an appropriate plan and respond to the query. For example,

How would you pile A on C on B?
```
I understand that a plan for performing pile on A and C and B is
by performing put on B and a table and then performing put on C
and B and then performing put on A and C.
```

Notice that in this case a plan is derived but not executed. So far we have demonstrated that the agent is able to interact with the user about its beliefs, and it can use the domain rules to answer queries about the domain. The agent can also understand natural language domain descriptions of domain-specific rules and plans and acts as contained in the following paragraphs

> *There is a table. The table is a support. Blocks are supports. Picking up is a primitive action. Before picking up a block the block must be*

clear. After picking up a block the block is not clear and the block is held. If a block is on a support then after picking up the block the block is not on the support and the support is clear. Putting is a primitive action. Before putting a block on a support the block must be held and the support must be clear. After putting a block on a support the block is not held and the block is clear and the block is on the support. After putting a block on another block the latter block is not clear.

A plan to achieve that a block is held is to pick up the block. A plan to achieve that a block is on a support is to put the block on the support. If a block is on a support then a plan to achieve that the support is clear is to pick up the block and then put the block on the table. A plan to pile a block on another block on a third block is to put the third block on the table and then put the second block on the third block and then put the first block on the second block.

Given the above description of a domain, and a situation

A is a block. B is a block. C is a block. C is on A. C is clear. B is clear and on the table:

the agent can use the domain description from above to plan and act in the situation. Thus it will be able to derive plans and perform actions required to fulfill requests such as

Pile A on B on C.

6 Concluding remarks

In this paper, we have described a model, the design, and aspects of implementation of an intensional representation for plans. These representations have been constrained by issues in cognitive modeling, belief representation, reasoning, and natural language understanding. Although the model presented is a simplified one, it serves as a starting point for creating a more sophisticated rational agent. We have been relaxing various assumptions to enhance the model. Though this work is still in progress we are discovering that SNePS and its underlying theories contribute effectively toward our goals[8]. We have designed and implemented intensional propositional representations for plans. This is a major advancement over operator-based descriptions of plans. Operator-based formulations of actions tend to alienate the discussion of operators themselves. Operators are usually specified in a different language than that used for representing beliefs about states. Moreover, plans (or procedural networks) constructed from these operators can only be accessed by specialized programs (critics, executors) and, like operators, are represented in still another formalism. Our representations for acts, actions, goals, and plans build upon and add to the intensional propositional representations of SNePS. This framework enables us to tackle various tasks mentioned above in a uniform and coherent fashion.

Our current system is being advanced in several directions. In the context of planning, there are issues associated with conjunctive goals[22], non-linear plans [12, 21, 2], and dealing with the effects of actions. As mentioned in [3] explicitly specifying the disbelieving of propositions as a result of performing some action is not natural. We propose to use belief revision (SNeBR) to detect inconsistencies after asserting the effects of an action. We have started to address the issue of modeling sensory acts and reactivity in such a framework. Some of the directions already in consideration are discussed in [5, 7].

Acknowledgements

Syed Ali designed and implemented the natural language component. We would like to thank Richard Wyatt and Hans Chalupsky for discussion and feedback on this project. Special thanks also to Fernando Perreira for providing valuable feedback on an earlier version of this paper while he was visiting Buffalo.

References

[1] Edsger W. Dijkstra. *A Discipline of Programming*. Prentice-Hall, Englewood Cliffs, NJ, 1976.

[2] Mark Drummond and Austin Tate. Ai planning: A tutorial and review. Technical Report AIAI-TR-30, Artificial Intelligence Applications Institute, University of Edinburgh, Edinburgh, November 1987.

[3] Mark E. Drummond. A representation of action and belief for automatic planning systems. In Michael P. Georgeff and Amy L. Lansky, editors, *Reasoning about Actions and Plans - Proceedings of the 1986 Workshop*, pages 189–212, Los Altos, CA, 1987. AAAI and CSLI, Morgan Kauffmann.

[4] Richard E. Fikes and Nils J. Nilsson. STRIPS: A new approach to the application of theorem proving to problem solving. *Artificial Intelligence*, 5:189–208, 1971.

[5] D. Kumar. An integrated model of acting and inference. In D. Kumar, editor, *Current Trends in SNePS–Semantic Network Processing System: Proceedings of the First Annual SNePS Workshop*, pages 55–65, Buffalo, NY, 1989. Springer-Verlag.

[6] D. Kumar, S. Ali, and S. C. Shapiro. Discussing, using and recognizing plans in SNePS preliminary report - SNACTor: An acting system. In *Proceedings of the Seventh Biennial Convention of South East Asia Regional Confederation*, pages 177–182, New Delhi, India, 1988. Tata McGraw-Hill.

[7] D. Kumar, S. S. Ali, J. Haas, and S. C. Shapiro. The SNePS acting system. In K. E. Bettinger and G. Srikantan, editors, *Proceedings of the Fifth Annual University at Buffalo Graduate Conference on Computer Science*, pages 91–100, 1990.

[8] Deepak Kumar and Stuart C. Shapiro. Architecture of an intelligent agent in sneps. In John Laird, editor, *SIGART Bulletin*. ACM Press, New York, NY, 1991.

[9] J. P. Martins and S. C. Shapiro. Belief revision in SNePS. In *Proceedings of the Sixth Canadian Conference on Artificial Intelligence*, pages 230–234. Presses de l'Université du Québec, 1986.

[10] J. P. Martins and S. C. Shapiro. Theoretical foundations for belief revision. In J. Y. Halpern, editor, *Theoretical Aspects of Reasoning About Knowledge*, pages 383–398. Morgan Kaufmann Publishers, Los Altos, CA, 1986.

[11] J. P. Martins and S. C. Shapiro. A model for belief revision. *Artificial Intelligence*, 35(1):25–79, 1988.

[12] Earl D. Sacerdoti. *A Structure for Plans and Behavior*. Elsevier North Holland, New York, NY, 1977.

[13] S. C. Shapiro. The SNePS semantic network processing system. In N. V. Findler, editor, *Associative Networks: The Representation and Use of Knowledge by Computers*, pages 179–203. Academic Press, New York, 1979.

[14] S. C. Shapiro. Generalized augmented transition network grammars for generation from semantic networks. *The American Journal of Computational Linguistics*, 8(1):12–25, 1982.

[15] S. C. Shapiro. The CASSIE projects: An approach to natural language competence. In *Proceedings of the 4th Portugese Conference on Artificial Intelligence*, pages 362–380, Lisbon, Portugal, 1989. Springer-Verlag.

[16] S. C. Shapiro. Cables, paths and "subconsious" reasoning in propositional semantic networks. In J. Sowa, editor, *Principles of Semantic Networks*, page 21. Morgan Kaufmann, San Mateo, CA, 1990. To appear.

[17] S. C. Shapiro and The SNePS Implementation Group. *SNePS-2 User's Manual*. Department of Computer Science, SUNY at Buffalo, 1989.

[18] S. C. Shapiro, D. Kumar, and S. Ali. A propositional network approach to plans and plan recognition. In *Proceedings of the 1988 Workshop on Plan Recognition*, page 21, Los Altos, CA, 1989. Morgan Kaufmann.

[19] S. C. Shapiro and W. J. Rapaport. SNePS considered as a fully intensional propositional semantic network. In N. Cercone and G. McCalla, editors, *The Knowledge Frontier*, pages 263–315. Springer-Verlag, New York, 1987.

[20] Stuart C. Shapiro, Beverly Woolf, Deepak Kumar, Syed S. Ali, Penelope Sibun, David Forster, Scott Anderson, James Pustejovesky, and Juergen Haas. Discussing, using, and recognizing plans–Project Report. Technical Report RADC-TR-90-404, Volume II (of 18), North-East Artificial Intelligence Consortium, Griffiss Air Force Base, NY, 1990.

[21] A. Tate. Generating project networks. In *Proceedings 5th IJCAI*, pages 888–93, 1977.

[22] R. Waldinger. *Achieving Several Goals Simultaneously*, pages 94–136. Ellis Horwood, Chichester, England, 1977.

Semantics of Property Inheritance
in a Hierarchic System with Explicit Negation[1]

Gabriel David[2]   António Porto
Departamento de Informática
Universidade Nova de Lisboa
P-2825 Monte da Caparica
Portugal
e-mail: {gtd,ap}@fct.unl.pt

Abstract

The purpose of this paper is to present a first step in a formal study of inheritance systems.

The kind of systems considered are those that support overriding (all definitions being taken as defaults) and multiple inheritance. The overriding is based on the explicit statement of negative information.

The basic entities are classes and properties. The system is hierarchic because it is made out of classes which are structured as a hierarchy. We consider both the basic case of properties restricted to atomic propositional formulas and their negations, and the extension to properties defined by rules in the Logic Programming style.

A formal definition of hierarchic systems is given for which a model-theoretic 3-valued semantics is introduced. This semantics is explicitly stated in terms of sets of individuals. It defines the notion of interpretation, the characterization of models, and what is meant by validity of formulas in such structures.

The inheritance mechanism is able to choose from a set of inherited default properties which ones must be overriden in order to guarantee that the local program has a model.

The notion of characteristic individuals of classes, introduced in our semantics, turns out to play a clarifying role of the relationship between semantic and syntactic aspects of inheritance systems.

1   Introduction

A common practice in scientific activity is the search for classifications established by recognizing common properties among individuals of a chosen domain. This induces the definition of taxonomies structured as hierarchies of classes with associated properties, from which information can be retrieved with the help of a more or less formalized kind of inheritance reasoning.

The purpose of this work is to present a first step in a formal study of such inheritance systems. Our study covers systems with overriding and multiple inheritance. The properties are defined by sets of clauses and the inheritance mechanism is based on computing

---

[1] Work done under partial support of Esprit BRA 3020 "Integration" and Portuguese JNICT project PEROLA
[2] Owns a scholarship from INIC.

the consequences of these sets in the class and then using them as defaults for the sub-classes. The overriding is done through explicit negation. Multiple inheritance is obtained by the consistent union of the sets of properties coming from the relevant superclasses. Clashes of inherited properties (p and $\neg p$) are solved by assuming a neutral position: p becomes undefined.

This led us to adopt a 3-valued approach which we find a more natural way of formalizing incomplete knowledge about the world. The semantics obtained can deal with potential contradiction and overriding in a simple way which does not rely on modifications of the program. In a previous work [DP91] we developed a 2-valued semantics based on a notion of completion. The main problems that arose were:

- the lack of symmetry induced by the preference for negative properties in the multiple inheritance case and

- a discrepancy between the conclusions derived from a distinguished standard model and those valid in the system, caused by the confusion between negative information and absence of information.

The paper starts with the simpler case of *atomic hierarchic systems* (AHS) where properties are restricted to atomic propositional formulas and their negations. The notions of interpretation and model are formalized supporting the definition of validity of formulas.

Then we extend the formalism to the case of general *hierarchic systems* (HS) where properties are defined by clauses with universally quantified variables.

2　Atomic hierarchic systems

This section is devoted to the simple case where properties are unstructured and independent of each other, except through negation.

To any given set $\mathcal{P}$ of property names we associate the set of *properties* $\mathcal{B}(\mathcal{P}) = \mathcal{P} \cup \{\neg p \mid p \in \mathcal{P}\}$ consisting simply of the property names and their negations.

Definition 1 *We define an atomic hierarchic system (AHS, for short) as being a 4-tuple* $\langle \mathcal{C}, \mathcal{P}, \prec, ld \rangle$ *where*

- $\mathcal{C}$ *is the set of* class names;

- $\mathcal{P}$ *is the set of* property names;

- $\prec$ *is the* hierarchic relation, *which must be an intransitive acyclic relation on* $\mathcal{C}$;

- ld *is a total function* $\mathcal{C} \longrightarrow \wp(\mathcal{B}(\mathcal{P}))$ *mapping each class name to a set of properties called its* local definition; *images of ld must be consistent:* $p \in ld(c) \Rightarrow \neg p \notin ld(c)$.

2.1 Pre-interpretation

A *pre-interpretation* I of an AHS is defined over a domain of individuals $\mathcal{D}_I$. We must provide interpretation functions for class names and for property names:

$$\kappa_I \;:\; \mathcal{C} \longrightarrow \wp(\mathcal{D}_I)$$
$$\pi_I \;:\; \mathcal{B}(\mathcal{P}) \longrightarrow \wp(\mathcal{D}_I)$$
$$\tau_I \;:\; \mathcal{C} \longrightarrow \wp(\mathcal{D}_I)$$

We define a *class* to be the set of individuals a class name is mapped to by the function κ_I. A property is mapped, by the function π_I, to a set of individuals, too. This coincidence reflects the duality between extension (class) and intension (its defining properties) of a set.

In the sequel the *characteristic subset* of a class will be related to the class itself. However, we want to bring to the semantic level the intuitive notion of an individual that is typical of a certain class, in the sense that all the characteristic properties of the class hold for the individual. This is the reason why we provide a second interpretation function (τ_I) for class names.

The denotations of class names and property names are defined directly from the interpretation functions:

$$
\begin{aligned}
c \in \mathcal{C} &\;\Rightarrow\; [\![c]\!]_I = \kappa_I(c); \\
p \in \mathcal{B}(\mathcal{P}) &\;\Rightarrow\; [\![p]\!]_I = \pi_I(p); \\
c \in \mathcal{C} &\;\Rightarrow\; \ll\!c\!\gg_I = \tau_I(c).
\end{aligned}
\tag{1}
$$

A set of properties is a generalized property. Its denotation is the intersection of the denotations of all the properties in it:

$$[\![\{p_1,\ldots,p_n\}]\!]_I = \bigcap_{i=1,\ldots,n} [\![p_i]\!]_I$$

Definition 2 *Auxiliary operators. The* complement *operation, $\tilde{x}$ or equivalently $\sim x$, is defined for properties and for generalized properties*

$$
\begin{aligned}
p \in \mathcal{P} &\;\Rightarrow\; \tilde{p} = \neg p \\
p = \neg q &\;\Rightarrow\; \tilde{p} = q \\
g \in \wp(\mathcal{B}(\mathcal{P})) &\;\Rightarrow\; \tilde{g} = \{\tilde{p} \mid p \in g\}.
\end{aligned}
$$

The consistent *operation is defined over sets of properties from which it filters out complementary pairs.*

$$consistent(g) = \{p \in g \mid \tilde{p} \notin g\}.$$

2.2 Inheritance mechanism

An AHS includes a function called *local definition* which directly associates a consistent set of properties $ld(c)$ (also written $|c|$) to each class c.

Definition 3 *Characteristic definition of a class c:*

$$<c> = |c| \cup consistent(\bigcup_{c \prec a} (<a> - \sim |c|))$$

The *characteristic definition* of a class c is the set of properties which are defined locally in c or which are (recursively) inherited from its superclasses. The inheritance mechanism allows for exceptions because local definitions that contradict inherited definitions override these ones. Notice that this construction involves a purely syntactical manipulation of objects in the AHS.

The *consistent* operation is needed here to exclude complementary pairs from inherited properties of a class. These could arise in a situation of multiple inheritance from incompatible classes. In such a situation the system should not commit itself to any of the possibilities [Tou86].

2.3 Models

Pre-interpretations are completely arbitrary.

Definition 4 *A pre-interpretation I is an* interpretation *of an AHS iff it respects two basic restrictions:*

$$c \in \mathcal{C} \;\Rightarrow\; \tau_I(c) \subseteq \kappa_I(c)$$
$$p \in \mathcal{P} \;\Rightarrow\; (\pi_I(p) \cap \pi_I(\neg p)) = \emptyset.$$

Typical individuals of a class must belong to it ($\ll c \gg_I \subseteq [\![c]\!]_I$); and an individual must not verify a property and its negation, because such an interpretation would be contradictory. These restrictions are so strong that we rule out all the pre-interpretations not respecting them.

Individuals either belong or do not belong to a class, but the treatment of properties is 3-valued. A property p may hold for an individual i ($i \in \pi_I(p)$), it may not hold ($i \in \pi_I(\neg p)$), or it may be undefined. Our basic intuition is to deal with p and $\neg p$ in a totally symmetric way, as if they were different properties, although strongly connected by a sort of built-in integrity constraint forcing them to be disjoint.

Definition 5 *An interpretation I is a* model *of an AHS S ($I \in mod(S)$) iff, for any two class names c and b,*

$$
\begin{aligned}
&1. \quad c \prec b \;\Rightarrow\; [\![c]\!]_I \;\subseteq\; [\![b]\!]_I \\
&2. \quad [\![c]\!]_I - \bigcup_{b \prec c} [\![b]\!]_I \;\subseteq\; \ll c \gg_I \\
&3. \qquad\qquad \ll c \gg_I \;\subseteq\; [\![<c>]\!]_I.
\end{aligned}
\tag{2}
$$

The first condition forces a model to correspond to the intuitive notion of taxonomy.

The second states that individuals in class c which do not belong to any of its subclasses must be characteristic individuals of c. The reverse does not hold. There may be characteristic individuals of c that also belong to a subclass of c.

The third condition assures that the characteristic subset of a class really collects characteristic individuals of that class, i.e. individuals that belong to the class and for whom all the properties in its characteristic definition hold. In other words, $\ll c \gg$ must be contained in the set of individuals in class c which are not exceptions to any of its characteristic properties.

Knowledge is only expressed through classes; the only way to distinguish between two individuals is by including them in different classes.

We can identify three dimensions of variability on models. First they depend on the domain and the interpretation function (κ) for class names. We call a given κ for a given domain a *configuration*. Given a configuration several possibilities for the extensions of both the characteristic subsets and the properties are allowed.

The three conditions for interpretations to be models can be viewed in a constructive way. Condition 1. validates a configuration. Condition 2. imposes a minimum on the characteristic subsets. Condition 3. builds the minimum extensions of the properties based on those subsets.

This construction suggests that among the models of a system we may distinguish a *standard model*, using some minimality criteria. Notice that the empty interpretation, where $\forall c, p\ \kappa_I(c) = \pi_I(p) = \emptyset$, is always a (trivial) model of any AHS. We want standard models to have non-empty classes.

Definition 6 *Standard models M_S are subject to three constraints:*

1. *$\forall c \in C$ $\#([c]_{M_S} - \bigcup_{b \prec c}[b]_{M_S}) = 1$ (# is the cardinality function)*

2. *extensions of characteristic subsets are minimal*

3. *extensions of properties (positive or negative) are minimal.*

This definition of standard models seems reasonable because any class must contain at least one individual in order to be relevant and distinct class names must have distinct denotations. The first constraint imposes a configuration. The second is equivalent, for the given configuration, to restrict condition 2. on models to the equality case. So we get classes with exactly one characteristic individual. The third constraint forbids any property not in the characteristic definition of a class to hold for the corresponding characteristic individual.

Proposition 1 *Standard models are unique if we abstract from the actual individuals.*

2.4 Validity

In this section we first characterize the denotation of formulas with respect to interpretations and then we define validity. Formulas are expressions of the form $c\!:\!g$ where c is a class name and g is a generalized property. They denote boolean values t, u, f standing respectively for *true*, *undefined*, and *false*. u is meant to cater both for situations where a given property is not defined and situations where a conflicting pair exists.

Definition 7 *The value of a formula* $c\!:\!g$ *in an interpretation* I *is*

$$[c\!:\!g]_I = \begin{cases} \mathbf{t} & \ll c\gg_I \subseteq [g]_I \\ \mathbf{f} & \exists p \in g \ \ll c\gg_I \subseteq [\bar{p}]_I \\ \mathbf{u} & otherwise \end{cases} \tag{3}$$

A formula f *is valid in a AHS* S *iff the value of* f *is* $\mathbf{t}$ *in every model of* S.

$$S \models f \ \Leftrightarrow \ \forall I \in mod(S)\ [f]_I = \mathbf{t} \tag{4}$$

This definition coincides with what is intuitively expected from the common notion of inheritance as expressed in the next proposition. It stresses the importance of the characteristic definition by establishing a relationship between this syntactic entity and the validity of certain formulas.

Proposition 2 *A formula* $c\!:\!p$ *is valid in an AHS iff the property* p *belongs to the characteristic definition of the class* c,

$$S \models c\!:\!p \ \Leftrightarrow \ p \in <c>$$

Validity is expensive to test from the definition due to quantification over all models. It would be better if we could devise an easier way to find out which properties hold for each class. This is the main goal behind the construction of the standard model M_S.

Proposition 3 *A formula is valid in an AHS iff it is true in its standard model*

$$S \models f \ \Leftrightarrow \ [f]_{M_S} = \mathbf{t}.$$

Thus we have obtained a perfect match between the conclusions derived from the basic definition of validity and truths in the standard model.

So the proposed semantics for an AHS S is the set of formulas which are $\mathbf{t}$ in its unique standard model.

Definition 8 *Semantics of an AHS.*

$$sem(S) = \{f|\ S \models f\} = \{f|\ [f]_{M_S} = \mathbf{t}\}$$

With this semantics the set of properties holding for classes in the system is exactly what should be expected from the quantification over all models. Moreover, it can distinguish whether a certain property does not hold or whether it is just undefined. $sem(S)$ is a 2-valued partial semantics equivalent to a 3-valued semantics in the following way ($p \in \mathcal{P}$):

$$S \models_3 c\!:\!p = \begin{cases} \mathbf{t} & c\!:\!p \in sem(S) \\ \mathbf{f} & c\!:\!\neg p \in sem(S) \\ \mathbf{u} & c\!:\!p, c\!:\!\neg p \notin sem(S) \end{cases} \tag{5}$$

The situation $c{:}p, c{:}\neg p \in sem(S)$ is impossible because it would arise only in a contradictory system. The semantics does not commit to any unsupported conclusions and it is not blocked by the occurence of conflicts in a multiple inheritance situation. In the saturated case where

$$c \in \mathcal{C}, p \in \mathcal{P} \Rightarrow S \models c{:}p \text{ or } S \models c{:}\neg p,$$

$sem(S)$ is also a 2-valued total semantics.

If we want to preserve the standard model under some kind of completion operation which saturates the model it is necessary to minimize the extension of the characteristic subsets against the more intuitive choice of maximizing it. In general, a completion tends to reduce the number of individuals which qualify as characteristic of a superclass because it can add some new properties to the previous definitions raising incompatibilities with classes that used to be simple specializations.

Example 1 *Multiple inheritance in an AHS.*

The definition of the atomic hierarchic system S is

$$
\begin{aligned}
S \;=\; \langle\;\; & \{a, r, q, b, n\}, \\
& \{p, d\}, \\
& \{r{\prec}a, q{\prec}a, n{\prec}r, n{\prec}q, b{\prec}r\}, \\
& \{a \to \{d\}, b \to \{\neg d\}, r \to \{\neg p\}, q \to \{p\}, n \to \{\}\}\;\rangle
\end{aligned}
$$

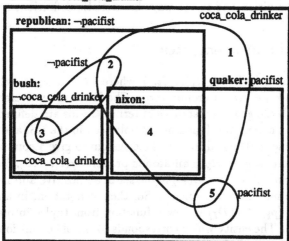

The characteristic definitions for the classes of S display the need for the *consistent* operator, in particular $<n>$:

$$<a> = \{d\},\; <r> = \{d, \neg p\},\; <q> = \{d, p\},\; <b> = \{\neg d, \neg p\},\; <n> = \{d\}.$$

The standard model, ranging over the standard domain $\mathcal{D}_{M_S} = \{1, 2, 3, 4, 5\}$, is:

$$\begin{array}{lll} \kappa(a) = \{1,2,3,4,5\} & \tau(a) = \{1\} & \pi(p) = \{5\} \\ \kappa(r) = \{2,3,4\} & \tau(r) = \{2\} & \pi(\neg p) = \{2,3\} \\ \kappa(q) = \{4,5\} & \tau(q) = \{5\} & \pi(d) = \{1,2,4,5\} \\ \kappa(b) = \{3\} & \tau(b) = \{3\} & \pi(\neg d) = \{3\} \\ \kappa(n) = \{4\} & \tau(n) = \{4\} & \end{array}$$

From here we can conclude

$$sem(S) = \{a\!:\!d, r\!:\!d, q\!:\!d, b\!:\!\neg d, n\!:\!d, r\!:\!\neg p, q\!:\!p, b\!:\!\neg p\}.$$

In $sem(S)$ we only listed the basic properties because generalized properties are easily obtained from these.

Property p creates an inconsistency in class n. So, in order to keep the possibility of a non-empty class, the complementary pair is dropped, leaving p undefined. $\triangle$

3   Adding rules

In this section we present a generalization of AHS's that encompasses the inclusion of conditional definitions for properties in classes. These properties may have arguments. We present the reviewed definition of a *hierarchical system* (HS) and we relate the new framework with the previous results. Then we go into further details of the construction of a class model.

The characterization of a HS differs from that of an AHS mainly in the notions of property and local definition and in the way charateristic definitions are built.

3.1   Properties and predicates

An atomic property is of the form $p(t_1, \ldots, t_m)$, where $p \in \mathcal{P}$ is a property name (equipped with the arity m) and $t_i \in \mathcal{H}$ is a ground term. The Herbrand universe $\mathcal{H}$ corresponding to the HS contains all the ground instances of terms. Terms are defined in the usual way out of the sets of all constant and function symbols used in the HS, and a set of variables. The Herbrand universe is attached to the whole system to give a common language to all the classes. Like before, a *property* is an atomic property $p(t_1, \ldots, t_m)$ or the negation of an atomic property $\neg p(t_1, \ldots, t_m)$. $\mathcal{B}(\mathcal{P})$ is the set of all positive and negative properties. But these properties may have arguments. So, their denotation, in an interpretation I, that used to be just $[\![p]\!]_I \in \wp(\mathcal{D}_I)$ is now a function from tuples into sets of individuals $[\![p]\!]_I : \mathcal{H}^m \longrightarrow \wp(\mathcal{D}_I)$. The entity which corresponds to the old definition is the application of a property name to a tuple $[\![p(a)]\!]_I \in \wp(\mathcal{D}_I)$.

As we have seen in the previous section the literals which are valid in the system are of the form $c\!:\!p$. In the rest of this section we will be concentrating on a single class at a time in order to find its class model. So we will sometimes drop the class name, when the abstraction is unambiguous, and use the designation 'literal' when talking about property p. In this intensional sense we can see a property as a predicate abstracted on one argument, the class. The connection is established through the characteristic subset $\ll c \gg$

and not through the taxonomic denotation $[\![c]\!]$, because we want to allow for exceptions in subclasses of c

$$M_S \models c\!:\!p \Leftrightarrow \ll\!c\!\gg \subseteq [\![p]\!].$$

This justifies our initial assignment of two denotations to a class symbol.

3.2 Local definition

The *local definition* is now a set of property definitions, instead of the properties themselves. A property definition is a conditional expression which, following the relationship between properties and predicates, we will often call clause. The set of all clauses is

$$\mathcal{E}(\mathcal{P}) = \{p \leftarrow g | p \in \mathcal{B}(\mathcal{P}), g \in \wp(\mathcal{B}(\mathcal{P}))\}.$$

A definition $p \leftarrow \emptyset$ is the same as asserting p. So $ld : \mathcal{C} \longrightarrow \wp(\mathcal{E}(\mathcal{P}))$ is a total function mapping each class name to a set of clauses called its local definition.

This characterization of ld is made in terms of (ground) properties. However, uninstantiated terms may be allowed instead of properties. Clauses containing such terms are considered universally quantified at the head and taken as a short hand for its full instantiation over the Herbrand universe.

A local definition must be consistent. Before explaining what is meant by consistency of a set of clauses we shall introduce an auxiliary function.

Definition 9 *Imediate consequence operator*

$$T_P(D) = \{p | p \leftarrow g \in P, g \subseteq D\}.$$

The heads of clauses are properties and so q and $\neg q$ may both be generated by T_P. Although they are closely related and interpreted as the negation of each other, we consider them as different properties, in the context of the application of the operator. This is akin to the renaming of negative literals as new atoms in [GL90]. The operator T_P is monotonic and so it has a least fixpoint [Llo87].

Definition 10 *Consequence operator*

$$T_P^*(D) = T_P \!\uparrow\! w(D).$$

This operator takes a set of literals D and produces all the consequences of the clauses in the program P. If we take for P the local definition of a class c then we see $|c|$ as an open definition, a function from sets of properties into sets of properties (literals)

$$T_P^* : \mathcal{B}(\mathcal{P}) \longrightarrow \mathcal{B}(\mathcal{P}).$$

Definition 11 *A set of clauses P is consistent iff $T_P^*(\emptyset) \cap \sim T_P^*(\emptyset) = \emptyset$ and $T_P^*(\emptyset)$ verifies all the clauses in P (see section 3.4).*

This means that a set of clauses may contain definitions for both p and $\neg p$ and remain consistent as long as p and $\neg p$ are not both generated by $T_P^*(\emptyset)$.

3.3 Inheritance mechanism

We want the characteristic definition of a class c ($<c>$) to be a set of properties as before, in the AHS. Intuitively, $<c>$ will collect all the ground literals which may be derived from the local definition combined with those which are inherited from the superclasses of c, in a way to be specified below. The resulting set of literals may be equated to a set of properties in the AHS formalism. So, the work done previously remains in force, including the conditions for an interpretation to be a model.

We are left with the problem of specifying an inheritance mechanism and then building $<c>$ from it and the local definition.

The *inheritance mechanism* is based on the following idea. All the (non-contradictory) properties which hold for the superclasses of a class c are collected in a consistent set Δ (potential contradictions in Δ may occur in the multiple inheritance case) and inherited by c unless they are overriden by a clashing property derived from $|c|$; subclasses of c inherit Δ updated with those properties which are implicitly defined locally in $|c|$. Inherited properties Δ are viewed as defaults some of which may be overriden if they clash with, or lead to clashes in, the set of consequences of $|c|$. So $<c>= h(|c|, \Delta')$ where $\Delta' \subseteq \Delta$ is such that $<c>$ is a class model of $|c|$. The specification of the inheritance function h has two degrees of freedom: the way consequences are derived from $|c|$ and the choice of Δ'.

Definition 12 *The set of inherited properties Δ^c of a class c is the consistent union of all its superclasses' characteristic definitions*

$$\Delta^c = consistent(\bigcup_{c \prec a} <a>).$$

A class inherits a set of properties and not a set of property definitions. Each local definition is compiled out with respect to the inherited properties before passing the updated set to its subclasses. This kind of inheritance is similar to *predicate inheritance* [MP91] as opposed to *clause inheritance*. The main difference to our approach lies in the way overriding is dealt with. In [MP91] two modes are introduced: extension and overriding, at the level of a complete predicate definition (set of clauses for the same predicate name). The two modes are needed because no explicit negation is allowed in the heads of clauses. Because we work with positive and negative literals, we are able to override only part of a predicate by stating just the contradictory property(ies). Thus we have a finer control over the inheritance process. Non contradictory properties *extend* the already existent ones for that predicate. To have a positive overriding effect either an intermediate dummy class is added to allow for the introduction of a double negative overriding or an inheritance mode may be added to the language.

3.4 Class model

We have already established that the connection between AHS's and their extensions to have rules in definitions, the HS's, is done through characteristic definitions and subsets. So we may concentrate on the, to a large extent, orthogonal problem of how to get $<c>$ out of c and its superclasses.

Definition 13 *A set of ground literals is a (partial or 3-valued) class pre-interpretation.*

Due to the presence of negative literals in clause heads, a class pre-interpretation I^c may be contradictory. A positive literal $p(a)$ in I^c means that $p(a)$ is true of c ($val(p(a)) = \mathbf{t}$); a negative literal $\neg p(a)$ means $p(a)$ is explicitly false ($\mathbf{f}$); if neither $p(a)$ nor $\neg p(a)$ belong to I_c then $p(a)$ is undefined ($\mathbf{u}$). This is the default case. Minimizing an interpretation in the set inclusion sense thus amounts to minimize explicit information, maximizing the set of undefined literals - this is the 3-valued counterpart of the maximization of falsehood in the 2-valued case.

The boolean values are ordered: $\mathbf{t} > \mathbf{u} > \mathbf{f}$. Negation is defined by: $\neg \mathbf{t} = \mathbf{f}, \neg \mathbf{f} = \mathbf{t}, \neg \mathbf{u} = \mathbf{u}$.

A set of literals is understood as their 3-valued conjunction

$$val(\{p_1, \ldots, p_n\}) = min(val(p_1), \ldots, val(p_n))$$

and a clause is verified if the head is greater than the body

$$val(p \leftarrow g) = val(p) \geq val(g).$$

The definition for $\leftarrow$ departs from other common formalizations of 3-valued logic like Kleene's or Bochvar's [Tur84], because $\mathbf{u} \leftarrow \mathbf{u}$ evaluates to $\mathbf{t}$ and not to $\mathbf{u}$, as it might be expected. The evaluation of a clause is always $\mathbf{t}$ or $\mathbf{f}$. As [Prz89] points out this is essential to LP in order to make it easier to find models and to keep the constructive side of rules in force.

Definition 14 *A class pre-interpretation I^c is a class model iff it verifies all the rules in $|c|$ and is non-contradictory.*

In a first attempt, $<c>$ could be chosen to be the least class model. There is always one since $|c|$ is required to be consistent. But this amounts to ignore inheritance, i.e. to set $\Delta' = \emptyset$ and the inheritance function to $h(|c|, \Delta') = LEAST(|c|)$. But, in general, we want to include in the model as much as possible of the inherited properties.

Definition 15 *A clash occurs in a pre-interpretation I when*

- *I contains a complementary pair (contradiction) or*

- *a rule $p \leftarrow g$ is not verified ($val(p) < val(g)$) (incompatibility).*

The notion of clash generalizes the notion of complementary pair. The second situation, called incompatibility, is a kind of *hidden* contradiction. The set of defaults which are involved in contradictions is called the *offending* defaults $\mathcal{O}$.

In order to get a deeper understanding of the clash removal process by simplification of defaults we introduce next a lattice of pre-interpretations L, associated to a class c which inherits the set of properties Δ. Each element I_X of L is a pre-interpretation with two components: $\Delta_X = \Delta - X$, where X is the set of arc labels from the top of L to I_X; and the image Γ_X of $T^*_{|c|}(\Delta_X)$. L is ordered by subset inclusion among defaults Δ_X. The arcs are labelled by the literal eliminated from Δ_X when going from I_X to an $I_{X'}$ which is immediately below.

As the operator T^* is monotonic, the top image $\Gamma_{\{\}}$ contains the images of all the other elements.

As $|c|$ is consistent, the bottom image Γ_Δ ($\Delta_X = \emptyset$) is the least model of $|c|$.

Intuitively, the inheritance function should give the greatest model, if there is one, or a composition of the alternative maximal models which can be found in the lattice.

Example 2 *Simple overriding.*

$$
\begin{aligned}
\Delta^c &= \{p, r\} &&\text{(inherited properties)} \\
|c| &= \{\neg r \leftarrow p\} &&\text{(local definition)} \\
<c> &= ? &&\text{(properties which hold in } c)
\end{aligned}
$$

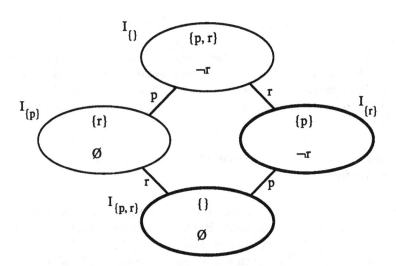

Setting the inheritance function $h(|c|, \Delta') = T^*_{|c|}(\Delta') \cup \Delta'$ there are in principle four possibilities to compute $<c>$, according to the combinations of defaults from Δ^c which remain in Δ'.

The bottom of the lattice is always a model

$$I_{\Delta^c} = h(|c|, \emptyset) = T^*_{|c|}(\emptyset) = LEAST(|c|).$$

$I_{\{\}}$ contains a contradictory pair $(r, \neg r)$, so clearly it is not a model.

Neither the pre-interpretation $I_{\{r\}}$ nor $I_{\{p\}}$ contain a contradictory pair, so it looks like both are models. However, a closer look leads to the conclusion that only $I_{\{r\}}$ is a model. The problem with $I_{\{p\}}$ is that $\Delta^c \setminus \{p\}$ assigns $val(r) = \mathbf{t}$ and $val(p) = \mathbf{u}$ while from $|c|$ we can conclude $val(\neg r) \geq val(p) = \mathbf{u}$ and this is incompatible with $val(r) = \mathbf{t}$.

The answer is $<c>=\{p, \neg r\}$ or $<c>= \emptyset$. In general we will be interested in the first case, the second being considered trivial. $\triangle$

$I_{\{p\}}$ in the example is not a model. There is a deep reason for this assymmetry. From $\{p \leftarrow, r \leftarrow, \neg r \leftarrow p\}$ it is possible to conclude $\neg p$ in classical logic by using case analysis or through the contrapositive $\neg p \leftarrow r$. But doing this is against the tradition of Logic Programming [GL90] where '$\leftarrow$' is viewed as an inference rule, in a constructive way, and not as a classical implication. So, the contrapositive does not hold in the sense that the clash removal process never introduces new information (new literals) but is restricted to remove literals from Δ. This operation, by itself, just changes literals from t to u, unless they are also defined independently.

Among the pre-interpretations we will distinguish two cases:

1. when there are contradictions among literals derived locally in Γ; it corresponds to a potential contradiction that is revealed by the presence of the defaults;

2. every contradiction involves one default; this is the basic overriding situation and so we will consider only this case at first.

Theorem 1 *In a class pre-interpretation I_X where the image Γ_X is consistent the only way to reduce the number of clashes is by throwing away one of the offending defaults $\delta \in \mathcal{O}$ (contradicted by Γ_X).*

This result is interesting because it means, in this case, that it is not needed to look into the bodies of the rules in search of a literal to eliminate.

Proof. The argument is very simple. Eliminating a literal δ from $\Delta_X - \mathcal{O}$ means setting its value to u because its opposite is not independently stated. The body of each active clause containing δ changes from (1) t to u, or (2) t to f. In case (1), the respective head may now remain t or, at best, become u. But as the contradictory default still holds, forcing the head literal to be f, everything we got was a change from an explicit clash to a hidden contradiction. In case (2), the withdrawal of δ caused another literal in the body to change from t to f, thus just transfering the problem to the definitions of this other literal. A non-offending default cannot be made false by the elimination process. $\square$

Corollary: in a lattice, a pre-interpretation without explicit contradictions is not a model if one of its immediate superiors contains a complementary pair and the corresponding arc is labelled by a non-offending literal.

So, in the example, cutting out p does not eliminate the clash in r which would eventually be drawn up from the defaults, anyway. The disadvantage of starting with p is that the final model obtained is not the maximal one.

Proposition 4 *If $\Gamma_{\{\}}$ is consistent there is a path to each maximal model labelled only with offending elements.*

A different situation arises when the image Γ is itself inconsistent. This means that the program contains clauses with complementary heads and that the clauses were activated by the defaults. Otherwise the program is inconsistent and not allowed. So it is possible to eliminate this kind of contradiction, which does not involve directly the offending set, still by eliminating the appropriate defaults.

The method presented here is based on unfolding the rules until their bodies only contain defaults or cycles are found. A fact unfolds to true of course. A cycle implies the value u for the corresponding head. So only the other case is relevant. The result of this program transformation is an explicit function from defaults into all the possible conclusions. Then it is a matter of finding the best set of defaults to erradicate, probably the smallest among the several minimal possibilities, which guarantees that the corresponding pre-interpretation is a model.

This method may be applied to the initial set of defaults thus including the offending set, or it can be a second step after the application of the basic overriding mechanism.

Example 3 *Induced contradictions in the image.*

$$\Delta^c = \{a, d, \neg p\} \qquad\qquad |c| = \left\{ \begin{array}{ccc} p & \leftarrow & a, \neg p \\ \neg p & \leftarrow & d \end{array} \right\}$$

The program is already in the required form (body only with defaults). So two admissible sets of defaults may be considered for elimination: $\{a, d\}$ and $\{\neg p, d\}$. But the pre-interpretation obtained with the first one is not a model. So the second one is chosen and the maximal set of defaults is $\{a\}$. This is the same result one would obtain by eliminating at first the offending set ($\{\neg p\}$), then applying the transformation to the reduced defaults which gives

$$\begin{array}{ccc} p & \leftarrow & a, d \\ \neg p & \leftarrow & d \end{array}$$

and then eliminating the common literal in both clauses b. $\qquad\qquad\qquad \Delta$

4   Final remarks

In conclusion, we think that the two basic intuitions that oriented this work, namely the symmetric treatment of explicit positive and negative properties and the adhesion to the LP paradigm in its constructive concern, payed off in simplicity and clarity when dealing with exceptions and incompleteness of knowledge.

The shift to the 3-valued logic framework inspired by the interest in modelling exceptions in the context of inheritance reasoning, is similar to the work of [GL90] directly addressed to extend LP with explicit (or, in their terminology, classical) negation. They also depart from the traditional CWA [Rei80] that is present even in other 3-valued semantics, like the Well Founded [VGRS90], as a preference for negative assumptions. We adopt the position of minimizing information (not truth) in the sense that our positive or negative conclusions are explicitly supported by the program. Everything else is considered undefined, i.e. we use a UAF rule, for *undefined as failure*, instead of the usual NAF.

In [GL90] the appearance of a contradiction spreads to the whole model: every literal becomes true, which amounts to annihilate its information content. This seems to be meaningful in the context of a single theory. In a HS, contradictions caused by multiple inheritance are just defaults and so may be fighted locally by setting the intervening literals to undefined.

In a flat (non-hierarchic) LP system the prevalent operator NAF, negation as failure, is often used to model a default policy. This happens, for instance, in [KS90] with the aim of explicitly representing exceptions in LP. Positive and negative literals are not symmetric. Negative represent exceptions and so are prefered. The goal is to obtain a reduction of programs to the standard SLDNF case. In HS, we rely on the structure represented by the hierarchy to specify as defaults properties inherited from superclasses. For that reason we deliberately omitted the NAF.

It is central to the inheritance mechanism described the problem of eliminating clashes by appropriately overriding defaults. Once more the hierarchy helped to find a criterium. A similar subject has been addressed in [PAA91] but there the set of variable literals was a priori restricted to be those which were true by NAF.

As a last remark we stress that we are aware of some of the limitations of our approach. For instance, the functional character that a rule possesses in the class where it is defined vanishes when the class model is computed and so is not inherited by the subclasses. This observation seems to point to an inheritance mechanism closer to *clause inheritance* [MP91]. This is one of our current research topics.

References

[DP91]   Gabriel David and António Porto. Semantics of inheritance in a propositional hierarchic system. Universidade Nova de Lisboa, 1991. RT 23/91-DI/UNL.

[GL90]   Michael Gelfond and Vladimir Lifschitz. Logic programs with classical negation. In David H. D. Warren and Peter Szeredi, editors, *Logic Programming*, page 579, Cambridge, MA, 1990. MIT Press.

[KS90]   Robert Kowalski and Fariba Sadri. Logic programs with exceptions. In David H. D. Warren and Peter Szeredi, editors, *Logic Programming*, page 598, Cambridge, MA, 1990. MIT Press.

[Llo87] John Wylie Lloyd. *Foundations of Logic Programming*. Springer-Verlag, Berlin, 1987.

[MP91]   Luís Monteiro and António Porto. Semantic and syntactic inheritance in logic programming. Universidade Nova de Lisboa, 1991. RT 24/91-DI/UNL.

[PAA91] Luís Moniz Pereira, José Júlio Alferes, and Joaquim Nunes Aparício. Contradiction removal within well founded semantics. In *Logic Programming and Non-Monotonic Reasoning'91*, 1991.

[Prz89]   Teodor C. Przymusinski. Three-valued formalizations of non-monotonic rea-
           soning and logic programming. In Ronald J. Brachman, Hector J. Levesque,
           and Raymond Reiter, editors, *Principles of Knowledge Representation and
           Reasoning*, page 341, San Mateo, CA, 1989. Morgan Kaufmann Publishers.

[Rei80]   Raymond Reiter. A logic for default reasoning. *Artificial Intelligence*, 13:81,
           1980.

[Tou86]   David S. Touretzky. *The Mathematics of Inheritance Systems*. Pitman, Lon-
           don, 1986.

[Tur84]   Raymond Turner. *Logics for Artificial Intelligence*. Ellis Horwood, Chichester,
           England, 1984.

[VGRS90]   Allen Van Gelder, Kenneth A. Ross, and John S. Schlipf. The well-founded
           semantics for general logic programs. *Journal of ACM*, 1990.

Time in Confluences: Dealing with Delays for Consistency-Checking

Amílcar Cardoso, Ernesto Costa

Laboratório de Informática e Sistemas, Universidade de Coimbra
Qt. Boavista, Lote 1, 1º, 3000 Coimbra, Portugal
amilcar@uc.ctt.pt, ernesto@uc.ctt.pt

Abstract

Most model-based approaches to diagnosis require a procedure which checks for the consistency of the observations, given a model of the diagnosed system. When dealing with a dynamically changing system such a procedure must take into account time-varying data. Additional difficulties arise when delays are involved in interactions between variables. The worst case occurs when some of the delays are completely unspecified.

This paper presents an approach to consistency-checking which handles qualitative models of dynamic systems exhibiting time lags. A component-centered ontology is adopted to model the structure of the physical system and an episode-based approach is adopted for representing its behavior over time. An example consisting of a physical process exhibiting transportation lags is used to illustrate the power of the approach. Algorithms are presented and illustrated by an output from an implementation in Prolog called C-CAT (Consistency-Checking Along Time).

The solution proposed represents an extension to Brian Williams' Temporal Constraint Propagation methodology. It also extends the applicability range of existing approaches to model-based diagnosis, permitting its use in tasks such as on-line diagnosis of dynamic systems.

1. Introduction

Qualitative reasoning is the basis for most of the recent work on common-sense approaches to tasks like interpretation, analysis, simulation, design and diagnosis of physical systems [e.g., 4, 8, 10, 15]. The key idea is to represent the behavior of such systems in a style as close as possible to the way humans think about their physical environment, i.e., accounting for the really important concepts with a minimum commitment to details. Qualitative reasoning allows computer programs to perform their tasks dealing with concepts such as *process*, *component*, *structure* and *causality*, at the expense of a quantitative detail that humans most of the time don't consider in their every-day reasoning. We think this is the main strength of qualitative reasoning. Moreover, the qualitative models used are more readable and easier to debug. Furthermore, handling causality allows the generation of human-like explanations. All these characteristics make qualitative reasoning an appealing tool to model-based diagnosis of physical systems. Suitable modelling techniques exist which enable reasoning about structure. We will adopt a component-centered approach from [4].

When dealing with dynamic environments the means to handle time in a convenient way must also be supplied. Several approaches exist to integrate temporal information in qualitative modelling and reasoning. The basic mechanisms we adopt are owed to B. C. Williams in his work on TCP [14], an episode-based methodology used to predict behavior.

This paper presents an approach to perform consistency-checking over a continuous stream of data collected from a dynamically-changing system. The approach is powerful enough to handle systems exhibiting time lags, even when their durations are almost completely unspecified. As consistency-checking is a basic step required for most algorithms to model-based diagnosis [e.g., 6, 7, 11, 12], this approach extends its use to tasks such as on-line diagnosis of a wide range of dynamic systems.

We review in Section 2 the basic concepts behind qualitative reasoning, under a component-centered ontology. In Section 3 we present the mechanisms adopted to represent behavior over time. Our approach to consistency-checking is presented in Section 4, with an example which illustrates its power and an output from the C-CAT program (Consistency-Checking Along Time) which implements the presented Algorithms.

2. Qualitative Modelling of Physical Systems

When qualitatively modelling a physical system, the numerical range of each variable involved is analyzed and splitted in continuous regions bounded by meaningful point values. Each of those regions and values will correspond to a *qualitative value*. Usually the single value 0 is chosen to split the range of each variable in two regions, the positive and the negative, leading to three qualitative values: "+", "-" and "0". We represent the qualitative value of a variable X in such a quantity space by $[X]$ and the qualitative value of a time derivative $d^n X/dt$ by $\partial^n X$ (we adopt this notation from [4]).

A physical system may be viewed, for modelling purposes, as being composed of a set of interconnected components. Adopting this ontology, the qualitative model of the device may be obtained by modelling both each component in a context-free fashion and the interconnections between them [4, 15]. Modelling is accomplished by qualitative versions of differential equations, called *Confluences*.

Qualitative states, corresponding to operating regions, are identifyed for each component when appropriate. Different qualitative states of a component are modeled by a different set of confluences. Within this framework, two kinds of behavior emerge which lead to two complementary perspectives: behavior through state transitions (interstate behavior) and behavior during qualitative states (intrastate behavior). In this paper we will restrict our analysis to intrastate behavior, although our approach may be easily extended to deal with interstate behavior.

For reasoning over confluences we will use *Constraint Propagation* [13]. Therefore, we will consider confluences as being *constraints* upon the *values* of variables and derivatives, which constitute the *cells* of a constraint-network.

For many reasoning tasks, like generation of causal explanations, there is the need to specify *how* behavior is produced. But given a confluence $A = B$, a problem exists on determining if A is cause or consequence. There are methodologies to ascribe a causal "flux" to the constraints in face of a set of input disturbances [e.g., 4, 5, 15]. As a result of their application, a confluence $A = B$ may be transformed in a *Qualitative-Causal Relation* $A \rightarrow B$, meaning "A causes B" <u>and</u> "A and B have the same qualitative value".

3. Representation for Behavior over Time

Time may also be modeled in a qualitative way, splitting its range in regions bounded by time points where significant events occur. When dealing with intrastate behavior, significant events consist in changes in the qualitative values of variables and derivatives (cells of the constraint network). Obviously, a change in the qualitative value of a cell must only perform a splitting in the time range of that same cell. Therefore the behavior of each cell over time must be modeled separately. Following [14], we will use two-dimensional *Histories* [9], called *Value Histories*. Instants where changes occur in the value of a cell split its time range in meeting intervals [2] where the value of the cell remains the same. A value/interval pair $e = (V, \alpha)$ is called an *episode*. For each cell X a value history $h(X)$ consisting of a sequence of meeting episodes $(e_0, e_1, ..., e_n)$ is built. To represent the fact that an episode e belongs to the history $h(X)$ we will write $e \in h(X)$. To denote that a particular episode e_i is the *i*th episode of a history h(X) we will use the binary function "EPN" (standing for "episode number") and write e_i = EPN(X,i).

To attain conciseness, episodes must be kept *maximal*, i.e., two consecutive episodes must have different values. Value histories made up of maximal episodes are called *Concise Histories* [14].

Within this representation framework, the time interval is taken as primitive. When reasoning over intervals of time, we will follow Allen & Hayes's interval-based temporal logic [1, 2].

3.1. Time in Confluences

We have already seen that confluences may be viewed as constraints over qualitative values of cells. When modelling the behavior of such cells by concise histories, the constraints between them must reflect a two-dimensional relation, i.e., they must be settled over qualitative values and also over time.

One possible solution consists in parameterizing confluences by time, as in [14]. For instance, a resistor may be modeled by Ohm's law, $V = RI$, whose qualitative version is the confluence $[V] = [I]$, as R is a positive constant. The corresponding *Parameterized-By-Time (PBT)* confluence is $[V(t)] = [I(t)]$, which means that the qualitative value of V equals the qualitative value of I at every *simultaneous* episode pair, i.e., $\forall \alpha \{(v, \alpha) \in h([V]) \wedge (i, \alpha) \in h([I]) \supset (v = i)\}$.

Parameterizing confluences by time enlarges their modelling power and permits a more complex temporal reasoning. Explicit representation for delays is provided, therefore reasoning about systems which exhibit time lags is possible.

3.2. Propagation through PBT-confluences

A PBT-confluence is a two-dimensional relationship that qualitatively restricts the values and intervals of a set of episodes. The calculus in the qualitative value dimension is performed as for normal confluences. The time domain of the results of such calculus is restricted by the time dimension of the confluence. This ordinarily corresponds to the TCP (Temporal Constraint Propagation) methodology [14] which is used to predict behavior.

When no delays are involved, PBT-confluences relate *simultaneous* fractions of episodes. Therefore, given a PBT-confluence restricting N episodes, its time domain consists in the intersection of the intervals of those episodes.

In the most general case, however, a PBT-confluence relates *non-simultaneous* fractions of episodes. More precisely, given a PBT-confluence which restricts a set E of episodes and associates to each of them a specific delay, its time domain is the intersection of the intervals of the set E_t of episodes which are the temporal translation of the episodes of E over the respective delays.

We denote the (positive) temporal translation of the history of a variable X over an interval σ as tt(X, σ). Under the episode-based approach we are adopting, this function may also be applied over other value/interval structures, like episodes. The (positive) temporal translation of an interval α over the interval σ will be denoted as ptt(α, σ). We will also consider that the operation of intersection between time intervals is denoted by "!" and defined as in [2].

Proposition 1 asserts the calcula to perform when all but one of the episodes restricted by a PBT-confluence are known and we want to deduce the remaining one:

Proposition 1. Given the PBT-confluence $A(t - \Delta t_A) + B(t - \Delta t_B) + ... + M(t - \Delta t_M) + N(t - \Delta t_N) = 0$ and the known episodes $EPN(A,i) = (V_A, \alpha_i)$, $EPN(B,j) = (V_B, \beta_j)$, ..., $EPN(M,k) = (V_M, \mu_k)$, a new episode $EPN(N,l) = (V_N, \eta_l)$ may be deduced such that

$$V_N = -V_A - V_B - ... - V_M \wedge \eta'_l = \alpha'_i \,!\, \beta'_j \,!\, ... \,!\, \mu'_k,$$

where $\alpha'_i = ptt(\alpha_i, \Delta t_A)$, ..., $\mu'_\kappa = ptt(\mu_k, \Delta t_M)$, $\eta'_i = ptt(\eta_l, \Delta t_N)$.

Once a new episode $EPN(N,l) = (V_N, \eta_l)$ is deduced, it must be integrated in the respective history h(N) if $\eta_l \neq \varnothing$. To keep h(N) concise, neighboring episodes of the new one must be analyzed and possibly a fusion operation must be performed to maintain episodes maximal.

4. Consistency-Checking

One of the basic steps for most diagnosis algorithms is the check for the consistency of the observations, given a model of the diagnosed system [e.g., 6, 7, 11, 12]. When dealing with a dynamically changing system, this task must be performed over the value dimension (as for static systems) and over the time dimension.

We consider that data from the physical system is continually being sampled at a convenient rate and that concise histories for variables and derivatives are being made up of them. We assume a discrete model for time where the sampling interval is considered as a *moment* [2].

The histories will grow incrementally as new data are being collected. We will denote as HIS(t) the histories we dispose at moment t.

Our goal is settling a support for the consistency of the histories thus created, given the PBT-confluences which model the behavior of the system. The support should embody some notion of causality. A causal support reflects the commonsense notion of consistency of time-changing data, consequences being supported by its causes. Also causal explanations could be generated from a trace of that support.

Basically, given a PBT-confluence where causality is defined, our approach consists in looking for *Sets of Supporting Episodes* (*SSE's*) of the causes-histories, which may consistently explain each episode of the consequence-history. The trace of the sets thus obtained will represent possible *justifications* for the consequent history. We will denote the set of supporting episodes for an episode $(V, \sigma) \in h(X)$ as SSE(X, V, σ).

To illustrate the methodology we introduce an example system consisting of one only component whose interactions between variables exhibit time lags.

4.1. An Example

Consider the Heat Exchanger represented in Figure 1, where a liquid flows through and is heated by condensing steam. Pressures along the liquid and steam paths are assumed to be constant.

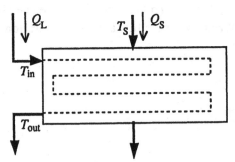

Fig.1: A simple Heat Exchanger

In most heat exchangers where a phase transition occurs a saturated steam is used, i.e., T_s is made equal to the saturation temperature, at the considered pressure, of the substance used. The energy transfer is made by condensation and the steam temperature remains approximately constant during the process. The energy balance for the process is given by[1]

$$Q_s \lambda_s = Q_L C_{P_L} (T_{out} - T_{in})$$ (1)

where λ_s is the condensing enthalpy of the steam, also called "latent heat of condensation", which we may consider approximately constant, and C_{P_L} is the specific heat at constant pressure of the liquid, also approximately constant.

Differentiating (1) w. r. t. time, we get

$$\lambda_s \frac{dQ_s}{dt} = C_{P_L} Q_L \frac{dT_{out}}{dt} - C_{P_L} Q_L \frac{dT_{in}}{dt} + C_{P_L} (T_{out} - T_{in}) \frac{dQ_L}{dt}$$ (2)

We may now obtain the confluences which model the device. From (1), we get

$$[Q_s] = [Q_L] * [T_{out} - T_{in}]$$ (3)

and from (2)

$$\partial Q_s = [Q_L] * \partial T_{out} - [Q_L] * \partial T_{in} + [T_{out} - T_{in}] * \partial Q_L$$

In normal conditions, $Q_s \geq 0$, $Q_L \geq 0$ and $(T_{out} - T_{in}) \geq 0$, therefore the second confluence becomes

$$\partial T_{out} = \partial Q_s - \partial Q_L + \partial T_{in}$$ (4)

For the sake of simplicity, let's consider that Q_L is positive and not changing, so the confluence (4) reduces to $\partial T_{out} = \partial Q_s + \partial T_{in}$. As Q_s and T_{in} are inputs and T_{out} an output, we may state the causal relation

$$\partial T_{out} \leftarrow \partial Q_s + \partial T_{in}$$ (5)

Figure 2 shows a possible evolution of the variables: initially the system is in static equilibrium and then two disturbances occur that make Q_s rise and T_{in} decrease.

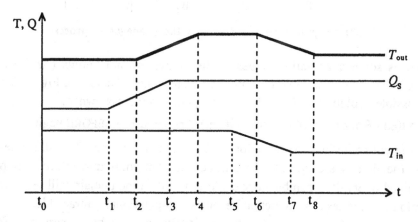

Fig.2: Linearized diagram for a possible evolution of Tin, QS and Tout

---

[1] The complete deduction of these equations is presented in [3].

T_{out} is influenced by three distinct processes: the mass transportation of liquid, the mass transportation of steam and the process of energy transfer as heat by condensing steam.

A more detailed analysis of the system will show that a constant delay Δt is involved in the influence of T_{in} over T_{out}. Also a variable delay Δt_S is involved in the influence of Q_S over T_{out} (Δt_S depends on Q_S and T_{in}).

Therefore, the behavior of the device may be represented by the PBT-confluence

$$\partial T_{out}(t) \leftarrow \partial Q_S(t - \Delta t_S) + \partial T_{in}(t - \Delta t) = tt(\partial Q_S, \Delta t_S) + tt(\partial T_{in}, \Delta t) \qquad (6)$$

The histories of the derivatives and their temporal translations for the evolution shown in Figure 2 are graphically represented in Figure 3. This Figure also shows how $h(\partial T_{out})$ may be deduced from $h(\partial Q_S)$, $h(\partial T_{in})$ and a complete specification of the delays, by executing temporal translations as stated by Proposition 1.

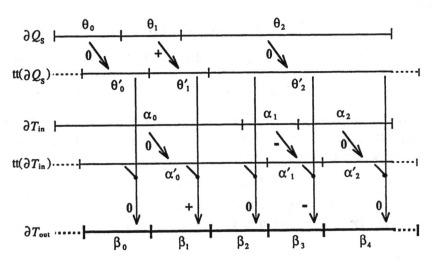

Fig.3: Graphical representation of the propagation process

However, as some quantitative values of the delays are not known (Δt_S varies over time), the behavior of T_{out} cannot be precisely determined. Therefore, Figure 2 presents only a possible evolution of T_{out}, which corresponds to the case where

$$ptt(end(\theta_1), \Delta t_S) \text{ BEFORE } ptt(begin(\alpha_1), \Delta t) \equiv end(\theta'_1) \text{ BEFORE } begin(\alpha'_1)$$

Under different conditions the behavior of T_{out} could be different. This illustrates that if some of the delays are completely unspecified, temporal translation will produce undetermined intervals, a combinatory explosion in the time domain will result from the propagation and the task of prediction becomes computationaly intractable.

It is, however, possible to theoretically establish a support for the consequence-history $h(\partial T_{out})$ given cause-histories $h(\partial Q_S)$ and $h(\partial T_{in})$, even in such situations. Moreover, it is shown in [3] how computational tractability may be guaranteed imposing only upper-bound limits to the delays.

4.2. Computing Sets of Supporting Episodes

Supposing that the histories for ∂T_{in}, ∂Q_S and ∂T_{out} are being built from data collected from the system, let's analyze how supporting episodes may be generated from observations along time and from PBT-confluence (6). We will use the histories represented in Figure 4 as an example. For computational efficiency, the analysis will be performed only when some significative changes occur, i.e., in the first moment of each episode (as represented in the Figure).

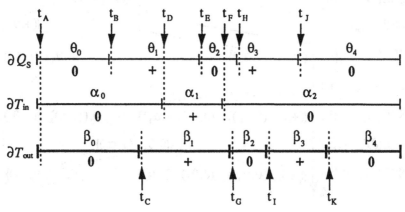

Fig.4: An Example of Histories

Figure 5 represents the SSE's for the episodes of $h(\partial T_{out})$, given the histories of Figure 4. We may see that more than one set of episodes may be a support for some of the episodes of ∂T_{out}. As a result, seven justifications exist for $h(\partial T_{out})$ represented by seven paths (e.g., path A).

This example illustrates the fact that more than one set of supporting episodes may be deduced from one SSE, as at t_D and t_E. It also shows that the same set of supporting episodes may be deduced from different ones, as at t_G and t_K, a graph-like structure resulting from the deduction process.

The generation of SSE's may be sketched in this way: at any one moment a collection of SSE's exists; given new information, new collections may be deduced from each SSE; a concise reunion of those collections results in a new collection of non-duplicated SSE's.

To implement this deduction process we use two algorithms. The first one, Algorithm A1, deduces a collection of sets of supporting episodes from a given SSE and new data in the histories. The second one, Algorithm A2, takes a collection of SSE's and new data in the histories, calls Algorithm A1 for each SSE of the collection, obtaining a new collection for each SSE, and finally performs an operation of concise reunion over those collections.

If the resulting collection contains no SSE's, an inconsistency is detected: there is no support for the new data in the histories.

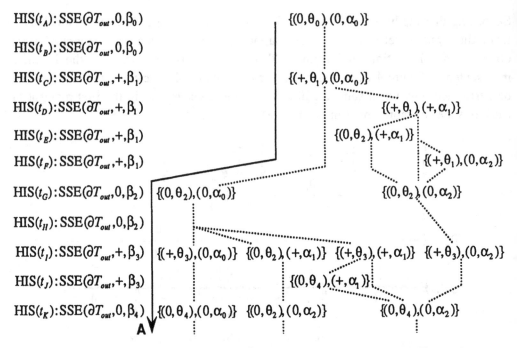

Fig.5: SSE's for the episodes of h(∂T_{out}), given the Histories of Figure 4

When no new episodes occur in the histories, the SSE's don't change either. Therefore, for the sake of computational efficiency the algorithms must be called only when a new episode exists in at least one of the histories. It is a function of whatever uses the algorithms to guarantee that this condition holds.

The basic algorithm to deduce a new collection of Sets of Supporting Episodes from an already settled SSE, given a most recent set of histories, is:

Algorithm A1 (Deduce a collection Σ of Sets of Supporting Episodes from a SSE)
Given:
  1. *The PBT-confluence $N(t) \leftarrow A_1(t - \Delta t_1) + A_2(t - \Delta t_2) + ... + A_m(t - \Delta t_m)$,*
     where all Δt_x's, which denote the delays involved in the influence of a
     variable A_x and the variable N, are unknown quantities;
  2. *HIS(t_i), consisting of the concise histories $h(N)$, $h(A_1)$, $h(A_2)$, ..., $h(A_m)$ built*
     until t_i;
  3. *A set of supporting episodes $SSE(N, V, \eta) = \{EPN(A_1, r_1), EPN(A_2, r_2), ...,*
     EPN(A_m, r_m)\}$ for the episode $EPN(N, u) = (V, \eta)$, where the interval η
     contains t_j, which is the last moment before t_i;

Deduce the collection Σ *of sets of supporting episodes, starting with* $\Sigma = \emptyset$:

   a) If the given SSE is consistent in the qualitative value dimension with the most recent episode of h(N), then include it in Σ.

   b) FOR each new episode E in HIS(t_i) DO:

     Case a: If $E = EPN(N,u+1) = (V', \eta')$ *then,*

       FOR p varying from 1 to m DO:

         — FOR each set of episodes $S = \{EPN(A_1,s_1), EPN(A_2,s_2), ..., EPN(A_m,s_m)\}$ *such that* $s_k = r_k + 1$ *for p episodes and* $s_k = r_k$ *for the remaining m - p episodes, if S is consistent in the qualitative value dimension with* (V', η'), *then S is a new SSE for EPN(N,u+1); therefore, include S in* Σ.

     Case b: If $[E = EPN(A_k, s_k)] \wedge [EPN(A_k, s_k-1) \in SSE(N, V, \eta)]$ *for any* $k \in [1, m]$ *(if that is the case,* $s_k - 1 = r_k$*), and the set*

$$S = \{\{EPN(A_1,r_1), EPN(A_2,r_2), ..., EPN(A_m,r_m)\} \setminus \{EPN(A_k,r_k)\}\} \cup \{EPN(A_k,s_k)\}$$

     is consistent in the qualitative value domain with (V, η), *then S is a new SSE for EPN(N,u); therefore, include S in* Σ.

If Algorithm A1 returns $\Sigma = \emptyset$, no set of supporting episodes could be deduced.

The algorithm to deduce a new collection of sets of supporting episodes from an already settled one, given a most recent set of histories, is:

Algorithm A2 (*Deduce a new collection* Σ' *of Sets of Supporting Episodes from an old one*)

   Given:

     1. The PBT-confluence $N(t) \leftarrow A_1(t - \Delta t_1) + A_2(t - \Delta t_2) + ... + A_m(t - \Delta t_m)$, *where all* Δt_x's *are unknown quantities;*

     2. HIS(t_i), consisting of the concise histories h(N), h(A_1), h(A_2), ..., h(A_m) built until t_i;

     3. A collection of sets of supporting episodes $\Sigma = \{SSE_1, SSE_2, ..., SSE_l\}$ *for* $EPN(N,u) = (V, \eta)$ *(i.e.,* $SSE_k = SSE(N, V, \eta)$ *for all* $k \in [1, l]$*), where the interval* η *contains* t_j, *which is the last moment before* t_i.

   Deduce the collection Σ' *of sets of supporting episodes for* $EPN(N,u') = (V', \eta')$, *where the interval* η' *contains the moment* t_i:

     a) For each set of supporting episodes SSE_k *deduce a new collection of sets of supporting episodes* Σ'_k *using Algorithm A1;*

     b) Deduce the collection $\Sigma'_U = \bigcup_k \Sigma'_k$;

     c) Deduce Σ' *by removing every duplication from* Σ'_U.

If Algorithm A2 returns an empty collection, i.e., $\Sigma' = \emptyset$, an inconsistency was detected.

When Algorithm A1 returns an empty collection the path containing the SSE from which no new collection could be deduced is pruned.

Figure 6 shows an output from a Prolog implementation of these Algorithms, called C-CAT. The histories are similar to those of Figure 4 and the deduced SSE's are similar to those of Figure 5.

```
****** CCAT - Consistency-Checking Along Time ******

Complete Histories (test data):
    History for d(v_Tout): [(0,50), (+,40), (0,35), (+,15), (0,0)]
    History for d(v_Qs): [(0,45), (+,37), (0,30), (+,10), (0,0)]
    History for d(v_Tin): [(0,32), (+,22), (0,0)]

At time 0, SSE's for (d(v_Tout),0,0):
    {(d(v_Qs), 0, 0), (d(v_Tin), 0, 0)}
                                                    At time 40, SSE's for (d(v_Tout),+,40):
                                                        {(d(v_Qs), +, 37), (d(v_Tin), +, 22)}
At time 15, SSE's for (d(v_Tout),+,15):                 {(d(v_Qs), +, 37), (d(v_Tin), 0, 0)}
    {(d(v_Qs), +, 10), (d(v_Tin), 0, 0)}                {(d(v_Qs), +, 37), (d(v_Tin), 0, 32)}
                                                        {(d(v_Qs), 0, 30), (d(v_Tin), +, 22)}
At time 22, SSE's for (d(v_Tout),+,15):
    {(d(v_Qs), +, 10), (d(v_Tin), +, 22)}          At time 45, SSE's for (d(v_Tout),+,40):
    {(d(v_Qs), +, 10), (d(v_Tin), 0, 0)}                {(d(v_Qs), +, 37), (d(v_Tin), +, 22)}
                                                        {(d(v_Qs), +, 37), (d(v_Tin), 0, 0)}
At time 30, SSE's for (d(v_Tout),+,15):                 {(d(v_Qs), +, 37), (d(v_Tin), 0, 32)}
    {(d(v_Qs), +, 10), (d(v_Tin), +, 22)}               {(d(v_Qs), 0, 30), (d(v_Tin), +, 22)}
    {(d(v_Qs), +, 10), (d(v_Tin), 0, 0)}                {(d(v_Qs), 0, 45), (d(v_Tin), +, 22)}
    {(d(v_Qs), 0, 30), (d(v_Tin), +, 22)}
                                                   At time 50, SSE's for (d(v_Tout),0,50):
At time 32, SSE's for (d(v_Tout),+,15):                 {(d(v_Qs), 0, 30), (d(v_Tin), 0, 32)}
    {(d(v_Qs), +, 10), (d(v_Tin), +, 22)}               {(d(v_Qs), 0, 45), (d(v_Tin), 0, 0)}
    {(d(v_Qs), +, 10), (d(v_Tin), 0, 0)}                {(d(v_Qs), 0, 45), (d(v_Tin), 0, 32)}
    {(d(v_Qs), +, 10), (d(v_Tin), 0, 32)}
    {(d(v_Qs), 0, 30), (d(v_Tin), +, 22)}

At time 35, SSE's for (d(v_Tout),0,35):
    {(d(v_Qs), 0, 30), (d(v_Tin), 0, 0)}
    {(d(v_Qs), 0, 30), (d(v_Tin), 0, 32)}
```

Fig.6: Output from C-CAT

4.3. Improvements to the Algorithms

The trace of the deduction may be recorded [3] so that the resulting paths, i.e., justifications, may be used for generation of explanations. For consistency-checking purposes only, such a recording is not necessary.

A situation is represented in Figure 5 that deserves special care: we can see that the episode $(0, \alpha_0)$ of $h(T_{in})$ is used in path A as support for all the episodes of $h(T_{out})$.

However, this violates the intuition that an episode should not be a support, in a particular path, for an observed behavior whose extent is greater than the episode's extent if the delay involved is constant. There are also situations where infinite paths are generated, which completely disables the consistency-checking procedure [3]. Completely unrestricted delays make the problem intractable.

Therefore, some knowledge on the delays is needed, i.e., some technique to prune the generated graph. One consists in reasoning over intervals' extents, which in this case means quantitatively reasoning over intervals' endpoints. This is, however, a too restrictive approach because delays in physical systems are seldom constant and difficult to compute with exactitude.

Other approach consists in heuristically defining a validity-term to the influence of each cause-episode on the consequence-history. Associating a validity-term for a variable in a PBT-confluence corresponds to defining *an upper-bound limit* for the non-specified delay involved in the interaction of that variable with the consequence-variable. Therefore, any path of the graph involving a cause-episode which is no longer valid will be purged. This approach is explored in [3], where more detailed explanations and more examples may be found. Note that each validity-term may be, depending on the actual physical system, either computed upon the quantitative model of the system description or settled by an expert on the domain (this is not, however, a concern of this paper).

5. Conclusions

We have presented an approach to consistency-checking of data collected from a dynamically changing system, which handles almost completely unspecified delays. It represents an extension to TCP methodology in the sense that TCP is used to predict behavior while we use the same basic modelling mechanisms to check for consistency. An output from a Prolog implementation of the presented algorithms, called C-CAT, was used to illustrate the approach.

Another contribution of this paper is to expand the applicability range of existing model-based approaches to diagnosis which need a consistency-checking procedure to perform their task. Constructing such a procedure using C-CAT enables the application of those approaches to on-line diagnosis of dynamic systems.

The fact that minimal commitment is imposed to the knowledge about delays enlarges even more the potential of this proposal.

Some open issues remain which must be considered. The approach should be extended to deal with a set of PBT-Confluences: this may be attained by developing a special Constraint Propagation Algorithm using C-CAT. Also an extension is needed to handle interstate behavior.

This work corresponds to a part of the project of an architecture to perform on-line monitoring and diagnosis of physical processes.

References

[1] J. F. Allen, 1984, *"Towards a General Theory of Action and Time"*, Artificial Intelligence, 23, 123-154.

[2] J. F. Allen and P. J. Hayes, 1989, *"Moments and Points in an Interval-Based Temporal Logic"*, Computational Intelligence, 5, 225-238.

[3] A. Cardoso and E. Costa, 1990, *"Time in Confluences: Dealing with Delays for Consistency-Checking (Extended Paper)"*, Tech. Report DEE-UC-003-90, University of Coimbra.

[4] J. de Kleer and J. S. Brown, 1984, *"A Qualitative Physics Based on Confluences"*, Artificial Intelligence 24 (1-3), 7-83.

[5] J. de Kleer and J. S. Brown, 1986, *"Theories of Causal Ordering"*, Artificial Intelligence 26 (1), 33-61.

[6] J. de Kleer and B. C. Williams, 1987, *"Diagnosing Multiple Faults"*, Artificial Intelligence 32 (1), 97-130.

[7] J. de Kleer, A. K. Mackworth and R. Reiter, 1990, *"Characterizing Diagnosis"*, Procs. AAAI-90, Vol.1, 324-330, Boston, MA, USA.

[8] K. D. Forbus, 1984, *"Qualitative Process Theory"*, Artificial Intelligence 24 (1-3), 85-168.

[9] P. J. Hayes, *"The Second Naive Physics Manifesto"*, 1985, in: J. H. Hobbs and R. C. Moore (Eds.), *"Formal Theories of the Commonsense World"*, 1-36, Ablex Publ. Corp., Norwood, NJ, USA.

[10] B. Kuipers, 1986, *"Qualitative Simulation"*, Artificial Intelligence 29 (3), 289-338.

[11] O. Raiman, 1989, *"Diagnosis as a Trial: The Alibi Principle"*, Model-Based Diagnosis Int. Workshop, 31-42, Paris, France.

[12] R. Reiter, 1987, *"A Theory of Diagnosis from First Principles"*, Artificial Intelligence 32 (1), 57-95.

[13] G. J. Sussman and G.L. Steele Jr., 1980, *"CONSTRAINTS: A Language for Expressing Almost Hierarchical Descriptions"*, Artificial Intelligence 14 (1), 1-40.

[14] B. C. Williams, 1986, *"Doing Time: Putting Qualitative Reasoning on Firmer Ground"*, Procs. AAAI-86, Vol.1, 105-112, Philadelphia, PA, USA.

[15] B. C. Williams, 1990, *"Temporal Qualitative Analysis: Explaining How Physical Systems Work"*, in: D. S. Weld and J. de Kleer (Eds.), *"Qualitative Reasoning about Physical Systems"*, 133-177, Morgan Kaufmann, San Mateo, CA, USA.

A TEMPORAL REPRESENTATION FOR
IMPERATIVELY STRUCTURED PLANS OF ACTIONS [1]

Eric RUTTEN [2]

CWI

(Centre for Mathematics and Computer Science)

Kruislaan 413

1098 SJ Amsterdam

The Netherlands

Abstract

The execution of plans of actions by a robot inspired the conception of various representations, from the point of view of planning in artificial intelligence and of execution control. Planning formalisms are often founded on predicate logic and its more recent extensions, particularly temporal logic. Robot programming languages, as far as concerning the task-level, feature control structures derived from computer programming languages, as well as ones more specifically related to real-time execution.

We propose a representation of plans of actions augmented by an imperative control structure, using a classical logical and temporal model. We therefore define, on the basis of an interval-based temporal logic, a set of imperative control primitives that define the temporal arrangement of the actions and subplans within their scope. After that, primitives for the reaction to evolutions in the environment are defined in the same formalism, in order to respond to constraints concerning interaction and adaptation to the external world.

1   Introduction

Context and motivation. Planning is historically linked to its application in robotics. The general motivation of the work presented here is an approach to robotics involving the presence of a human operator (as in teleoperation) or user (from the designer to the end-user). This approach is a complement to the total-autonomy approach. In our case, automatic plan generation is changed for hand-writing of plans, for which a planning assistance should be provided, in relation also to the execution monitoring of these plans. Planning can then be assimilated to a form of high-level (i.e. task-level) programming of robots: a progamming language is then required. It must enable the expression of a temporal arrangement of actions, under the form of a control flow guiding the execution of primitive tasks.

Still, a logic-based model of actions and plans, following a current approach in automatic planning, is also usefull:

---

[1]The work described in this paper was performed at IRISA / INRIA, 35042 Rennes, France.

[2]supported by an ERCIM fellowship (European Research Consortium in Informatics and Mathematics: CNR (Italy), CWI (The Netherlands), GMD (Germany), INESC (Portugal), INRIA (France), RAL (United-Kingdom)).

- as a definition of the behavioural semantics of the planning language, in relation to its execution involving real-time programming problems;

- as a support of planning assistance, e.g. under the form of simulation to which the work presented in this paper has been applied [11], or in the perspective of the possible use of automatic planning as well.

Problem addressed. Within this framework, the specific problem addressed in this paper is a modelling problem: the building of a representation of plans of actions, on which the aforementioned treatments will be based.

In order to express the control structure of a plan of actions, our work consists in:

- determining the primitives of the planning language: we make the choice of an imperative language, featuring classical programming control structures, and also less classical ones, more directly related to the reactive and real-time aspect of robotics;

- defining the behaviour or semantics of these primitives, considering their logical and temporal aspects.

Thus, the work presented here is a combination of a time and action representation formalism with robot programming methods and languages involving real-time issues. It is shared between the application of a theoretical knowledge representation formalism, and the significance of the model with regard to the application domain.

Organization of the paper. In the following section, we will consider how the problem of plan representation is treated in the litterature, as a planning problem and as a task-level robot programming problem. We then briefly introduce the basic items of the model, using an interval-based temporal logic. Plans are first built on these, using classical control structures, characterized by the fact that they are temporally independent of the execution environment. Next, we extend the language with elements enabling to relate the execution to changes in the environment. These capabilities are illustrated by an example in a space telerobotics environment.

2 Existing plan representations

Due to space limitations, we will only outline a deeper study [10]. Our interests correspond to two ways of looking at plans of actions, that are not often integrated.

Planning in artificial intelligence. On one hand, A.I. planning has given an important set of results concerning the search problems involved in the generation process [7]. We are more interested in the representations of *operators* or primitive actions, considered to be directly executable by some agent or effector. This effector is generally taken to be a robot, seen from an abstract point of view. The well-known *STRIPS* representation defines an action by its preconditions and effects in terms of manipulations of a logic predicates data-base. A plan is then an organized collection of operators. The form that this organization can take is the object of many different works; the representation of plans, as a set of actions, is mostly directed by automatic generation considerations. It has not yet evolved into a generally accepted standard [5].

Temporal representations. One approach was that of using temporal logics, in order to capture the temporal dimension of the changes in the world as well as the disposition of actions: an important and wide-spread litterature concerns the subject. Particularly, interval-based models of time allowed to express relations between properties as well as actions [1]; Vere introduced another temporal model [13]. Sandewall e.a. [12] and Ghallab e.a. [6] proposed declarative representations of plans, in terms of temporal relations between the actions.

The only representation that we know of that is at once temporal and imperative is proposed by Hultman e.a. [9], and features temporal definitions of sequence, parallelism, conditional statement, iteration, and a form of reactivity, in relation to Sandewall e.a.'s model [12]. This latter approach, and that of [6] is linked to the development of a mobile robot and its programming environment, which leads us to the link between such a temporal model and command languages executable by a robot.

Robotics and languages. From this point of view, the determination of a plan of actions for a robot can be seen as a programming problem, characterized by an evolutive environment, particular objects (movements, servo-control, geometry), and a real-time control tightly concerned with the fundamental problems of reactivity [14]. In the litterature in this domain, it is difficult to find general approaches; robot programming is mostly considered at a lower level, where many problems are still open. At the level interesting us, i.e. the task-level, several specific solutions present some similarities, however. These languages are based on hierarchical execution architectures and present classical programming languages control structures such as sequence, conditionals, and various interpretations of parallelism, and they are often completed with control strutures specifying the execution of an action or a plan *when* some condition is encountered. In computer programming languages, the classical control structures have been thoroughly worked upon, while newer approaches concerned with automata and the theory of real-time and reactive programming have given way to more specifically temporal control primitives [3].

The work presented in this article aims at combining planning, particularly in its temporal representations, and task-level robot programming, particularly in its imperative real-time aspects. This is attempted by the definition of the elements of a language presenting reactive constructs, in terms of a temporal and logical model of the world and of the actions.

3 Basic items

Interval-based temporal logic. The basic temporal formalism that we use has been worked out in the litterature: it is inspired from Allen's works [1]. The temporal primitive is the interval: it is interpreted in the usual way, as a "chunk" of time, convex, and with a duration. Two intervals can have relative positions described by Allen's relations *before (b), meets (m), overlaps (o), starts (s), during (d), finishes (f), equals (=)* and their inverses *after (a), met-by (mi), overlapped-by (oi), started-by (si), contains (di), finished-by (fi)*. A relation between two intervals I_1 and I_2 can be disjunctive: it is then noted between parentheses, e.g. a non-strict inclusion can be defined by: I_1 in $I_2 \equiv I_1$ $(s\ d\ f\ =)$ I_2. A predicate $lasts(I,D)$ will allow us to relate an interval I with a duration D.

The temporal facts model the properties of the world, represented under the general form: $true(Interval, Property)$, meaning that the *property* is true on the extent of the time *interval*. The interpretation is the classical one in the litterature. In particular, negation is provided with the "strong" interpretation, i.e. $not(P)$ is true on I if P isn't true on any sub-interval of I:

$$true(I, not(P)) \Longleftrightarrow (\forall i)(\ i\ in I \Longrightarrow \neg true(i, P)\ ).$$

Primitive actions. We consider actions at task-level, meaning that they are described by their conditions and effects on a logical representation of the execution environment. Their temporal dimension is defined by a duration of their execution interval, and the relations between it and the truth intervals of concerned temporal facts: preconditions, conditions and effects.

A primitive action is defined by a five-tuple, noted:

$$action(\ A,\ Duration,\ Preconditions,\ Conditions,\ Effects\ ).$$

The preconditions describe what must be verified in the world immediately before the execution of the action, the effects describe what becomes true as a result of this execution, and the conditions describe what must be true in the environment on all the duration of the action. The latter give the relation between the duration of the action and temporal facts in the environment, making the difference with atemporal models. They allow to describe "*keep-actions*", that keep a condition true during their execution, as defined by Sandewall e.a. [12], corresponding to their "*prevail-conditions*". The way such an action takes place in time is illustrated by fig. 1.

The execution of actions and plans on an interval is represented by: $exec(I,A)$: this is a property, meaning that action A can executed from begining to end on the interval I. The definition of the temporal disposition of a given action A, defined by $action(A, D, P, C, E)$, is:

Definition 1 :
$$
\begin{aligned}
exec(I,A) \Longleftrightarrow \ & lasts(I, D) \\
& \wedge (\forall p \in P)(\exists I_p)(\ true(I_p, p) \wedge I_p\ (m\ o\ fi\ di)\ I) \\
& \wedge (\forall c \in C)(\exists I_c)(\ true(I_c, c) \wedge I\ in\ I_c) \\
& \wedge (\forall e \in E)(\exists I_e)(\ true(I_e, e) \wedge I\ (d\ s\ o\ m)\ I_e)
\end{aligned}
$$

The preconditions describe what must be verified in the world at least immediately before the execution of the action, that is to say on an interval I_p such that: $I_p\ (m\ o\ fi\ di)\ I_a$. The conditions describe what must be true in the environment over the whole duration of the action: each c of them must be true on an interval I_c, that contains the action interval I_a, i.e. I_a in I_c. The effects describe what becomes true as a result of this execution, and must be true immediately after the action interval; they may however be true already before (e.g. the action of opening an already open door shouldn't give way to a failure, or else this aspect of the action must be modelled in the form of an explicit condition). The relative disposition of the action interval I_a and an effect interval I_e is then: $I_e\ (di\ si\ oi\ mi)\ I_a$ or: $I_a\ (d\ s\ o\ m)\ I_e$.

A particular example of action is *nothing*, that has no duration, no conditions and no effects: $action(\ nothing,\ 0,\ [\ ],\ [\ ],\ [\ ])$.

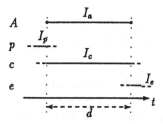

Figure 1: A primitive action in time.

Undefined duration actions. The duration of actions is not always known: some of them have no intrinsic duration, changing at each execution. We therefore give ourselves another kind of actions, with an undefined duration, for which the execution interval will be determined by the control structure of the plan, as will be seen in section 5. They otherwise have the same characteristics as the primitive actions. They are noted:

$$u\text{-}d\text{-}action(\ A,\ Preconditions,\ Conditions,\ Effects\ ),$$

and are defined, for an action A defined by $u\text{-}d\text{-}action(A,P,C,E)$, by:

Definition 2 :
$$exec(I,A) \iff (\forall p \in P)(\exists I_p)(\ true(I_p,p) \wedge I_p\ (m\ o\ fi\ di)\ I)$$
$$\wedge(\forall c \in C)(\exists I_c)(\ true(I_c,c) \wedge I\ in\ I_c)$$
$$\wedge(\forall e \in E)(\exists I_e)(\ true(I_e,e) \wedge I\ (d\ s\ o\ m)\ I_e)$$

An example, similar to *nothing*, is *pause*: $u\text{-}d\text{-}action(pause,\ [\ ],\ [\ ],\ [\ ])$.

4 Environment-independent control primitives

We consider a plan as a set of actions provided with a control structure. A plan is then either a primitive action, either sub-plans, that are plans themselves recursively, framed in a control structure. We will here give some control primitives allowing to build such a structure, with a temporal definition, that can be refined or completed [10].

They are independent of the environment in the sense that they are temporally defined only in terms of their components, and not in terms of the environment.

Classical control structures.

Sequence noted *seq(PList)*, where *PList* is a list of sub-plans of the form $[P_1|P]$, P_1 being the first in the list, and P the remainder of the list: its execution starts with that of P_1, that meets that of P, that in turn finishes the execution of the sequence (see fig. 2).

Definition 3 :
$$exec(I,seq([P_1|P])) \iff (\exists I_1,I_P)\ (I_1\ s\ I\ \wedge\ I_1\ m\ I_P \wedge I_P\ f\ I$$
$$\wedge\ exec(I_1,P_1)\ \wedge\ exec(I_P,seq(P))\ ).$$

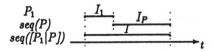

Figure 2: Sequence in time.

Conditional noted $cond(C, P_{true}, P_{false})$, where C is the condition evaluated on a sub-interval starting the global interval I, and a plan is chosen according to the result (see fig. 3).

Definition 4 :

$$exec(I, cond(C, P_{true}, P_{false})) \Longleftrightarrow (\exists I_c)(\quad I_c \; s \; I \wedge$$
$$(\;(true(I_c, C) \wedge exec(I, P_{true}))\vee$$
$$(true(I_c, not(C))\wedge exec(I, P_{false})))\;).$$

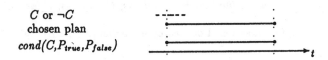

C or $\neg C$
chosen plan
$cond(C, P_{true}, P_{false})$

Figure 3: Conditional statement in time.

It is possible to extend this to a *case* statement.

Parallelism noted *par(B)*, to specify that several sub-plans have to be executed "at the same time". It is nevertheless not necessary to impose identical execution intervals, as Hultman e.a. do [9], as the different branches can have different execution durations. Our parallel construct is interpreted as a **cobegin-coend** of the branches constituted by the sub-plans in B. This means all branches start together and the parallel construct is executed until the last branch ends. In terms of intervals, it means that there exists one branch executing on the global interval, and all are executed on intervals starting or equal to this interval (see fig. 4):

Definition 5 :

$$exec(I, par(B)) \Longleftrightarrow (\exists b_1 \in B) \quad (\;exec\;(I, b_1)\;)$$
$$\wedge \; (\forall b_2 \in B) \quad (\exists I')(exec(I', b_2) \wedge \; I' \; (s \; =) \; I).$$

Abstraction.

This is needed in order to be able to structure the plans hierarchically.

Abstracting sub-plans The reuse of a plan P can be done by giving a name, defining it to be a compound action A, which is noted: *c-action(A, P)*, and defined by:

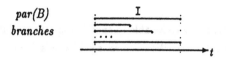

Figure 4: Parallelism in time.

Definition 6 :

exec(I, A) $\iff$ c-action(A, P) $\wedge$ exec(I, P)

Decomposing actions In the same way, complex actions like a shown in fig. 5 can be decomposed into primitive ones, like for example: *c-action(a , seq([a_1, a_2]))* with:

action(a_1, d_1, [ ], [p_1, p_2], [not(p_2), p_3]), and a_2: *action(a_2, d_2, [p_1, p_2], [p_3], [p_2]).*

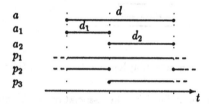

Figure 5: A compound action in time : *action-c(a,seq([a_1,a_2]))*.

Definition of derived control structures Another use of compound actions is to construct other control primitives from the basic ones, such as a form of iteration:

c-action(while(C, body),
            cond(C, seq([body,
                            while(C, body)]),
                nothing   ))

Other primitives can be defined, namely those defining the relation between two sub-plans for each of Allen's thirteen relations [10].

5   Reaction to the environment

The control primitives seen up to now are defined independently from the environment, only in terms of their components. In order to take into account a richer interaction with the evolution of this environment, another kind of control primitives has to be introduced, characterized as being reactive. From the point of view of their temporal definition, it means that the definition of the execution interval will be given in relation with the truth intervals of facts describing the environment.

Reaction at action level.

At the action level, it is interesting to be able to specify that the execution interval of an action is determined by "external" constraints. We will first see how this can be done in the frame of the global plan.

For example, it can be determined by the execution of a plan in parallel (see fig 6), as in the case of the structure "*as-long-as*": *a-l-a(P,A)* such that:

Definition 7 :

$$exec(I, a\text{-}l\text{-}a(P,A)) \iff exec(I,P) \land exec(I,A)$$

which can be extended to sets of actions. The execution interval of the undefined duration action A is specified to be that of the plan P.

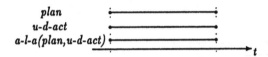

Figure 6: Reaction at action level: *a-l-a(P,A)* in time.

A reactive control structure can be defined by the association of the execution interval of an undefined duration action A to the truth interval of a condition C, by noting: *while-c(C,A)* with the definition:

Definition 8 :

$$
\begin{aligned}
exec(I, while\text{-}c(C,A)) \iff \\
(\exists I_c, I_{nc})(\quad & true(I_c, C) \land I\ (f\ =)\ I_c \\
\land\ & true(I_{nc}, not(C)) \land I\ m\ I_{nc} \\
\land\ & exec(I, A)\ ) \\
\lor\ (\exists I_{nc})(\quad & true(I_{nc}, not(C)) \land I\ in\ I_{nc} \\
\land\ & lasts(I, 0)\ )
\end{aligned}
$$

In the disjunction, the first part is illustrated in fig. 7: the execution interval I finishes or equals the truth interval of C: I_c, and meets the truth interval of $not(C)$. The second part of the disjunction represents the case where *while-c(C, A)* is executed when C is not verified: in this case, A is not executed, and the construct terminates instantly.

Another comparable structure is: *until-c(C,A)*.

Reaction at plan-level: the rules.

Another form of reactivity is to specify that, in reaction to the satisfaction of a condition, a plan should be executed; i.e. a *rule* states that the reaction plan is executed *as soon as* or *when* the condition is true.

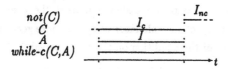

Figure 7: Reaction at action level: *while-c(C,A)* in time.

Simple rules The specification of the execution of a plan R in reaction to a condition C is noted: *when(C,R)*. We want the reaction to happen as soon as the condition is satisfied on a truth interval I_C. If I_C is not on the beginning of the interval I (see fig. 8), i.e. if I_C $(d\ f\ oi)$ I, then its negation is on an interval I_{nc} such that I_{nc} $(o\ s)$ I. In order to avoid that C be satisfied on an interval *in* I and *before* I_C without a reaction firing, it must be specified that: I_{nc} m I_C. This situation is temporally described by:

$$(\exists I_C)(\quad I_C\ (d\ f\ oi)\ I \wedge true(I_C,C)$$
$$\wedge\quad (\exists I_{nc})\quad (I_{nc}\ (o\ s)\ I \wedge I_{nc}\ m\ I_C \wedge true(I_{nc},non(C))\ )$$
$$\wedge\quad (\exists I_R)\quad (I_R\ (s\ si\ =)\ I_C \wedge I_R\ f\ I \wedge exec(I_R,R)\ )\ )$$

One can notice that from I_{nc} $(o\ s)$ $I \wedge I_{nc}$ m I_C, it can be deduced that I_C $(d\ f\ oi)$ I, by transitivity; the formulation is thus redundant, but we hope it advantages its clarity.

In another possible execution, the execution interval I of the rule is that of the reaction plan R: this corresponds to the case where condition C is satisfied on the beginning of the rule, i.e. on I_C such that I_C $(o\ s\ fi\ di\ si\ =)\ I$. This is temporally described by:

$$(\exists I_C)(\quad I_C\ (o\ s\ fi\ di\ si\ =)\ I \wedge true(I_C,C) \wedge exec(I,R)\ )$$

Finally, if the condition is not satisfied at all on I, the reaction plan is not executed:

$$(\exists I_C)(\ I\,inI_C \wedge true(I_C,non(C))\ )$$

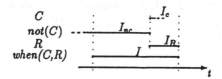

Figure 8: Reaction at plan level: a rule in time.

The *when* primitive is thus defined by:

Definition 9 :
$$exec(I,when(C,R)) \Longleftrightarrow$$
$$(\exists I_c)(\quad (\ I_c\ (o\ s\ fi\ di\ si\ =)\ I \wedge true(I_c,C) \wedge exec(I,R)\ )$$
$$\vee\ (\ I_c\ (d\ f\ oi)\ I \wedge true(I_c,C)$$
$$\wedge (\exists I_{nc})(I_{nc}\ (o\ s)\ I \wedge I_{nc}\ m\ I_c \wedge true(I_{nc},not(C))\ )$$
$$\wedge (\exists I_R)(I_R\ (s\ si\ =)\ I_c \wedge I_R\ f\ I \wedge exec(I_R,R)\ )\ )$$
$$\vee\ (\ I\ in\ I_c \wedge true(I_c,not(C))\ )\ )$$

where the three sub-formulas of the disjunction treat the cases of the satisfaction of the condition on the beginning of the rule interval I, of a more general disposition illustrated by fig. 8, or of the absence of the condition on the rule interval.

The behaviour of the rule can be defined in other ways: the reaction plan can be specified to be executed each time the condition is verified: $whenever(C,R)$. A possible interpretation is that of "sequential" reactions, i.e. waiting the end of the execution of R before reacting to a possible other satisfaction of C [10].

Using the rules.

These reactive structures have the characteristic of giving way to executions where the interval is not fully determined by the definitions. When considering their use in the frame of a control structure, they can be related to the undefined duration actions seen earlier, though their temporal disposition is less simple, because we do not want the reaction plan to be interrupted, when there is a reaction.

Association to a plan As in definition 7, associating a rule D to the parallel execution of a plan P is a way to determine its interval. This is noted: $assoc(P, D)$.

Its intuitive interpretation is that, during the execution of a sub-plan P, the satisfaction of condition C will cause the execution of R; once the plan is terminated, the rule will cease to be executed.

In an execution where the rule D is executed on the interval I_D terminating before the interval I_P of plan P, the primitive $assoc(P,D)$ is executed on I such that $(I = I_P \wedge I_D (s =) I)$. Another possible execution is that where P is executed on I_P terminating before I_D. In this case, the $assoc$ primitive has its interval I terminated by the rule's one, so that R is not interrupted: $(I = I_D \wedge I_P (s =) I)$. A third execution is the one where C is never satisfied on the execution interval of P, which determines the interval of $assoc$, as well as that of the associated rule D: $when(C,R)$: $(I_P = I \wedge I_D = I)$.

Thus the definition:

Definition 10 :
$$exec(I, assoc(P, D)) \Longleftrightarrow (\exists I_P, I_D)(\quad exec(I_P, P) \wedge exec(I_D, D) \wedge$$
$$(\ (I = I_P \wedge I_D \ s \ I)$$
$$\vee (I = I_D \ \wedge I_P \ s \ I)$$
$$\vee (I = I_P \ \wedge I_D = I)\ )\ )$$

The association is extendable to repetitive rules and to sets of simple or repetitive rules.

Association to a condition Another way of using a rule is to associate its execution interval with the truth interval of a given condition in the environment, for example while this condition is true: $while\text{-}c\text{-}r(C, D)$.

Its interpretation is that the rule D is executed as long as the condition C is true in the environment; i.e. the rule D is deactivated when C is not satisfied any more in the environment.

As for the association to a plan, we distinguish three cases following the execution of the rule D:

- either it is executed on an interval I_D such that I_D terminates before I_C, the reaction having been executed: then *while-c-r(C, D)* is executed on I such that their relations are: $(I \ (f \ =) \ I_C \ \wedge \ I_D \ (s \ =) \ I)$.

- either it is I_C that terminates before I_D, in the case where the reaction plan is executed on an interval overlapping I_{nc}. Then, I is determined by: $(I \ = \ I_D \ \wedge \ I_C \ (o \ s \ =) \ I)$.

- otherwise, if C is not satisfied on I, then the rule is not executed at all.

It is thus defined by:

Definition 11 :
$$exec(I, \text{ while-c-r}(C,D)) \Longleftrightarrow (\exists I_C, I_{nc}, I_D)(\quad true(I_C, C) \wedge \ true(I_{nc}, not(C)) \wedge I_C \ m \ I_{nc}$$
$$\wedge \ exec(I_D, D) \wedge$$
$$(\ (I \ (f \ =) \ I_C \ \wedge \ I_D \ (s \ =) \ I)$$
$$\vee (I \ = \ I_D \ \wedge \ I_C \ (o \ s \ =) \ I) \ ) \ )$$
$$\vee (\exists I_{nc})(\quad true(I_{nc}, non(C)) \wedge I \ in I_{nc} \wedge \ lasts(I, 0) \ )$$

As before, it is extendable to repetitive rules, and to sets of simple or repetitive rules.

6 Examples of application

The planning language was used in a simulation application that we are going to illustrate only briefly: we do not have enough space here to give all the definitions of actions and the complete model of the world but more complete descriptions are made elsewhere [10, 11].

The simulator implements a part of the model, in that it takes as input the plans written using some of the previously described control structures, and, given an initial situation, it gives as output a temporal database containing temporal facts (i.e. facts associated to a time interval) for the actions and the properties of the world. In this particular application, the intervals for negated post-conditions are in fact "clipped" in order to be terminated by the corresponding action's interval.

6.1 A space telerobotics example

It is inspired by studies realized at MATRA-ESPACE [2] for the European space station COLUMBUS.

The environment On this station, there is a bi-arm manipulation system, with *arm1* and *arm2*, both *available* in the initial situation, *arm1* being in the rest position *restpos1*, and *arm2* in the rest position *restpos2*. A *tool* is stocked at position *toolbox*, where it is *free*. A removable *ORU* (Orbital Replaceable Unit) is at position *posORU*, and *fixed* on a *support*.

The situation corresponds to the following set of properties, each associated with an interval into a temporal fact: *available(arm1), available(arm2), position(arm1, restpos1), position(arm2, restpos2), free(tool), position(tool, toolbox), position(ORU, posORU), fixedon(ORU, support)*.

The actions In the considered environment example, we define the action of 1 *mn* duration for an *arm*, to *ungrasp* an *object*:

$$action(\quad ungrasp(Arm,Obj),\ 1\ mn,$$
$$[held(Obj,Arm)]\ ,$$
$$[held(Obj,Arm)]\ ,$$
$$[not(held(Obj,Arm)),\ available(Arm)]\ ).$$

This action has as precondition and condition that the *object* must be *held* by the *arm*, and as effects that the object is not held anymore by the arm, and that the arm becomes *available*.

An action with reciprocal effects is to *grasp* an object. It is decomposed into two stages, in order to specify that the *arm* ceases to be *available* from the start of the action, and that the *object* is *held* only at the end. It is defined by:

$$c\text{-}action(\ grasp(Arm,Obj),\ seq([\ grasp1(Arm,Obj)\ ,\ grasp2(Arm,Obj)\ ])\ )$$

with:

$$action(\quad grasp1(Arm,Obj),\ 0,$$
$$[\ ]\ ,$$
$$[available(Arm),\ position(Obj,Pos),\ position(Arm,Pos)\ ]\ ,$$
$$[not(available(Arm))]\ )$$

for which the conditions are that the arm and the object be at the same position, and that the arm be available, and for which the effect is that the arm is not available anymore.

At the end of this first action, the *object* is not yet *held*; this is where the second part of the composed action begins:

$$action(\quad grasp2(Arm,Obj),\ 1\ mn,$$
$$[\ ]\ ,$$
$$[position(Obj,Pos),position(Arm,Pos)]\ ,$$
$$[held(Obj,Arm)]\ )$$

This is a particular example of composed action such as illustrated in fig. 5.

A useful undefined duration action is for an *arm* to *hold* an *object*: it is an action meant to maintain a condition, since it has no effect as such, but must ensure the prehension of the *object* by the *arm*.

$$ud\text{-}action(\quad hold(Arm,Obj),$$
$$[\ ],$$
$$[held(Obj,Arm)],$$
$$[\ ]\ ).$$

The other actions used in the next plan example are defined this way, but we can not describe them all here.

A plan   One of the missions of the modelled bi-arm manipulation system is to manipulate *ORUs* (Orbital Replaceable Units): in the simplified version presented here, the plan of *detaching* an *ORU* from its *support* can be described as follows: while an *arm1* moves to a *toolbox* to fetch a *tool*, the other one *arm2* goes to *grasp* the *ORU*. Then, the *arm2* holds the *ORU*, *as-long-as* the *arm1* does the following: *insert* the tool in the *ORU*, *actuate* it, bring it back to the tool box, come back and grasp the *ORU*, that is then held by the two arms. This illustrates in particular the use of undefined duration actions, in the framework of the *as-long-as* control structure: it represents a particular synchronisation scheme between the branches at the execution, that the real-system controller will have to manage.

The corresponding plan is:

$$
\begin{aligned}
seq([\quad par([\quad &seq([\quad moveto(arm1,toolbox),\\
&\qquad\qquad grasp(arm1,tool),\\
&\qquad\qquad moveto(arm1,ORU)]),\\
&seq([\quad moveto(arm2,ORU),\\
&\qquad\qquad grasp(arm2,ORU)])\\
]),\\
a\text{-}l\text{-}a(\quad &seq([\quad insert(arm1,tool,ORU),\\
&\qquad\qquad actuate(arm1,tool,ORU),\\
&\qquad\qquad moveto(arm1,toolbox),\\
&\qquad\qquad ungrasp(arm1,tool),\\
&\qquad\qquad moveto(arm1,ORU),\\
&\qquad\qquad grasp(arm1,ORU)]),\\
&hold(arm2,ORU))\\
])
\end{aligned}
$$

Given such a plan, and a definition of each of the primitive or composed actions used in it, it is then possible to describe its effects on its environment, modelled by temporal facts. Graphical outputs in the form of chronograms are produced for fully specified quantitative dates and durations [10, 11].

6.2   An example of reactive control structure

The simulator does not treat the reactive control structures. However, their definition is used in another application, where the language is used as a programming language for plans of robot-tasks, to be executed by a particular robotic architecture, using a high-level real-time reactive language [4].

An example of the use of reaction (suggested by one of the referees for this paper) concerns the process of moving an arm to a toolbox, taking into account that the robot accepts the commands: *start-moving-direction(X)* and *stop-moving*, and a property *be-at(arm,X)*, X denoting the position.

A movement action can be seen as a compound action like *grasp* (see above), with a first action consisting in starting from the previous position, and a second action consisting in actually doing the move, with, as effect, that the destination position is reached [10]. Here however, we take

The actions involved here are:

action(start-moving-direction(X), ε, [halted], [ ], [moving-to(arm,X), not(halted)]) and:

action(stop-moving, ε, [moving-to(arm,X)], [ ], [halted, not(moving-to(arm,X))]).

The durations are specified to be ε: the actions only consist in emitting some message to the robot, and their durations are not significant here.

A plan representing the process, defined as a compound action, is as follows:

$$c\text{-}action(\quad move\text{-}to(X),$$
$$seq(\ start\text{-}moving\text{-}direction(X),$$
$$when(\ be\text{-}at(arm,X),\ stop\text{-}moving)\ )\ )$$

7 Conclusion

A temporal model for an imperative language for structured plans.

We propose a model of plans of actions provided with an imperative control structure. They are defined on the basis of a unified temporal formalism inspired by Allen's interval-based logic, allowing to describe as well the environning world and its evolution as the temporal arrangement of the plans. Control primitives are described, first independently from the environment, in that they have a temporal disposition depending only on the components they frame. Then, other primitives are defined in reaction to the environment, taking into account truth intervals of properties in the world.

In relation with execution monitoring [11], the model provides a basis for a better defined task-level robot programming language. This model was applied to space telerobotics missions concerning a bi-arm robot: this experiment provided a testbed for an early version of the model, and inspired some of its extensions.

Extensions.

Other extensions and future work concern the present limitations of the model:

- the model itself: a more complete study of the elements of the model, the way they can be combined together, and their properties is necessary to determine their significance, their useability, and to extend and/or modify them accordingly.

- its application to task-level robot programming, in the framework of a robot controller architecture developed at INRIA–Sophia Antipolis, is the occasion of confronting it to particular execution architectures, and testing its applicability [4]. This is done in relation with a model of robot tasks using particular concepts of the synchronous reactive systems and the high-level real-time language ESTEREL [3] and its specific temporal semantics.

- the links of the model to planning as a generation process can be explored, on the base of the common formalism of actions. In particular, it would be interesting to relate it to formal approaches to planning, and temporal plan generation [8].

References

[1] J.F. Allen. Towards a general theory of action and time. *Artificial Intelligence*, 23:123–154, 1984.

[2] G. André, G. Berger, A. Elfving. The Bi-Arm Servicer, a multi-mission concept and a technological model for space robotics. In *Proceedings of the 2nd European In-Orbit Operations Technology Symposium*, Toulouse, France, September 1989, ESA SP-297 (December 1989).

[3] G. Berry. *Real-time programming: special purpose or general purpose languages*. In *Proceedings of the IFIP World Computer Congress*, San Francisco, 1989 (Invited talk).

[4] E. Coste-Manière, B. Espiau, E. Rutten. *Task-level robot programming combining object-oriented design and synchronous approach: a tentative study*. Research Report INRIA, to appear, June 1991.

[5] DARPA Santa Cruz Workshop on Planning, W. Swartout *ed.*, *AI Magazine*, 9(2):115–131, Summer 1988.

[6] M. Ghallab, R. Alami, R. Chatila. *Dealing with time in planning and execution monitoring*. In R. Bolles ed. *Robotics Research 4*. MIT Press, 1988.

[7] J. Hendler, A. Tate, M. Drummond. AI Planning: Systems and Techniques. *AI Magazine*, 11(2):61–77, Summer 1990.

[8] J. Hertzberg, A. Hortz. Towards a theory of conflict detection and resolution in nonlinear plans. In *Proceedings of the IJCAI '89*, pages 937–942, Detroit, Michigan, August 1989.

[9] J. Hultman, A. Nyberg, M. Svensson. *A software architecture for autonomous robots*. Technical report n° LAIC-IDA-89-TR1, Department of Computer and Information Science, University of Linköping, Sweden, 1989.

[10] E. Rutten. *Représentation en logique temporelle de plans d'actions dotés d'une structure de contrôle impérative. Application à l'assistance à l'opérateur en téléopération*. Thèse de Doctorat de l'Université de Rennes I, 13 Juillet 1990. (in French).

[11] E. Rutten, J.C. Paoletti, G. André, L. Marcé. A task-level language for operator assistance in teleoperation. In *Proceedings of the International Conference on Human Machine Interaction and Artificial Intelligence in Aeronautics and Space*, Toulouse, Septembre 1990.

[12] E. Sandewall, R. Rönnquist. A representation of action structures. In *Proceedings of the AAAI '86*, pages 89–97, Philadelphia, August 1986.

[13] S. Vere. Planning in time: windows and durations for activities and goals. *IEEE Pattern Analysis and Machine Intelligence*, PAMI 3:246–267, May 1983.

[14] R. Voltz. Report of the robot programming languages working group. NATO Workshop on Robot Programming Languages. *IEEE Journal of Robotics and Automation*, RA 4(1):86–90, February 1988.

Maximal Intervals: An Approach to Temporal Reasoning[*]

Cristina Ribeiro[†] and António Porto
Departamento de Informática
Universidade Nova de Lisboa
2825 Monte da Caparica Portugal
e-mail:{mcr,ap}@fct.unl.pt

Abstract

Temporal reasoning is recognized as a key problem in many AI areas, namely knowledge bases, natural language processing and planning. The ability to deal with partial knowledge is particularly important in a temporal domain. We describe a temporal language that accounts for incompletely specified temporal information about propositions. The language is semantically based on the notion of *maximal interval*, the denotation of a proposition being a set of maximal intervals where it holds. The main differences between classical formalisms such as those by Allen, McDermott, Shoham and Kowalski and our approach are briefly discussed. In a partial KB, abduction on the temporal order is generally needed to answer a query, and the answer is then conditional on the abduced facts. To comply with the intended semantics, an implicit form of temporal consistency has to be enforced, and this presents the main challenge to the design of the inference mechanism. We present here the syntax and declarative semantics of a propositional version of the language of maximal intervals and a first discussion of the problems in designing an inference system adequate to work with this temporal framework.

Keywords: temporal reasoning, knowledge representation, deductive databases.

1 Introduction

Temporal reasoning is recognized as a fundamental part of a system aimed at the formal treatment of commonsense knowledge. Temporality is an outstanding feature when modelling many aspects of the physical world, and its various implications have been focused upon in such application areas as knowledge bases, natural language processing and planning. The ability to deal with partial knowledge is particularly important in a temporal

---

[*]This research was supported by Portuguese JNICT project PEROLA.
[†]Owns a scholarship from INIC.

domain. The scope of our work is the representation and inference with incomplete temporal knowledge [PR90a]. We will be using a knowledge base as the example application, as the kind of inference required to answer temporal queries to a KB illustrates the issues we want to address.

The approaches that have been taken so far consider as basic entities some form of temporally qualified propositions, using either periods or instants as the basic structure for time. The representation of a temporal fact is then the association of a proposition with a temporal extent. The problem of relating the validity of a proposition at one time with its validity at some other time posed many questions as to the temporal categorization of propositions.

We propose a scheme based on the idea of characterizing each proposition in terms of the set of disjoint maximal time intervals in which it holds. Temporal statements about the world are then viewed as supplying partial information about the elements of those sets.

An important aspect is the separation between a language for storing the temporal information about propositions and a language for making arbitrary temporal statements. We call the first the language of maximal intervals, **MI** for short, and the second the external language. These are intended for use in a knowledge based system, where they correspond respectively to the KB language and an interface language.

This paper presents a brief justification for the difference in perspective between some classical approaches to temporal reasoning and our own. The separation of the temporal language in two levels is motivated in this context. The syntax and declarative semantics of **MI** are introduced, and a first approach to an inference system described.

2 Background

Existing approaches to temporal reasoning in AI comprise the schemes where events are basic entities, such as the situation calculus [MH81] and the event calculus [KS86] and those that take time as the primitive notion and therefore consider intervals or points as the entities to which knowledge is to be referred. This second group includes [All84] [McD82] [Sho87].

In every approach to knowledge representation where time is focused upon, there is usually some discussion about the role of events or actions. Intuitively, we tend to see as dissimilar in nature the validity of a property for a stretch of time and the occurrence of an event over a time period, and this suggests representing them by different constructs in a temporal language. This is the motivation behind the proposals where both the time line and the event concepts are required for representing time-related knowledge, like those originated in [All84] [McD82].

When time is taken to be primitive, the next choice is between points and periods as basic temporal entities. Only one of these is required for a minimal framework, so we must choose one as basic and derive the other [vB83]. Allen's theory is based on time intervals, McDermott and Shoham take points as basic.

When an apriori distinction is made between what we shall call "properties" and "events" the separation is usually based on the characteristic of "temporal homogeneity". For a proposition *Prop* holding during interval I, it can be stated as

$$holds(I, Prop) \Leftrightarrow \forall_{I'} \, I' \subseteq I \Rightarrow holds(I', Prop)$$

The general tendency is to axiomatize properties as homogeneous and events otherwise.

The situation calculus [MH81] introduced the idea of considering time implicit in the ordering of events. A situation is a static picture of the world, and events trigger the evolution from one situation to the next. Kowalski's event calculus was introduced as an upgrade to the situation claculus, in which concurrent events are handled. It was not intended as a temporal language, but rather as a way of dealing with temporal matters in the context of Horn Clause Logic with Negation by Failure. It also deals with intervals, but only those limited by events.

Allen considers three types of basic propositions: properties, events and processes. Predicates $HOLDS$, $OCCUR$ and $OCCURRING$ apply to these three categories respectively, associating an interval with each proposition. Properties obey an axiom imposing homogeneity. For events the minimum interval for their occurrence is considered, and the converse of homogeneity holds: if event e occurs over interval I, it does not occur over any of its subintervals. For processes a more vague temporal behaviour is stated, namely that a process occurring in an interval must be occurring at some of its subintervals.

McDermott considers properties and events, a property holding over a collection of time points and an event holding over a collection of pairs of time points. Their temporal behaviour is similar to the corresponding objects in Allen's theory.

In Shoham's approach [Sho87] all propositions are qualified with an interval of validity, regardless of their nature, and nothing is a priori assumed about the validity of a proposition in subintervals of those where it is known to be valid. He then suggests numerous criteria for classifying propositions according to their temporal behaviour, with varying degree of discrimination and granularity. It is argued that classifications such as the one based on homogeneity are not the only possibility, and so it is better to separate the classification mechanism and customize it for every application.

3 A logic of temporal information

We propose to address the issue of temporal reasoning by first trying to establish what kind of temporal information to deal with.

Our first issue is a precise definition of what an atomic proposition is, and is concerned with the level at which time is to be considered in the knowledge base. Many discussions about the classification of temporal statements stem from the consideration of arbitrary propositions as basic objects in a temporal logic. We agree with Shoham's argument on the classification of propositions: If arbitrary statements about the world are to be taken as atomic propositions, then it is better not to assume an a priori classification of them in a temporal language, and rather do it as a second step, tailoring the classification to the application. Our point of view is that prior to the discussion of how to classify propositions, we must define what we intend to have as the atomic objects to which temporal reasoning is to be applied. Allen considers the proposition "I am walking from home to the store" as a process and "I walked from home to the store" as an event. What distinguishes these two propositions are strictly temporal matters: the second is in the past and therefore transmits the sense of accomplishment whereas the first is referred to the present moment. If two propositions differing only in temporal aspects are viewed as different basic objects by a temporal language, then it is likely that classifications in this language get arbitrarily complex.

We chose to start from basic propositions that have the common property of having no embedded temporal references. Corresponding to the two sentences above, we would have a basic proposition of the form "I walk from home to the store". It looks natural that a language whose objective is to associate a temporal incidence to propositions should operate on non-temporal propositions. We stress this fact because it is not the case with the temporal formalisms referred to earlier. The interesting point is that when the temporal references are factored out, the distinction between properties and events, common to several of the proposed formalisms, is not clear cut any more. The proposition "running for 20 minutes" is considered of type event (or gestalt in Shoham's classification) because if it holds for an interval I it will not hold for any of its subintervals. But this characteristic is induced by the temporal reference within, and is no characteristic of "running". In the same sense, the event in the example above, interpreted as "I walked (exactly) from home (exactly) to the store" has a temporal reference in that the precise duration of the move is implicit. If a less strict interpretation is assumed, as it usually is the case, we can say that "walk from home to the store" may be considered valid in subintervals of an interval where it is known to hold.

Having defined what constitutes an atomic proposition P we now try to view the temporal information about P in the most compact form. This is why we introduce the definition of *maximal intervals* for a proposition.

Definition 1 *An interval I is maximal for P if P holds over I and there is no interval containing I where P also holds.*

We are resorting to the commonsense notion of a proposition holding in an interval in order to motivate the concept of maximal intervals in an informal way. But our temporal scheme is built the other way round, by starting with intervals specified by their end points and looking at propositions as sets of such intervals.

It is apparent that this definition of interval is restricted, and is not suited for the general use of intervals in natural language, but we claim that it will be useful as a basic level in a temporal reasoning system.

Maximality of intervals is a characteristic that permits the ontological shift from "intervals of validity for a proposition" to "temporal information for a proposition". If a KB were allowed to contain, along with a clause associating proposition P with interval I, a multitude of other clauses associating P with various subintervals of I, on the grounds that they are also valid, inference would become both inefficient and hardly meaningful. When searching for an interval of validity for a given proposition, we might sometimes get too many intervals and sometimes fewer than would be possible. As our interest is as much in effective inferencing as in knowledge representation, maximal intervals offer a balance between expressive power and adequacy for inference.

An apparent drawback of this solution is that we rarely have information about maximal intervals for the propositions we store in a KB. This is why we must have a good account of incomplete information about them. We establish time instants as the basic temporal entities, and create special objects to stand for the end points of intervals, whenever they are not fixed. Allowing ordering constraints among all end points, we have the expressive power for the essential knowledge about the temporal ordering of intervals. We can store partial information relating arbitrary periods of time to propositions as constraints on the end points of maximal intervals of the propositions.

Essential to our approach is the decoupling of **MI** from the user interface language. The distinctions among categories of propositions belong to the user interface language. User statements are transformed into KB statements where only maximal intervals may appear. We are thus able to have no redundant temporal information in the KB. Suppose a fact

$$for(1, \alpha, P)$$

is in the KB stating that $\langle 1, \alpha \rangle$ is a maximal interval for P. If new information about P holding during $\langle 1, 2 \rangle$ is acquired, we must analyse the existing facts before turning this into a maximal interval in the KB. As we talk about arbitrary intervals in the interface language, this fact means there exists a maximal interval of P for which $\langle 1, 2 \rangle$ is a subinterval. This can be expressed as

$$for(\beta, \gamma, P), \beta \prec 1, \gamma \succ 2$$

and can be launched as a goal. We want as solution (the update) the constraint $\alpha \succ 2$, which guarantees that one maximal interval already in the KB contains the one mentioned in the new fact.

We view some problems that have been tied to classification of propositions according to temporal behaviour as having less to do with temporal issues than with the modelling of the world. It is often argued, for instance, that propositions such as "Maria is writing" are not homogeneous, because if someone is writing for one hour there is no guarantee that she is writing every minute during that hour. The problem with this kind of argument is that the two references to 'write' above do not have the same meaning. The meaning of the second 'write' corresponds to a fine-grained analysis of the write process, but the first one refers to writing as a more uniform and global activity, and occasional stops are not seen as interrupting it. We have to accept that these two semantic accounts for 'write' are legitimate and it is a problem of natural language interpretation to find out which one is meant in a given occurrence of the word. Both can be captured by sets of maximal intervals, and these may even be related to show their semantic affinities. Maximal intervals may be seen as a "homogeneous residue" to such semantic analysis as the one made above. When a precise semantics is given to complex entities that require temporal characterization we can get down to elementary temporal information in terms of maximal intervals.

Allen [All84] presented a theory of action based on his temporal logic, where such notions as conditions for actions, causality and intention are regarded. Modelling these requires a solid theory of time, so that the complex temporal mechanisms involved may be decomposed into simpler low-level operations. Work on the modelling of action conditions and granularity of knowledge for a knowledge base application [PR90b] led us to conclude that more effort in a basic temporal language is required before attempting such tasks.

4 The temporal ontology

Our ontology is based on points. We take points in time as the basic entity, and build intervals as pairs of points. Intervals that begin and end in the same point are valid. A basic proposition is represented by a set of maximal intervals.

There is a total order on points, with greatest and least elements. Partial orders on time are sometimes proposed apparently to account for the incompleteness of the temporal references. We chose a total order to comply with the commonsense notion of time, and use ordering constraints on time points to reflect the incompleteness of temporal information.

Several interval-based temporal reasoning systems have been proposed and opinions diverge as to the use of intervals or points as the basic objects. Allen [All83] presented an algebra of intervals where time points are dispensed with. The temporal relation of two time intervals is expressed as a disjunction of the thirteen basic relations that can hold between them, such as *before, meets* or *overlaps*. A graph representation for these relations is established where the arc between two nodes is labelled with the relation between the corresponding intervals. His interval algebra is used to compute the relation between any pair of intervals, in order to have consistency in the graph. Allen's consistency algorithm tests consistency up to three nodes, and improvements to five nodes were developped [vB89]. In [VK86] it has been shown that testing for general consistency is NP-hard, and a tractable point algebra was presented as an alternative. A subset of the interval algebra translates directly into the point algebra. It is important to note that not all possible assertions about the relation of intervals are expressible in the interval algebra, where all 2^{13} assertions for the temporal ordering of *two* intervals are possible. Allen argues that assertions such as

$$(A \, before \lor meets \, B) \, or \, C \, after \, B$$

are not usual in common language and are the kind used only in temporal puzzles. But the same might be said about many of the disjunctive relations for two intervals. We want to have a temporal reasoning system operating on a large number of intervals, and therefore must have a computationally effective way of dealing with consistency. Most interval relations used in natural language are more naturally expressed as point relations. Adopting point algebra, we have tractable consistency tests at the cost of expressive power in the basic language. We exclude explicit disjunctive knowledge of the form $A \, before \lor after \, B$ but are able to represent the implicit disjunctions that arise from incomplete knowledge.

There are no structures in our language corresponding to the sets of disjoint intervals. This contrasts with the proposal in [Lad86], where these sets, called non-convex intervals, are the basic temporal entities. In *MI* the sets of disjoint intervals are present only in the semantic analysis.

5   The *MI* language

KB statements are formulas, written as logical implications. Its form is similar to Horn clauses, the difference being in the implicit quantifications for the temporal variables. We are assuming that variables in the body are universally quantified, but those appearing only in the head have existential quantification. What becomes excluded here is the implication between a conjunction of facts and a new fact exhibiting no temporal dependency towards its premises. We consider such rules meaningless in a temporal KB.

The facts on a KB represent acquired information about the world. The temporal anchoring of facts may be incompletely specified, but this partial information always corresponds to ordering constraints on the end points of maximal intervals for those facts. In the language special terms are used as the equivalent of existentially quantified variables to denote those time points. When we have the fact

$$for(1, \alpha, alive), \alpha \prec 20$$

what we know is that there exists an $\alpha \leq 20$ such that the interval $\langle 1, \alpha \rangle$ is a maximal interval for the proposition *alive*. The use of terms such as α correspond to the classical procedure of skolemizing existential variables.

MI supports only two relations: the total order on time points, $\prec$, used to express temporal constraints, and the relation *for*, between what we generally call *predications* and the (end points of) corresponding maximal intervals. All terms are interpreted over an infinite universe of ordered time points. KB statements are formulas, and temporal terms are split in three groups—constants, variables and mobiles. Variables correspond to universally quantified time points and mobiles to existentially quantified ones. This syntactic distinction will be crucial for the inference mechanism; mobiles are akin to terms built out of Skolem constants and functions, but we need to distinguish them from the other constants in use. We use mobiles to model time points for which some information exists (for example being the end point of the interval for a fact) but whose precise anchorage is yet unknown. Mobiles are global syntactic entities (much like constants) and may therefore be shared among several statements. Variables as usual are local to clauses. In the following we present the syntax and semantics of the propositional version of *MI*.

5.1   Syntax

We define:

$\mathcal{C}$: the set of constants

$\mathcal{M}$: the set of mobiles

$\mathcal{M}_f$: the set of mobile functions, each equiped with an arity greater than 0

$\mathcal{V}$: the set of variables

$\mathcal{P}$: the set of proposition symbols.

Mobile functions behave as function symbols in a classic language. Here they are restricted to play the role of Skolem functions.

The set of *atomic terms* is defined as $C \cup V \cup M$.

The set of *terms* is recursively defined asfollows:

- Every atomic term is a term

- If $m \in M_f$ is a mobile function with arity n and $T_1, \ldots T_n$ are terms, $m(T_1, \ldots T_n)$ is a term.

The *atomic formulas* are constraint formulas and predicative formulas.

A *constraint formula* has the form $t_1 \prec t_2$, where t_1 and t_2 are terms.

A *predicative formula* has the form $for(t_1, t_2, p)$ where t_1, t_2 are terms and $p \in P$.

A *clause* is

$$H \leftarrow B$$

where H, the "head", is an atomic formula and B, the "body", is a (possibly empty) conjunction of atomic formulas

$$B = b_1, \ldots, b_n \ (n \geq 0)$$

Whenever the head is a constraint formula the body is empty and the constraint always involves a mobile.

A *definite clause* is a clause with nonempty head. A *fact* is a definite clause with empty body. A *goal* is a clause with empty head. A KB is a set of definite clauses.

5.2 Semantics

Next we define interpretations and satisfiability.

An interpretation $\mathcal{I}$ is a 6-tuple $\langle \mathcal{T}, \leq, \mathcal{I}_C, \mathcal{I}_M, \mathcal{I}_{M_f}, \mathcal{I}_P \rangle$. $\mathcal{T}$ is the domain for the temporal entities, a set of time points. $\leq$ is a reflexive total order relation on $\mathcal{T}$. To this we associate the non-reflexive total order $<$, defined as follows:

$$\forall_{p_1, p_2 \in \mathcal{T}} \ (p_1 < p_2) \Leftrightarrow (p_1 \leq p_2) \wedge \neg(p_2 \leq p_1)$$

Over $\mathcal{T}$, the set of intervals is defined as

$$S = \{\langle t_1, t_2 \rangle : t_1, t_2 \in \mathcal{T}, t_1 \leq t_2\}$$

and dually for the end points (beginning and ending) of an interval

$$\forall_{i \in S} \ i = \langle t_1, t_2 \rangle \Rightarrow b(i) = t_1, \ e(i) = t_2$$

We build a set $\mathcal{D}$ whose elements are sets of intervals from S with the property that no two overlapping intervals belong in the same set. Formally

$$\mathcal{D} = \{s \in \wp(S) : \forall_{i_1, i_2 \in s} \ i_1 \neq i_2 \Rightarrow i_1 <> i_2\}$$

where $i_1 <> i_2$ is to be read as 'i_1 is disjoint from i_2' and may be defined as

$$\forall i_1, i_2 \in S \ i_1 <> i_2 \Leftrightarrow (e(i_1) < b(i_2)) \vee (e(i_2) < b(i_1))$$

$\mathcal{I}_C, \mathcal{I}_M, \mathcal{I}_{M_f}$ and $\mathcal{I}_P$ are total functions of the following kinds:

- $\mathcal{I}_C\colon \mathcal{C} \to \mathcal{T}$ associates a time point with each constant symbol

- $\mathcal{I}_M\colon \mathcal{M} \to \mathcal{T}$ associates a time point with each mobile constant

- $\mathcal{I}_{M_f}\colon$ is a function that maps each mobile function m of arity n to a function $\mathcal{T}^n \to \mathcal{T}$

- $\mathcal{I}_P\colon \mathcal{P} \to \mathcal{D}$ associates a set of disjoint intervals with each proposition symbol.

This last interpretation function leads to an implicit notion of consistency of intervals for the same predication. In fact, allowing overlapping intervals for the same predication would violate the intention that those intervals be maximal.

A *variable assignment* α is a function $\mathcal{V} \to \mathcal{T}$. For any given interpretation $\mathcal{I}$ and variable assignment α we define the denotations of arbitrary terms as follows

$$
\begin{array}{llll}
c \in \mathcal{C} & \Rightarrow & [\![c]\!]_{\mathcal{I}}^{\alpha} & = \mathcal{I}_C(c) \\
m \in \mathcal{M} & \Rightarrow & [\![m]\!]_{\mathcal{I}}^{\alpha} & = \mathcal{I}_M(m) \\
m \in \mathcal{M}_f & \Rightarrow & [\![m(T_1,\ldots T_n)]\!]_{\mathcal{I}}^{\alpha} & = \mathcal{I}_{M_f}(m)([\![T_1]\!]_{\mathcal{I}}^{\alpha},\ldots [\![T_n]\!]_{\mathcal{I}}^{\alpha}) \\
v \in \mathcal{V} & \Rightarrow & [\![v]\!]_{\mathcal{I}}^{\alpha} & = \alpha(v) \\
p \in \mathcal{P} & \Rightarrow & [\![p]\!]_{\mathcal{I}}^{\alpha} & = \mathcal{I}_P(p)
\end{array}
$$

Now we define $\mathcal{I} \models_{\alpha} p$, the satisfiability of a formula p wrt an interpretation $\mathcal{I}$ under a variable assignment α

$$
\begin{array}{lll}
\mathcal{I} \models_{\alpha} t_1 \prec t_2 & \text{iff} & [\![t_1]\!]_{\mathcal{I}}^{\alpha} \leq [\![t_2]\!]_{\mathcal{I}}^{\alpha} \\
\mathcal{I} \models_{\alpha} for(t_1,t_2,p) & \text{iff} & \langle [\![t_1]\!]_{\mathcal{I}}^{\alpha}, [\![t_2]\!]_{\mathcal{I}}^{\alpha} \rangle \in [\![p]\!]_{\mathcal{I}}^{\alpha} \\
\mathcal{I} \models_{\alpha} (p_1,p_2) & \text{iff} & \mathcal{I} \models_{\alpha} p_1 \text{ and } \mathcal{I} \models_{\alpha} p_2
\end{array}
$$

Satisfaction is defined only for clauses, as the only (implicitly) quantified formulas, in the usual way:

$\mathcal{I} \models H \leftarrow B$ iff for all variable assignments α, $\mathcal{I} \models_{\alpha} H$ whenever $\mathcal{I} \models_{\alpha} B$. As usual, a model for a KB is an interpretation satisfying all of its clauses.

6 Inference

Having described *MI* and the declarative semantics which give it the properties we consider essential for temporal reasoning, we now turn to the design of an inference system where such properties will correspond to built-in mechanisms. We shall not propose here an ultimate solution to the inference system, but present some of the problems that emerge when trying to establish its general scheme.

In the presence of a partial KB, we have to devise mechanisms that will produce informative answers to a query. The idea of an instance of a query as a strict logical consequence of the KB seems too limited, as few interesting conjunctions of facts are likely to be logical consequences of the KB. The kind of answers we consider are logical implications between a set of conditions and an instance of the query. Logical consequence still holds, from the KB to this implication. It has become common in nonmonotonic reasoning to refer to such conditions as abductions, and we shall also use this terminology.

The only relation we will "abduce" is the temporal order on time points, $\prec$. This corresponds to the generation of possible orderings among facts for which some temporal information exists. This mechanism of assuming extra information on the temporal order is also meaningful in terms of *MI* semantics. A KB with incomplete knowledge of the ordering of time points qualifying its predications admits multiple models. In each model, the total order on time points establishes either $\alpha \prec \beta$ or $\beta \prec \alpha$ for every pair of temporal tokens α and β. Whenever we assume $\alpha \prec \beta$ in the inference process, we are only choosing one possibility for the order relation concerning α and β, and therefore reducing the number of models that satisfy the query. This "abduction" on the ordering of instants is a natural mechanism in commonsense reasoning and provides for much of its richness.

6.1 Consistency

We define consistency of a KB expressed in *MI* as the non-existence of overlapping intervals for the same predication. A partial KB has several models and in the context of a derivation the KB is extended with the abductions made up to the moment. Applying the deduction theorem, the derivation of a goal G in KB K extended with the set of abductions A is equivalent to the derivation of the implication $A \Rightarrow G$ in K. The problem arises that along a derivation we want to be sure that at any time the KB plus the abductions has at least one model. For each mobile in the KB, there may be constraints that lead to an inconsistency. These constraints may not be abduced.

The consistency problem can be illustrated by the following paradigmatic example, with two facts for the same predication:

$for(1, \alpha, p).$ $1 \prec \alpha.$

$for(\beta, 3, p).$ $\beta \prec 3.$

The problem is that there are values for the mobiles for which no model exists, such as $\alpha = 4$, because of the restriction of non-overlapping intervals for the same predication. As mobiles are global entities in a KB (clauses for different predications may share the same mobile) maintaining consistency is a global task and will be the central problem in the inference.

In short, our consistency problem has two aspects: consistency of the point algebra that implements the interval relations and temporal consistency of predications. The first amounts to verifying the total order on the time points, the second requires that maximal intervals be non-overlapping. Comparing again our approach with other systems designed to reason with intervals, it is obvious that only the first problem is dealt with there, as the second is a consequence of our interpretation of propositions.

6.2 Approaches

Several approaches to inferencing with maximal intervals have been tried. The most obvious starting point is to use resolution on the KB regarded as a set of Horn clauses.

Unification must be specialized as it deals only with temporal variables and must account for constraints on their values and relative order. It is quite easy to get possible intervals for each predication in a goal, but the problem remains of assuring consistency of such intervals with the intended models for the KB. A solution is to launch a "consistency check", expressed as a goal of "non-contradiction". This goal generates all intervals for the same predication in order to prove that the given interval is temporally consistent with all those and thus constitutes a solution. The question posed by this consistency check is that all intervals for a predication have to be found each time we want to validate a single interval. Moreover, as mobiles are shared among predications, behaving as global entities to which constraints are applied, it is not enough to look at the intervals for a given predication in order to enforce temporal consistency. New consistency checks are required for those other propositions having end points changed by the abductions made.

The second approach is a step towards making this inference more efficient, and consists in turning the problem around: if we have to compute all intervals for a predication in order to enforce consistency, then we can just compute them all once and then select solutions from the set. Compared to the first approach this one avoids some unnecessary repetition of work, but as before all the burden of assuring consistency of the KB is put on the query evaluation process.

Still another way to look at inference is to consider that the KB must be kept consistent at each update, and the inference for a predication has only to test an "integrity formula" for the KB. At each update some of the work of the consistency checks is performed by deriving the formula. Building this integrity formula amounts to generating all KB facts bottom-up, producing the ordered sets of intervals for each predication (subject to multiple choices due to the partial knowledge about the temporal order) and then expressing the possible combinations of such sets in a logical form. The process of obtaining this integrity formula is hardly incremental, and we can easily see that it does not allow an efficient way to test consistency during a derivation. If we take the example in fig. 1, for instance, the consistency formula for a KB containing only those facts could be written as

$$(\alpha = 3 \wedge \beta = 1) \ \vee \ \alpha < \beta$$

where the disjunction accounts for the choice between two classes of models for the KB: those where there is a single maximal interval for p in $\langle 1, 3 \rangle$ and those where at least two intervals for p lay there. We can imagine a KB where clauses for other predications exist and suppose the consistency formula is the same. In the derivation of a goal, the consistency formula has to be tested each time an abduction is made. We assumed this formula is a static one, and so we are always testing the same formula. By using the static consistency formula no use would be made of the fact that the disjunctions in the formula are exclusive as they correspond to effective choices in the possible models of the KB (and consequently on the ordering of facts in the world). If one choice is made during a derivation, a comittment has to be taken towards it, in order to avoid unnecessary computation.

The above considerations lead us to conclude that an effective approach to inference with maximal intervals must include two aspects. The first is the compilation of static information in the KB into data structures where temporal consistency of intervals is easily tested. The second is a dynamic mechanism to modify these structures according to the constraints from the goal and the abductions made. This way a balance is established between tasks that can take place during update and those that must be performed in the derivation of an answer. Keeping a dynamic global structure for constraints, the comittment to the abductions made is implicit, and accounts for enforcing both maximality of intervals and consistence of the $\prec$ relation.

6.3 Some Considerations

When looking at all the problems we have stated one might wonder if complexity in inference is a consequence of adopting maximal intervals or if equivalent problems arise in the temporal formalisations proposed by Allen, McDermott, Shoham or Kowalski. The answer to this brings to light the difference in our approach. All these temporal formalisms are designed to talk about arbitrary intervals, associating them with propositions and reasoning about their temporal relationships. Both McDermott and Shoham interpret propositions as sets of time entities, and we have followed the same path. But their sets have no general characterization, and Shoham advocates this temporal classification should be made after the basic temporal framework has been laid. From the considerations made here, it is likely that this classification will account for considerable complexity in an inference system. From the point of view of Shoham's classification process, it is apparent that our sets of intervals are a particular case. Kowalski's event calculus, although presented as a formalism based on events, has a great concern with obtaining intervals for predicates. In that sense we can compare it to an interval calculus. As intervals are always limited by events, we can also view it as as calculus of maximal intervals. The beginning and end of an interval are associated to transitions of truth values of predicates. But in order to obtain temporal consistency of predicates in the event calculus one must write specific axioms for that purpose, and the execution of such axioms leads to the same kind of difficulties for the inference system.

7 Solving a goal in the KB

In *MI* we have a way of talking about single time intervals where propositions hold, but the notion of a set of maximal intervals is associated with each proposition. In natural language, information is not usually communicated via maximal intervals, but we can always transform non-maximal intervals into constraints on maximal intervals. We have thus considered two languages, *MI* as an internal language and an external language for dealing with arbitrary intervals. A query about an interval expressed in the external language is turned into a query about a maximal interval via the user interface.

The answer to a query posed to a KB expressed in the propositional language *MI* amounts to expressing an interval for each predication in the query. This interval belongs to the denotation of the predication in all models of the KB, if no abduction is performed. If a set of constraints is abduced, the interval belongs to the denotation of the proposition in all models of the KB plus the abductions.

8 An example

We now use the well known Yale Shooting Problem (YSP) [HM86] to illustrate the use of *MI*. This example has been devised to show the difficulties raised by the "frame problem". We address here only the temporal reasoning problems within the frame problem. It is generally understood that other issues concerning knowledge modelling are also involved [Sho87].

The YSP scenario has an initial state in which a person is alive and a gun unloaded. Then the gun is loaded. At some later time it is shot. We want to be able to derive intervals for "alive' and "loaded' that are consistent with the model of maximal intervals for the propositions. One formulation for the YSP in **MI** is as follows:

(1) $for(1, 1, load)$.

(2) $for(3, 3, shoot)$.

(3) $for(1, \alpha_3, alive)$. $\alpha_3 \succ 1$.

(4) $for(L, f_4(L), loaded) \leftarrow for(L, L, load)$. $f_4(L) \succ L$.

(5) $for(f_5(S), S, alive) \leftarrow for(S, S, shoot), for(A, B, loaded), A \prec S, S \prec B$. $f_5(S) \prec S$.

The first two clauses model the events of *load* and *shoot* by point-like intervals for the corresponding predications. The third captures the *alive* initial condition. The remaining give conditions for *loaded* from *load* and for *alive* from *loaded* and *shoot*. As we are going to reason in terms of maximal intervals, we are forced to model as incompletely specified any interval whose limits are not already known, such as in (3) above. Also we are stating explicitly the condition that the pair of time points constitutes an interval, namely that they are ordered in time. Functions $f_4(L)$ and $f_5(S)$ are mobile functions and correspond to Skolem functions.

Suppose a query Q1

$$? - for(1, A, alive), A \succ 4$$

This goal may unify with clauses 3 and 5 above. Our derivation proceeds by trying these possibilities, and generates conditions of disjointness for the maximal intervals found. In this case two intervals are derived: $\langle 1, \alpha_3 \rangle$, with constraint $\alpha_3 \succ 1$ and $\langle f_5(3), 3 \rangle$ with constraints $f_5(3) \prec 3$ and $3 \prec f_4(1)$. Depending on the abductions made, three possible configurations for the set of intervals for *alive* emerge:

$$3 \prec f_4(1) \rightarrow \{\langle 1, 3 \rangle\}$$

$$\alpha_3 \prec f_5(3), 3 \prec f_4(1) \rightarrow \{\langle 1, \alpha_3 \rangle \langle f_5(3), 3 \rangle\}$$

$$f_4(1) \prec 3 \rightarrow \{\langle 1, \alpha_3 \rangle\}$$

In the general case, deriving these configurations would involve enforcing disjointness for the intervals in other predications. But here there are single intervals for *load*, *shoot* and *loaded* in the KB. Only the third configuration is unifiable with the goal. The solution is then

$$f_4(1) \prec 3 \rightarrow \{\langle 1, \alpha_3 \rangle\}$$

meaning that *loaded* must have stopped before *shoot*.

If we have now query Q2

$$? - for(1, A, alive), for(1, 4, loaded), A \succ 4$$

we can reason as before for the *alive* predication, and find conditions such that $\langle 1, 4 \rangle$ is a maximal interval for *loaded*. But the conjunctive goal fails, as the abductions required to satisfy both are incompatible.

We intentionally did not model this problem in more detail than it was originally proposed. It follows that, according to our model of propositions, certain "counterintuitive" inferences are licensed, such as those where more than one maximal interval for *alive* is present. To prevent this, axioms for the temporal behaviour of *alive* are required.

This example shows the expected behaviour of the inference system when solving a simple temporal query. Several points are not addressed here: how do questions referring to arbitrary intervals in the user language translate to *MI* queries, how is a conditional answer turned into an answer in the user language and what meaning is to be assigned to the mobiles that appear in the abductions that are a part of the answer. As to the last one, we point out that, although symbols like α_3 or $f_4(X)$ may not appear suggestive in our KB, each one has an intended meaning, α_3 being the end of an interval for *alive* beginning in 1 and $f_4(X)$ the end of an interval for *loaded* beginning in X. This meaning is induced by their occurrence in clauses for the predications mentioned. The condition on the answer to query Q1 can be rephrased in natural language as "the end of the interval for *loaded* beginning in 1 is after 3", and no meaningless symbols occur here.

9 Conclusions and ongoing work

We presented a propositional temporal language and showed how it can be used for building a temporal knowledge base. Maximal intervals were introduced as an outstanding feature. In order to allow the manipulation of the intrinsically incomplete knowledge, the temporal relations between the end points of intervals are kept as constraints.

We are presently working on the inference mechanism for the propositional logic. The main features are a structure to store constraints on points and mechanisms to keep the consistency of the constraints on time points and the maximality of intervals.

Maximal intervals are a solution to the problem of storing temporal information but any user interfacing a knowledge base needs a temporal language dealing with arbitrary time intervals, as used for instance in natural language. We currently investigate what was called here the external language.

One important feature still missing in the propositional language is point arithmetic. We intend to have it soon, and be able to account for the duration of intervals.

In the near future we intend to make the extension to a first order language, and incorporate negative information making use of its temporal symmetry.

References

[All83] James Allen. Maintaining Knowledge About Temporal Intervals. *Communications of the ACM*, 26(11):832–843, 1983.

[All84] James Allen. Towards a General Theory of Action and Time. *Artificial Intelligence*, (23):123–154, 1984.

[HM86] Steve Hanks and Drew McDermott. Default reasoning, nonmonotonic logics and the frame problem. In *Proceedings of the 5th National Conference on Artificial Intelligence*, pages 328–333, AAAI, 1986.

[KS86] Robert Kowalski and Marek Sergot. A logic-based calculus of events. *New Generation Computing*, 4(1):67–95, 1986.

[Lad86] Peter Ladkin. Time representation: a taxonomy of interval relations. In *Proceedings of the 5th National Conference on Artificial Intelligence*, pages 360–366, 1986.

[McD82] Drew McDermott. A Temporal Logic for Reasoning About Processes and Plans. *Cognitive Science*, (6):101–155, 1982.

[MH81] J. M. McCarthy and P. J. Hayes. Some Philosophical Problems from the Standpoint of Artificial Intelligence. *Readings in Artificial Intelligence*, 1981.

[PR90a] António Porto and Cristina Ribeiro. *Maximal Intervals: A Logic of Temporal Information*. Technical Report DI-28, Departamento de Informática, FCT-UNL, 1990.

[PR90b] António Porto and Cristina Ribeiro. Representação de conhecimentos acerca de eventos temporais. In *Actas do 2º Congresso Iberoamericano de Inteligência Artificial*, 1990.

[Sho87] Yoav Shoham. *Reasonig about Change*. The MIT Press, 1987.

[vB83] J. F. A. K. van Benthem. *The logic of time*. Volume 156 of *Studies in Epistemology, Logic, Methodology and Philosophy of Science*, D. Reidel Publishing Company, 1983.

[vB89] Peter van Beek. Approximation algorithms for temporal reasoning. In *Proceedings of the 11th International Joint Conference on Artificial Intelligence*, pages 1291–1296, 1989.

[VK86] Marc Vilain and Henry Kautz. Constraint propagation algorithms for temporal reasoning. In *Proceedings of the 5th National Conference on Artificial Intelligence*, pages 377–382, 1986.

Consistency Driven Planning

Martin Decker   Guido Moerkotte
Holger Müller   Joachim Posegga*

Universität Karlsruhe
Fakultät für Informatik
Postfach 6980, 7500 Karlsruhe, FRG

{moer|mueller|posegga}@ira.uka.de

Abstract

This paper describes a novel approach to planning. The presented algorithm is based on a consistency maintaining procedure for computing possible worlds out of given worlds and applications of operators. Worlds are represented by facts, rules, and consistency constraints. In order to avoid the frame and qualification problems we state neither frame axioms nor qualification axioms. Instead, general consistency constraints are used. As a result an execution of an action which asserts its postconditions to the current state of the world may result in inconsistency. A repair mechanism then generates possible changes (repairs) to the inconsistent world such that the resulting world describes the actual consistent state of affairs, i. e. a possible world after the execution of an action.

The generated repairs serve two purposes: as they describe possible worlds in which the action's postconditions hold, they can be used to reason about these worlds and eliminate those which have undesired properties. Moreover, the repairs are used to guide the linear planner such that the generated plans lead to the selected possible world.

1 Introduction

We describe an approach to planning based on deduction. The advantages of deductive systems are well-known; they have clear semantics (namely the semantics of the underlying logic) and are quite well understood from a theoretical point of view. However, in practical applications deduction techniques tend to be rather inefficient, unless applied carefully.

STRIPS [3] and the situation calculus [5, 6] show two extremes of using deduction within a planner. In STRIPS, deduction is only used for checking preconditions of actions, while situation calculus does *everything* by deduction using a theorem prover. The latter does not seem appropriate when one is interested in building usable planners, since small toy problems already overwhelm state-of-the-art provers with inferences [2].

---

*Part of the research was performed while the author was visiting the Dept. of AI, University of Edinburgh, Scotland. This visit was supported by the Commission of European Communities under grant ERBSCI*CT000301 - (SC1000301).

The approach we propose lies between these two extremes. We use deduction for modelling states and transitions between states, but leave the actual search for a plan to a specialized algorithm. This avoids the semantic problems of STRIPS [7] and rules out the most important reason for inefficiency. Additionally, incompleteness of linear planners, e.g., the Sussman Anomaly, can be avoided. The rest of the introduction informally describes the basic ideas of our approach. Subsequent sections elaborate and formalize these ideas.

Assume we have a description of an initial world W_0 in a planning scenario (in a suitable first-order language), and a set of domain constraints C that must always hold. If an operator op is executed, we want to compute the subsequent world W_1. The first problem to be faced is the frame problem [8]. Ginsberg and Smith [4] offer the following solution: put the action's postconditions into W_1 and copy all formulas from W_0 to W_1. Then delete as few formulas coming from W_0 as possible until W_1 becomes consistent with C. The qualification and ramification problem can be treated in a similar way.

Our approach adopts this idea but uses a deductive database for modelling states and a repair mechanism which allows us to automatically detect and remove inconsistencies in the database (see [9]). There are two important advantages over the Ginsberg and Smith approach. First, we avoid the problem that syntactically different but semantically equivalent axiomatizations yield different results [13] by a careful choice of the language's syntax. And, secondly, we not only allow formulas from W_0 to survive in W_1, but also generate new ones if necessary[1]. This is advantageous, because it allows us to compute more information than is given by the original goal *before* the actual planning starts. Thus we perform a completion of the goal. This completed description gives valuable information for the plan search. Sussman's conjunctive goal problem (see figure 1) will illustrate this.

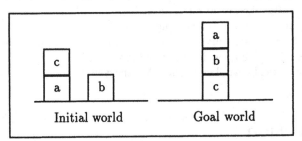

Figure 1: The conjunctive goal problem

W_0 is given by the facts $\{on(a, table), on(c, a), on(b, table)\}$, the goal G is $\{on(a,b), on(b,c)\}$, and C is a set of appropriate domain constraints for the blocks world (like "no object must be at two places", "blocks must not 'fly around' but rest on something that is fixed", etc)[2]. In order to get a complete description of the goal state W_G, we add G to W_0 resulting in

$$W_G = \{on(a, table), on(c, a), on(b, table), on(a, b), on(b, c)\}.$$

This violates several constraints: block 'a' is at two places, thus '$on(a, table)$' must be

---

[1] There is of course a price to be paid for that: a *complete* description of the world is required.

[2] We will list these explicitly in a later section, when we come back to this example. At this point there's no need to bother with too much details.

deleted. For the same reason '$on(b, table)$' must go[3]. We now have $W_G = \{on(a, b), on(b, c),$ $on(c, a)\}$, which is an impossible 'circular' tower, therefore '$on(c, a)$' also disappears. The result is –in this case– a world holding only the goal. However, this still violates a constraint, namely that every object must be at a certain place. Block 'c' is not, so we must find a place for it. The only choice here is *adding* '$on(c, table)$', so finally $W_G = \{on(a, b), on(b, c), on(c, table)\}$, the goal state of figure 1. As it can be seen, we arrived at a complete description of the goal state.

How does this relate to deductive databases, inconsistencies in them, and regaining consistency? Assume the initial world is modelled as a database state, and the goal is transformed into the transaction $[add(on(a, b)), add(on(b, c))]$. It is executed on the database and causes some constraints to be violated. By means described in [9], the following so–called 'repair' transaction is computed: $[del(on(c, a)), add(on(c, table)),$ $del(on(a, table)), del(on(b, table))]$. Executing this transaction leads to a consistent database, and gives valuable information on finding a plan for the goal[4]: we have to look for a sequence of actions 'performing' the combined goal and repair transactions. Here it's [move(c,a,table); move(b,table,c); move(a,table,b)], a plan that can easily be found by a linear planning algorithm.

To summarize, the key idea of our approach is to borrow ideas from deductive database technology for modelling worlds in planning and to use techniques for detecting and resolving inconsistencies to model transitions from one world to another. By these means, we compute a complete description of a possible goal world and use this information to guide a dedicated (linear) planning algorithm. As the main driving force is regaining consistency we call our approach *Consistency Driven Planning*.

The rest of the paper is organized as follows. In sections 2 and 3 the basic notions for representing planning domains are defined. An axiomatization of the Sussman Anomaly together with the proceeding of the planner is given in section 4. Section 5 introduces a planning algorithm designed to exploit our framework. In section 6 we discuss a more complex example: the river crossing problem. In section 7 we present a solution for the dumbbell problem. Section 8 concludes the paper.

2   Computing Possible Worlds

Looking at current research in databases one will notice that the problem of computing possible worlds has its parallel in the area of deductive databases: a possible world directly corresponds to a database state. Hence, the task of computing the resulting state of the world in a planning scenario after the execution of an action corresponds to the computation of updates in databases after a transaction. Usually a deductive database does not offer the expressiveness of full first-order logic, but a restricted language that can be handled efficiently. Therefore we employ a restricted predicate calculus to describe possible worlds. Two major limitations are made to the predicate calculus. First, as in deductive databases, only ground atoms – without function symbols – are used. Second, in order to guarantee domain independence, the permitted formulas are required to be

---

[3]Recall that only formulas coming from W_0 may be deleted.

[4]The general situation is, of course, more complicated; we give a more complex example in a later chapter.

range-restricted. We use the common definition of range-restrictedness as introduced in [11].

Subsequently, variables are denoted by x, y, z and a ground atom is called a *fact*. *Rules* are restricted to definite Horn-clauses. Then, a *possible world* is a triple $W :=$ $(W_{facts}, W_{rules}, W_{constr})$ where W_{facts} is a set of facts, W_{rules} is a set of rules defining the derived predicates, and W_{constr} is a set of closed range-restricted formulas called consistency constraints (for an example world see section 4). For a possible world $W :=$ $(W_{facts}, W_{rules}, W_{constr})$ we define the *completion* as

$$Comp(W) :=$$
$$\{a | a \text{ is a fact}, W_{facts} \cup W_{rules} \models a\} \cup \{\neg a | a \text{ is a fact}, W_{facts} \cup W_{rules} \not\models a\}$$

thus incorporating Reiter's closed-world assumption [12]. For a formula f, $Comp(W) \models f$ is abbreviated by $W \models f$. A world $W := (W_{facts}, W_{rules}, W_{constr})$ is called *consistent* iff $Comp(W) \cup W_{constr}$ is free of contradictions.

For a_i $(1 \leq i \leq n)$ being facts, a *world transition* is defined as a finite set $WT :=$ $\{o_1(a_1), ..., o_n(a_n)\}$ of *instructions* where $o_i \in \{add, del\}$. A world transition changes the facts in W_{facts}. $WT(W)$ denotes the world resulting from the world transition WT if applied to the world W. In the presentation of the planning algorithm we will use the mapping Γ which maps a state transition to a set of closed literals defined as $\Gamma(WT) :=$ $\{a | add(a) \in WT\} \cup \{\neg a | del(a) \in WT\}$. In order to model constant parts of possible worlds, *protected predicates* are introduced whose facts may not be affected by a world transition.

Let WT be a world transition, $W := (W_{facts}, W_{rules}, W_{constr})$ a possible world and there exists at least one consistency constraint $c \in W_{constr}$ such that $Comp(W) \cup \{c\}$ is inconsistent, then WT is called a *repair* for W_{constr} iff $Comp(WT(W)) \cup W_{constr}$ is consistent and WT is minimal. The main idea for the computation of repairs is to use derivation trees whose leaves contain the required information. E. g. the deducible fact a is (partly) responsible for the violation of a consistency constraint. In order to regain consistency the SLDNF tree for a (which by definition contains all derivations of a) is searched for a minimal set R of leaves such that the removal inhibits any derivation of a. For non-derivable facts which have to be added to regain consistency the main idea remains the same but the procedure is somewhat more complicated. For further details the reader is referred to [9, 10].

3 Describing Operators and Goals

An *operator specification* is defined as

> **declare** opsym$(x_1, \dots, x_n)$
> > **Pre** <precondition>
> > **Post** <postcondition>
> **end**

where *opsym* is the name of the operator, x_i $(1 \leq i \leq n)$ are variables, <precondition> is a set of range-restricted formulas, <postcondition> is a set of literals. Further, the two sets of the operator specification may contain only $x_1 \ldots x_n$ as free variables. $opsym(x_1, \ldots, x_n)$ is called the *head* of an operator specification.

An *operator op* is a head of an operator specification, where all parameters are replaced by constants. $Pre(op)$ and $Post(op)$ refer to the fully instantiated sets of <precondition>, <postcondition>, respectively. If L is a set of literals L^+ is the set of atoms of L and L^- is the set of atoms which appear negated in L. $\overline{L} = \{a | a \in L^-\} \cup \{\neg a | a \in L^+\}$ denotes the inversion of the signs of the literals in L. With the definitions above, some basic notions of planning can be formalized: A *goal* G is a set of closed, range-restricted formulas, and a *planning problem* is a triple (W_0, OP, G), where W_0 is a consistent initial world, OP a set of operator specifications, and G a goal.

For uniformity reasons, we assume that a goal G implicitly introduces an operator $goal()$, where $Pre(goal()) := G$ and $Post(goal())$ is empty.

Each plan $[op_1, \ldots, op_n]$ defines a unique sequence of possible worlds $W_1, \ldots, W_n$:

- $W_{facts,i} := (W_{facts,i-1} \setminus Post^-(op_i)) \cup Post^+(op_i)$

whereas $W_{rules,i} = W_{rules} = W_{rules,0}$ and $W_{constr,i} = W_{constr} = W_{constr,0}$ remain unchanged.
A plan is called a *solution* for a planning problem, iff

- $op_n = goal()$,

- $\forall i \in \{1, \ldots, n\} : Comp(W_{i-1}) \models Pre(op_i)$, and

- $\forall i \in \{1, \ldots, n\} : W_i$ is consistent.

In terms of planning, this means that before inserting an operator into an operator sequence two things have to be verified: (i) the preconditions of the operator must be satisfied, and (ii) the resulting world must be consistent.

4 The Sussman Anomaly

We want to illustrate our planning algorithm with a short example from the blocks world. Figure 1 depicted the initial state and the goal state of the blocks world.

Figure 2 shows the corresponding formalization of the initial world W_0. In this examples and also in the following ones the predicate *is* is a protected predicate.

The rules and constraints $W_{rules,0}$ and $W_{constr,0}$ verbally read as follows:

rule_1:   an object which stands on another one is supported by that object
rule_2:   every object supports all objects that stand on it
constr_1:   everything can be at one place only
constr_2:   only one block can be on another
constr_3:   every block is supported by the table
constr_4:   only blocks can stand on other objects

The only operator needed within our blocks world is the move operator, specified as follows:

Initial Facts $W_{facts,0}$:
  $is(a, block),\ is(b, block),\ is(c, block),\ is(table, table),$
  $on(c, a),\ on(a, table),\ on(b, table)$

Rules $W_{rules,0}$:
  $rule\_1:\ \forall x_1, x_2:\quad on(x_1, x_2) \Rightarrow supported\_by(x_1, x_2)$
  $rule\_2:\ \forall x_1, x_2, x_3:\quad on(x_1, x_2) \wedge supported\_by(x_2, x_3) \Rightarrow supported\_by(x_1, x_3)$

Constraints $W_{constr,0}$:
  $constr\_1:\ \forall x_1, x_2, x_3:\quad on(x_1, x_2) \wedge on(x_1, x_3) \Rightarrow x_2 = x_3$
  $constr\_2:\ \forall x_1, x_2, x_3:\quad is(x_1, block) \wedge on(x_2, x_1) \wedge on(x_3, x_1) \Rightarrow x_2 = x_3$
  $constr\_3:\ \forall x_1:\qquad\qquad is(x_1, block) \Rightarrow supported\_by(x_1, table)$
  $constr\_4:\ \forall x_1, x_2:\qquad\ \ on(x_1, x_2) \Rightarrow is(x_1, block)$

Figure 2: The initial world W_0 of the blocks world

declare move(x_1, x_2, x_3)
    pre $is(x_1, block), is(x_2, block) \vee x_2 = table, is(x_3, block) \vee x_3 = table$
           $on(x_1, x_2), \forall x_4 \neg on(x_4, x_1), \neg x_2 = x_3$
    post $on(x_1, x_3), \neg on(x_1, x_2)$
end

Roughly, the algorithm can be specified as follows:

init $plan := [goal()]$
while no solution has been generated
   begin
      (1) determine a repair R for a op_i in $plan = [op_1, \ldots, op_n]$ where the pre-
           condition of op_i is not satisfied in W_{i-1} or W_i is inconsistent, s. t. for
           $W_{i-1} := R(W_{i-1})$ these problems would disappear
      (2) select an operator op that performs some of the instructions of R
      (3) insert the operator op somewhere before op_i into the plan
   end

Each of these three steps are choice points, i. e., usually the planner has to choose one out of several possible results and has to store the remaining results in order to allow backtracking. In the following example we assume that the algorithm always performs optimal choices. For the Sussman Anomaly the planner works as foilows:

Initialization

    The planning algorithm starts with the plan $[goal()]$. The precondition of the special operator $goal()$ is the goal $G = \{on(a, b), on(b, c)\}$.

First execution of the loop body

    Step 1.1: (Determine a repair) *To satisfy the precondition of the operator $goal()$*

a list of repairs is computed by a repair mechanism described in [9]. After that, the planner selects an arbitrary repair R at the first choice point.

The repair mechanism finds exactly one repair

$$R = \{add(on(a,b)), add(on(b,c)), add(on(c,table)),$$
$$del(on(a,table)), del(on(b,table)), del(on(c,a))\}$$

for the world W_0 and the goal G such that $Comp(R(W_0)) \cup W_{constr,0} \cup G$ is consistent. Note, that the repair mechanism derives a new fact $on(c,table)$ from W_0 and G. The expression $add(on(c,table))$ denotes that $on(c,table)$ must be derivable in an actual goal world.

Step 1.2: (Select an operator) *The task for the planner is to look for a sequence of actions 'performing' the transaction R proposed by the repair mechanism. The planner matches the literals of $\Gamma(R)$ with the postcondition of the operators examing whether the postcondition Post(op) of an operator op contains some ground literals which are also appearing inside $\Gamma(R)$. If there are several possible operators a single one is selected (second choice point).*

In our example we have three *del/add* pairs in R, each matching the literals of the postcondition of the move operator specification. The planner selects the pair $< del(on(c,a)), add(on(c,table)) >$ which is performed by *move(c,a,table)*.

Step 1.3: (Insert the operator in the plan) *The algorithm can insert the selected operation in the generated plan at some position before the operation whose repair is just transformed into a plan (third choice point).*

The only possible position for *move(c,a,table)* is directly before *goal()*.

Second execution of the loop body

Step 2.1: (Determine repairs) *If the repair that is associated with an operator is still not converted into a list of operators no new repairs are generated.*

Only two out of six instructions of the repair R are so far achieved by the plan $[move(c,a,table), goal()]$. Thus, no new repairs are generated.

Step 2.2: (Select an operator) Analogously to step 1.2, the operator $move(b,table,c)$ is chosen for the pair $< del(on(b,table)), add(on(b,c)) >$.

Step 2.3: (Insert the operator) The operator is inserted in the second position of the generated plan:

$$[move(c,a,table), move(b,table,c), goal()]$$

Third execution of the loop body

Step 3.1: (Determine a repair) Two instructions of the repair R still have to be established. Therefore, no new repairs are generated.

Step 3.2: (Select an operator) The planner chooses $move(a, table, b)$ for the last pair $< del(on(a, table)), add(on(a, b)) >$

Step 3.3: (Insert the operator) By insertion of $move(a, table, b)$ in the third position of the plan we generate a solution

$$[move(c, a, table), move(b, table, c), move(a, table, b), goal()]$$

for the planning problem, since all intermediate worlds are consistent and the preconditions of all operators are satisfied.

Some details of the algorithm could not be exhibited due to the simplicity of the above example. First, we have successively inserted the selected operators into the partial generated plan. This special order is not necessary. And, secondly, we reached a solution in step 3.3 without encounting the problems of unsatisfied preconditions or inconsistent intermediate worlds. These two problems can be treated in the same way as the original planning problem. Thus repairs are generated and matched against the postcondition of operators by further iterations of the loop.

5   The Planning Algorithm

In the previous section we introduced the main ideas of our planner through an example. In this section we want to present a formalization of this ideas. The Sussman example already contains a general but informal description of the planner. Every step has some preliminary remarks which refer to the general algorithm. To get a formal description we only need to transform the remarks into a formal representation. Figure 3 shows the result of such a transformation.

The algorithm consists of two main parts: an initialization and a while loop. During the initialization we introduce the variables *plan* and *list_of_repair_sets*. The value of *plan* is a list of operators. We denote these operators by $op_1, \ldots, op_n$. We use the distinguished operator $goal()$ of which the precondition is the goal G and the postcondition is empty. The operator $goal()$ is always the last operator of *plan*. This guarantees that a solution transforms the initial world W_0 into a goal world. During the computation for each operator op_i of *plan* a set of repairs can be computed. In order to associate the repairs to the operator op_i we store the set of repairs in the i-th position of the list *list_of_repair_sets*. *repairs*$_i$ denotes the repairs of the operator op_i.

The second main part of the algorithm is the while loop. The condition of the loop checks whether the current plan is a solution. If a solution is found, the condition of the loop is false and the algorithm stops. If the condition is true, i. e., there exists at least one operator such that its precondition is unsatisfied or the subsequent world is inconsistent, the algorithm selects one of these operators.

The conditional of the first step of the loop body checks whether it is necessary to compute a new set of repairs for the selected operator op_i. If for the operator op_i no repairs have been computed, *repairs*$_i$ is empty. During the first execution of the loop body this is the case for the operator $goal()$. Therefore we have to compute a first set of repairs for $goal()$. Each repair R of this set transforms the initial world into a goal world $R(W_0)$ since $Post(goal())$ is empty and $Pre(goal())$ is the goal G.

input A planning problem (W_0, OP, G)

init   1. $plan := [goal()]$

        /* $plan$ is a list of operators. op_i denotes the i-th operator of $plan$. They implicitly define the worlds $W_1, \ldots, W_n$ as described in sec. 3 where n is the length of the current plan. */

        2. $list\_of\_repair\_sets := [\emptyset]$

while there exists an index i such that
        $Comp(W_{i-1}) \not\models Pre(op_i)$ **or** W_i is not consistent.

        /* Not all preconditions of op_i are satisfied, or the subsequent intermediate world is inconsistent. */

do   1. **if** $repairs_i = \emptyset$ **or** $\exists R \in repairs_i : \Gamma(R) \subseteq Comp(W_{i-1})$

        then $repairs_i :=$ the set of all repairs R such that
            $Comp(R(W_{i-1})) \models Pre(op_i)$ /* Precondition satisfied after applying R */
            and
            successor world $op_i(R(W_{i-1}))$ is consistent
        fi

        2. Assume $repairs_i = \{R_1, \ldots, R_k\}$.
        choose some index j and some literal q such that
            $q \in \Gamma(R_j)$ **and** $q \notin Comp(W_{i-1})$

        3. $repairs_i := \{R_j \mid q \in \Gamma(R_j)\}$

        4. **choose** an operator op such that $q \in Post^+(op) \cup \overline{Post^-(op) \setminus Post^+(op)}$

        5. **choose** a position $pos \in \{1, \ldots, i\}$ and

           • insert op at position pos into $plan$
           • insert $\emptyset$ at position pos into $list\_of\_repair\_sets$

od

output : the solution $[op_1, \ldots, op_n]$.

Figure 3: The Planning Algorithm

The set of new repairs is determined with respect to the operator op_i and the world W_{i-1} which is determined by the partial plan $[op_1, \ldots, op_{i-1}]$ and the initial world W_0. During further computations new operators can be inserted before op_i into the plan. Therefore it is sometimes necessary to determine a new set of repairs for op_i in order to consider these changes of the plan. We have decided that after one repair R is satisfied, i. e., the formula $\exists R \in repairs_i : \Gamma(R) \subset Comp(W_i)$ is true, the algorithm shall compute a new set of repairs for op_i.

In the second step we choose a ground literal q such that one repair R_j has an instruction of which the execution achieves q and the literal q is not satisfied in the previous world W_i. The operator *choose* is indeterministic. In a concrete implementation we have to replace the *choose* operator with a special search strategy.

In the third step we gather all repairs R_j which have an instruction that achieves q.

At this point we could also use a *choose* operator to select only one repair but in order to reduce the search space we have decided to gather the repairs instead of introducing a further choice point.

In the last two steps we choose an operator *op* that achieves the literal q and we insert *op* somewhere before op_i into the generated plan. The special set construction of step 4 reflects the effects of operators in plans. E. g. two operators which differ only in their postconditions $\{f\}$ and $\{f, \neg f\}$, respectively, have always the same effect 'add f to the world' when they are applied on a world.

In our implementation we have restricted the insertion of new operators into *plan* by the usage of protected subgoals. We declare the literal q between *pos* and i as a protected subgoal. Every insertion of an operator op' into a position *pos'* is forbidden if *pos'* lies in the scope of a protected subgoal q and the subgoal q is unsatisfied after the execution of op'.

6   The River Crossing Problem

The computation of a solution for the Sussman anomaly of section 4 was rather straightforward. Because of our 'optimal-choice assumption' the algorithm had to compute only one repair and could directly transform the single repair into a solution.

Now we present the more complicated river crossing example. A farmer wants to transport his goose, his dog and his bag full of corn from the left side of the river to the right side. For the farmer only a small boat is available that can only carry him and another object. The specification of the operator *move* allows that the farmer can alone traverse the river in the boat. During the transportation the farmer has to observe that he does not leave the dog and the goose or the goose and the corn behind since then the dog would eat the goose or the goose would eat the corn, respectively.

Although we again assume that the planner conducts optimal the computation of a solution requires the capability of the planner to manage unsatisfied preconditions and inconsistent intermediate worlds. In this example we restrict the choose operators in such a way that the algorithm corresponds to the means ends analysis:

init *plan* $:= [goal()]$
$\quad R :=$ **choose** a repair such that $R(W_0)$ is a goal world

while there exists an instruction I in the repair R that is not performed

1. **choose** an operator op_{i_k} that performs the instruction I: $\Gamma(I) \in Post(op_{i_k})$
2. let $plan = [op_1, \ldots, op_{i_{k-1}}, goal()]$
   insert op_{i_k} directly before $goal()$: $plan := [op_1, \ldots, op_{i_{k-1}}, op_{i_k}, goal()]$
3. **choose** a subplan $[op_{i_{k-1}+1}, \ldots, op_{i_k-1}]$ such that

$$plan := [op_1, \ldots, op_{i_{k-1}}, op_{i_{k-1}+1}, \ldots, op_{i_k-1}, op_{i_k}, goal()]$$

   is a solution or the only violated condition for a solution is that the precondition of $goal()$ is not satisfied. Especially, the intermediate worlds must be consistent.

Initial Facts $W_{facts,0}$:
  $is(farmer,obj)$, $is(dog,obj)$, $is(goose,obj)$, $is(corn,obj)$, $is(left,loc)$, $is(right,loc)$,
  $pos(farmer,left)$, $pos(dog,left)$, $pos(goose,left)$, $pos(corn,left)$

Constraints $W_{constr,0}$:
  $constr\_1$: $\forall x \exists y :$ $is(obj,x) \Rightarrow pos(x,y) \wedge is(loc,y)$
  $constr\_2$: $\forall x,y,z : pos(x,y) \wedge pos(x,z) \Rightarrow y = z$
  $constr\_3$: $\forall x :$ $pos(goose,x) \wedge pos(dog,x) \Rightarrow pos(farmer,x)$
  $constr\_4$: $\forall x :$ $pos(goose,x) \wedge pos(corn,x) \Rightarrow pos(farmer,x)$

Operator: declare $move(x,l_1,l_2)$
                pre: $is(obj,x)$, $is(loc,l_1)$, $is(loc,l_2)$, $l_1 \neq l_2$
                        $pos(farmer,l_1)$, $pos(x,l_1)$
               post: $pos(farmer,l_2)$, $pos(x,l_2)$, $\neg pos(farmer,l_1)$, $\neg pos(x,l_1)$
              end

Goal G: $pos(farmer,right)$, $pos(goose,right)$, $pos(corn,right)$, $pos(dog,right)$

Figure 4: Axioms for River Crossing

Figure 4 shows the formalized planning problem. The world W_0 in the figure 5 depicts the initial situation.

After the initialization the planner works as follows:

First execution of the loop body

The repair mechanism concludes from the goal and the second constraint: 'every object can be at one place only' the single repair

$R = \{$ del(pos(farmer, left)), add(pos(farmer, right)),
         del(pos(goose, left)),   add(pos(goose,right)),
         del(pos(corn, left)),   add(pos (corn,right)),
         del(pos(dog, left)),   add(pos(dog,right)) $\}$

The planner chooses $op_1 = move(goose,left,right)$ as first operator. Note, that any other choice would result in an inconsistent world.

Second execution of the loop body

The precondition of op_1 is satisfied and the intermediate world W_1 is consistent. Only the precondition of $goal()$ is unsatisfied in W_1. Therefore the planner determines from R an operator $op_2 = move(dog, left, right)$ and inserts op_2 between op_1 and $goal$ into the plan: $plan := [op_1, op_2, goal()]$.

Third execution of the loop

The precondition of operator op_2 is unsatisfied. In the world W_1 the farmer is not on the left side of the river. A repair $\{ del(pos(farmer,right)), add(pos(farmer,left))\}$ is computed and transformed into the operator $op_3 = move(farmer,right,left)$. op_3

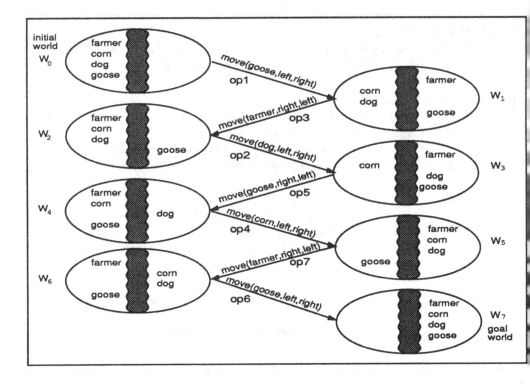

Figure 5: Worlds and Operators for River Crossing

corresponds to a subplan in the means ends analysis. Therefore we insert op_3 directly before op_2: $plan := [op_1, op_3, op_2, goal()]$.

Fourth execution of the loop body

Since the only fault of the current plan is the unsatisfied precondition of $goal()$ (W_3 is not a goal world) we determine a further operator $op_4 = move(corn, left, right)$ and insert it into $plan$: $[op_1, op_3, op_2, op_4, goal()]$.

Fifth execution of the loop body

As in the third execution of the loop body we have to move the farmer from the right side to the left one in order to achieve a world that satisfies the precondition of op_4. At this point we perform a good choice by the application of the operator $op_5 = move(goose, right, left)$. We not only move the farmer but also the goose from the right side to the left side. This choice prevents us from generating an inconsistent world W_4. Since we employ the means ends analysis we insert op_5 before op_4: $plan := [op_1, op_3, op_2, op_5, op_4, goal()]$.

Sixth and seventh execution of the loop body

Analogous to the executions 2 and 3 we determine the last two operators. Figure 5 shows the solution together with the inital- and the goal world and all intermediate worlds $W_1, \ldots, W_6$.

7 The Dumbbell Problem

This section shows how our approach deals with the qualification and ramification problem. Both problems can be characterized as follows:

Qualification Problem: the number of preconditions that must be fulfilled in order to execute an action can be immense.

Ramification Problem the number of things that are changed by an action can also be very large.

A system that needs frame axioms all qualifications and ramifications for each action must be listed explicitly[5]. This often prevents efficient handling of the axiomatization. In order to show the important points, we need not refer to the planning algorithm; the mechanism for maintaining consistency alone manages the frame problem, independent of the way the actual planner works.

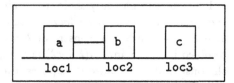

Figure 6: The Dumbbell Scenario

$is(a, block)$ $is(b, block)$ $is(c, block)$
$is(connected, a, b)$
$is(loc1, location)$ $is(loc2, location)$ $is(loc3, location)$
$on(a, loc1)$ $on(b, loc2)$ $on(c, loc3)$

Figure 7: Facts for the Dumbbell Problem

Figure 6 and 7 describe the dumbbell scenario: in a blocks world, two blocks are connected. If one of them is moved, the other will move, too. Assume there is only one operation, namely *move*. A qualification for *move* is that the target location must be free. If we want to move *a* from *loc1* to *loc2*, this action is qualified, first. However, the action will also cause *b* to move itself to another location (in this case *loc3*), so, a ramification eliminates the prior qualification. But there is an additional qualification then: *loc3* must be free. An approach based on frame axioms requires all these ramifications and qualifications to be listed explicitly, which is possible for this simple scenario, but troublesome in larger domains.

The constraints that are needed to handle this in our approach are shown in figure 8: the loc-constraints are the usual requirements for the blocks world and say that nothing can be at two locations, no two things can be at one location, and everything is somewhere. The meaning of the connected rules is obvious.

---

[5]In a situation-calculus based approach with n predicates specifying a state of the world and m actions, $n \cdot m$ frame axioms are needed.

loc-constr-1:	$\forall x,y,z:$	$on(x,y) \wedge on(x,z) \Rightarrow y = z$
loc-constr-2:	$\forall x,y,z:$	$on(x,y) \wedge on(z,y) \Rightarrow x = z$
loc-constr-3:	$\forall x \exists y:$	$is(x,block) \Rightarrow on(x,y) \wedge is(y,location)$
connected-rule-1:	$\forall x,y:$	$is(connected,x,y) \wedge on(x,loc1) \Rightarrow on(y,loc2)$
connected-rule-2:	$\forall x,y:$	$is(connected,x,y) \wedge on(x,loc2) \Rightarrow on(y,loc3)$

Figure 8: Constraints and rules for the Dumbbell Problem

Assume we want to have a at $loc2$, thus $on(a,loc2)$ is the goal to achieve. If this is added to the initial world, the following repair is generated to make the resulting world consistent again:

$$R \;=\; \{ \;\; \neg on(a,loc1), \neg on(b,loc2), \neg on(c,loc3), \\ on(b,loc3), on(c,loc1) \;\; \}$$

This computation proceeds in principle as follows. If we assert $on(a,loc2)$, but also have $on(a,loc1)$, constraint 1 is violated. The only choice to repair it is deleting $on(a,loc1)$, expressed by the literal $\neg on(a,loc1)$. Now, $on(b,loc2)$ violates two constraints: constraint 1, because b is both at $loc2$ and $loc3$, and constraint 2, because both b and c are at the same place[6]. This is resolved by removing $on(b,loc2)$ and $on(c,loc3)$. Finally, both b and c cause problems with constraint 3, because it requires a location for each existing block. The only choice to repair this is obvious. Note that a goal world will be complete, if it satisfies the repair set.

Last not least, some remarks to finding a plan for this problem. First, an appropriate 'move' operator must not have the precondition that the target location is empty, because we want to handle qualifications implicitly. When looking for a plan, we have to find a sequence of 'move's that 'perform' the repair; $[move(a,loc1,loc2), move(c,loc3,loc1)]$ would do the job. However, this does not mean that the goal world is actually achievable: the intermediate world is inconsistent, because c blocks $loc3$. This plan could only be carried out if we had two actors that can 'move' in parallel. The current implementation of our planner does not handle parallel actions, but future research will investigate this.

8 Concluding Remarks

We have described a novel approach to planning based on deduction. The deductive system consists of a deductive database enhanced by a procedure for maintaining consistency. The approach is called *consistency driven planning*, and was motivated by the observation that database states directly correspond to possible worlds in planning.

We have shown how such a deductive machinery can be tightly integrated into a linear planning algorithm exhibiting several advantages over previous linear planners, e.g., the qualification and ramification problem can be handled elegantly. Moreover, the resulting planner is known to be complete [1].

The experiences with the implementation of the introduced planning algorithm made so far are promising. Future research will investigate the development of non-linear planners based on the *consistency driven planning* paradigm. Other possible areas for further

---

[6] $on(b,loc3)$ is derivable with rule 2 and the fact $(a,loc2)$.

research concern the introduction of disjunctions or even general formulas for the add and delete sets, and the integration of evaluable function symbols in order to cope with arithmetics, for instance.

References

[1] M. Decker. Entwurf und Implementierung eines Planers basierend auf einem Konsistenzerhaltungsmechanismus einer deduktiven Datenbank. Diplomarbeit, 1991.

[2] J. Dix, J. Posegga, and P.H. Schmitt. Modal Logic for AI Planning. In *First Intern. Conf. on Expert Planning Systems*, Brighton, UK, July 1990. IEE.

[3] R. Fikes and N. Nilsson. STRIPS: A new approach to theorem proving in problem solving. *Artificial Intelligence*, 2:189 ff., 1971.

[4] M. L. Ginsberg and D. E. Smith. Possible worlds planning I + II. *Artificial Intelligence*, 35, 1988.

[5] C. Green. Application of theorem proving to problem solving. In *Proc. 1st IJCAI*, Washington D.C., 1969.

[6] R. Kowalski. Logic for problem solving. DCL TechReport 75, DAI, Edinburgh, Scotland, 1974.

[7] Vladimir Lifschitz. On the semantics of STRIPS. In Michael P. Georgeff and Amy L. Lansky, editors, *Reasoning about Actions and Plans, Proceedings of the 1986 Workshop*, Los Altos, CA, 1987. Morgan Kaufmann.

[8] John McCarthy and Pat Hayes. Some philosophical problems from the standpoint of artificial intelligence. In B. Meltzer and D. Michie, editors, *Machine Intelligence 4*. Edinburgh University Press, Edinburgh, Scotland, 1969.

[9] G. Moerkotte. *Inkonsistenzen in deduktiven Datenbanken (Inconsistencies in deductive databases)*. Informatik Fachberichte Nr. 248. Springer-Verlag, 1990.

[10] G. Moerkotte and P.C. Lockemann. Reactive consistency control in deductive databases. tech. report 3/90, Universität Karlsruhe, 1989.

[11] J.-M. Nicolas. Logic for improving integrity checking in relational data bases. *Acta Informatica*, 18, 1982. 227-253.

[12] R. Reiter. On closed world data bases. *In: H. Gallaire And J. Minker (Eds.)*, Logic And Data Bases, Plenum, New York, 1978. 227-253.

[13] Marianne Winslett. Theory Revision Semantics for Use in Reasoning about Actions. In *Proc. AAAI-88*, 1988.

AN EFFICIENT APPROACH TO PLANNING IN ASSEMBLY TASKS

Carlos Ramos ; Eugénio Oliveira
Faculdade de Engenharia da Universidade do Porto
4099 Porto Codex - PORTUGAL

ABSTRACT

Assembly Robotics is considered a good testbed to evaluate AI planning algorithms. In most cases, these algorithms are tested on simulated and simplified robotic environments. However, the application of such algorithms to real assembly tasks fail since the usual approach, restrictive to the blocks world, is too poor to be generalized for real-life robotic problems. On the other hand, these algorithms are very expensive to be applied on Robotics, where real time problems are often found.

The aim of this paper is to describe our on-going work concerning the implementation of an Intelligent and Efficient Planner, the so called High Level Planner (HLP), to deal with real Assembly problems. In our approach some important features such as the conversion of Computer Vision outputs (object positions and orientations) to some inputs used by the Planner (symbolic relationships) as well as the execution of the high level plan by a real robot (RENAULT-APRA) are taken into account.

HLP is implemented in PROLOG and is member of a Multi-Agent Community together with other four agents: Object Identifier (VISION), World Descriptor (WD), Models (MODELS) and the Low Level Executor (LLE).

The HLP generates efficient plans which are automatically translated to a robot level language by the LLE which directly controls the robot. Two alternative searching methods can be chosen in the plan formulation. The first one uses Best First algorithm, being appropriated for real time constraints dealing. The other algorithm, using a kind of Branch and Bound, needs some more time to be executed, but the best plan is obtained. Both algorithms consider an efficient pruning of incorrect paths of the planning tree.

1-INTRODUCTION

Planning is essentially a problem involving searching. Unfortunately, for large dimension problems, the combinational explosion during searching process may happen. The approach that we propose bears in mind this problem. In our work, a great effort was done to choose the best heuristics to guide the search. Another important topic is how to avoid the consideration of incorrect or no promising paths. The system that we will describe is designed to be integrated in a flexible assembly system. It involves the interface with a Computer Vision System in order to convert the usual outputs of Image Analysis to the symbolic inputs of the Planning System. Moreover, the generated plan is not only displayed at the computer monitor but it is also translated to the appropriated instructions which are executed by the Renault-APRA robot.

The framework used to encapsulate the overall system is the Distributed Artificial Intelligence [Ramos-89]. The agents involved in our robotic testbed are the following: HLP (High Level Planner), LLE (Low Level Executor), WD (World Descriptor), VISION and MODELS. HLP is an automatic generator of plans able to use operators in order to convert the initial configuration of objects in the desired configuration. LLE gets the plan, formulated by HLP, and translates it into orders which are understood by the robot. WD uses spatial reasoning to convert the numeric output of VISION in the symbolic relationships needed as input to HLP. Besides, WD is also concerned with the geometric constraints handling. VISION is a 3D object identifier using camera and laser. MODELS concentrates different object representations to be used by the other agents. Each agent is seen as the union of the associated Intelligent System (Planning or Image Analysis algorithms) with an upper layer having the following main modules: the Self-Knowledge to represent the Intelligent System, the Acquaintances to represent the others Agents, the Communications layer and a Monitor to schedule and control the tasks execution as well as to interact with other modules [Oliveira-91].

In section 2 some related work will be referred. The following sections will describe the work we are doing concerning the implementation of an intelligent planning module in a real Assembly Robotic System. Section 3 will explain the principles and methodologies behind HLP (High Level Planner), an automatic generator of plans [Ramos-91a)]. Section 4 is related with the connection between Computer Vision numeric outputs and High Level Planner symbolic inputs. Section 5 establishes the importance of models namely in which concerns information about grasping positions of the objects. Finally, section 6 collects the main conclusions taken in the previous sections.

2 - RELATED WORK

The first system involving planning ideas was GPS [Newell-63]. GPS introduces means-end-analysis where the operators are chosen in order to make the current state more similar to the desired goal state. STRIPS [Fikes-72] uses three lists for each kind of operation (ADD, DELETE and PRECONDITION lists). Unfortunately, the generation of efficient plans is not certain. Hierarchical Planning appears with ABSTRIPS [Sacerdoti-74] where planning is achieved as an hierarchy of abstraction spaces. NOAH [Sacerdoti-77] establishes first the preconditions of application of an operator and only then the ordering of the operators is chosen. "Critics" were introduced in order to establish the interactions between parts of the plan. NONLIN [Tate-77] uses ordering links to treat interactions between parts of the plan.

Unfortunately, the application of the planners described before to real robotic problems rises some important difficulties mainly due to their pure symbolic nature. They didn't care how to get the symbolic description of the world state from the usual outputs of Computer Vision. A great effort must be done to incorporate numerical and geometric constraints such as the decision of how to grasp objects and how to change their stable states by means of regrasping operations. Besides, some of them are too heavy to be applied in on-line assemblies.

Nowadays, other approaches are being used to deal with Assembly Robotics. Let us focus our attention in just a few of them. Homem de Mello [Mello-91] proposes the use of an AND/OR graph instead of directed graphs. A relational model is based in quintuples: parts, contacts, attachments, relationships and attribute-functions. A constraint of this approach is that it imposes that no more than two parts are joined at each time. HANDEY [Lozano-

Perez-89] includes a sensory system and is able to perform grasping and regrasping operations for pick and place problems. SPAR [Hutchinson-90] uses a three-level hierarchy with operational, geometric and uncertainty-reduction goals. SPAR is able to perform sensing operations during execution and to generate error-recovery plans. The main limitations of SPAR are: there is no subsystem to detect the positions and orientations of objects and the absence of the collision avoidance study.

3-EFFICIENT PLAN GENERATION IN HLP

HLP is intended to be used for real assembly tasks. The main goal of HLP is the efficient generation of a plan suitable to be handled by the Low Level Executor (LLE). The HLP algorithm uses forward chaining (the plan is derived from the initial state to the final desired state). Despite, the same algorithm could be adapted to backward chaining. Since forward chaining makes the interleaving of planning and execution easy, this strategy was chosen in order to achieve a faster execution of the plan.

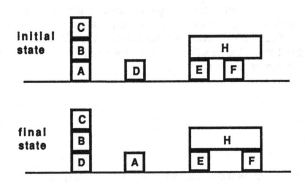

Figure 1 - An example for the pre-processing phase

A pre-processing module analyses the initial and final states (both symbolic and geometrical description) to discard goals that are already done. First of all, symbolic relationships are grouped (e.g. in fig. 1 the states on(h.e) and on(h.f) are grouped into a composed state on(h.[e.f])). A goal is considered as accomplished whenever the intended object locations (positions, orientations and stable states) and symbolic relationships have been successfully reached as well as to the the objects where the stacking or insertion is to be performed.

Fig. 1 shows an example with specific initial and final states. Notice that only the relationship on(e.floor) is already accomplished. Objects a, d and f are already correct in which concerns the goals symbolic description, but their locations are incorrect. The object h is in its correct location, being also on the desired objects but one of the objects under h (object f) is not in the desired location. The object b is in the correct location but it is on the incorrect object (a in spite of d). Finally the example shows the state on(c.b) in the initial and final situation. This last case was intentionally introduced because some planners consider the state as accomplished and later they detect that something is wrong and use a special procedure to solve the problem. Here, there is no need of these considerations because the object under c (object b) is not in accordance with its desired symbolic relationship.

When an object is in all the ways correctly placed it is marked and the goals involving this object in the first argument, are considered as already satisfied. The use of a pre-processing module is more efficient than the use of critics to solve conflicts.

Now, the objective is to satisfy grouped, or compound, final goals (those that are not marked as being in the final state description). To illustrate the plan generation we will choose an example where Best-First approach solution cost differs from Branch and Bound solution cost (this is not the usual case in assembly tasks).

Fig. 2 shows the description of the initial and final states of an assembly task involving 11 objects. Notice that only the goal on(base1,[floor]) was considered as being already accomplished. Therefore, the grouped goals to accomplish are the following (in_v is used to describe vertical insertions while in_h is used to describe horizontal insertions):

in_v(vert1,[base1]);
in_v(vert2,[base1]);
on(base2,[floor]);
in_v(vert3,[base2]);
in_h(hor1,[vert2,vert3]);
in_v(vert4,[base2]);
in_v(vert5,[hor2,base2]);
on(base3,[floor]);
in_v(vert6,[base3]);
on(hor2,[vert4,vert6]);

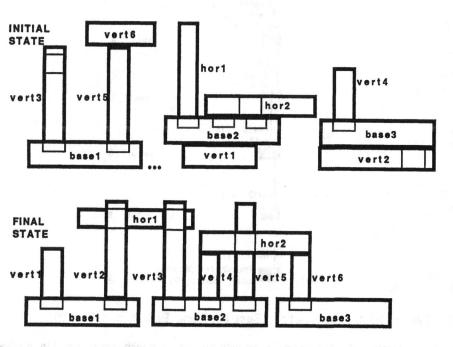

Figure 2 - An example of the initial and final states

Figure 3 shows the paths to the final state obtained by the two methods. Branches are labeled only by the name of the objects instead of the operator. The cost of partial goals is embraced by parenthesis. The solution achieved using Best First approach is the one in the left side, being the other solution given by an algorithm similar to Branch and Bound.

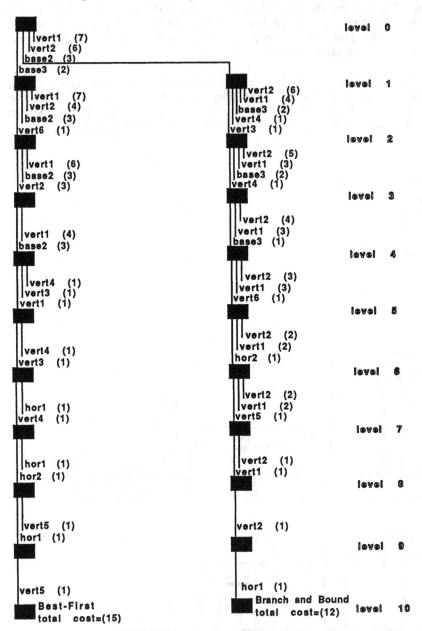

Figure 3 - Two paths for the solution (Best First and Branch and Bound)

Each state is associated with one operator (on with put_on, in_v with insert_v and in_h with insert_h). The generation of the appropriated plan can be seen as a dynamic building of a tree, where the state of the world, at each moment, is represented in the nodes and the applied operators to accomplish a goal are represented by an arc from one state to another. The main heuristic used in the plan generation with Best First method is to choose the operator that reaches one compound goal moving the least number of objects. Only those compound goals having in the second argument names of objects marked as being in the correct position (or the floor) are considered as candidates to the heuristic selection. This is obvious according the heuristic function. If, for example, we try to evaluate the cost to accomplish in_v(vert3,[base2]) and if base2 is not in the correct position we must, firstly, put base2 on floor. However, there is a goal on(base2,[floor]) having an inferior cost than in_v(vert3,[base2]) since the execution of the last one involves also the execution of the first one.

Let us trace the first step in the solution using Best First algorithm. In the first level, four candidate goals are evaluated:

on(base3,[floor]) with cost 2 (vert4 and base3);
on(base2,[floor]) with cost 3 (hor2, hor1 and base2);
in_v(vert2,[base1]) with cost 6 (vert6, vert5, vert3, vert4, base3 and vert2);
in_v(vert1,[base1]) with cost 7 (vert6, vert5, vert3, hor1, hor2, base2 and vert1);

Notice that in the third hypothesis there is no need to move vert3 and in the last hypothesis there is no need to move vert6 and vert5. However, these movements are done to free the space around the destination of the objects vert2 and vert1 respectively. One must pay attention to possible collisions between the robot arm and the objects producing unexpected changing of the world state, during plan execution.

Therefore, the first hypothesis is chosen in order to go from the initial state (level 0) to the next level (where goal on(base3,[floor]) is satisfied). In the lists, above, the operator, associated with the state, is applied to the last object of the list (base3) after putting all other objects of the list (only vert4 in this first case) on the floor. The planner is able to correctly derive the right sequence of actions to remove objects from the top of a specific object. We represent these intermediate movements to the floor by a special operator put_on_floor(X). This is different from put_on(X,[floor]) since the last one refers to the accomplishment of a final goal while in put_on_floor(X) an intermediate movement to the floor is performed in order to access another object.

Similar considerations could be established to the other levels of the tree represented in figure 3 (each level represents the satisfaction of a specific goal),being the final plan as follows:

```
put_on_floor(vert4)
put_on(base3,[floor])           : level 1
insert_v(vert6,[base3])         : level 2
put_on_floor(vert5)
put_on_floor(vert3)
insert_v(vert2,[base1])         : level 3
put_on_floor(hor1)
put_on_floor(hor2)
put_on(base2,[floor])           : level 4
insert_v(vert1,[base1])         : level 5
insert_v(vert3,[base2])         : level 6
insert_v(vert4,[base2])         : level 7
put_on(hor2,[vert4,vert6])      : level 8
insert_h(hor1,[vert2,vert3])    : level 9
insert_v(vert5,[hor2,base2])    : level 10
```

The total cost of the plan execution is 15 (15 movements of objects) using the Best First approach. This plan is quickly derived (almost immediately) being useful for real time applications. Otherwise, if time is not important, the planner may use the Branch and Bound approach. In figure 3 the solution obtained by Branch and Bound is also shown. This last solution has the cost of 12 and the plan is the following:

```
put_on_floor(hor1)
put_on_floor(hor2)
put_on(base2,[floor])        : level 1
insert_v(vert3,[base2])      : level 2
insert_v(vert4,[base2])      : level 3
put_on(base3,[floor])        : level 4
insert_v(vert6,[base3])      : level 5
put_on(hor2,[vert4,vert6])   : level 6
insert_v(vert5,[hor2,base2]) : level 7
insert_v(vert1,[base1])      : level 8
insert_v(vert2,[base1])      : level 9
insert_h(hor1,[vert2,vert3]) : level 10
```

Our implementation of Branch and Bound is also efficient to deal with this specific case. As in the Best First approach, the incorrect paths or paths leading to lost of work are pruned. On the other hand, pure Branch and Bound use is expensive since it is very common to switch from a node near the solution to another far from the solution but with a small cost. The reader has already observed that our trees have a pre-defined number of levels, equal to the number of grouped or compound final goals. The minimum partial cost to go from one level to the following one is 1. Therefore, the minimum cost of a solution passing by a node in a specific level will be the cost until the node plus the difference between the number of levels and the level of the node. Our implementation of Branch and Bound compares such minimum costs because in this way we avoid the excessive switching between nodes close to the solution to nodes still far from the solution.

Notice that this example was studied to give different solutions by means of the application of the two methods (the order of goals was changed to give the total cost of 15 in Best First since our first experiment with Best First leads to the cost of 13). The reader can formulate new examples or generate them randomly to verify that usually both methods give solutions with the same cost.

For the example exposed in this section we have obtained the following time results using a PROLOG interpreter: 2 seconds for Best First and 4 seconds for Branch and Bound.

In this example a regrasping procedure would be needed, but this is a job for LLE agent [Ramos-91 b)].

Finally, it is convenient to notice that a great effort was done to achieve a convenient knowledge representation for data and knowledge involved in the plan generation. There is a way in which the user asks the HLP about the reasons underlying its choices. Below, we will exemplify the explanation facilities in the case of the plan generated by Best First approach.

Whenever the user chooses the explanation support option, control is passed to the user after the satisfaction of a specific goal. For the example explained in this section one may ask why was the goal put_on(base3,[floor]) accomplished first or why was not chosed another one. Questions can be put in a short form as it is shown in the following dialogue example:

<Why base3?
>Because the cost to put base3 in the correct symbolic state and location is the lower one (2). Only 2 objects {vert4 and base3} need to be moved.
<Why not base2?
>Because the cost to put base2 in the correct symbolic state and location is 3 while the cost to put base3 in the correct symbolic state and location is 2. In the case of base2 3 objects are moved {hor2, hor1 and base2} while in the case of base3 only 2 objects need to be moved {vert4 and base3}.
<Why not hor1?
>Because the objects vert2 and vert3 are not in the correct symbolic state and/or location.
<Why not base1?
>Because base1 is already in the correct symbolic state and location.
<Why not cube?
>Unknown object for this task.
<Why not base3?
>Are you kiding?

The user is also able to ask the system about goals that have already been accomplished or about goals to achieve as well as the partial costs leading the previous level with the current level.

We think that the knowledge representation structures we use will facilitate the possibility of re-plan whenever it is desired.

4- CONVERTING COMPUTER VISION OUTPUTS IN PLANNING INPUTS

In our cooperative community of agents a conflict is derived from the mismatch of different knowledge representations: the Object Identifier (VISION) is only able to output numeric values associated with the position (X,Y,Z), orientation (Angle) and stable state (SState) of the identified objects, but HLP works on symbolic relationships (such as on(A,B) or in(C,D)).

To resolve this conflict a new agent (WD) was introduced to convert the output coming from VISION to the input suitable to HLP. The main symbolic relationships envisaged were: when an object is on another one; when an object is inserted in a vertical or horizontal hole of another one; and obviously when an object is on the floor.

The World Descriptor will not only need, as inputs, the positions, orientations and stable states of objects, but also the models of objects (from MODELS). The World Descriptor is mostly interested in the description of supporting faces of objects. These faces are represented by a list of coordinates (x,y) of vertices and by the height (H) of the same supporting face. It is very simple to derive the real position of an object supporting face using the (x,y) list, face height (H), object position (X,Y,Z) and orientation (Angle). The symbolic relationships on and in are then easily computed intercepting the supporting faces of similar height. For illustrative purposes, figure 4 shows three possible cases for a situation on(A,B).

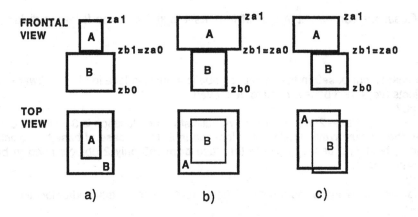

Figure 4 - From object locations to symbolic relationships

The lists of vertices define a polygon when projected on the floor (XY plane). In 4a) the polygon A is contained in the polygon B. On the other hand, 4b) illustrates the polygon B contained in the polygon A. Finally, in 4c) there are interceptions between both polygon lines.

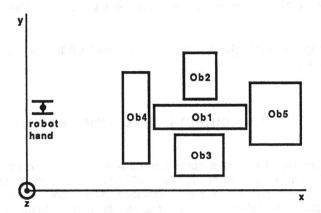

Figure 5 - Geometric Constraints must be visible to Planners

The extraction of other relationships are being implemented to solve some problems related with grasping procedures, where no direct contact between objects exist. As an example, figure 5 illustrates the top view of a scene relating to a situation where the object Ob1 cannot be reached directly by the robot hand. In this case there is need to change the position of objects Ob2 and Ob3 or, alternatively, the positions of objects Ob4 and Ob5. A symbolic relationship must be introduced to make visible the proximity of objects.

5 - SOME FEW WORDS ABOUT MODELS FOR GRASPING

MODELS is an agent where the main features of objects are represented. In section 3 we have seen that models of faces are good to deal with conversions between object locations and symbolic relationships. Models are also important for the sensorial agents (namely for Object Identifiers). Here, we will point out the important features of models to deal with grasping. An Intelligent grasp algorithm must decide where and how to grasp the objects. For example, in the final state considered in fig. 2 it is not expected to perform a good horizontal insertion of <u>hor1</u> in <u>vert2</u> and <u>vert3</u> if we try to grasp <u>hor1</u> around the mass center. MODELS must define a region where the appropriated grasping is possible. Therefore, the grasping algorithm will decide to grasp the object according to the goal it is trying to satisfy.

Figure 6 shows how to describe, by a predicate, the grasping model of an object. The first argument is the name of the object, the second is its stable position, the third is a list with possible angles of grasping, the fourth informs, for each grasping angle, about the maximum and minimum heights between which grasping is possible, and finally the last argument informs about the horizontal deviation around the position of the object in plane XY.

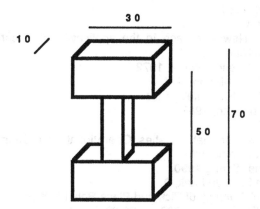

`grasp_model(obj,3,[0,1.571],[[50,70],[50,70]],[[-15,15],[-5,5]])`

Figure 6 - A grasping model

6 - CONCLUSIONS

From the previous sections we may point out the following conclusions:
• the pre-processing module of HLP makes the pruning of goals that are already accomplished in the description of the initial state of the object's world;
• plan generation uses one of two alternative searching methods: Best First or Branch and Bound;
• the heuristic function of Best First approach computes the number of objects to move in order to accomplish a goal. The lower cost is chosen;
• at each level the tree is pruned for the sake of efficiency;
• Best First approach is here really fast, the answer being obtained immediately. We claim that it can be used in real time environments. Another advantage of Best First is that this approach gives almost always a plan with the same cost of Branch and Bound.
• the advantage of Branch and Bound here is that the best plan is always generated. The difference in which concerns plan execution time is not so big as it was initially supposed

since some optimizations were made in Branch and Bound to avoid excessive switching between nodes which are close to the solution to nodes still far from the solution;
• the explanation support makes it easy to the user the understanding of HLP strategies;
• traditional difficulties in the connection between Vision outputs and inputs of symbolic Planners are overcomed by the existence of the World Descriptor agent;
• at the level of the plan execution, our agents take into account the way the objects are grasped.

REFERENCES AND LITERATURE

[Camarinha-89]   Sistema de Programação e controle de estações robóticas
                   uma arquitectura baseada em conhecimento
                   Dissertação de Doutoramento,
                   UNL,Lisboa,1989
                   Camarinha, L.

[Fikes-72]   STRIPS: A New Approach to the application of Theorem Proving to
                   Problem Solving
                   Artificial Intelligence, Vol. 2, 1972
                   Fikes, R. E and Nilsson, N. J.

[Huhns-87]   Distributed Artificial Intelligence
                   Morgan Kaufmann, 1987
                   Huhns, M.N.

[Hutchinson-90]   Spar: A Planner that satisfies Operational and Geometric Goals in
                   Uncertain Environments
                   AI Magazine, Spring 1990
                   Hutchinson,S. H. and Kak, A. C.

[LozanoPerez-89]   Task-Level Planning of Pick-and-Place Robot Motions
                   Computer IEEE, March 1989, pp 21-29
                   Lozano-Perez,T. ; Jones,J.L. ; Mazer, E. ; O'Donnell, P.A.

[Mello-91]   A Correct and Complete Algorithm for the Generation of Mechanical
                   Assembly Sequences
                   IEEE Transactions on Robotics and Automation, v. 7, n. 2,
                   pp 228-240, April 1991
                   Mello, L. and Sanderson, A.

[Newell-63]   GPS : A Program that simulates Human Thought
                   in Computer and Thought, Feigenbaum, E. and Feldman, J.
                   N.Y., McGraw-Hill, 1963
                   Newell, A. and Simon, H.

[Oliveira-91]   Towards a Generic Monitor for Cooperation
                   Workshop on BlackBoard Systems, AAAI Conference, L.A., 1991
                   Oliveira, E. and Qiegang L.

[Ramos-89]   Cooperation Between Vision and Planning Agents in a simple Robotic
                   Environment
                   Intelligent Autonomous Systems 2, Amsterdam, 1989
                   Ramos, C. and Oliveira, E.

[Ramos-91a)]   The Generation of Efficient High Level Plans and the Robot World
                   Representation in a Cooperative Community of Robotic Agents
                   ICAR-91-5th International Conference on Advanced Robotics,
                   Pisa, 1991
                   Ramos, C. and Oliveira, E.

[Ramos-91b)]   Intelligent Task Planning and Execution on Assembly Robotics
                    EURISCON-91 - European Robotics and Intelligent Systems Conf.
                    Corfu, Greece, 1991
                    Ramos, C. and Oliveira E.

[Sacerdoti-74]   Planning in a Hierarchy of Abstraction Spaces
                    Artificial Intelligence, Vol. 5, pp 115-135, 1974
                    Sacerdoti, E. D.

[Sacerdoti -77]   A Structure for Plans and Behavior
                    Elsevier, New York, 1977
                    Sacerdoti, E. D.

[Tate-77]   Generating Project Networks
                    5th International Joint Conference on AI, 1977
                    Tate, A.

Towards a Theory of the Repair Process

Gerhard Friedrich, Georg Gottlob, Wolfgang Nejdl*

Christian Doppler Laboratory for Expert Systems

Technical University of Vienna, Paniglgasse 16

A-1040 Vienna, Austria

e-mail: nejdl@vexpert.dbai.tuwien.ac.at

Abstract

This paper describes and formally defines the diagnosis and repair process considering repair as the main goal of this process. Other research on model-based diagnosis so far has been dealing only with the replacement of all components in a diagnosis as a repair action which we will show to be inadequate in many applications. We will then describe several key concepts necessary for a theory of a repair process and give a general definition of the repair process. Finally, we analyze the special case of component oriented repair and briefly mention how these concepts can enhance a conventional diagnosis system.

1 Introduction

This paper deals with the question of how to formally define the model-based diagnosis and repair process. We consider repair (i.e., restoration of specified system purposes) as the main goal of this process. Interestingly enough, this issue has been considered so far in only a few papers ([6] and [5]). In contrast to these papers we will develop a formal theory of repair in the context of diagnosis from first principles. The notion of therapy as a specialized kind of repair has been discussed in [2].

We will start by showing that the prevalent notion of repair as "replacement of all components in a diagnosis" is inadequate in many applications and how it has to be extended. We will discuss in Section 2 several key concepts necessary for a theory of a repair process and give a general definition of the repair process. Finally, in Section 3 we discuss the special case of component-oriented repair and also briefly discuss how these concepts can focus a conventional diagnosis engine.

---

*Part of this work was done while the author was spending a sabbatical at Xerox PARC.

Redundant Systems

Example 1 Redundant Switch Network

Consider the circuit in Figure 1 consisting of switches and bulbs where all switches are closed. For simplicity reasons, we further assume a sufficient power supply and correctness of the bulbs. Therefore, we expect all bulbs to be *on*, which can be expressed by $\forall i$: $light(b_i) = on$.

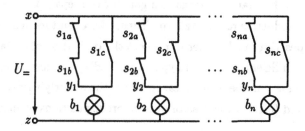

Figure 1: Switch Network

Observing all bulbs to be *off*, a consistency-based diagnosis approach produces $2n$ conflict sets $\langle S_{1a}, S_{1b} \rangle, \langle S_{1c} \rangle, \ldots, \langle S_{na}, S_{nb} \rangle, \langle S_{nc} \rangle$. Generating all minimal diagnoses yields a set containing 2^n diagnoses. This number is not reduced by a probability-based focus, if all fault probabilities are equal. Conventional diagnosis systems will proceed by performing n additional measurements between the switches S_{ra} and S_{rb} for $r = 1 \ldots n$ if these measurements are possible.

Reconsidering the major purpose of the system (i.e., to supply all consumers with energy), the straightforward repair action would be to repair just the n switches labeled with c, $\{S_{rc} \mid r = 1 \ldots n\}$.

This example indicates that a loose coupling of diagnosis and repair, where we take measurements to identify a leading diagnosis and then do repair, is an oversimplification of the task to be solved.

A repair-oriented approach results in several improvements for our example and for redundant systems in general. First, we save additional measurements if we concentrate on finding a sufficient repair set. Second, a minimal repair set is often smaller than a minimal diagnosis set, saving additional repair costs and minimizing the duration of the repair (repairing for example only 1 out of n components). Real life applications include all fault tolerant systems.

Focussed Repair   Another important characteristic of the repair process is its orientation and consequent focusing on a specific system purpose. While repairing components, only components which contribute to this specific function are considered. Although a device may be large, focusing on a specific purpose considers only relatively few components in most cases. In the ARTEX system developed at our department for diagnosing audio switching systems (which uses mainly heuristic diagnosis), the repair focuses on one out of hundreds of audio paths, namely the one, where a wrong output is detected.

Symptom Therapy Another notion of repair, which has been discussed in [2], is the concept of avoiding certain fault patterns as a goal for the repair process. This strategy is useful especially for abductive reasoning formalisms, where fault models play the dominant role in the system description. In order to prevent the derivation of certain symptoms, we have to invalidate a sufficient number of hypotheses leading to these symptoms. Symptom therapy is often necessary in medicine in cases, where the underlying causes are not known or cannot be removed (e.g., in the case of genetic predispositions or incurable diseases).

Compensation In the case of compensation, we do not (or cannot) exchange faulty components, but can influence their output behavior by changing their input parameters. As complex systems can usually not be guaranteed to work 100% correctly, compensation is used in most complex systems. Breaking harder when breaks are slowly beginning to fail is just one example.

Structural Changes Especially in emergency situations we use additional (usually primitive) components to change the structure of a device. This allows us to re-establish (primitive) functions of the device. Examples include emergency situations (using a wire to simulate a closed switch), passive redundancy, devices with self-reconfiguring ability or substitution of different components with a different type.

2 The Repair Process

Section 1 shows, that the process of performing diagnosis plus repair (we will call that *repair process* from now on) is much more sophisticated and has more variants than previous papers on model-based diagnosis have assumed. In almost all of these papers, the repair process has (implicitly) been defined as a simple two-phase process consisting of first finding the most plausible diagnosis candidate and then exchanging all components in this diagnosis.

However, as we have seen in the previous section, many application examples suggest a more sophisticated approach to the repair process using an alternating sequence of diagnosis and repair:

- Gain new knowledge (observations, device checks) in order to identify the (most plausible) system state (diagnosis).

- Make changes in the system state in order to ultimately get a system which fulfills its purpose (repair).

2.1 System States, Purpose and Theory Revision

In order to define the concept of the repair process formally, we will define the notions of *plausible system state*, *purpose* and *theory revision for integrating observations and actions* in the following sections. We will define these concepts in the framework of first order logic. However, they can be easily adapted to other contexts.

2.1.1 System State

Definition 1 (Plausible System State) A *(plausible) system state* Σ is a logical formula describing the view a user has of the actual world. Σ includes three different parts:

- Σ_{SD}: A set of first order sentences describing the structure and behavior of the system and its components.

- Σ_{COMP}: A set of first order sentences containing only mode literals associating modes (e.g., *ok* or *ab*) with components.

- Σ_{PAR}: A set of first order sentences describing the actual world in addition to the system description. These sentences include the observations made during the repair process and express the internal state of a system (including e.g., the values of physical parameters persisting after some repair actions).

where

$$\Sigma = \Sigma_{SD} \wedge \Sigma_{COMP} \wedge \Sigma_{PAR}$$

This system state can be seen as a set of plausible worlds (consisting of logical formulas) which represent the various states the user is willing to assume for the system. We represent one possible world by indexing the appropriate formulas, such as $\Sigma_w, \Sigma_{SD_w}, \Sigma_{COMP_w}, \Sigma_{PAR_w}$. $W(\Sigma)$ denotes the set of plausible worlds and w or $w(\Sigma) \in W(\Sigma)$ one of these plausible worlds.[1]

Such a world should be seen not only as a set of (propositional) facts (like most papers on belief revision do), but as a set of formulas. We can then include a disjunction of equally preferable facts in one world and do not have to split this world into a lot of

---

[1] In this paper, the term "world" usually denotes a plausible model of the actual world, not to be confused with the actual world itself.

different (equally preferred) ones. We are also able to include the system description and similar axioms. On the other hand, by keeping the possible models of such a complex world in mind, we can still define a model-based belief revision operator, which does not care about syntactic details in our axioms when they are not relevant.

System States in Diagnosis Systems To illustrate these concepts we will describe the system state Σ in a conventional model-based diagnosis system $(SD, COMP, OBS)$ considering only minimal diagnoses.

First, we have

$$\Sigma_{SD} \equiv SD$$

which does not change during the diagnosis process assuming non-destructive observations. Hence, Σ_{SD} is the same in all plausible worlds and can be seen as a set of integrity constraints.

Starting without any observations ($OBS = \emptyset$), the assumption that all components are functioning correctly is the minimal diagnosis, and we have

$$\Sigma_{COMP} \equiv \bigwedge_{c \in COMP} mode(c, ok)$$

Considering only minimal diagnoses means that we consider only worlds with a (set-theoretically) minimal set of faulty components. The plausibility of worlds in a conventional diagnosis system is solely determined by Σ_{COMP_w}.

Integrating additional observations *obs* is represented as

$$\Sigma' = \Sigma \circ_B obs$$

where $\circ_B$ is a theory revision operator integrating a formula *obs* into Σ, such that Σ' is again consistent and includes *obs*. Conflicting observations are integrated into Σ by changing Σ_{COMP}, and the plausible worlds $w \in W(\Sigma)$ correspond to the minimal diagnoses and their context.

The context mechanism of an (unfocused) ATMS describes all possible worlds, indexed by Σ_{COMP_w} and including the system model as Σ_{SD_w}.

As observations do not affect the actual system (only our view of it), we can assume $\Sigma_{PAR} \equiv OBS$, as all relevant parameters can be derived when needed. If we allowed actions affecting the system then Σ_{PAR} would have to include all our beliefs about the physical state of the system including persistency of (derived) values after such actions.

Initial System State The initial system state represents the assumptions one is willing to make before starting the repair process.

In usual field diagnosis situations where we have no conflicting observations, we assume that all components are working correctly. Only after observing conflicting values, we have to revise our correctness assumptions, but still use a minimality criterion for this revision.

On the other hand, if we want to make a final manufacturing test over all components, we usually assume that all components may be broken and try to prove with an (exhaustive) set of tests and measurements that everything is correct.

2.1.2 Purpose

The second important concept for the repair process is the notion of a purpose of the system, which has to be (re-) established by the repair actions.

Definition 2 (Purpose) A purpose of a system is a first order sentence T representing the correct function of the system.

For the switch network depicted in Figure 1, the purpose we used was $\bigwedge_{i=1...n} light(b_i) = on$. The redundant power supply can be described by $\bigwedge_{i=1...n} mode(s_{ia}, ok) \wedge mode(s_{ib}, ok) \wedge mode(s_{ic}, ok)$.

Relative importance of purpose goals can be defined by a partial ordering, using a current purpose goal T_i as initial focus, but including more important purpose goals $T_j > T_i$, if evidence for a failure of T_j is detected during the repair process.

Sometimes a purpose of a system depends on the situation (e.g., defined by the inputs) this system is used in. Such a situation dependent purpose T' can simply be expressed by a T of the form *preconditions* $\rightarrow T'$.

We will not discuss the integration of time into purpose and repair in this paper. Basically, all concepts described in this paper are still necessary in such a case. However, extensions are required to handle concepts like mean time to failure (MTTF) and similar notions from reliability theory which are necessary for preventive maintenance or regular maintenance tasks.

Checking the Purpose We can now formally define, what it means for a purpose to be guaranteed in the current system state.

Definition 3 (Guaranteed Purpose) A purpose T is guaranteed in a current system state Σ, iff

$$\Sigma \models T$$

This means, that we have to be able to make enough actual observations in order to guarantee the purpose. In the extreme if we are not allowed to take observations anywhere, we have to rely solely on assumptions about the correctness of components. In the other extreme, we do not have to make any assumptions if we take measurements everywhere.

This dependence on available observations has to be considered whenever we formulate the purpose of a system. Although we can express the purpose of redundancy in our switch network (by the sentence $\forall i : mode(s_{ia}, ok) \land mode(s_{ib}, ok) \land mode(s_{ic}, ok)$), we have to be able to look at the single switches to verify this. The bulbs are no indicators for this purpose goal.

Purpose and Repair Additionally, the purpose has to be related to the repair capabilities such that the system is repairable.

Definition 4 (Complete Repair for a World) A *complete repair* for a world $w \in \Sigma$, a purpose $\mathcal{T}$, a set of repair capabilities $\mathcal{R}$, is a sequence $\langle \rho_1, \ldots, \rho_n \rangle$ of sets of repair actions $\rho_i \subseteq \mathcal{R}$ for $i = 1, \ldots, n$ such that

$$\Sigma_{SD_w} \land \Sigma_{COMP_w} \land \Sigma_{PAR_w} \circ_A \rho_1 \ldots \circ_A \rho_n$$

is satisfiable and

$$\Sigma_{SD_w} \land \Sigma_{COMP_w} \land \Sigma_{PAR_w} \circ_A \rho_1 \ldots \circ_A \rho_n \models \mathcal{T}$$

The operator $\circ_A$ is a revision operator updating a theory such that it incorporates the state change describing the repair actions resulting in a new consistent theory. We will discuss the concept of revision operators for this task in Section 2.1.3.

Definition 5 (Complete Repair for a System State) A sequence of sets of repair actions $\langle \rho_1, \ldots, \rho_n \rangle$ is a *complete repair* for a system state Σ representing a set of worlds $W(\Sigma)$, iff it is a complete repair for each world $w \in W(\Sigma)$.

Once we can guarantee the purpose for Σ, the repair process is finished. In the following we will use the term *complete repair* with respect to the system state except where indicated otherwise.

We will call a complete repair sequence *irreducible* if there exists no proper subsequence which is a complete repair. An irreducible complete repair sequence guarantees the purpose under the precondition, that the assumptions made for initial system state and theory revision operator apply.

2.1.3 Theory Revision

The third main concept for repair is the integration of different actions into the system state Σ describing the actual device. Basically, we have to incorporate two different kinds of actions into Σ:

Observations: They do not affect the system to be repaired. Observations gather additional knowledge in order to make our view of the actual world more accurate.

Repair actions: They change the system. No additional knowledge about the actual world is gained. However, our model of the world (the system state) has to be changed reflecting these actions. The goal of repair actions is to re-establish (part of) the purpose of a system.

All other actions can be subsumed under these two types. (Test actions for example can not re-establish the purpose of the system, but can be handled by the same revision operator as repair actions.)

Revision Operators To incorporate the logical formulas representing these actions, we have to use two different belief revision operators, one ($\circ_B$) for adding knowledge, and one ($\circ_A$) for describing the results of actions.

The operators have to deal with the task that they often have to incorporate conflicting information into a theory. Both also have to minimize the resulting changes of the theory in some way. However, the minimal changes reasonable for the two different types of operations differ significantly.

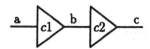

Figure 2: Two Buffers

Example 2 Consider the circuit depicted in Figure 2. After measuring $a \neq c$, the plausible worlds we usually consider are [c1] and [c2].

On the one hand, if we incorporate the observation $a = b$, c1 gets an alibi and we can assume $mode(c1, ok)$ (at least for the current set of inputs). The only remaining plausible world is [c2].

On the other hand, after (successfully) repairing $c1$ we also assume $mode(c1, ok)$ and therefore $a = b$ (i.e., the same facts as before). However, the remaining plausible worlds are now [ ] and [c2], as we might have repaired the correct or the faulty component!

This difference is due to the fact, that o_A changes both the actual world and our view (the set of plausible worlds) of it, but o_B changes only our view of the actual world. Therefore, o_A takes a set of plausible worlds and changes the facts in these worlds transforming old worlds into new ones. o_B on the other hand integrates additional information about which world is correct, deleting some old worlds, confirming other old ones and making new worlds plausible.

If we define minimal change operators for incorporating new knowledge (observations) into a theory according to the (domain independent) axioms described in [3], one suitable revision operator would be the one described in [1]. If we change the axioms from [3] in a minimal way to make them applicable for minimizing the results of actions, the operator described in [8] is a suitable one.

All of the above mentioned axioms and operators are totally domain independent and are based on minimizing change in propositional models. Additional operators can be defined if more knowledge is available.

In this paper, we will not further discuss the notion of a sensible belief revision operator for adding new knowledge (observations) and refer the reader instead to the notions of plausible diagnoses in model-based diagnosis systems. For incorporating actions, we will analyze a simple pessimistic revision operator and mention how to employ more complex operators.

The effect of o_A on Σ can also be used to distinguish between the different kinds of repair actions. Structural changes do not change Σ_{COMP}, repair by component replacement does not change Σ_{SD}, and compensation of failures does not change Σ_{SD} and Σ_{COMP}.

2.2 A General Repair Scheme

We can now give a general scheme for a repair algorithm using the concepts developed in the previous section.

Algorithm Scheme 1 A *repair process* can be defined as follows:

1. Assume an initial system state Σ (consisting of Σ_{SD}, Σ_{COMP} and Σ_{PAR}). Σ represents a set of worlds corresponding to the view of the diagnostic agent, e.g., the plausible worlds he considers.

2. Assume an initial purpose $\mathcal{T}$, which has to be fulfilled by the system and which will be considered as the focus for the repair process.

3. *If* the purpose T is guaranteed by the current Σ, *then stop.*

4. Generate sequences of possible sets of repair operations which could be performed in the next step and evaluate their utility. The set of operations consists of observations, test actions, and repair actions. Consequences of these repair sequences are computed by appropriate belief revision operators.

5. Choose the best (known) sequence and execute it. This will change the system state to a new current system state Σ' (according to the belief revision operators used) and possibly T to T'.

6. *go to 3*

The therapy algorithm defined for repair in abductive systems in [2] is a special case of this algorithm scheme.

In most dynamic systems a monitoring phase is included before the actual repair process. During this monitoring phase, the system is checked if it guarantees its purpose. Only after it does not guarantee a minimal purpose, the repair process begins.

3 Component-Oriented Repair (CR)

In this section we analyze the notion of component-oriented repair in more detail, as it is probably the most important kind of repair.

$ABM(c)$ represents the set of possible fault modes of a component, $\mathcal{OK}(N) = \{mode(c, ok) \mid c \in N\}$ for any set N of components, and $\mathcal{C}(M)$ is the set of components mentioned in any set $M \subseteq \{mode(c, m) \mid c \in COMP, m \in (\{ok\} \cup ABM(c))\}$.

Definition 6 (Diagnosis) A diagnosis for $(SD, COMP, OBS)$ is a set $M = \{mode(c_1, m_1), \ldots, mode(c_n, m_n)\}$ where $c_i \in COMP$, $m_i \in ABM(c_i)$ for all $i = 1, \ldots, n$, and $c_i \neq c_j$ for all $i \neq j$ such that

$$SD \cup OBS \cup M \cup \mathcal{OK}(COMP - \mathcal{C}(M))$$

is consistent and a component has always to be in exactly one behavioral mode. [2]

For CR we will use the following conventions:

Worlds: Σ_{COMP} represents the set of worlds corresponding to the set of diagnoses $DIAG$ returned by the diagnosis process:

$$\Sigma_{COMP} = \bigvee_{M \in DIAG} (M \cup \mathcal{OK}(COMP - \mathcal{C}(M)))$$

---

[2] In a logical sentence we use conjunction of all set elements instead of union.

Repair Actions: ρ represents a set of repair actions $\rho \subseteq \mathcal{R}$, where the set of possible repair actions $\mathcal{R}$ is $\{mode(c,m) \mid c \in COMP, m \in (\{ok\} \cup ABM(c))\}$. We allow a component to be replaced by a faulty one in order to fulfill the purpose.

Definition 7 (Belief Revision Operators for CR) A belief revision operator $\circ_A$ which integrates component-replacement repair actions into a system state Σ can be stated as

$$(\Sigma_{SD} \wedge \Sigma_{COMP} \wedge \Sigma_{PAR}) \circ_A \rho = \Sigma'_{SD} \wedge \Sigma'_{COMP} \wedge \Sigma'_{PAR}$$

such that

- The repair actions do not alter the system description, hence $\Sigma'_{SD} = \Sigma_{SD} = SD$.
- $\Sigma_{SD} \cup \rho$ is satisfiable, hence a component occurs at most once in the repair set.
- We assume as repair action only *successful* component replacements, i.e., replacements, where the mode of the new component does not change after it is put into the system. Therefore, exchanging a component c changes Σ_{COMP} in the following way:
$$\Sigma'_{COMP} = \Sigma_{COMP}\{mode(c,old)/mode(c,new)\}$$
where $mode(c,old)$ is the mode of the exchanged component and $mode(c,new)$ the mode of the new component.
- The only freedom left is Σ'_{PAR}. We will discuss two revision operators $\circ_A$ which differ on the construction of Σ'_{PAR}.

In order to generate repair sets efficiently a very important task is to limit the search space for an irreducible complete repair set. We have the following definitions:

Definition 8 (Purpose Assuring Set) A purpose assuring set R is a set $R \subseteq \{mode(c_i, m_i) \mid c_i \in COMP, m_i \in (\{ok\} \cup ABM(c_i))\}$ such that

$$SD \cup R \cup \phi \models \mathcal{T}$$

and

$$SD \cup R \cup \phi$$

is satisfiable, for all ϕ, where ϕ consists of mode literals mentioning those components which are not included in R (i.e., ϕ has the form $\{mode(c_j, m_j) \mid c_j \in COMP - \mathcal{C}(R)\}$ where $m_j \in (\{ok\} \cup ABM(c_j))$).

A purpose assuring set is a set of component behaviors (ok or a fault mode) such that the purpose of a system is fulfilled. The behavior of other components does not matter for guaranteeing the purpose.

Definition 9 (Kernel Purpose Assuring Set) A kernel purpose assuring set is an irreducible purpose assuring set.

The following theorem establishes a link between kernel purpose assuring sets and repair sets. This is important since kernel purpose assuring sets can be generated prior to diagnosis and serve as a starting point for generating repair sets.

Theorem 1 For each kernel purpose assuring set K it holds that

$$(\Sigma_{SD} \wedge \Sigma_{COMP} \wedge \Sigma_{PAR}) \circ_A K \models \mathcal{T}$$

for each Σ_{COMP} and Σ_{PAR}. Therefore, each kernel purpose assuring set is a complete repair for each Σ.

This follows from definition 8 and 9 and our success assumption for repair actions. Also $\Sigma' = (\Sigma_{SD} \wedge \Sigma_{COMP} \wedge \Sigma_{PAR}) \circ_A K$ cannot be inconsistent, as we can always produce a consistent Σ' by assuming $\Sigma'_{PAR} = true$.

Corollary 1 Each kernel purpose assuring set is a superset of an irreducible complete repair set.

An irreducible complete repair set may be smaller because adding Σ_{PAR} to $SD \cup K$ may reduce K to $K' \subset K$ so that $SD \cup K' \cup \Sigma_{PAR} \models \mathcal{T}$. On the other hand, complete and irreducible repair sets are possible, which are not subsets of any kernel purpose assuring sets, if we take persistency of observations into account and the purpose goal is stated in a situation dependent way.

Corollary 2 A repair set ρ for a set of diagnoses $DIAG$ and a kernel purpose assuring set K is:

$$\{mode(c,m) \mid mode(c,m) \in K, \exists n : n \neq m \; \exists M \in DIAG :$$

$$mode(c,n) \in (M \cup \mathcal{OK}(COMP - \mathcal{C}(M)))\}$$

This corollary can be simplified if we assume that the kernel purpose set only contains components behaving correctly:

$$\rho = \bigcup_{M \in DIAG} \{mode(c,ok) \mid c \in \mathcal{C}(M)\} \cap K$$

Corollary 3 If the system state Σ makes no assumptions about the mode of the components (i.e., $\Sigma_{COMP} = true$ — all possible worlds are plausible), then the notion of complete repair set and kernel purpose assuring set coincide.

CR with No Persistency (CRNP) This pessimistic approach makes no assumptions about the persistency of the observations and the internal parameters of the system, hence $\Sigma'_{PAR} = true$. This is useful if we consider the output of a pure diagnosis process, e.g., a set of diagnoses, as a set of candidates for repair. It follows that all complete repair sets characterized by Corollary 2 are also irreducible repair sets.

CR with Persistency (CRP) If we want to further reduce repair sets, we have to take persistency of observations and parameters into account and describe, how they change due to repair actions. We can for example use the causal theory framework discussed in [4] which minimizes unexplained changes.

4   Diagnosis and Repair

It is an interesting question, in which cases repair and diagnosis yield the same results. In the following we assume that a pure diagnostic reasoning system supplies us only with a set of diagnoses consisting of suspect components and therefore appeal to a CRNP-oriented view of repair.

Theorem 2 (For CRNP) If K is a kernel purpose assuring set for $(SD, COMP, T)$ and $COMP = C(K)$ then for all diagnoses M the repair set $\rho = M$ is complete and irreducible, e.g., the diagnosis is equivalent to repair.

In case of CRP, this is not valid in general, as a diagnosis may be further reduced for repair.

If we assume that $SD \cup \{\neg mode(c, ok) | c \in COMP\}$ is satisfiable , e.g., the assumption that all components are faulty is a possible diagnosis (which is the case for most systems) then the above theorem holds also in the other direction.

Definition 10 (Redundancy) A system model is redundant with respect to a specific purpose if there exist at least two different kernel purpose assuring sets for this purpose.

Remark 1 (For CRNP) If a system model is not redundant and well modeled then there exists one unique, complete and irreducible repair set for all diagnoses.

Even if we do not want to construct a completely repair-based system, we can still use some of the concepts discussed above to enhance a conventional model-based diagnosis system. We are then in several cases able to avoid the discrepancy between diagnoses and repair sets and can therefore directly use the output of the diagnosis system for repair.

Redundancy: We aggregate redundant sets of components into one higher level component. If this component is found to be faulty, it corresponds to an *abstract diagnosis*[3] of the form "$n - m + 1$ components are faulty" (in case of m out of n redundancy). If we have to distinguish between these redundant components, we can use *abstract measurement selection* (suggesting to take "1 out of n measurement points").

Focusing: The diagnosis focus is chosen depending on the repair purpose. The system model has to be designed according to the repair strategy using the corresponding abstraction level.

Structure: We can include structure changing repair actions into the model, such that they will be computed as diagnoses (preferably with high probability).

Probabilities: Updating probabilities of worlds (diagnosis candidates) as a result of repair actions is straightforward, as we consider the effect of a repair action on each of the worlds separately. Including probabilities for failure rates of new components to be exchanged for faulty ones is straightforward, too. Probability can also be a good way to encode the notion of "plausible world".

Finally, consider again the circuit depicted in Figure 1 and its purpose $\forall i$: $light(b_i) = on$. With respect to the purpose each set of switches $\{s_{ia}, s_{ib}, s_{ic}\}$ is only responsible for connecting x and y_i. It should therefore be aggregated into one abstract component s_i. The corresponding set of (abstract) repair actions is then $\{mode(s_1, ok), \ldots, mode(s_n, ok)\}$, each of which can be realized either by $\{mode(s_{ia}, ok), mode(s_{ib}, ok)\}$ or by $\{mode(s_{ic}, ok)\}$.

Furthermore, taking our correctness assumptions into account, a set of rules of the form

$$mode(s_i, ok) \rightarrow light(b_i) = on$$

would be sufficient for the repair process, getting as abstract diagnosis "The connection between x and y_i is not functioning correctly."

5 Conclusion

The current notion of diagnosis in model-based reasoning systems fails to solve the problem of repairing a system in the general case. Consequently this paper defines the notion of *repair* and *repair purpose* to formalize the *repair process* and its goals extending the notion of *diagnosis process*. We have further analyzed some common kinds of repair actions and

---

[3] The general notion of an abstract diagnosis was introduced in [7].

finally have shown how these concepts can enhance a conventional diagnosis engine if the system model reflects these concepts as described in this paper.

Acknowledgements

The third author thanks Johan de Kleer and the other members of the SERA group at Xerox PARC for providing him with an excellent research environment.

References

[1] Mukesh Dalal. Investigations into a theory of knowledge base revision: Preliminary report. In *Proceedings of the National Conference on Artificial Intelligence (AAAI)*, pages 475–479, St. Paul, Minneapolis, August 1988.

[2] Gerhard Friedrich, Georg Gottlob, and Wolfgang Nejdl. Hypothesis classification, abductive diagnosis and therapy. In *Proceedings of the International Workshop on Expert Systems in Engineering*, Vienna, September 1990. Springer Verlag, Lecture Notes in Artificial Intelligence, Vo. 462.

[3] Peter Gärdenfors. *Knowledge in Flux*. MIT Press, 1988.

[4] Hector Geffner. Causal theories for nonmonotonic reasoning. In *Proceedings of the National Conference on Artificial Intelligence (AAAI)*, pages 524–530, Boston, August 1990. Morgan Kaufmann Publishers, Inc.

[5] Ashok Goel and B. Chandrasekaran. Functional representation of designs and redesign problem solving. In *Proceedings of the International Joint Conference on Artificial Intelligence (IJCAI)*, pages 1388–1394, Detroit, August 1989. Morgan Kaufmann Publishers, Inc.

[6] Jeff Pepper and Gary S. Kahn. Repair strategies in a diagnostic expert system. In *Proceedings of the International Joint Conference on Artificial Intelligence (IJCAI)*, pages 531–534, Milano, August 1987. Morgan Kaufmann Publishers, Inc.

[7] Vijay A. Saraswat, Johan de Kleer, and Olivier Raiman. Contributions to a theory of diagnosis. In *First International Workshop on Principles of Diagnosis*, pages 33–38, Stanford, July 1990.

[8] Marianne Winslett. Reasoning about action using a possible models approach. In *Proceedings of the National Conference on Artificial Intelligence (AAAI)*, pages 89–93, Saint Paul, Minnesota, August 1988.

DECLARATIVE SOURCE DEBUGGING

Miguel Calejo[1] and Luís Moniz Pereira

Logic Programming and Artificial Intelligence Group
Universidade Nova de Lisboa (UNL)
2825 Monte da Caparica
Portugal

Abstract

We explore the idea of basing declarative debugging on the search for buggy *textual formulas* in the program, rather than on the search for computed buggy *formula instances*. The motivation is to build declarative debuggers requiring less oracle queries, at the cost of loosing information about the variable bindings of the diagnosis. This new approach we call *declarative source debugging*, as opposed to *declarative execution debugging*.

A motivating example for pure Prolog is given, consisting of an append computation with a wrong solution. Afterwards we present a declarative source debugging algorithm, and simulate it on some other examples. Under an (aparently reasonable) assumption the number of queries needed to derive a diagnosis is logarithmic with the *number of program source clauses*, rather than with the number of derivation nodes as in conventional declarative debugging, when using no case-dependent information.

Our conclusions carry over easily to other bug symptom types not exemplified and to impure Prolog, by adopting the conceptual framework of [Pereira Calejo 88, 89] and thereby uniformizing their treatment. This is reported in [Calejo 91].

Introduction

This paper focuses on the concept of declarative source debugging, neglecting references to other authors and omiting technical preliminaries. Please refer to [Calejo 91].

---

[1] FAX: +351 1 295 5641 Phone: +351 1 726 5147   Applelink:IT0083

MacNET/Connect:calejom   Internet: mc@fct.unl.pt

Searching for bugs instead of bug instances

Given a computation producing a false solution, conventional declarative debuggers search for a *bug instance* (an instance of a source program clause, with false head and true body goals).

It is possible to use a divide and conquer strategy over the AND tree of clause instances. For example, the Divide and Query algorithm [Shapiro 82] optimizes (i.e., minimizes) the number of queries, if the AND tree is a single chain of nodes and if no domain-specific information is available: the number of queries is then logarithmic with the number of tree nodes[2].

Let's redefine the purpose of a declarative (*source*) debugger to be as follows: search for *a clause which has an instance which is a bug instance*. This possibility was raised in [Pereira Calejo 88] (where, by the way, references to other work can be found), but not explored.

Example A buggy "append" predicate follows with a wrong solution
```
append([1,2,3,4,5],[6],[1,2,3,4,5,6,7,8]):
    (c1)    my_append([X|A],B,[X|C]) :- my_append(A,B,C).
    (c2)    my_append([],L,K).        % bug: K≠L
```

The AND tree of this solution is (the labels on the left denoting the source clauses that matched the goals):

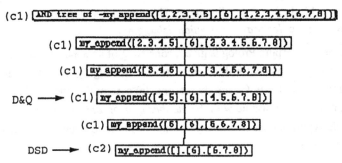

Divide and Query would pick the middle goal node for querying the oracle, plus an aditional query or two until finding the bug.

Now, notice that under the node my_append([],[6],[6,7,8]) there are only instances of clauses (one in fact: c2) which have no instances above the node: above the node there are only instances of clause c1. A *declarative source debugger* should query about that node first. Were it to be stated correct by the oracle, there would be a bug instance higher in the tree, in a region containing only instances of clause c1, and *no additional queries would be needed*; being wrong (as in fact it is), then clause c2 has a bug instance, and again no additional queries are needed.

---

[2] More complicated AND trees are still tackled by Divide & Query with a logarithmic cost K log n, where K depends on the tree branching factor; however the algorithm is no longer optimal since it ignores the *form* of the tree. A lookeahead search over possible queries and answers would be optimal, but more costly to implement.

Therefore, for this example 2 queries are needed for a "declarative source debugger", rather than 4 for a "conventional declarative debugger", always in the worst case[3].

This example suggests that while a conventional declarative debugger can find a bug instance with a number of queries logarithmic with the number of AND tree nodes, a declarative source debugger might be able to find a bug with a number of queries dependent on the number of source *clauses* in the program - a much more interesting prospect, since logic programs are apt to use recursion.

What should a declarative source debugger be ?

We now present our first attempt at a declarative source debugging algorithm, for the wrong solution problem for pure Prolog, to keep the exposition clear. It is easily generalized for the missing solution, inadmissible goal and wrong output bug symptom types, for impure Prolog, by adopting the conceptual framework in [Pereira Calejo 88,89a]; this is to appear in [Calejo 91], together with other declarative source debugging algorithms.

First, a couple of **definitions**: for a solution G, $CI(G)$ is the set of uniquely named clause instances[4] matching nodes in the[5] AND tree of G, and $C(G)$ is the set of all source program clauses with (computed) instances in $CI(G)$. CO denotes the union of all sets $C(X)$, and CIO the union of all sets $CI(X)$, for all existing correct(X) statements of the oracle[6].

We recall the Divide and Query algorithm due to Shapiro, a standard declarative execution debugging algorithm:

> Given a wrong solution T, if $\#(CI(T)\backslash CIO)=1$ then the clause instance matching T's node is a diagnosis.

> Otherwise query the oracle about a goal solution G, such that $\#(CI(G)\backslash CIO) \approx \#(CI(T)\backslash(CI(G) \cup CIO])$ - i.e. it "splits the tree in half". If G is wrong, continue the algorithm recursively with G as wrong solution, else with T; (and CIO will be larger due to the additional correctness statement).

---

[3] We count the initial incorrectness statement for the top node as a query, because it contains the same type of information that a query does (i.e., whether some literal is wrong or correct).

[4] By "uniquely named clause instances" we mean that 2 syntactically similar clause instances matching different tree nodes are considered different.

[5] We refer to *the* computational AND tree of G, rather than to *an* AND tree of G, because we're referring to the concrete AND tree of an actual computation; we're not referring to all possible derivations, which may be more than one due to non-determinism.

[6] Whether X denotes or not a logical literal (so that for example subsumption could be used to avoid redundant queries) depends on the assumptions about the logic programming dialect at hand. This issue being irrelevant to the focus of this paper, we remit the reader to [Calejo 91] and consider that X denotes a particular goal solution term derived from our present computation.

We now present the new declarative source debugging algorithm.

THE SECURE ALGORITHM

Recall that given a correct solution G under a wrong solution A, there is always a buggy instance of a clause BC under A but not under G.

Correctness assumption: We start assuming that *BC*, the buggy clause we look for, *has no instances under G*. In other words, *all clauses with instances under a correct solution are (temporarily) assumed correct*. The present declarative source debugging algorithm starts with this assumption, and will resort to a "declarative execution debugging" algorithm if the assumption is untenable.

SECURE starts with a wrong solution T, and a consistent oracle theory (possibly empty) consisting of statements about computation results of the present program (in our present setting, goal solutions). It is called "secure" because as soon as it detects that the correctness assumption is untenable it retracts it and falls back into assumption-free Divide and Query. Some times it finds a wrong clause *instance*, rather than just a wrong source clause.

1.   If $CO \supseteq C(T)$,

1.1.   Then {we have run out of source suspects, the assumption is untenable}

      1.1.1. Proceed with the divide and query algorithm above, with T as a wrong solution and using the existing oracle statements, and obtain a diagnosis.

1.2.   Else {there are source suspects left consistent with the assumption}

      1.2.1. Consider the number of suspect clauses not yet assumed correct, N_S = #(C(T)\CO), i.e. the cardinality of the set resulting from the subtraction of CO from C(T).

      1.2.2. If N_S=1, then:

          Let D be the (only) source clause in C(T)\CO.

          1.2.2.1.   If CI(T)\CIO contains only instances of D, terminate returning D as the diagnosis; else attempt to *validate* the diagnosis:

          1.2.2.2.   Find the instance DI of clause D in CI(T)\CIO about which there are more statements by the oracle (be it about the body goals or about the head): DI=(H<-B); if there's more than one such instance, choose the one for which CI(H)\CIO is minimal (because we expect H to be wrong)

          1.2.2.3.   Query about the remaining clause goals/head (i.e, those for which there are yet no oracle statements), until either all are queried, a body goal is stated wrong, or the head is stated correct;

          1.2.2.4.   If DI is a bug instance, then terminate returning it as the diagnosis, else proceed above at 1.1 as follows: if DI has a wrong body goal Bi, consider T=Bi; else continue considering T as the lowest bug manifestation.

      1.2.3. else: select the node G matching a clause instance in CI(T)\CIO, such that #(C(G)\CO) $\approx$ N_S/2. If this criterium selects more than one node Gi, then:

          1.2.3.1. Choose node Gi for which #(CI(Gi)\CIO) $\approx$ #(CI(T)\[CI(Gi) $\cup$ CIO]) - the best according to the divide and query algorithm.

      1.2.4. Query the oracle (i.e., ask the user to extend it with a statement, possibly affecting CO) about the correctness of G.

      1.2.5. If G is wrong, then proceed at step 1 above with G instead of T, else proceed at step 1 but still with T as the wrong solution.

SOME PROPERTIES OF SECURE

If SECURE returns a diagnosis for top goal's wrong solution Top using step 1.2.2., the number of queries to the oracle will be O(K*log(#C(Top)) + L), i.e. logarithmic with the number of source clauses in the program that were used to deduce Top, plus the maximum number of literals L in a program clause. This is because at each iteration the current "source suspect set", C(T)\CO, is made smaller by half, and on termination L queries may be needed to validate the diagnosis. K is a factor dependent on the branching factor of the AND tree of Top, L[7].

If the result is a diagnosis obtained with an auxiliar divide and query algorithm (using step 1.1.1), the number of queries will in general be $O(L*\log(\#CI(Top)) + K*\log(\#C(Top)) + L)$, to address those cases where the queries made while believing the assumption were poorly chosen according to the divide and query criterium.

We now present an example showing the need for the query overhead of the diagnosis validation steps

Example
```
r(X,Y) :- p(X), p(Y).
p(X) :- q(X).
q(a).   q(b).
```

Take the intended model to be {r(a,a), p(a), q(a), q(b)}. Therefore, for wrong solution r(a,b) there's a bug instance p(b):-q(b), an instance of the second source clause. Now, when the oracle states solution p(a) to be correct, SECURE will assume the second clause to be correct. Its diagnosis validation stage checks the validity of the assumption, and in this case retracts it, falling back on divide and query.

More Examples

How reasonable is the correctness assumption ? Given our difficulty in analysing pros and cons formally, due to the diversity of logic programs, we examine how SECURE digests some examples from the declarative debugging literature. For these the SECURE assumption was found valid.

Following is a table with the maximum number of queries necessary until diagnosis, for each of the examples given in appendix. The initial bug manifestation is counted as a debugger query.

Example	#CI(Top)	#C(Top)	D&Q queries	SECURE, part I	Validation
Partition	6	3	4	2	1
Insertion sort	17	5	5	3	0
Quicksort	26	7	6	4	2
Simple rule engine	8	4	4	3	0
Sieve of Erastosthenes	19	8	6	4	0

The first column gives the number of nodes in the AND tree for the wrong solution, and the second the number of source clauses matching goals in it. These are the initial numbers of suspects for declarative execution debugging and for declarative source debugging, respectively. The "SECURE, part I" column contains the number of queries until obtaining an assumed diagnosis.

---

[7] In other words, we still didn't figure it out. It is however directly related with the branching factor of the execution tree.

The rightmost column contains the additional diagnosis validation queries for SECURE. In a practical programming environment, as soon as the debugger has a diagnosis to be validated it can show it to the user, so that he can decide on whether to accept the diagnosis without validation or to answer additional queries; the debugger could also show instances of the (hypothetically) wrong clause on request, which may constitute useful information.

Conclusion

We presented the idea of basing declarative debugging (also) on information relating a computation trace with the program source clauses producing it, instead of ignoring it as in all previous work.

Apart from this information, implicitly available for all other declarative debugging frameworks, no other information is necessary to improve the query performance of a declarative debugger. For example, intelligent execution strategies, additional information concerning term-level bugs and heuristics [Pereira 86, Pereira Calejo 88], use of abstractions on computation results [Lichtenstein Shapiro 88] and oracle assertions [Drabent et al. 88] can be combined with the present approach. This is explored in [Calejo 91].

A tentative algorithm was presented, called SECURE, that relies on an assumption which if proven false makes the algorithm resort to an assumption-free declarative execution debugging algorithm.

The assumption is, for the wrong solution case, that "buggy clauses have no instances under a correct solution". Although false in general, this assumption is adequate for the examples we simulated; however more experimentation is needed to find out its real usefulness. The query performance in such favorable cases is logarithmic with *the number of clauses in the program*, rather than with the number of execution nodes as in conventional algorithms like Divide and Query. If the assumption needs to be lifted the performance degrades to that of (assumption-free) Divide and Query.

Our experimentation was done on our HyperTracer environment [Calejo 91], designed for declarative execution debugging; we still didn't design an implementation geared for declarative source debugging, which should benefit itself from the SECURE assumption.

References

[Calejo 91]   Miguel Calejo, A Framework for Declarative Prolog Debugging, PhD thesis, Universidade Nova de Lisboa (in preparation)

[Calejo Pereira 89] Miguel Calejo and Luís Moniz Pereira, The HyperTracer Debugging Environment, technical report, DI/UNL

[Drabent et al. 88] W. Drabent, S. Nadjm-Tehrani and J. Maluszynski, "Algorithmic Debugging with Assertions" in META88 Proceedings (eds. J. Lloyd), MIT Press, Bristol, 1988.

[Lichtenstein Shapiro 88]   Y. Lichtenstein and E. Shapiro, "Abstract algorithmic debugging" in 5 th International Conference and Symposium on Logic Programming (eds. K. Bowen and R.A. Kowalski), MIT Press, Seattle, 1315--1336, 1988.

[Pereira 86]   Luís Moniz Pereira, Rational debugging in logic programming, in Procs. of the 3rd International Logic Programming Conference, E.Shapiro (ed.), Lecture Notes in Computer Science 225, Springer Verlag 1986.

[Pereira Calejo 88]   Luís Moniz Pereira and Miguel Calejo, A framework for Prolog debugging, Procs. 5th Int. Conf. on Logic Programming, Kowalski and Bowen (eds.), MIT Press 1988.

[Pereira Calejo 89]   Luís Moniz Pereira and Miguel Calejo, Algorithmic Debugging of Prolog Side-Effects, Procs. of the 4th Portuguese AI Conference, J.P.Martins and E. Morgado (eds.), Lecture Notes in Artificial Intelligence, Springer-Verlag 1989.

[Shapiro 82]   Ehud Y. Shapiro, Algorithmic Program Debugging, MIT Press 1982.

Appendix

Following are the examples on which we simulated SECURE.

For each example we present the program, the wrong solution and its AND tree[8]. The name of each source clause matching a solution node is between parenthesis. The queries done by "Divide and Query" are pointed out by (D&Q). The queries done by SECURE are pointed out by arrows, numbered according to the query order. Sometimes there are two possible sequences for SECURE, shown with different arrow lengths. You may check the query performance summary table above.

E1. PARTITION

```
(c3) partition([X|A],Y,B,[x|C]) :- Y<X, partition(A,Y,B,C). % bug:x
(c4) partition([X|A],Y,[X|B],C) :- Y>=X, partition(A,Y,B,C).
(c5) partition([],_,[],[]).
```

Wrong solution: `partition([1,5,3,4,2],3,[1,3,2],[x,x])`.

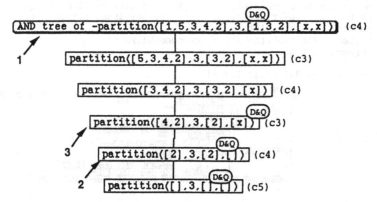

This is a simple example, but sligthly more complicated than `append` because the use of each source clause is interleaved along the recursion chain.

E2. INSERTION SORT

From [Shapiro 82, page 50]:

```
(c6)  isort([X|A],B) :- isort(A,C), insert(X,C,B).
(c7)  isort([],[]).
(c8)  insert(X,[Y|A],[X,Y|A]) :- X=<Y.
(c9)  insert(X,[Y|A],[Y|B]) :- insert(X,A,B). % bug: missing test
(c10) insert(X,[],[X]).
```

---

[8] Since some of the pictures are too small, the authors will provide the original MacDraw II file by email to anyone asking it.

Wrong solution: `isort([4,1,2,3,5,6],[1,2,3,5,4,6]).`

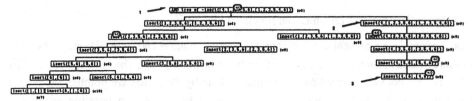

E3.   QUICKSORT

Another example from [Shapiro 82], here with only 1 bug left, so that we can start diagnosing a wrong solution.

```
(c11)   qsort([],[]).
(c12)   qsort([X|L],L0) :-
                partition(L,X,L1,L2),
                qsort(L1,L3),
                qsort(L2,L4),
                qappend([X|L3],L4,L0).   % bug
(c13)   partition([X|L],Y,[X|L1],L2) :- X<Y, partition(L,Y,L1,L2).
(c14)   partition([X|L],Y,L1,[X|L2]) :- Y=<X, partition(L,Y,L1,L2).
(c15)   partition([],X,[],[]).
(c16)   qappend([X|L1],L2,[X|L3]) :- qappend(L1,L2,L3).
(c17)   qappend([],L,L).
```

Wrong solution: `qsort([2,3,1,5],[2,1,3,5]).`

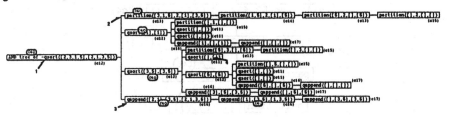

E4.   SIMPLE RULE ENGINE

An example from [Brayshaw Eisenstadt 88]: a simple rule engine, where the rules are taken correct but the engine is buggy. Since the tree is too large, we only show the rightmost half, the part visited by either of the diagnosis algorithms.

```
:-
        op(850,fx,not), op(900,xfx,:), op(870,fx,if),
        op(880,xfx,then), op(800,xfx,was), op(600,xfx,from),
        op(540,xfy,and), op(550,xfy,or), op(300,fx,'derived by'),
        op(100,xfx,[gives,eats,has,isa]).

(c18)   explore(Goal,Goal is true was 'found as fact',true) :-
                fact : Goal.
(c19)   explore(Goal,Goal is false was 'found as a fact',false) :-
                fact : (not Goal).
(c20)   explore(Goal,Goal is TVal was 'derived by' Rule from Proof,TV) :-
                Rule:if Cond then Goal,
                explore(Cond,Proof,TV).
(c21)   explore(Goal and Goals,Proof and Proofs,true) :-
                explore(Goal,Proof,true),
                explore(Goals,Proofs,true).
(c22)   explore(Goal and Goals,Proof,false) :-
```

```
                    explore(Goal,Proof,false),   % bug ;
                    explore(Goal,Proof,false).
(c23)   explore(Goal or Goals,Proof,true) :-
                    explore(Goal,Proof,true) ;
                    explore(Goals,Proof,true).
(c24)   explore(Goal or Goals,Proof and Proofs,false) :-
                    explore(Goal,Proof,false) ; % bug ,
                    explore(Goals,Proofs,false).
```

```
fact: buttercup gives milk.
fact: (not buttercup eats meat).
fact: (not buttercup has hair).
```

```
m_rule: if
        A has hair
        or
        A gives milk
     then
        A isa mammal.
```

```
c_rule: if
        A isa mammal
        and
        A eats meat
     then
        A isa carnivore.
```

Wrong solution:

```
explore(buttercup isa carnivore, How, Truth),
  How = buttercup isa carnivore is false was 'derived by' c_rule from
        buttercup isa mammal is false was 'derived by' m_rule from
                          buttercup has hair is false was 'found as a fact' and _P
```

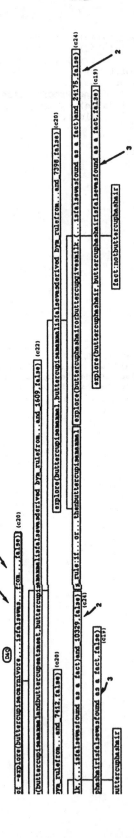

E5. SIEVE OF ERASTOSTHENES

From [Av-Ron 84]:

```
(c25)   primes(Limit,Ps) :- integers(2,Limit,Is), sift(Is,Ps).
(c26)   integers(Low,High,[Low|Rest]) :-
            Low =< High, !, M is Low+1,
            integers(M,High,Rest).
(c27)   integers(_,_,[]).
(c28)   sift([],[]).
(c29)   sift([I|Is],[I|Ps]) :- remove(I,Is,New), sift(New,Ps).
(c30)   remove(P,[],[]).
(c31)   remove(P,[I|Is],Nis) :-        % bug: shouldn't remove I
            user_not( 0 is I mod P ), !, remove(P,Is,Nis).
(c32)   remove(P,[I|Is],[I|Nis]) :-       % bug: shouldn't keep I
            0 is I mod P, !, remove(P,Is,Nis).
```

Wrong solution: `primes(7,[2,4])`. There are two Divide and Query sequences, and therefore one is shown with symbols.

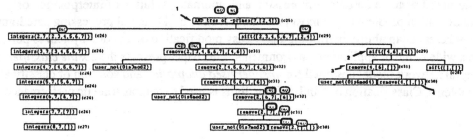

A NEURAL APPROACH
TO DATA COMPRESSION AND CLASSIFICATION

Klaus Peter Kratzer
Fachhochschule Ulm
Prittwitzstr. 10, D-7900 Ulm (Donau)

Abstract: Recently, neural networks have evolved as an alternate approach instead of rule-based systems for data compression and automated solution of interpolation or classification problems. The most prominent feature of the neural processing paradigm is its inherent adaptability permitting fairly easy modification of a neural system to perform in a wide range of application environments. This paper presents the *cosine classifier*, a neural network model designed for *unsupervised adaptation* and solution of classification problems. Classification of hand-written digits is used to demonstrate its performance.

1 Neural Information Processing

A neural information processing system is based on a grossly simplified model of the physiological/neurobiological system in the human brain. Hopefully, simple operations on many primitive microstructures will map to complex macro-operations for simulation of symbolic information processing on lower levels of abstraction. The physiological term *neuron* for a brain cell is transferred to computer science terminology and stands for a primitive processing unit with scant arithmetical capabilities. However, as a *complex* called *neural network* these units can perform astonishing feats (cf. [5, 7, 8]).

A further noteworthy property of this class of models is their special emphasis on *communication*. The state of a processing unit is defined by its *state of activation*, usually a scalar value. Thus, neural information processing amounts to switching patterns of activation within a neural complex. The processing units are interconnected according to some predefined topology; to simulate synaptic information transfer, each connection is associated with a *weight* as measure for the influence exerted by one processing unit upon another one. The configuration of weights is the sole means of knowledge representation within a neural network. Therefore, knowledge is not crystallized in the shape of symbols and symbol relationships; rather, it is represented on a sub-symbolic level and usually distributed among many connections. Figure 1 shows an example of a network structure, in this case a so-called *feed-forward network* accepting *stimuli* formatted as vectors of activation which are processed and filtered via several intermediate layers and passed on as *reactions* to the outside world.

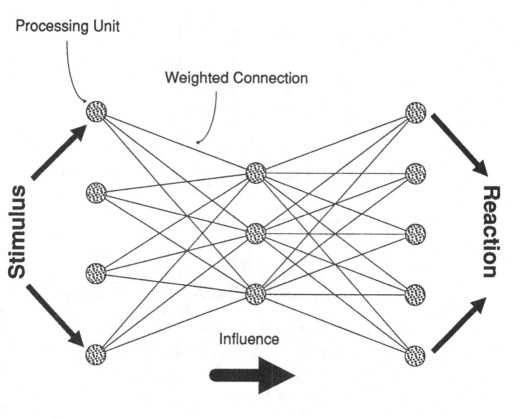

Fig. 1: Structure of a Neural Network

The prime reason for the "renaissance" of neural information processing from the early Eighties up till now is the remarkable *adaptability* of such systems; other authors tend to refer to *facilities for learning* which sounds impressive, but is maybe a bit pretentious. The weight configuration bearing all application knowledge is not tediously designed; instead, it is generated step-by-step while the network is exposed to representative sample data together with desired reactions. As compared to conventional programming this approach offers two advantages:

- You do not have to define a concise model of your application world.

- The definition of the desired function of the neural network is descriptive in an extensional way, which eventually facilitates compression of bulk data to fairly manageable structures.

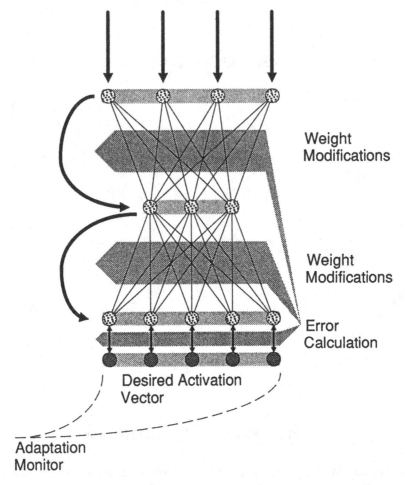

Fig. 2: Supervised Adaptation

Figure 2 presents the steps to be taken using so-called *supervised adaptation*. After activating the network its reaction is monitored and compared to the desired reaction. If the network produces an erroneous result, the error measure is distributed among all processing units according to their "responsibility" for faulty behavior, and weights are slightly adapted. This leads to a weight configuration with minimal deviation from the desired behavior as expressed by the set of sample data. It depends on the number of processing units and the chosen topology how perfectly those data can be reproduced --- and how sensibly the network responds to stimuli *not* presented during adaptation.

This mode of adaptation is based on the assumption that there is some superior authority (i.e., the network designer) to select sample data and to decide what the proper reaction is supposed to be. Some network models, however, support *unsupervised adaptation* by which the network modifies its weight configuration *autonomously*. The network "watches" its surroundings --- as a matter of fact, just a tiny section thereof --- and

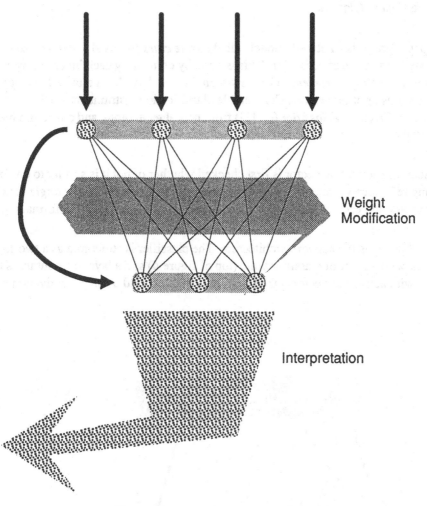

Fig. 3: Unsupervised Adaptation

develops an internal structure reflecting equivalences and similarities of the stimuli received. In contrast to supervised learning the evolutionary development of the network is even less biased by the network designer, since no desired reaction is expressed and no assumptions on the internal representation have to be made (see figure 3).

A network adapting in unsupervised mode and presented with maybe noisy stimuli (e.g., visual representations of digits or letters) will eventually detect common traits of the input data, *without any notion of the meaning of such signals*. This property can be exploited for classification tasks. To be useful, however, such a network must be supplemented by an *interpretation*. All possible reactions of the network have to be marked-up to map them to the terminology of its human operator.

2 The Cosine Classifier

This paper presents a network model called *cosine classifier* used to categorize stimuli
presented as vectors of activation. This is done by comparing each incoming vector with a
set of self-developed *reference vectors* which, in turn, have been retained from previous
presentations of other vectors. Comparable classification instruments are the
Carpenter/Grossberg classifier (cf. [1]) from neural technology and clustering methods
from statistics.

An incoming activation vector is first checked whether or not it is similar to one of the
existing reference vectors. The degree of similarity is measured by the *angle* between the
input vector and each of the reference vectors disregarding all length information.

Figure 4 presents the network architecture. The classifier is structured as a two-layered
network with a layer of classifier units (top of figure 4) and a layer of input units to be
loaded with activation vectors taken from the outside world. A single activation may be

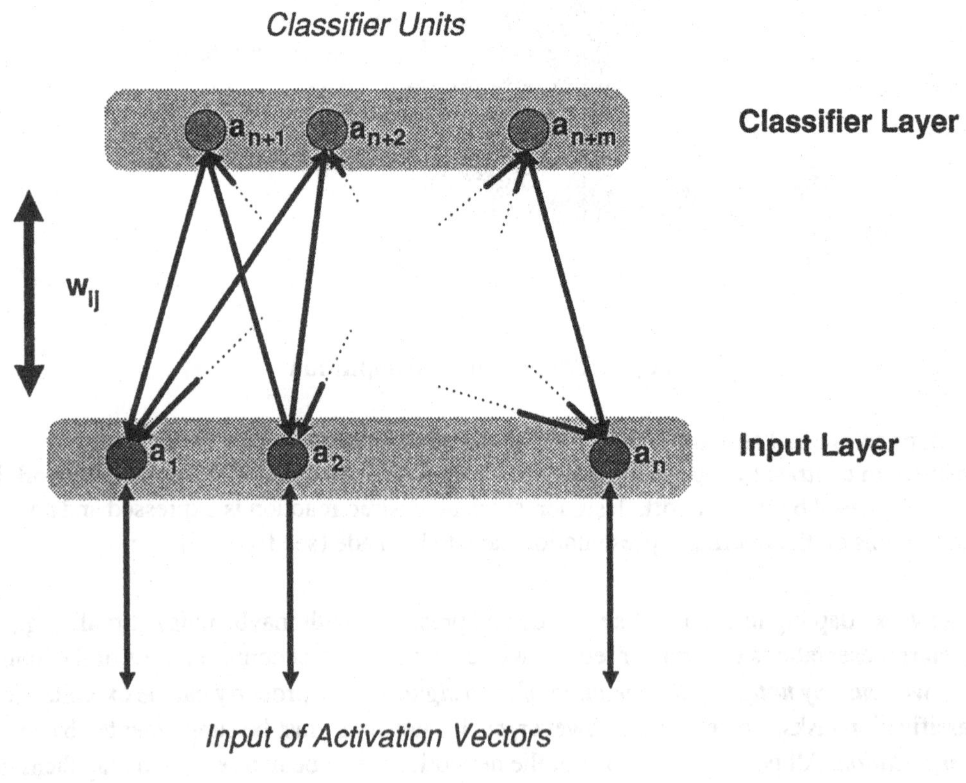

Fig. 4: Architecture of the Cosine Classifier

any scalar numeric value. All "knowledge" captured in the network is represented by reference vectors denoted by weights w_{ij} assuming

$$1 \leq i \leq n \quad \text{and} \quad n+1 \leq j \leq n+m$$

Thus, the reference vector assigned to classifier unit j reads as

$$\vec{w_j} = \begin{pmatrix} w_{1j} \\ w_{2j} \\ \cdot \\ \cdot \\ \cdot \\ w_{nj} \end{pmatrix}$$

Each reference vector is nomalized to size 1. There is *no* predetermined number of classifier units; contrary to the static layout of most neural models, this one must be dynamically extensible.

As soon as an activation vector $\vec{a_{raw}}$ is received, it has to undergo a *size normalization procedure*. Thus, input units are finally activated as:

$$a_i = \frac{a_{i,raw}}{\sqrt{\sum_i a_{i,raw}^2}}$$

As shown in figure 5, dismissal of length information is uncritical, even beneficial, in most cases. This holds in particular if only binary activations are used.

The cosine of the angle φ between the activation vector $\vec{a}$ and each of the reference vectors $\vec{w}$ serves as measure for their degree of similarity. This value is calculated quite efficiently as

$$\cos \varphi = \frac{\vec{a} \cdot \vec{w}}{|\vec{a}| \cdot |\vec{w}|}$$

Since it is known that

$$|\vec{a}| = |\vec{w}| = 1$$

this calculation is reduced to computing the dot product of both vectors:

$$\cos \varphi = \vec{a} \cdot \vec{w}$$

After having performed this calculation for each reference vector, a search for the classifier unit j^* with maximum activity is conducted.

$$a_j = \sum_i w_{ij} a_i$$
$$a_{j^*} = \max_j \{ a_j \}$$

Along the lines of the so-called *winner-take-all* procedure (cf. [2]) classifier unit j^* retains its activation while all other classifier units are reset to zero.

The complexity and the precision of the classification procedure are determined by a pre-defined *similarity coefficient* ρ. This value is selected from the interval

$$0 < \rho < 1$$

The degree of similarity recorded as a_{j^*} is now tested against ρ. If

$$a_{j^*} > \rho$$

holds, the reference vector is to be modified so as to point to the center of all input vectors that have already been detected by classifier unit j^*. Therefore, each classifier unit is equipped with a counter ζ_j that records how many assignments of input vectors to this classifier unit have occurred --- in the past and at present. Each assignment will therefore entail a slight correction of the reference vector involved (see figure 6).

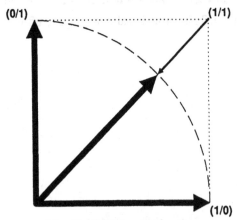

Fig. 5: Size Normalization

Fig. 6: Modification of a Reference Vector

First, ζ_j^* has to be incremented; the subsequent modification of j^* reads as follows:

$$\vec{w_j}^* \leftarrow \frac{\zeta_j^*-1}{\zeta_j^*}\,\vec{w_j}^* + \frac{1}{\zeta_j^*}\,\vec{a}$$

Since only normalized reference vectors are permitted, a final adjustmend reads as:

$$\vec{w_j}^* \leftarrow \frac{1}{\sqrt{\sum_i w_{ij}^{2*}}}\,\vec{w_j}^*$$

The cosine classifier is now ready to accept a new input vector.

If the test for acceptable similarity did *not* produce a positive result, the classifier must be extended by a classifier unit j^+ which is initialized as follows:

$$\zeta_j^+ \leftarrow 1$$
$$\vec{w_j}^+ \leftarrow \vec{a}$$

Again, a new stimulus may now be fed to the classifier.

An overview of this algorithms reads as follows:

Find a similarity coefficient ρ.
Repeat forever ...
    Activate input units.
    Normalize input vector.
    Compute activation of classifier units.
    Select the unit with maximum activation.
    If its reference vector is acceptably similar to the input vector ...
        Modify the reference vector as described above.
    otherwise ...
        Create and initialize a new classifier unit using the current input vector.

In contrast to other classifier models, this concept does not guarantee that an input vector once assigned to a classifier unit will always be recognized by the same unit. Rather, the cosine classifier shows considerable *plasticity* (cf. [2]) insofar as slow and continuous changes in the classifier's operational environment are reflected by changes, and sometimes switches, in the roles of the classifier units.

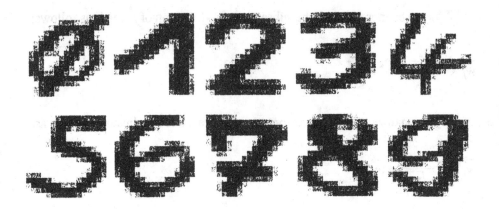

Fig. 7: Samples from the Training Data Set

3 Simulation Results

A first test of the classifier's usefulness was made in the field of pattern recognition. The adaptation was based on a training set of 10,000 hand-written digits (European style) which were normalized in size, rasterized, and fed into the classifier's 256 input units as 16×16 gray-scale matrices flattened to vectors. Figure 7 shows some of those sample input vectors.

Some of the reference vectors created after one pass through the data set are shown in figure 8. As long as the classifier units are highly frequented, the associated reference vectors are overlays of all accepted input vectors whose common traits show as dark shading of significant features. A close look reveals problems concerning the mix-up of

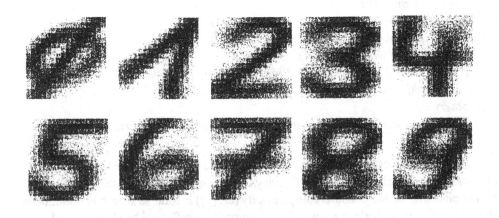

Fig. 8: Highly Frequented Reference Vectors

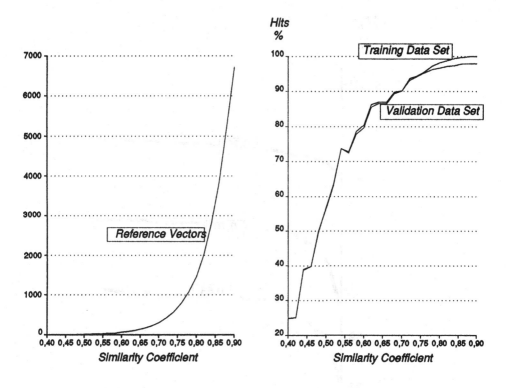

Fig. 9: Network Performance with Direct Coding

similar digits with different semantics; the reference vector representing *3* shows faint traces of some *8*'s which had been assigned.

A subsequent mark-up run is used to add an interpretation to each classifier unit. This is simply done by running the training set once more against the classifier --- this time without changing the network. However, record is kept which classifier unit reacted to which digit value. Thus, each classifier unit's preferred digit is to be used as interpretation.

In most cases, neural networks are not simply used to reproduce reactions, but to react properly to patterns not previously presented. So, to check the network's potential for *generalization* a validation data set of another 10,000 digits was run against the marked-up classifier.

The left side of figure 9 shows a mapping of the similarity coefficient ρ against the number of reference vectors created; on the right it is mapped against the hit rate for the training set (reproduction) and the validation set (generalization). Evidently, there is a marked ability to generalize since the spread between training hits and validation hits amounts to a mere half percent on average. With increased ρ we encounter a dispropor-

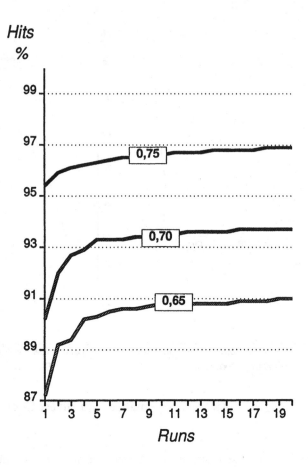

Fig. 10: Fine-Tuning by Multiple Runs

tionate raise of the number of classifier units which only pays off in terms of reproduction. Structures with $\rho > 0,8$ are clumsy to handle and, as a matter of fact, not particularly desirable in an application environment --- a hit rate of 100% is surely attainable, but most of the cost in memory and execution time would have to be attributed to improved reproduction with stagnant ability to generalize.

Multiple passes through the training data set render a significant increase of the hit rate while adding only few (less than 1%) further classifier units (see figure 10). The improvement is mainly caused by fine-tuning of existing reference vectors.

All results presented so far had been achieved by *direct transfer* of application data to the 256 units in the input layer. Preliminary reduction of data complexity renders even better performance. One of the principal tools used in neural technology is *coarse coding* (cf. [3]). The basic principle is to use the average of the activation value at a given location plus the activation of neighboring locations to activate an input unit. Thus, neigborhoods

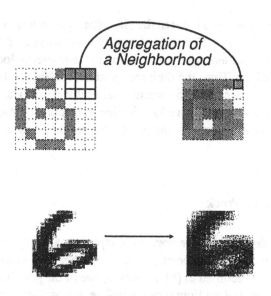

Fig. 11: Coarse Coding

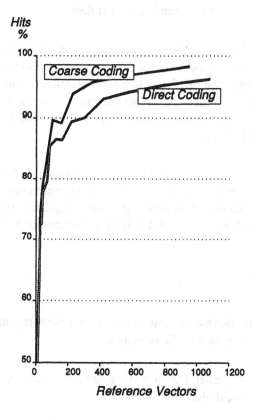

Fig. 12: Performance Improvement by Coarse Coding

overlap which blurs the picture and induces the classifier to react less sensitive to trifle dislocations of important features. Figure 11 shows an example of an 8×8 raster which is reduced to a 6×6 raster by condensing the activiation at the reference locations with that of all directly adjacent locations. Thus, the digit recognition problem can be transferred from a 256-dimensional vector space to a 196-dimensional vector space. The cost/performance ratio is improved significantly (see figure 12). Further reduction in dimension, however, would blur the picture to a degree where the probability for the occurrence of mix-ups would be intolerable.

4 Conclusions & Further Work

Of course, the problem described in the previous chapter cannot only be solved with the cosine classifier; costs and performance of a number of other approaches (perceptrons and polynomial classifiers) are recorded in [6]. However, one of the principal characteristics of this classifier is its *two-layered* configuration; therefore, it is well-suited for parallel architectures. An implementation of the cosine classifier on a transputer complex showed an improvement in performance nearly proportional to the increase in parallelism and hardly any discernible cost for communication overhead.

Further work has been directed at the enhancement of the unsupervised adaptation scheme by a supervised component. If mark-ups of reference vector and input vector are known, the ρ-criterion can be amended insofar as to invoke creation of a new classifier unit if those mark-ups diverge *or* similarity is unsatisfactory. Results with this procedure were excellent, with a reproduction rate constantly close to 100% and the ability to generalize depending on the selection of ρ.

In the future, emphasis should be moved to applications *outside* the area of pattern recognition. Integration with database systems for data compression and with knowledge-based systems to exploit plasticity should be prime targets. Many hopes rest on neural techniques --- and only successful field applications will help avoid disappointment.

5 Acknowledgements

This project has been funded by the state of Baden-Württemberg under grant "Integration of Neuro-Components into an XPS Environment".

Thanks are due to Dr. U. Kreßel, Daimler-Benz Research Institute Ulm, for discussion, helpful comments, and validation data.

References

[1] Carpenter, G.A. und Grossberg, S.: *Neural Dynamics of Category Learning and Recognition: Attention, Memory Consolidation, and Amnesia*, in: Davis, J., Newburgh, R. und Wegmann, E. (eds.): *Brain Structure, Learning, and Memory*, AAAS Symposium Series 1986.

[2] Grossberg, S.: *Competitive Learning: From Interactive Activation to Adaptive Resonance*, Cognitive Science, November 1987.

[3] Hinton, G.E., McClelland, J.L. und Rumelhart, D.E.: *Distributed Representations*, in: [8].

[4] Kohonen, T.: *Self-Organization and Associative Memory*, Berlin 1987.

[5] Kratzer, K.P.: *Neuronale Netze - Grundlagen und Anwendung*, München 1990.

[6] Kreßel, U., Franke, J. und Schürmann, J.: *Polynomklassifikator versus Multilayer-Perzeptron*, 12th DAGM Symposium, 1990.

[7] Lippman, R.P.: *An Introduction to Computing with Neural Nets*, IEEE ASSP Magazine, April 1987.

[8] Rumelhart, D.E. und McClelland, J.L.: *Parallel Distributed Processing: Explorations in the Microstructure of Cognition*, Cambridge MA 1986.

Generalization for a propositional calculus: a constraints-based approach

Raoul Vorc'h

IRISA 22 avenue Général Leclerc 35042 Rennes Cédex France
e-mail: vorch@irisa.fr

Abstract

In order to provide a propositional tableau-based theorem prover with learning capabilities, we describe generalization mechanisms that characterize the concepts of valid and non-valid formulae. Our generalization language is founded on the notion of formula schemata enriched with a system of constraints. We show how the most "attractive" generalizations of a given instance can be found. Successes or failures of proofs are handled within a same formalism.

Keywords: Generalization, Explanation, Semantic Tableaux, Sequents, Schemata, Constraints

1 Introduction

In order to improve the efficiency of problem solvers, learning methods are used to discover new rules (also called *macro-rules* or *macro-operators*) or control knowledge (*meta-rules*). In both cases, explanation-based learning techniques have been shown useful [Korf 85, Mitchell et al. 86, Minton et al. 89].

Actually, the field of automated theorem proving has not yet benefited from numerous works that have been undertaken within the domain of problem solving, while both domains are very close. Although the satisfiability problem for a propositional formula is NP-complete, one can expect learning to improve the performance of a theorem prover within particular domains and with respect to specific performance criteria, such as *speed* (to prove the theorems) or *power* (the class of problems that can be (effectively) solved).

O'Rorke [Ororke 89] has experimented learning methods for the LT theorem prover, which deals with propositional calculus as it is described in the *Principia Mathematica* [Whitehead et al. 62]. This calculus consists of a set of axiom schemata and two inference rules. The theorem prover is provided with a learning from example mechanism that may produce new axiom schemata. Comparing several versions of the system (without learning, with rote learning and with explanation-based learning), O'Rorke has shown that learning abilities (especially explanation-based learning) may improve performances.

Here, we propose to address the generalization problem for a cut-free sequent calculus (called system G in [Gallier 86]), which is a proof-system related to the semantic tableaux technique.

This proof system exhibits several interesting properties. Formulae don't need to be normalized (vs. the required clausal form in resolution for instance) and their structures are preserved by the inference rules. This is a fundamental point for the learning process: preserving the structure of formulae will allow the theorem prover to fit with the structures of the encountered formulae.

The proof search is convergent: it leads to a proof of the validity of the primary formula or to a counter-model for that formula (that is, an explanation that may be exploited).

Furthermore, by using a meta-level deduction system, it is easy and natural to define new inference rules from the obtained generalizations.

In section 2, we recall some definitions about the referred proof system. Then, we describe our learning framework (section 3) and define the language of constrained schemata (section 4). In section 5, we study a specific interpretation of the constraints and define some interesting schemata. Generalization from instances is described in section 6. In section 7, we show some consequences of the extension of the chosen interpretation. In the conclusion, some related works and open problems are evoked.

2   The formal system

We recall briefly some definitions about the proof system G, that is about semantic tableaux [Smullyan 68, Gallier 86].

The language (of instances) is the standard propositional language. The set of atomic propositions is $\mathcal{A} = \{p,q,...\}$. We use $\wedge$, $\vee$, $\neg$ and $\Rightarrow$ to denote the standard connectives. A *sequent* is a set S of signed formulae (noted F^- or F^+). $\{F_1^-, ..., F_n^-, F_{n+1}^+, ..., F_m^+\}$ is also written $F_1, ..., F_n \rightarrow F_{n+1}, ..., F_m$, following Gentzen's usual notation, where $F_1, ..., F_n \rightarrow F_{n+1}, ..., F_m$ is interpreted as $(F_1 \wedge ... \wedge F_n) \Rightarrow (F_{n+1} \vee ... \vee F_m)$.

There are two inference rules for each connective. For example, the rules for the $\Rightarrow$ connective are: $S \cup \{A^-, B^+\} \vdash S \cup \{(A \Rightarrow B)^+\}$ and $S \cup \{A^+\}, S \cup \{B^-\} \vdash S \cup \{(A \Rightarrow B)^-\}$. Axioms are all sequents that contain two conjugate atoms, i.e $\{S \cup \{A^-, A^+\}, A \in \mathcal{A}\}$.

A *deduction tree* for a sequent S is a tree labelled with sequents such that the root is labelled by S and the other sequents are obtained by inversing the inference rules (two deduction trees are depicted in figure 1 and 2). Remark: atoms are indexed, in order to distinguish occurrences of a same atom in the primary sequent.

If all the leaves of a deduction tree are axioms then the tree is called a *proof tree* (a proof tree for $\rightarrow p \Rightarrow q \vee q \Rightarrow p$ is given in figure 1).

$$\rightarrow p \Rightarrow q \lor q \Rightarrow p \qquad\qquad \rightarrow p_1 \Rightarrow q_1 \lor q_2 \Rightarrow p_2$$
$$\rightarrow p \Rightarrow q, q \Rightarrow p \qquad\qquad \rightarrow p_1 \Rightarrow q_1, q_2 \Rightarrow p_2$$
$$p \quad\rightarrow q, q \Rightarrow p \qquad\qquad p_1 \quad\rightarrow q_1, q_2 \Rightarrow p_2$$
$$q, p \quad\rightarrow p, q \qquad\qquad q_2, p_1 \quad\rightarrow p_2, q_1$$

Fig. 1: proof tree P for $\rightarrow p \Rightarrow q \lor q \Rightarrow p$

$$(p_1 \Rightarrow q_1) \land (q_2 \Rightarrow p_2) \quad\rightarrow p_3 \Rightarrow r_1$$
$$p_1 \Rightarrow q_1, q_2 \Rightarrow p_2 \quad\rightarrow p_3 \Rightarrow r_1$$
$$p_3, p_1 \Rightarrow q_1, q_2 \Rightarrow p_2 \quad\rightarrow r_1$$
$$p_3, q_2 \Rightarrow p_2 \rightarrow p_1, r_1 \qquad\qquad q_1, p_3, q_2 \Rightarrow p_2 \rightarrow r_1$$
$$q_1, p_3 \rightarrow q_2, r_1 \qquad\qquad p_2, q_1, p_3 \rightarrow r_1$$

Fig. 2: model tree M for $(p \Rightarrow q) \land (q \Rightarrow p) \rightarrow p \Rightarrow r$

A sequent that contains only atomic formulae and that is not an axiom will be called a *model sequent*. A deduction tree that has a leaf labelled with a model sequent is called a *counter-model tree* or simply a *model tree*.

For instance, all leaves of the deduction tree M depicted in figure 2 are labelled with axioms, except $p_2, q_1, p_3 \rightarrow r_1$, which is a model sequent.

3 Generalization framework

Explanation-based learning methods use a proof that an instance belongs to a target concept to find a generalization of this "example". Let us recall the basic definitions of the Explanation-Based Generalization (EBG) method defined in [Mitchell et al. 86].

A *concept* is a set of instances. A *concept definition* is a necessary and sufficient condition for belonging to the concept. A *generalization of an instance* is a concept definition that characterizes a concept containing the instance. An *operationality criterion* is a predicate over concept definitions that specifies an expected form for these definitions.

The EBG problem is the following: given a domain theory, a target concept definition (which is not operational), an instance of the concept and an operationality criterion, find a generalization of the instance that is a sufficient concept definition (i.e. that characterizes a subset of the concept), and that is operational.

As pointed in [Minton et al. 89] many target concepts may be defined in order to improve the efficiency of a problem solver: for each target concept, one just has to define a domain theory that allows explanations.

Here, our goal is to find new axiom schemata and thus, our target concept is the set of valid formulae.

One can adopt the following instance of the EBG problem for that target concept.

Domain theory: it is the proof system itself, which may be enriched with a particular theory for a particular domain.

Target Concept Definition: the set of all formulae deducible from the theory.

Instance of the concept: a given valid formula.

Operationality criterion: in a first approach, we consider that a definition is operational if it can be evaluated in the same way that the definition of the initial axioms of the proof system, that is by comparing atomic occurrences.

As the inference system may also be used to prove that a formula is non-valid, we will also be interested in charaterizing these formulae.

Furthermore, as defined in [Mitchell 82], the generalization space may be structured using a partial order: a generalization g is *more specific than* a generalization g' (or g' is *more general than* g), noted $g \preceq g'$, if all the instances recognized by g are also recognized by g'. g and g' are equivalent ($g \equiv g'$) if $g \preceq g'$ and $g' \preceq g$.

4 Generalization language: constrained schemata

In this section, we define our generalization language. The notion of formula schemata is a natural way to describe sets of formulae: intuitively, a formula schemata describes the set of all "concrete" formulae that may be obtained when the schema is instanciated. For instance, the schema $x \lor y$ may be instanciated to give $p \lor q, p \Rightarrow q \lor q \Rightarrow p ...$

Constraints are used to characterize subsets of all these potential instances.

4.1 Schemata

Schemata are built using another set $\mathcal{V} = \{x, y, z, ...\}$ of symbols (called *variables*) instead of $\mathcal{A}$. Thus, one can define *formula schemata*, *sequent schemata* and *deduction tree schemata* (or simply *deduction schemata*). A sequent schema and a deduction schema are noted $\mathcal{S}, \mathcal{D}$, respectively.

A *sequent frame* is a sequent schema where there are no multiple occurrences of a same variable. By extension, we call *deduction frame* a deduction schema whose root is a sequent frame. A sequent frame and a deduction frame are noted $\mathcal{F}_S, \mathcal{F}_D$, respectively.

More generally, we note T (resp. $\mathcal{T}, \mathcal{F}_T$) an instance (resp. a schema, a frame). Finally we note $\mathcal{I}nst$ the set of all formulae and we note $\mathrm{Var}(\mathcal{T})$ the set of all variables of a schema $\mathcal{T}$.

Definition (instanciation) *An instanciation for a schema $\mathcal{T}$ is a function ϕ from $\mathrm{Var}(\mathcal{T})$ to $\mathcal{I}nst$. ϕ is said to be atomic if its range is a subset of $\mathcal{A}$.*

$$\rightarrow x \Rightarrow y \lor z \Rightarrow w$$
$$\rightarrow x \Rightarrow y, z \Rightarrow w$$
$$x \quad \rightarrow y, z \Rightarrow w$$
$$z, x \quad \rightarrow w, y$$

Fig. 3: Frame $\mathcal{F}_D$ for proof P

T is an *instance* of $\mathcal{T}$ if and only if T=$\phi\mathcal{T}$ for an instanciation ϕ. We also say that $\mathcal{T}$ *recognizes* T.

Given an instance T, we call *frame for T* a frame $\mathcal{F}_T$ such that T=$\phi\mathcal{F}_T$ for an atomic substitution ϕ. We need to distinguish distinct occurrences of a same atom (we have used indexes in the figures) that appear in a sequent instance:

Definition (atomic occurrence) *Given a sequent S and a frame $\mathcal{F}_S$ for S (S=$\phi\mathcal{F}_S$), we call atomic occurrence any couple $(x, \phi(x))$ where $x \in Var(\mathcal{F}_S)$.*

Example: $\rightarrow x \Rightarrow y \lor z \Rightarrow w$ is a sequent frame for $\rightarrow p \Rightarrow q \lor q \Rightarrow p$ (the corresponding instanciation is defined by $\phi(x)=\phi(w)=p$ and $\phi(y)=\phi(z)=q$). Atomic occurrences are $(x,p),(y,q),(z,q),(w,p)$ (p_1, q_1, p_2 and q_2 in the figure). $\mathcal{F}_D$ (figure 3) is a deduction frame for the proof P (figure 1).

There is a bijection between the set of all variables of the frame and the set of all atomic occurrences, which is noted ϕ'.

In the example of figure 1, $\phi'(x)=p_1$, $\phi'(y)=q_1$, $\phi'(z)=q_2$ and $\phi'(w)=p_2$.

4.2 The constraints and their semantic

4.2.1 Expected properties

Let S be a sequent that verifies a target property $\mathcal{P}$ (e.g. validity). Let $\mathcal{S}$ be a sequent schema that recognizes S.

We note $\mathcal{I}nst(\mathcal{S})$ the set of all instances recognized by $\mathcal{S}$. Among these instances, we are particulary interested in those that verify (as S) the property $\mathcal{P}$. We note $\mathcal{P}(\mathcal{I}nst(\mathcal{S}))$ that subset.

The role of a system of constraints is to characterize at best such a subset. Let $\mathcal{S}_c$ be the sequent schema with constraints. We are looking for the following properties:

Completeness: For any instance such that $\mathcal{P}$, we want to be able to find a generalization of the instance such that all the instances recognized by the generalization also satisfy $\mathcal{P}$.

Maximality: We wish $\mathcal{I}nst(\mathcal{S}_c)$ to be as "close" as possible to $\mathcal{P}(\mathcal{I}nst(\mathcal{S}))$ (however we always need $\mathcal{I}nst(\mathcal{S}_c) \subseteq \mathcal{P}(\mathcal{I}nst(\mathcal{S}))$, otherwise $\mathcal{S}_c$ has no interest with respect to $\mathcal{P}$).

Granularity: The instance language is often a sub-language of the generalization one, so that one can interpret an instance as a particular generalization. A more abstract level of description may be preferred if it offers a simpler description language. We adopt such an abstract bias (which is natural with regard to the target properties): we accept to be unable to discriminate between syntactical variants of a same formula.

4.2.2 Constrained schemata: syntax

A system of constraints simply consists of two finite binary relations over the variables of the schemata, that define positive and negative constraints, respectively.

Definition (system of constraints) *Let T be a schema. A system of constraints for T is a couple $C = (C_+, C_-)$ such that C_+ and C_- are two sets of couples from $Var(T) \times Var(T)$.*

C_+ (resp. C_-) is called a *positive specialization* (resp. a *negative specialization*) and its elements are called *positive constraints* (resp. *negative constraints*). We note $C \subseteq C'$ if $C_+ \subseteq C'_+$ and $C_- \subseteq C'_-$. We note $C \cup C'$ the system $(C_+ \cup C'_+, C_- \cup C'_-)$ (similar notation for $C \cap C'$). In order to distinguish the two kinds of constraints, we note a positive constraint $x = y$ and a negative one $x \neq y$.

Definition (constrained schema) *A constrained schema is a couple $T_c = (T, C)$ where C is a system of constraints for T.*

4.2.3 Constrained schemata: semantics

Definition (interpretation) *An interpretation is given by a binary relation over $\mathcal{I}nst$. This relation is noted $=^i$ and its complementary relation $\neq^i$.*

Definition (instanciation for a constrained schema) *Let $T_c = (T, C)$ be a constrained schema. An instanciation for T_c is an instanciation ϕ for T that is consistent with the constraints:*
$$\forall xy \in Var(T), [x = y \in C_+ \Rightarrow \phi(x) =^i \phi(y)] \wedge [x \neq y \in C_- \Rightarrow \phi(x) \neq^i \phi(y)].$$

The "power" of a schema (i.e. its ability to recognize the most instances) is settled by the choice of an interpretation. In the next section, we give some properties about the simplest (and the more restrictive) interpretation.

5 Syntactical properties of schemata

The chosen interpretation (I1) is simply the syntactical equality between atoms (that is $=^i$ is defined by $\{(p,p), p \in \mathcal{A}\}$). We give some general properties of $\mathcal{T}(T)$, the set of all generalizations that recognize a given instance T.

5.1 A lattice of schemata

Let $x = y$ and $y = z$ belonging to a system of constraints. Then, the constraint $x = z$ will always be satisfied ($=$ is transitive): $x = z$ is an *induced* constraint. By a same way, if $x = y$ and $y \neq z$ belong to the system of constraints, then $x \neq z$ is an induced constraint.

More generally, all induced constraints from a given system of constraints are obtained by applying two closures and a product:

1) reflexive symmetric and transitive closure of C_+ (C_+^*).

2) symmetric closure of C_- (C_-^*).

3) product of C_+^* and C_-^*: $C_+^* \times C_-^* = \{x' \neq y', \exists (x \neq y) \in C_-^*, (x = x') \in C_+^*, (y = y') \in C_+^*\}$.

We note C^* (closure of C) the system $(C_+^*, C_+^* \times C_-^*)$.

Proposition *Let T be a schema, C and C' be two systems of constraints for T. $(T,C) \preceq (T,C')$ iff $C'^* \subseteq C^*$.*

In particular, two systems of constraints (for a same schema) are equivalent if they have the same closure.

Proposition *Let $\mathcal{F}_T$ be a frame for T. Any element of $T(T)$ may be defined by a schema $(\mathcal{F}_T,C)$.*

Given a constrained schema $\mathcal{S}_c \equiv (\mathcal{F}_T,C)$, $(\mathcal{F}_T,C^*)$ is a canonical form of $\mathcal{S}_c$.

Proposition *$(T(T),\preceq)$ has a complete lattice structure and the associated operators may be defined as follows:*

$(\mathcal{F}_T,C) \cap (\mathcal{F}_T,C') = (\mathcal{F}_T,C^* \cup C'^*)$ *(union of the constraints)*

$(\mathcal{F}_T,C) \cup (\mathcal{F}_T,C') = (\mathcal{F}_T,C^* \cap C'^*)$ *(intersection of the constraints)*

As a consequence, there is a (unique) most general schema (mgs(T)) and a (unique) most specific schema (mss(T)).

Remark: Plotkin and Reynold have used such a lattice to structure sets of terms and atomic formulae [Plotkin 70, Reynolds 70].

5.2 Particular schemata

Let $\mathcal{F}_T$ be a frame for an instance T and ϕ be the instanciation such that $T = \phi \mathcal{F}_T$.

Proposition (mgs(T) and mss(T)) *mss(T) $\equiv (\mathcal{F}_T,C)$ with $C_+ = \{x = y, \phi(x) =^i \phi(y)\}$ and $C_- = \{x \neq y, \phi(x) \neq^i \phi(y)\}$. mgs(T) $\equiv (\mathcal{F}_T,C_\emptyset)$ ($C_\emptyset$ is the system $(\emptyset,\emptyset)$).*

Remark: mss(T) recognizes exactly all syntactical variants of T and mgs(T) recognizes all the instances that have the same structure as T (with any atom).

A schema that has only positive (resp. negative) constraints is called positive (resp. negative) schema.

Proposition (msps(T) and msns(T)) *Let $(\mathcal{F}_T,C)$ be the canonical form of mss(T) (i.e $C = C^*$). There is a (unique) most specific positive (resp. negative) schema msps(T) $\equiv (\mathcal{F}_T,(C_+,\emptyset))$ (resp. msns(T) $\equiv (\mathcal{F}_T,(\emptyset,C_-))$).*

Example: $\mathcal{F}_S = \to x \Rightarrow y \vee z \Rightarrow w$ is a frame for the (sequent) instance S $= \to p \Rightarrow q \vee q \Rightarrow p$ (S $= \phi\mathcal{F}_S$ with $\phi(x)=\phi(w)=p$ et $\phi(y)=\phi(z)=q$).

mgs(S) $\equiv (\mathcal{F}_S,(\emptyset,\emptyset))$.

mss(S) $\equiv (\mathcal{F}_S,(\{x = w, y = z, w = x, z = y, x = x, y = y, z = z, w = w\}, \{x \neq y, x \neq z, y \neq w, z \neq w, y \neq x, z \neq x, w \neq y, w \neq z\}))$. An equivalent form (but not canonical) is $(\mathcal{F}_S,(\{x = w, y = z\}, \{x \neq y\}))$.

msps(S) $\equiv (\mathcal{F}_S,(\{x = w, y = z, w = x, z = y, x = x, y = y, z = z, w = w\}, \emptyset))$. An equivalent form is $(\to x \Rightarrow y \vee y \Rightarrow x, C_\emptyset)$.

msns(S) $\equiv (\mathcal{F}_S,(\emptyset, \{x \neq y, x \neq z, y \neq w, z \neq w, y \neq x, z \neq x, w \neq y, w \neq z\}))$.

5.3 Interesting generalizations

We are particularly interested in the following schemata:

A *valid sequent schema* (resp. *model sequent schema*) is a sequent schema that recognizes valid sequents (resp. non-valid sequents), only.

A *proof schema* (resp. *model tree schema*) is a deduction schema that recognizes proof trees (resp. model trees), only.

Definition (proof/model specialization) *Let $(\mathcal{F}_D,C)$ be a constrained deduction frame.*

C_+ is a proof specialization if for any leaf there is a negative variable x^- and a positive one y^+ with $x = y \in C_+$.

C_- is a model specialization if $\mathcal{F}_D$ has a leaf $\mathcal{F}_S$ that contains only variables and such that $\{x \neq y, x^-, y^+ \in \mathcal{F}_S\} \subseteq C_-$.

Proposition (characterization property) *Let $\mathcal{D}_c \equiv (\mathcal{F}_D,C)$ be a canonical deduction schema (i.e $C = C^*$).*

$\mathcal{D}_c$ is a proof schema iff C_+ is a proof specialization.

$\mathcal{D}_c$ is a model tree schema iff C_- is a model specialization.

Furthermore, there is a direct link between a proof schema and a valid sequent schema (resp. between a model tree schema and a model sequent schema):

Proposition (characterization property) *A sequent schema is a valid sequent schema (resp. a model sequent schema) iff it has a proof schema (resp. a model tree schema).*

6 Generalization from instances

First, we address the generalization of valid sequents ("succes" of proofs). Then, we consider the generalization of non-valid sequents ("failure" of proofs).

6.1 Generalization from a valid instance

Let S be a valid sequent. mss(S) is a valid sequent schema (it recognizes syntactical variants of S, only). We want to obtain more general schemata. We define for this purpose two generalization mechanisms: variabilization and regression.

6.1.1 Variabilization

First, one can suppress negative constraints, which do not participate in the validity property. Thus, msps(S) is a valid sequent schema. Example: $S = \rightarrow p \Rightarrow q \vee q \Rightarrow p$ is a valid sequent. $mss(T) \equiv (\rightarrow x \Rightarrow y \vee z \Rightarrow w, (\{x = w, y = z\}, \{x \neq y\}))$. Thus, $\rightarrow r \Rightarrow s \vee s \Rightarrow r$, which is recognized by mss(S), is a valid sequent.

$msps(S) \equiv (\rightarrow x \Rightarrow y \vee z \Rightarrow w, (\{x = w, y = z\}, \emptyset))$.

$\rightarrow p \Rightarrow p \vee p \Rightarrow p$ is recognized by this schema and is thus a valid sequent.

Remark that msps(S) is just a variabilization of S (cf. its equivalent form $((\rightarrow x \Rightarrow y \vee y \Rightarrow x, C_\emptyset))$.

This is a generalization that can be obtained from rote learning. One must use particular proofs to get more general schemata.

6.1.2 Regression

Regression of a proof essentially consists in finding the sufficient constraints that allowed the deduction tree to be a proof.

Let P be a proof tree for S (see figure 1 for example). In each leaf of P (there is only one leaf in our example) one can find (at least) a pair of conjugate atoms, which is called *connection*. In the example, (p_1, p_2) and (q_2, q_1) are connections.

Given a sequent (a leaf) S we note $C(S)$ the set of its connections, and given a deduction tree D, we note $C(D)$ the set of all connections for all leaves of D. By extension we will also say that $C(D)$ is a set of connections for the root of D. $E \subseteq C(D)$ is a *spanning set of connections* for D if for any leaf S of D, we have $C(S) \cap E \neq \emptyset$.

For instance, $\{(p_1, p_2), (q_2, q_1)\}$ is a spanning set of connections for $S = \rightarrow p_1 \Rightarrow q_1 \vee q_2 \Rightarrow p_2$ (figure 1). It is not minimal: $\{(p_1, p_2)\}$ and $\{(q_2, q_1)\}$ are also spanning sets of connections for S.

Remark: a deduction tree is a proof tree iff it has a spanning set of connections.

The regression procedure for a proof will produce a proof specialization from a set of connections, keeping in each axiom leaf (at least) one connection.

Regression procedure

Given a set of connections E, let PS(E) be the positive specialization defined by: $PS(E) = \{x = y, (\phi'(x), \phi'(y)) \in E\}$ (remember that $\phi'(v)$ is the atomic occurrence which is associated to the variable v).

Given a proof tree P and a frame $\mathcal{F}_D$ for P, the procedure REGR$(\mathcal{F}_D,$D$)($E,$\mathcal{C}_+)$ builds a spanning set of connections and a positive specialization $\mathcal{C}_+$:

procedure REGR$(\mathcal{F}_D,$D$)($E,$\mathcal{C}_+)$;
begin
case
. D is not a leaf (i.e D has one or two (main) sub-trees) $\rightarrow$
    E:= $\emptyset$; $\mathcal{C}_+$:=$\emptyset$;
    for all sub-tree D' of D (frame $\mathcal{F}_D$') **do**
    REGR$(\mathcal{F}_D$',D',$)($E',$\mathcal{C}_+$'); E:=E $\cup$ E'; $\mathcal{C}_+$:= $\mathcal{C}_+\cup \mathcal{C}_+$'
. D is a leaf (i.e. an axiom) $\rightarrow$
    let c be a connection of D
    E:={c}; $\mathcal{C}_+$:=PS(E)
esac
end.

Note that finally $\mathcal{C}_+$ is simply PS(E). We note Regr(D,E) the deduction schema $(\mathcal{F}_D,($PS(E)$,\emptyset))$ and Regr(S,E) the sequent schema $(\mathcal{F}_S,($PS(E)$,\emptyset))$ (S (resp $\mathcal{F}_S$) is P root (resp. $\mathcal{F}_D$ root)).

Proposition *PS(E) is a proof specialization.*

Thus, Regr(D,E) is a proof schema and Regr(S,E) is a valid sequent schema.
    Example: PS$\{(p_1,p_2)\}$)= $\{x=w\}$. The corresponding valid sequent schema is $(\rightarrow x \Rightarrow y \vee z \Rightarrow w,(\{x=w\},\emptyset))$, which is equivalent to $(\rightarrow x \Rightarrow y \vee z \Rightarrow x,\mathcal{C}_\emptyset)$. $\rightarrow p \Rightarrow q \vee r \Rightarrow p$ (not recognized by msps(S)) is recognized by this schema, and thus is a valid sequent.
    PS$(\{(q_2,q_1)\})$ produces $(\rightarrow x \Rightarrow y \vee z \Rightarrow w,(\{z=y\},\emptyset))$, which is equivalent to $(\rightarrow x \Rightarrow y \vee y \Rightarrow w,\mathcal{C}_\emptyset)$. Then one can recognize a sequent like $\rightarrow p \Rightarrow q \vee q \Rightarrow r$.
    Remark that PS$(\{(p_1,p_2),(q_2,q_1)\})$ produces msps(T).

Proposition *msps(S) $\preceq$ Regr(S,E).*

The characterization of the *most general schemata* is related to the *minimal* spanning sets of connections. Remark that even if a unique connection is selected in each leaf, the set of connections which is given by the regression procedure is not necessary minimal. For example: suppose that the proof tree has two (axiom) leaves S1 = $p_1 \rightarrow p_2$ and S2 = p_1, $q_1 \rightarrow p_2$, q_2. (p_1,p_2) is the unique connection of S1 and is necessary selected. In S2, both (p_1,p_2) and (q_1,q_2) are connections. A minimal spanning set of connections is obtained if (p_1,p_2) is also selected in S2. Otherwize, the obtained spanning set $(\{(p_1,p_2), (q_1,q_2)\}$ is not minimal.

6.2 Generalization from a non-valid instance

The mechanisms are similar. Here, negative constraints are used to characterize model sequent schemata. We develop this section by analogy with the previous one, following an example. Let $S = (p_1 \Rightarrow q_1) \wedge (q_2 \Rightarrow p_2) \rightarrow p_3 \Rightarrow r_1$. S is a non-valid sequent: the deduction tree of figure 2 is a model tree for S.

6.2.1 Variabilization

Let $\mathcal{F}_S = (x \Rightarrow y) \wedge (z \Rightarrow u) \rightarrow v \Rightarrow w$ be a frame for S. $\mathrm{mss}(S) \equiv (\mathcal{F}_S, (\{x = u, x = v, y = z\}, \{x \neq y, x \neq w, y \neq w\}))$ is a model sequent schema.

To generalize mss(S) one can suppress positive constraints, (keeping all *induced negatives* ones). Thus we get $\mathrm{msns}(S) \equiv (\mathcal{F}_S, (\emptyset, \{x \neq y, x \neq w, x \neq z, y \neq u, y \neq v, y \neq w, z \neq u, z \neq v, z \neq w, u \neq w, v \neq w\}))$. As in the positive case, that schema may just be interpreted as a variabilization related to a rote learning.

6.2.2 Regression

Thanks to the model tree M of figure 2 and its model sequent $SM = p_2, q_1, p_3 \rightarrow r_1$, one can produce a model specialization. That sequent gives a set of disconnections: a *disconnection* is a pair of atomic occurrences of opposite sign, but which are not concerned with the same label. $\mathcal{D}(SM)$, the set of all the disconnections given by SM is $\{(p_2, r_1), (q_1, r_1), (p_3, r_1)\}$.

A *spanning set of disconnections* for a deduction tree includes the disconnections $\mathcal{D}(SM)$ of a model leaf SM. Given a set E of disconnections, the negative specialization obtained by regression is $\mathrm{NS}(E) = \{x \neq y, (\phi'(x), \phi'(y)) \in E\}$.

If E is a spanning set then NS(E) is a model specialization and thus characterizes a model deduction tree schema and a model sequent schema.

In our example, we obtain $\mathrm{NS}(\mathcal{D}(SM)) = \{u \neq w, y \neq w, v \neq w\}$.

$\mathrm{Regr}(S, \mathcal{D}(SM)) \equiv ((x \Rightarrow y) \wedge (z \Rightarrow u) \rightarrow v \Rightarrow w, (\emptyset, \{u \neq w, y \neq w, v \neq w\}))$ is a model sequent schema (which is of course more general than msns(S)).

6.3 Discussion

The defined mechanisms are suitable to address the EBG problem of section 3. All generalizations are operational (like the evaluation of the initial axiom schemata, we just have to look for conjugate atoms).

Valid sequent schemata (which may be used as new axiom schemata) may also produce inference rules: from a valid sequent schema $\Gamma \rightarrow \Delta$, one can propose the $\Gamma \vdash \Delta$ rule, and also (using the cut rule) $\Delta \rightarrow \Theta \vdash \Gamma \rightarrow \Theta$.

The system of constraints which has been defined satisfies the completeness and granularity properties of section 4.

The maximality property for atomic instanciations is also satisfied. More precisely, one can find a finite family of most general schemata that exactly recognizes $\mathcal{P}(\mathcal{I}nst(S))$ (we could use a single constraint system introducing the disjunction). That last point (maximality) is not satisfied when general instanciations are used.

7 Other interpretations for constraints

Given two interpretations I and I', we say that constraints are weaker (resp. stronger) in I' if they allow more (resp. less) instanciations than in I. Note that when positive constraints become weaker, negative constraints become stronger (and reciprocally).

In order to increase the power of our generalizations we are looking for new interpertations.

We now extend the instanciation range to all formulae and we consider the following candidates for a new $=^i$ relation: *syntactical equality* (I2), *logical equivalence* (I3), *logical implication* (I4).

7.1 New characterizations

Let us take the sequent schema $S_c= (\to x \Rightarrow y \lor z \Rightarrow w, (\{x = w\}, \emptyset))$ (which is a valid sequent schema for I1) and let us define four instanciations as follows:

$\phi_1 : \phi_1(x) = \phi_1(w) = p.$
$\phi_2 : \phi_2(x) = (p \land r), \phi_2(w) = (p \land r)$
$\phi_3 : \phi_3(x) = (p \land r), \phi_3(w) = (r \land p)$
$\phi_4 : \phi_4(x) = (p \land r), \phi_4(w) = p.$

We take any instanciation of y and z (two atoms a and b for example).

Only ϕ_1 is consistent for I1. $\phi_1 S= \to p \Rightarrow a \lor b \Rightarrow p.$

ϕ_1 and ϕ_2 are consistent for I2. $\phi_2 S= \to (p \land r) \Rightarrow a \lor b \Rightarrow (p \land r).$

ϕ_1, ϕ_2 and ϕ_3 are consistent for I3. $\phi_3 S= \to (p \land r) \Rightarrow a \lor b \Rightarrow (r \land p).$

All these instanciations are consistent for I4. $\phi_4 S= \to (p \land r) \Rightarrow a \lor b \Rightarrow r.$ What about valid sequent schemata and model sequent schemata for these new interpretations?

Proposition (valid sequent schemata) *I1, I2, I3 et I4 have exactly the same valid sequent schemata.*

In particular, S_c is a valid sequent schema for (I2,I3,I4) if and only if it is a valid sequent schema for I1. (Thus, in the example, as S_c is a valid sequent schema, all the instances $\phi_i S$ described before are valid sequent schemata).

Unfortunately, we lose the model sequent schemata. More precisely, we only keep those of the model sequent schemata whose "negation" is a valid sequent schema (the "negation" of $(\mathcal{F}_1, ..., \mathcal{F}_n \to \mathcal{F}_{n+1}, ..., \mathcal{F}_m, \mathcal{C})$ is $(\neg((\mathcal{F}_1 \land ... \land \mathcal{F}_n) \Rightarrow (\mathcal{F}_{n+1} \lor ... \lor \mathcal{F} F_m)), \mathcal{C}))$.

7.2 Consequence for the learning process

We have seen that all the valid sequent schemata for I1 are also valid sequent schemata for the other interpretations. Thus, one can adopt the following process:

1) **Production** of valid sequent schemata: we use the generalization mechanisms described before. For instance, thanks to the proof P of $\rightarrow$p $\Rightarrow$q $\vee$ q $\Rightarrow$p, we produce the valid sequent schema $S_c = (\rightarrow$x $\Rightarrow$y $\vee$ z $\Rightarrow$w,$(\{x = w\}, \emptyset))$.

2) **Use** of valid sequent schemata: one can choose any interpretation for the evaluation. For example, S_c recognizes (p $\wedge$r) $\Rightarrow$a $\vee$ b $\Rightarrow$(r $\wedge$p) (instanciation ϕ_3).

What about the operationality criterion? Let us distinguish two cases:

1) The new definition of $=^i$ is considered as operational.

Schemata may be used directly. Although this point of view is unrealistic in general (the operationality definition rejoins the concept definition itself), it may be adopted if some restrictions are made on the nature of these instanciations.

2) The new definition of $=^i$ is not considered as operational.

However, we can use it for some kind of partial evaluation. For example, let $S_c \equiv (S, (\{x = w\}, \emptyset))$ be a valid sequent schema. S_c is only operational for atomic instanciations. Suppose that we know two formula schemata $\mathcal{F}$ and $\mathcal{F}'$ such that $(\mathcal{F} \rightarrow \mathcal{F}', \mathcal{C})$ is valid. Let us define a substitution θ by $\theta(x) = \mathcal{F}$, $\theta(y) = \mathcal{F}'$. $S_c' \equiv (\theta S_c, \mathcal{C})$ is also a valid sequent schema.

Example: $S_c = (\rightarrow$ x $\Rightarrow$y $\vee$ z $\Rightarrow$w,$(\{x = w\}, \emptyset))$ is a valid sequent schema. (u $\wedge$v $\rightarrow$t,$\{v = t\}, \emptyset)$) is valid. Let $(\theta(x) = u \wedge v, \theta(y) = t)$. $S_c' \equiv (\rightarrow$ (u $\wedge$v) $\Rightarrow$y $\vee$ z $\Rightarrow$t,$(\{v = t\}, \emptyset))$. $\rightarrow$ (p $\wedge$ r) $\Rightarrow$a $\vee$ b $\Rightarrow$r is now recognized whereas it was not (operationaly) recognized before.

8 Conclusion

We have proposed a generalization language founded on the notion of constrained schemata that is suitable to characterize the concepts of valid formulae (resp. non-valid formulae) and to provide a propositional tableau-based theorem-prover with learning abilities.

The formalism exhibits several levels of description corresponding to the chosen interpretation of the constraints.

We have characterized several generalization mechanisms, including explanation-based ones, using proof (or counter-proof) regression. We have shown that is possible to produce interesting generalizations from instances and to use them at several abstraction levels. Furthermore, sucesses and failures of proof are handled within a same formalism.

As pointed out in [Harmelen et al. 88], there is a link between EBG and partial evaluation: the formal system provides a general definition of the concept of validity, which is evaluated to give schemata, according to the encountered instances.

This system of constraints may be related to *networks of constraints* [Mackworth 77]. In this latter framework, induced constraints correspond to *constraint propagation*.

Here, we were principally interested in *dynamic* learning, that is learning from the proofs that are produced by the system. *Static* forms of learning (that is learning from an analysis of the formulae of a particular domain) are also possible using the same proof system [Belleannee et al. 91].

We have not dealt with the *utility problem*, that is the problem of characterizing the actual value of the produced generalizations (i.e. their abilities to actually improve the performance of the prover) [Minton et al. 89]. This problem must be addressed by means of a global approach, dealing with the dynamical aspects of a problem solving system. However, one can also look for local criteria to estimate the quality of the obtained generalizations. Results from the domain of constraint networks may be useful in that respect.

References

[Belleannee et al. 91] Belleannée (C.) and Nicolas (J.). – Static learning for an adaptative theorem prover. *In: Proccedings of EWSL 91 (European Working Session on Learning).* pp. 298–311. – Springer-Verlag.

[Gallier 86] Gallier (J.H.). – *Logic for Computer Science: Foundations of Automatic Theorem Proving.* – Harper and Row, New-York, 1986.

[Harmelen et al. 88] Harmelen (van F.) and Bundy (A.). – Explanation based-generalisation = partial evaluation. *Artificial Intelligence*, vol. 36, 1988, pp. 401–412.

[Korf 85] Korf. – Macro-operators: a weak method for learning. *Artificial Intelligence*, vol. 26, 1985, pp. 35–77.

[Mackworth 77] Mackworth (A.K.). – Consistency in networks of relations. *Artificial Intelligence*, vol. 8, 1977, pp. 99–118.

[Minton et al. 89] Minton (S.N.), Carbonel (J.G.), Knoblock (C.A.), Kuokka (D.R.), Etzioni (O.) and Gil (Y.). – Explanation based learning: A problem solving perspective. *Artificial Intelligence*, vol. 40, 1989, pp. 63–118.

[Mitchell et al. 86] Mitchell (T.M.), Keller (R.M.) and Kedar-Cabelli (S.T.). – Explanation based learning: A unifying view. *Machine Learning*, vol. 1, 86, pp. 47–80.

[Mitchell 82] Mitchell (T.M.). – Generalization as search. *Artificial Intelligence*, vol. 18, 1982, pp. 203–226.

[Ororke 89] O'Rorke (P.). – Lt revisited: Explanation-based learning and the logic of principia mathematica. *Machine Learning*, vol. 2, 1989, pp. 117–159.

[Plotkin 70] Plotkin (G.D.). – A note on inductive generalization. *Machine Intelligence*, vol. 5, 1970, pp. 47–80.

[Reynolds 70] Reynolds (J.C.). – Transformational systems and the algebraic structure of atomic formulas. *Machine Intelligence*, vol. 5, 1970, pp. 135–152.

[Smullyan 68] Smullyan (R.M.). – *First Order Logic.* – Springer-Verlag, 1968.

[Whitehead et al. 62] Whitehead (A.N.) and Russel (A.N.). – *Principia Mathematica.* – Cambridge University Press, London, 1962.

Adaptive Learning
Using A Qualitative Feedback Loop

Lothar Winkelbauer
International Institute for Applied Systems Analysis
Advanced Computer Applications
A-2361 Laxenburg, Austria
phone: 02236/71 521/298, email: winkel@iiasa.ac.at

Christian Stary
Florida International University
School of Computer Science
University Park, Miami, Florida 33199, USA
phone: (305) 348-2440, email: stary@scs.fiu.edu

Abstract

Most of the example-based learning algorithms developed so far are limited by the fact that they learn unidirectionally, i.e., they just transform the presented examples into a fixed internal representation form and do not adapt their learning strategy according to the results of this transformation process. Only a few learning algorithms incorporate such a feedback from an evaluation of the learned problem representation to the input for the next learning step. But all those rely on quantitative evaluation of the problem representation only, qualitative criteria are always neglected.

In this paper we present the automatic learning environment ALEX which allows for adaptive learning by applying a **feedback loop** based on quantitative and qualitative evaluation of the problem representation. We follow the idea that the **quality** of a problem representation determines further knowledge acquisition activities in a certain problem domain. Hence, we derive qualitative evaluation criteria for problem representations and exemplify their successful applicability for an inductive learning strategy, namely example-based learning, in ALEX.

1 Introduction

Knowledge acquisition has been identified as the bottleneck in developing AI-applications e.g., Carbonell, 1989. It involves problem definition, concept clustering and refinement, and problem-solving strategies. Most knowledge acquisition strategies developed so far are limited by the fact that they learn unidirectionally, and thus lack adaptive behavior (Dietterich, 1989). For instance, example-based learning algorithms merely transform the presented examples into a fixed internal representation and do not adapt their learning strategy according to the results of this transformation process. To achieve steady progress in knowledge acquisition, learning strategies have to adapt according to the results of the addressed transformation process. Thus, evaluation of the already learned representation is the key to achieve adaptive behavior.

Only a few knowledge acquisition strategies incorporate **feedback** from an evaluation of the learned problem representation to the input for the next learning step e.g., Van der Velde, 1988. Similar to analytical learning approaches such as SOAR (Laird et al., 1986), feedback loops enhance the ability to replicate the success of learning efficiently. In most of all feedback systems the evaluation of the problem representation mostly relies on quantitative criteria, usually accuracy in the coverage of the problem domain, or the efficiency (e.g., number of rules generated) of the problem representation. There are only few approaches e.g., Bergadano et al., 1988, which use quality constraints for concept descriptions. Thus the problem representation is only evaluated according to its performance, the quality (i.e., the meaning, etc.) of the generated representation is neglected. Even more than quantitative criteria, qualitative criteria can be used to identify "weak spots" in the problem representation learned so far, in order to determine the learning strategy for the next acquisition phase. Feedback loops applying qualitative evaluation criteria can significantly improve the coverage of the problem domain.

In the following, the automatic learning environment ALEX is introduced, which supports adaptive learning by using a feedback loop between the evaluation of its problem representation and the learning strategy in the next learning step. The evaluation is based on quantitative and qualitative criteria, which are developed throughout the presentation of ALEX.

2 The Learning Environment ALEX

ALEX has been developed to enable the application and evaluation of knowledge acquisition strategies in different problem domains (Winkelbauer and Fedra, 1990). It consists of an example generation

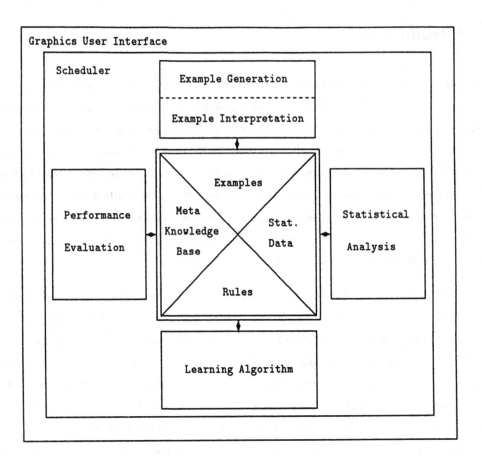

Figure 1: The Learning Engine

module (i.e., a tutor software system representing the application domain); the learning subsystem; an analysis component; and the user interface and control structure integrating these components (Figure 1).

As the core of the learning subsystem the incremental learning algorithm **ID-H** has been developed, based on the incremental application of **hybrid clustering**. This extends Quinlan's ID3 concept (Quinlan, 1986; Manago and Kodratoff, 1989) in terms of applicability to different problem domains and transparency and concept-orientation of its internal representation of knowledge.

To improve the overall performance of the learning environment a **feedback loop** between the results of a learning step and the input of the next learning step has been introduced. Therefore the learning environment can *automatically* direct its learning strategy according to its assessment of its current performance from learning step to learning step.

2.1 Knowledge Representation

In ALEX three different types of knowledge are represented: the training examples presented, the meta knowledge used in ID-H for the hybrid clustering, and the knowledge acquired.

The *examples* are first stored as an unstructured list of attribute/value tuples. Once domain-specific knowledge has been learned, the examples are stored together with the learned knowledge, making it possible to trace from which examples which concept has been learned.

Meta knowledge is required to coordinate the learning process throughout the learning system and to perform and control the tasks of the knowledge acquisition strategy. In the knowledge acquisition strategy, meta knowledge is required to restructure the knowledge representation of the learned concepts. The meta knowledge provides a possibility to tune the learning process, i.e., the trainer/developer can influence the behavior of the knowledge acquisition strategy significantly by modifying the meta knowledge without changing the knowledge acquisition strategy itself.

The internal representation of the *knowledge acquired* is a decision tree. Each level of the tree corresponds to an attribute of an example. The branches on one level represent the different values/ranges/classes of attribute values. The decision tree can be easily interpreted as a set of production rules, where one route through the tree from the root node to one leaf node can be considered one rule. The more attributes the examples have, the deeper the tree. The more branches the tree has, the more complex the knowledge and the bigger the search space for the knowledge acquisition strategy. The less levels and branches, and thus nodes, there are in the tree, the more general are the rules and the more efficient their application.

2.2 Qualitative Evaluation of Knowledge Representation

Usually, the quality of knowledge is determined by its usability and expressiveness (Bergadano et al., 1988). In the following we elaborate these criteria to make them pragmatically usable.

2.2.1 How to Derive Quality Constraints

In order to achieve reliable knowledge as the result of automated knowledge acquisition we elaborate usability and expressiveness by applying the *generic task* model (Bylander et al., 1987). The model is based on the following knowledge sources:

1. *The type of problem*, in particular the type of input and the type of output;

2. *The representation of task-relevant knowledge* with respect to the generality of the task e.g., diagnosis;

3. *The problem-solving strategy which has to be learned.*

Obviously, "the initial problem statement determines what to represent and assists in identifying missing information required for problem solving" (Baalen, 1989). The initial problem statement can either be a set of parameters (as in the case of conventional ML) or a comprehensive partitioned description of a problem like the one addressed by Baalen. For the latter, "a good representation is one that captures constraints of a problem directly in its structure and behavior rather than learning the constraints to be enforced by the problem solver using that representation." (Baalen,1989) The implications of the above for currently used knowledge acquisition techniques are:

- Constraints have also to be captured by the structure of a problem description e.g., by the set of parameters selected for knowledge representation;

- A high-quality learning environment has to have the ability to refine a problem description in a proper representation;

- Learning by selected inputs (according to the refinement e.g., feedback loops) provides for comprehensive problem representation.

2.2.2 Quality Based on Structure

The structure of a problem description (eventually including the way to solve the problem) can be identified as all kinds of static and dynamic entities and relationships which allow a concept of the problem domain to be built.

STRUCTURE-CRITERION

To represent a thing means to resemble its structure into a representation scheme.

The criterion postulates, whenever we can identify structural items such as entities to describe a problem space, we have to map them to a computable scheme. ALEX meets the identified structure criteria because:

- All identified structural items can be mapped to an entire computable representation scheme, namely the decision tree;

- Each level of the decision tree corresponds to an attribute of the problem domain;

- The decision tree explicitly represents all modifications and rearrangement of the internal representation of what has been learned (high transparency). For example, step-wise refinement of structure can be achieved by specifying branches in the decision tree;

- The decision tree enables hierarchical classification, considered as one of the most appropriate modeling techniques;

- The internal knowledge representation can easily be translated into production (IF – THEN) rules, a computable representation scheme.

CONSTRAINTS ENFORCED BY STRUCTURE

" A representation captures a constraint, when, expressed in that representation, the constraint follows from the meaning postulates of the representation" (Baalen, 1989)

For example, a function symbol in FOL captures the notion of a 'function' by capturing the 'single valued' constraint (among other things). More precisely, the single valuedness of a concept is captured when it is represented as a function because single valuedness then follows from the meaning postulates.

$$\forall x \forall y \forall F[x = y \rightarrow F(x) = F(y)]$$

The system has learned, if it provides a structure that allows representation of the complete range of values that are relevant for the problem representation. ALEX acts this way by providing a dedicated level in the decision tree for each attribute without restricting the number of nodes (which represent particular values and/or subranges of the value domain).

2.3 Hybrid Clustering

The learning algorithm now used in ALEX is ID-H, which is based on an ID-like core. But this ID-like component of ID-H by itself does not provide enough flexibility according to application domains, i.e., its performance varies very much, depending on the structure and sequence of the training examples. In particular, for numeric attributes its performance is highly unsatisfactory.

To overcome these problems in ID-H on top of the basic concept of ID3 the technique of incremental **hybrid clustering** has been developed which is based on ideas from conceptual clustering, used as in the CLUSTER knowledge acquisition strategies by Michalski and Stepp (Stepp and Michalski, 1986) and the work of Fisher related to the COBWEB algorithm (Fisher, 1987; Fisher, 1989). Hybrid clustering extends Quinlan's ID3 concept in terms of applicability to different problem domains and transparency and concept-orientation of its internal representation of the knowledge. The basic idea is to summarize similar attribute values of examples with the same output behavior to clusters (i.e., classes), thus **generalizing** the acquired knowledge, which up to that point only represents a rather efficient way of storing the examples.

This generalization is done in the following two ways:

- **Numeric Clustering:**

  Under the assumption that the examples contain numeric attributes as well, a clustering of the numeric attributes in the form of **numeric ranges** can be introduced.

  This is done by summarizing all adjacent branches of the decision tree i.e., examples or groups of examples, with the same result in one branch representing the value range which covers them all. Thus, all future examples with an attribute value within that range are assumed to have the same result as defined by that branch of the decision tree.

  This kind of clustering can only be applied to numeric attributes, but it proved to be very efficient in this case, since it reduces the number of branches and thus the number of nodes in the decision tree significantly and therefore improves the performance and transparency of the learning results.

- **Symbolic Clustering:** A more general way of clustering that can be applied to all kinds of attributes is the clustering according to **symbolic ranges**. In this case all branches with the same result which represent attribute values which correspond to a certain symbolic range (e.g., light red, dark red and orange can be summarized as red) can be collated. This does not only lead to an improvement in terms of efficiency, but also introduces a completely new language and thus a new meaning in the knowledge representation. Symbolic clustering can be applied recursively, allowing for a hierarchical aggregation of basic and intermediary symbolic terms to terms representing higher-level concepts (e.g., first step: light red and dark red can be summarized as red; second step: red and green can be summarized as colored).

However, which symbols or numeric values can be summarized under which symbolic term must be defined prior to the learning and therefore need to be stored in a meta knowledge base, which is to a large degree domain-specific. Some flexibility can be introduced by allowing the knowledge acquisition strategy to modify the pre-defined concept hierarchies according to the training examples and the knowledge already learned.

2.4 A Sample Learning Step

The construction, extension and transformation of the decision tree such that it covers all new and previously presented examples constitutes one *learning step*. To demonstrate how restructuring of the knowledge representation is supported in ALEX consider the following decision tree with 12 end nodes as the starting point for a *hybrid clustering* step.

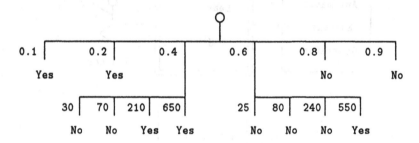

Since all attribute values of the examples are numerical, the technique used is collating neighboring value ranges with the same result value, according to the symbolic classes given in the attribute definitions. This is done in two steps (i.e., one on each level), producing the following tree with 6 end-nodes:

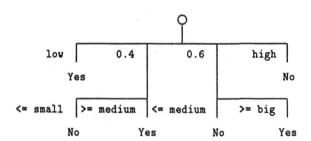

Thus the level of complexity of the tree has been reduced from 20 to 6 end-nodes (i.e., rules), the coverage of the rules has been extended, and where possible, symbolic values are used, thus making the rules more meaningful as well.

3   Adaptive Learning Using Feedback

In each learning step a *new* problem representation is generated. The quality of the learning strategy used in the current learning step can be measured as the efficiency and the quality of this problem representation. Thus the results of a quantitative and qualitative evaluation cf the problem representation can be used to adapt, and thus improve, the learning strategy for the next learning step by providing feedback between the old and the new learning strategy (see Figure 2).

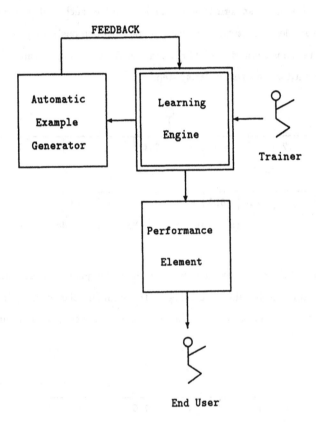

Figure 2: The Feedback Loop

3.1 Quantitative Evaluation

Nearly all learning systems are evaluated using quantitative criteria. The usual quantitative criteria used throughout the literature (e.g., Norton, 1989) are:

- accuracy: i.e., the coverage of the problem domain, usually measured comparing the learned problem representation against the whole set of examples representing the problem domain;

- robustness: degree of variation of results obtained, when the learned knowledge is tested against slightly modified test sets;

- cost of classification: capturing the properties of a description related to its storage and use (Bergadano et al., 1988).

In most cases this evaluation is just used to describe the learning method and to compare it with others. Some learning systems apply this criteria during the construction of the representation to evaluate alternative representation possibilities *a priori* to incorporating a new example in the representation. However, only few (e.g., Emde, 1989) use the results of this evaluation *a posteriori* (i.e., after one learning step) to provide feedback for the learning strategy in the next learning step.

In ALEX, as a first evaluation step a statistical performance analysis is carried out by testing the learned rules against various pre-selected test sets. The statistical analysis concentrates on the *accuracy* criterion, where, due to the huge number of examples necessary to describe the whole problem domain, the test sets usually only represent a randomized cross-section of the whole set of examples. But instead of determining only one overall value of accuracy, in the quantitative evaluation procedure of ALEX the test examples are divided into different groups (i.e., equidistant intervals for numeric attributes, symbolic ranges for qualitative attributes) and for each of these groups a separate accuracy evaluation is performed. Thus it is possible to find out where the "weak spots" of the current representation are. This information is used to direct the generation of examples in the next learning step to these problem spots, thereby *directing* the learning to those areas where the highest levels of improvement of accuracy and coverage can be expected. So far robustness and cost are neglected in the statistical evaluation procedure of ALEX, but it can be expected that they can be used in a way similar to that of the accuracy criterion.

3.2 Qualitative Evaluation

In the following we investigate how far quality constraints can be applied to the behavior of an adaptive learning process.

BEHAVIOR-CRITERION

> *Structure enables different behavior, which means to enforce a problem's constraints by keeping them invariant in their structure.*

Any condition, such as a certain range of values for an attribute, may change the instances of attributes (e.g., number of occurrences), but should not touch the initial structure. Since this criterion can be satisfied in ALEX with the decision tree, all modifications concerning behavioral changes can be made explicit. In particular, by

- the height and width of the decision tree, the behavior of the learning environment becomes explicit knowledge. Within a certain layer, the number of values concerning an attribute may increase without changing the initial structure (one attribute at a layer) of the tree;

- representing the results of hybrid clustering, the input for the feedback loop can be provided appropriately. Thus, the learning process can be monitored easily.

3.3 Adapting the Learning Strategy for the next Learning Step

In systems based on "learning from examples" a key point of the learning strategy is which examples are presented to the learning system, and in which sequence they are presented. In ALEX this is controlled by the feedback from the results of the evaluation procedure to the new learning strategy. The quantitative evaluation is used to determine where the "problem areas" i.e., critical attributes and uncertain value ranges in the problem domains are, and the qualitative evaluation can show which examples could be used for restructuring the decision tree in order to obtain a representation of higher generality and comprehensibility. The example generation in the next learning step then mainly produces examples from those areas, concentrating the learning to where the highest improvements in terms of accuracy and coverage can be expected.

In order to select examples for restructuring the decision tree, we evaluate the additional information content achieved by the previous learning step and concerning the active problem-solving process. Additional information content (i.e., constraints concerning the operational part in the original problem domain) can be reflected by differentiated attribute values or a shift towards a subtree for a certain type of examples. Since adaptation is a dynamic process, there has to be some evaluation of how far problem-solving processes have been covered by the structure. Anyhow, these additional constraints concerning the dynamics of problem solving are accessible in each iteration of the feedback loop. We base our qualitative evaluation on the following criteria:

CONSTRAINTS ENFORCED BY BEHAVIOR

If a certain behavior occurs which cannot be covered by the already acquired structure and behavioral constraints, then new constraints have to be enforced by the behavior.

This quality criterion can be met, if the structure can be enhanced in case of novel problem-solving behavior. The increase of correlations and interdependencies indicates the degree of restriction for further generalization. The behavior is that of unification, allowing $F(x)$ to unify $F(y)$ only if x unifies with y, where F is a function symbol. It is to measure to what extent the operational part of a structure can be used for more general problems (which can be tested by rerunning the acquisition algorithm). To optimize the example selection, ALEX acts as follows:

- The results of hybrid clustering are accessible for evaluation, since they are represented by the decision tree immediately. It can be determined immediately, if the entire example has changed (parts of) the tree. Hence, example selection i.e., feedback processing occurs in each learning step.

- Feedback loops allow optimization about *how* to learn. If no changes in the previous learning step have occurred, further meta-knowledge for the next example selection is required. In order to generate meta-knowledge, the following quality criterion has to be applied.

INCREMENTAL CAPABILITY

Incrementation is a process which always concerns particular elements of the already acquired knowledge. It selects only those concepts for refinement which enrich the comprehensiveness of the problem representation.

This criterion is achieved by the steady refinement of the static and dynamic problem domain representation. Since hybrid clustering supports generalization, it is possible to generate a problem domain description for a *class* of problems.

The feedback provided from this evaluation can result in modifications of the associations defined between symbolic concepts in the meta knowledge and the attribute values, and in reshaping the decision tree. Since such reshaping operations can be performed within the hybrid clustering process, these changes are not carried out immediately after the evaluation. Implementing them as changes of the meta knowledge controlling the clustering part of the learning strategy of the next learning step is much more efficient. The developed qualitative criteria can be used to evaluate the complete learning strategy (choice of examples, representation, learning algorithm). The first attempt to implement them in order to apply them *automatically* after each learning step has been made by formulating rules operating on the learned knowledge, as well as on the meta knowledge used during the learning process.

Nevertheless, criteria concerning the orthogonality of parameters, correlations between attributes, etc. have to be developed. These criteria focus on the capability of a knowledge acquisition strategy to generate constraints among the descriptive items of the problem specification. If orthogonality constraints are applied, the order within a parameter set may change to represent the correlation by order of the parameters, or the cardinality of the set increases. Since in ALEX the initial learning step determines the order of parameters in the description set of the problem domain, orthogonality constraints cannot be fully supported. ALEX may simply indicate the necessity for modifications in the attribute set of a problem description by applying the incremental behavior criterion, but it cannot automatically improve the significance of particular description items, because the refinement is merely achieved for attributes of examples, and not for a set of attributes.

4 Conclusion

Although knowledge acquisition for reliable (robust and accurate), as well as flexible knowledge representation is considered to be the major bottleneck in the development of AI-applications, there is no consensus about the reasons and methods for overcoming it. There is a great variety of proposals, ranging from theoretical approaches e.g., Hoffmann, 1990, to method-oriented ones e.g., Bergadano et al., 1988. We have chosen a more pragmatic approach by equipping the automatic learning environment ALEX, which uses an incremental learning strategy, with a feedback loop between the evaluation of the representation created in one learning step and the learning strategy in the next learning step. The evaluation is based on quantitative and qualitative criteria, which may, also, serve as guidelines for upcoming developments, as well as evaluation criteria for existing acquisition strategies.

The introduction of the feedback loop enables ALEX to automatically adapt its learning strategy, thus making the overall learning process much more efficient and the resulting problem representation more comprehensible.

Acknowledgements

The research project described in this paper is funded by the Austrian *Fonds zur Förderung der wissenschaftlichen Forschung (FWF)* under Project No. P6323P.

The contributions of Dr. Milan Kubat in the implementation and testing of the first prototype version of ALEX are gratefully acknowledged.

References

Baalen, J.V. (1989) Towards A Theory of Representation Design. MIT, AI-Lab, Technical Report 1128, January 1989.

Bergadano, F.; Matwin, St., Michalski, R.S.; Zhang, J. (1988): Measuring Quality of Concept Descriptions. In: Proceedings EWSL '88, [eds.] Sleeman, D; Richmond, J., pp. 1-14.

Bylander, T.; Chandrasekaran, B. (1987): Generic Tasks for Knowledge-Based Reasoning: The "Right" Level of Abstraction for Knowledge Acquisition. International Journal of Man-Machine Studies, Vol. 26, pp. 231-273.

Carbonell, J.G. (1989) Paradigms of Machine Learning. Artificial Intelligence, Vol. 40, pp. 1-9.

Dietterich, T.G. (1989) Limitations on Inductive Learning. In: Proceedings of the 6th International Workshop on Machine Learning, pp. 124-129.

Emde, W. (1989) Lernen im geschlossenen Kreislauf. (Closed Loop Learning). Wissensbasierte Systeme. 3. Internationaler GI-Kongreß. Oktober. München. Springer-Verlag. pp. 72-84.

Fisher, D. (1989) Noise-tolerant Conceptual Clustering. Proceedings of the Eleventh International Joint Conference on Artificial Intelligence. August 20-25. Detroit, Michigan. Morgan Kaufmann. San Mateo, CA. pp. 825-830.

Fisher, D. (1987) Knowledge Acquisition Via Incremental Conceptual Clustering. Machine Learning 2: 139–172. Kluwer Academic Publishers.

Hoffmann, A.G. (1990): General Limitations on Machine Learning. Proceedings of the ECAI '90, pp. 345-347.

Laird, J.E. Rosenbloom, P.S., and Newell, A. (1986): Chunking in Soar: The Anatomy of a General Learning Mechanism. Machine Learning 1, pp. 11-46.

Manago, M. and Kodratoff, Y. (1989) Toward a New Generation of ID Algorithms. In: Proceedings of the IJCAI-89. Workshop on Knowledge Discovery from Data. Detroit, MI.

Norton, S.W. (1989) Generating Better Decision Trees. In: Proceedings of the IJCAI-89. pp. 800-805.

Quinlan, J.R. (1986) Induction of Decision Trees. Machine Learning, No.1. pp. 81-106.

Quinlan, J.R. (1988) An Empirical Comparison of Genetic and Decision-tree Classifiers. Proceedings of the Fifth International Conference on Machine Learning. June 12-14. Ann Arbor, Michigan. Morgan Kaufmann. San Mateo, CA.

Stepp, R.E. and Michalski, R.S. (1986) Conceptual Clustering: Inventing Goal-oriented Classifications of Structured Objects. In Michalski, R.S., Carbonell, J. and Mitchell, T.M. [eds.] Machine Learning. An Artificial Intelligence Approach. Vol. II. Morgan Kaufmann Publishers, Inc. Los Altos. California. pp. 471-498.

Van de Velde (1988) Learning through Progressive Refinement. In: Proceedings EWSL '88, [eds.] Sleeman, D., Richmond, J., pp. 211-226, October.

Winkelbauer, L. and Fedra, K. (1991) ALEX: Automatic Learning in Expert Systems. In: Proceedings Seventh IEEE Conference on Artificial Intelligence Applications. February 24-28, 1991, Miami Beach, Florida. IEEE Computer Society Press. Los Alamitos, California. pp.59-62.

Lecture Notes in Artificial Intelligence (LNAI)

Lecture Notes in Computer Science

Vol. 503: P. America (Ed.), Parallel Database Systems. Proceedings, 1990. VIII, 433 pages. 1991.

Vol. 504: J. W. Schmidt, A. A. Stogny (Eds.), Next Generation Information System Technology. Proceedings, 1990. IX, 450 pages. 1991.

Vol. 505: E. H. L. Aarts, J. van Leeuwen, M. Rem (Eds.), PARLE '91. Parallel Architectures and Languages Europe, Volume I. Proceedings, 1991. XV, 423 pages. 1991.

Vol. 506: E. H. L. Aarts, J. van Leeuwen, M. Rem (Eds.), PARLE '91. Parallel Architectures and Languages Europe, Volume II. Proceedings, 1991. XV, 489 pages. 1991.

Vol. 507: N. A. Sherwani, E. de Doncker, J. A. Kapenga (Eds.), Computing in the 90's. Proceedings, 1989. XIII, 441 pages. 1991.

Vol. 508: S. Sakata (Ed.), Applied Algebra, Algebraic Algorithms and Error-Correcting Codes. Proceedings, 1990. IX, 390 pages. 1991.

Vol. 509: A. Endres, H. Weber (Eds.), Software Development Environments and CASE Technology. Proceedings, 1991. VIII, 286 pages. 1991.

Vol. 510: J. Leach Albert, B. Monien, M. Rodríguez (Eds.), Automata, Languages and Programming. Proceedings, 1991. XII, 763 pages. 1991.

Vol. 511: A. C. F. Colchester, D.J. Hawkes (Eds.), Information Processing in Medical Imaging. Proceedings, 1991. XI, 512 pages. 1991.

Vol. 512: P. America (Ed.), ECOOP '91. European Conference on Object-Oriented Programming. Proceedings, 1991. X, 396 pages. 1991.

Vol. 513: N. M. Mattos, An Approach to Knowledge Base Management. IX, 247 pages. 1991. (Subseries LNAI).

Vol. 514: G. Cohen, P. Charpin (Eds.), EUROCODE '90. Proceedings, 1990. XI, 392 pages. 1991.

Vol. 515: J. P. Martins, M. Reinfrank (Eds.), Truth Maintenance Systems. Proceedings, 1990. VII, 177 pages. 1991. (Subseries LNAI).

Vol. 516: S. Kaplan, M. Okada (Eds.), Conditional and Typed Rewriting Systems. Proceedings, 1990. IX, 461 pages. 1991.

Vol. 517: K. Nökel, Temporally Distributed Symptoms in Technical Diagnosis. IX, 164 pages. 1991. (Subseries LNAI).

Vol. 518: J. G. Williams, Instantiation Theory. VIII, 133 pages. 1991. (Subseries LNAI).

Vol. 519: F. Dehne, J.-R. Sack, N. Santoro (Eds.), Algorithms and Data Structures. Proceedings, 1991. X, 496 pages. 1991.

Vol. 520: A. Tarlecki (Ed.), Mathematical Foundations of Computer Science 1991. Proceedings, 1991. XI, 435 pages. 1991.

Vol. 521: B. Bouchon-Meunier, R. R. Yager, L. A. Zadek (Eds.), Uncertainty in Knowledge-Bases. Proceedings, 1990. X, 609 pages. 1991.

Vol. 522: J. Hertzberg (Ed.), European Workshop on Planning. Proceedings, 1991. VII, 121 pages. 1991. (Subseries LNAI).

Vol. 523: J. Hughes (Ed.), Functional Programming Languages and Computer Architecture. Proceedings, 1991. VIII, 666 pages. 1991.

Vol. 524: G. Rozenberg (Ed.), Advances in Petri Nets 1991. VIII, 572 pages. 1991.

Vol. 525: O. Günther, H.-J. Schek (Eds.), Large Spatial Databases. Proceedings, 1991. XI, 471 pages. 1991.

Vol. 526: T. Ito, A. R. Meyer (Eds.), Theoretical Aspects of Computer Software. Proceedings, 1991. X, 772 pages. 1991.

Vol. 527: J.C.M. Baeten, J. F. Groote (Eds.), CONCUR '91. Proceedings, 1991. VIII, 541 pages. 1991.

Vol. 528: J. Maluszynski, M. Wirsing (Eds.) Programming Language Implementation and Logic Programming. Proceedings, 1991. XI, 433 pages. 1991.

Vol. 529: L. Budach (Ed.) Fundamentals of Computation Theory. Proceedings, 1991. XII, 426 pages. 1991.

Vol. 530: D. H. Pitt, P.-L. Curien, S. Abramsky, A. M. Pitts, A. Poigné, D. E. Rydeheard (Eds.), Category Theory and Computer Science. Proceedings, 1991. VII, 301 pages. 1991.

Vol. 531: E. M. Clarke, R. P. Kurshan (Eds.), Computer-Aided Verification. Proceedings, 1990. VIII, 372 pages. 1991.

Vol. 532: H. Ehrig, H.-J. Kreowski, G. Rozenberg (Eds.), Graph Grammars and Their Application to Computer Science. Proceedings, 1990. X, 703 pages. 1991.

Vol. 533: E. Börger, H. Kleine Büning, M. M. Richter, W. Schönfeld (Eds.), Computer Science Logic. Proceedings, 1990. VIII, 399 pages. 1991.

Vol. 534: H. Ehrig, K. P. Jantke, F. Orejas, H. Reichel (Eds.), Recent Trends in Data Type Specification. Proceedings, 1990. VIII, 379 pages. 1991.

Vol. 535: P. Jorrand, J. Kelemen (Eds.), Fundamentals of Artificial Intelligence Research. Proceedings, 1991. VIII, 255 pages. 1991. (Subseries LNAI).

Vol. 536: J. E. Tomayko, Software Engineering Education. Proceedings, 1991. VIII, 296 pages. 1991.

Vol. 539: H. F. Mattson, T. Mora, T. R. N. Rao (Eds.), Applied Algebra, Algebraic Algorithms and Error-Correcting Codes. Proceedings, 1991. XI, 489 pages. 1991.

Vol. 540: A. Prieto (Ed.), Artificial Neural Networks. Proceedings, 1991. XIII, 476 pages. 1991.

Vol. 541: P. Barahona, L. Moniz Pereira, A. Porto (Eds.), EPIA '91. Proceedings, 1991. VIII, 292 pages. 1991. (Subseries LNAI).

Vol. 543: J. Dix, K. P. Jantke, P. H. Schmitt (Eds.), Nonmonotonic and Inductive Logic. Proceedings, 1990. X, 243 pages. 1991. (Subseries LNAI).